Teachers
and Reform

Teachers and Reform

Chicago Public Education, 1929–1970

JOHN F. LYONS

UNIVERSITY OF ILLINOIS PRESS
Urbana and Chicago

Library of Congress Cataloging-in-Publication Data
Lyons, John F.
Teachers and reform : Chicago public education,
1929–1970 / John F. Lyons.
p.   cm. — (Working class in American history)
Includes bibliographical references and index.
ISBN-13 978-0-252-03272-1 (cloth : alk. paper)
ISBN-10 0-252-03272-1 (cloth : alk. paper)
1. Public schools—Illinois—Chicago—History—
20th century. 2. Education—Illinois—Chicago—
History—20th century. 3. Educational change—
Illinois—Chicago.
I. Title.
LA269.C4L96   2008
371.0109773'11—dc22   2007046832

For my parents,
Eileen and Michael Lyons.

Contents

Acknowledgments

This book could not have been completed without the help of a number of people and institutions. A two-year fellowship from the University of Illinois at Chicago, the John and Grace Nuveen International Scholar Award, also from the University of Illinois at Chicago, the King V. Hostick Award from the Illinois Historic Preservation Agency, and the Albert Shanker Fellowship for Research in Education from the American Federation of Teachers provided me with the finance and time to undertake my research. Many librarians and archivists handed over their facilities and resources to enable me to study the fascinating history of Chicago and its system of public education. I particularly wish to thank the interlibrary loan department of the University of Illinois at Chicago and the library staff at Joliet Junior College for tracking down my numerous esoteric requests. The much-missed Archie Motley and the staff at the Chicago Historical Society enlightened me with their vast knowledge of Chicago history, and Daniel Golodner and the staff at the Walter Reuther Library in Detroit made my research trips to the Motor City enjoyable and rewarding.

I learned as much, if not more, about the Chicago public schools from the oral histories I undertook than I did from the books, reports, newspapers, and documents I pored over alone in the archives. I would like to thank all those retired Chicago schoolteachers and administrators who graciously agreed to be interviewed for this book. They informed me about the daily work lives of schoolteachers, their role in the community, and their attempts to use union organization to better their working lives.

To turn my research into a book required the help of many. My greatest intellectual debt is to Eric Arnesen. His enthusiasm for the project, his vast knowledge of U.S. and labor history, and his insistence that history is about writing clearly and succinctly has made this book better in every way. I also wish to thank Bill Ayers, Perry Duis, Leon Fink, Richard Fried, Michael Perman, Kate Rousmaniere, Leo Schelbert, and Wayne Urban for commenting on various drafts of the book. The classroom lectures, seminars, and books of many scholars have shaped my thinking along the way. Robin Cohen, Elizabeth Faue, Richard Hyman, Marion Miller, Janet Nolan, and Mary Kay Vaughan have proved particularly inspiring. To turn my doctoral dissertation into this book required the expertise of James Barrett and an anonymous reader at the University of Illinois Press. The excellent work of Laurie Matheson, Rebecca Crist, and Drew Bryan improved the manuscript and guided me through the publication process. My colleagues in the Social and Behavioral Sciences Department at Joliet Junior College have provided an intellectually stimulating environment in which to work.

The book also benefited from conversations with family and friends. Ray Kennedy, Anthony Maravillas, Mark Martin, Greg Rohlf, and Jeff Sobczynski made university life an enjoyable experience. Thanks to Dorothy, Mike, and Eddie Callan for hosting me on research trips to Detroit. I would like to thank my dad, brother Mike, sister Mary, Enrico Fiorani, Michele Callan, Giorgia Fiorani, Kate Place, Ruben Manrique, and Manchester City Football Club for years of support and fun. My mum passed away before this book was published, but her ideas and values animate every page. As the book was heading toward publication, my daughter Sinéad was born, and she proved to be a wonderful distraction. My greatest debt goes to Joanie Callan, for inspiration, support, and love and for enlightening me about the reality of the Chicago public school system today.

* * *

Portions of chapter one appeared in "Chicago Teachers Unite," *Chicago History* (Spring 2004): 32–47; "The Limits of Professionalism: The Response of Chicago Schoolteachers to Cuts in Education Expenditures, 1929–1933," *Journal of Illinois History* 1 (Autumn 1998): 4–22; and in "Regional Variations in Union Activism of American Public Schoolteachers" in *Education and the Great Depression: Lessons Learned from a Global History,* ed. E. Thomas Ewing and David Hicks, (New York: Peter Lang, 2006): 19–35. Portions of chapter 4 appeared in "Cold War and Anticommunism," in *The Encyclopedia of Chicago*, ed. James R. Grossman, Ann Durkin Keating, and Janice L. Reiff (Chicago: University of Chicago Press, 2004). Small portions of chapter 5 appeared in "1960 New York Teachers' Strike" in *The Historical Encyclopedia of American Labor*, ed. Robert Weir. and James P. Hanlan (Westport, Conn.: Greenwood, 2004).

List of Abbreviations

AFL	American Federation of Labor
AFL-CIO	American Federation of Labor–Congress of Industrial Organizations
AFSCME	American Federation of State, County, and Municipal Employees
AFT	American Federation of Teachers
BTC	Black Teachers Caucus
CATA	Chicago African-American Teachers Association
CCCO	Coordinating Council of Community Organizations
CCPE	Citizens Committee on Public Expenditures
CFL	Chicago Federation of Labor
CIO	Congress of Industrial Organizations
CORE	Congress of Racial Equality
CSC	Citizens Schools Committee
CTF	Chicago Teachers Federation
CTU	Chicago Teachers Union
ETU	Elementary Teachers Union
FWHST	Federation of Women High School Teachers
IFT	Illinois Federation of Teachers
ISFL	Illinois State Federation of Labor
MTC	Men Teachers Club
MTU	Men Teachers Union
NAACP	National Association for the Advancement of Colored People

NEA	National Education Association
OCD	Office of Civilian Defense
PTA	Parent Teacher Associations
PTU	Playground Teachers Union
SCMWA	State, County, and Municipal Workers of America
TAC	Teachers Action Committee
TCQE	Teachers Committee for Quality Education
TFIS	Teachers for Integrated Schools
TRCE	Teachers for Radical Change in Education
UAW	United Auto Workers
UE	United Electrical Workers
UFT	United Federation of Teachers
UFWA	United Federal Workers of America
UPWA	United Public Workers of America
USO	United Service Organization
UTC	United Teachers Committee
VEC	Volunteer Emergency Committee
WTUL	Women's Trade Union League

Teachers
and Reform

Introduction

Public school teachers and their unions are a major component of the modern U.S. labor movement and an influential force in public education. At the beginning of the twenty-first century, the American Federation of Teachers (AFT) has approximately 900,000 members and the National Education Association (NEA) nearly three times as many. In school districts across the country, teachers' unions bargain with their employers and often resort to strikes to satisfy their demands. Prior to the 1960s, however, teachers' strikes and collective bargaining agreements between teachers and school authorities were rare, and membership in teachers' unions was confined to a dedicated minority. In 1960, more than forty years after it was founded, the AFT had fewer than 60,000 members. Public sector workers had no legal right to organize, bargain with employers, or strike, and most school boards ignored those local teachers' unions that had organized. Both the AFT and the NEA eschewed strikes, and the latter portrayed itself as a professional organization little interested in bettering teachers' wages or attaining collective bargaining rights.

In the early years of the twentieth century, the center of teacher unionism was found in Chicago. Chicago elementary school teachers organized the Chicago Teachers Federation (CTF), which became the first teachers' union to affiliate with a local labor council in 1902 and led the way in forging a national organization in 1916. After the Chicago Board of Education banned the federation in 1916 and the CTF disaffiliated from organized labor the following year, the CTF declined in membership and influence. Because of the distress of the Great Depression, Chicago public school teachers once again turned to organized labor when they formed the Chicago Teachers Union (CTU) in 1937. The CTU attracted a majority of Chicago teachers and remained the largest and most influential AFT local until the 1960s. Although formed during the 1930s, the CTU, like the vast majority of teachers' unions, did not attain bargaining rights with the Board of Education or engage in strikes until the 1960s.

The story of the CTU suggests a number of questions for the study of public school teachers and their unions. Why did Chicago teachers join the CTU in such large numbers while teachers in other areas remained aloof from unions until the 1960s? Did public school teachers form and join unions to improve the schools, as the unions claimed, or simply to gain economic improvements for themselves, or a combination of the two? Why did teachers in Chicago and the rest of the nation wait until the 1960s to gain collective bargaining rights and to engage in their first strike? What strategy did the CTU use to achieve its goals and what changes did the union bring to Chicago public education?

With relatively few teachers engaging in union activism before the 1960s, those scholars who have pioneered the study of teacher unionism have focused much of their attention on explaining the failure of American teachers to strike or unionize. Researchers have noted that most public school teachers were women and originated from middle-class and rural families, which traditionally proved less responsive to collective action and organized labor than the male urban working class. Others have argued that teachers' individual responsibility for their work, either in the school or preparing and grading at home, meant they had little contact with their fellow workers, which hindered collectivity. To sustain authority over students and the respect of the school authorities, a teacher had to maintain his or her dignity, show conformist attitudes to the pupils, and maintain conservative appearance and behavior.[1]

To explain the unwillingness of teachers to unionize, other scholars suggest that public school teachers adhered to an ideology of professionalism. In the early years of the twentieth century, school authorities increased educational credentials for public school teachers and promised them greater salaries, more employment security, and higher social status. Teachers believed that their professional standing made them middle-class, this argument contends, prompting them to identify with their employers rather than with the working class and to reject labor unions and militant workplace action. An ideology of professionalism "effectively paralyzed and then slowed the unionization of teachers," historian Marjorie Murphy argues. "Only in the

last twenty years have teachers effectively challenged the confining defini-
tions of professionalism."[2]

While conservatism and professionalism could restrain the union activism of teachers, it is just as true that a desire to attain the unfulfilled promises of professionalism and to preserve traditional work practices inspired
teachers to unionize. Many teachers joined unions when authorities failed
to deliver the desired economic and psychological rewards of professional
status. Some schoolteachers who took pride in their teaching turned to unions
because they wanted to maintain control over their work routines, which
school administrators, politicians, and business elites threatened. As Murphy
recognizes, professionalism was "Janus-faced." It could "inure teachers to a
hierarchical system" or it could raise expectations of autonomy and higher
wages that, if unfulfilled, could act as a spur to collective action. Yet Murphy
and others focus on the restraining influence of professionalism and fail to
discover why and under what circumstances public school teachers, including those in Chicago, built influential and enduring teachers' unions.[3]

To understand why some teachers joined unions and others did not requires us to pay particular attention to the larger historical context in which
teachers worked and lived. Economic and social conditions that influenced
the funding and quality of the schools, the strength and tradition of local
private sector unions, and the acceptance of unions by school administrators
and local politicians played a large part in the teachers' decision to join a
union. In Chicago, the poorly run and underfunded public school system ran
out of money just as the Great Depression was approaching. Chicago public
school teachers, who had been promised the gains of professional status,
worked in a deteriorating school system and found themselves unpaid and
unappreciated. A city with a long tradition of labor militancy and progressive political movements nurtured teacher unionism and helped teachers
forge a new union in 1937 to attain their pay and status. Dependent on the
Chicago Federation of Labor (CFL) for support, the Chicago Democratic
Party machine and its supporters in the public schools avoided conflict with
the CTU and tolerated union activity.

In addition to the issue of unionization, scholars have debated whether
teachers joined unions to pursue monetary gains or to reform the public
schools. Since teachers founded the AFT in 1916, the organization has portrayed itself as a union fighting for better salaries and benefits for its members
and improvements in the public schools. Indeed, teachers' unions across
the land asserted that they wanted improved pay and conditions for teachers in order to provide quality education for the students. Higher salaries

would attract superior teachers to the school system and upgrade the quality of education for the students, they claimed. Lower class sizes and teacher aides helped students obtain greater individual attention from teachers and allowed instructors more time for preparing and improving lessons. After teachers gained collective bargaining rights and engaged in bitter strikes in the 1960s and 1970s, political scientists, sociologists, and journalists argued that teachers' unions advanced their own selfish ends at students' expense.[4] Even today, teachers' unions are at the center of many educational debates. They are accused of hindering educational reform, protecting underperforming teachers, closing the schools for selfish motives, increasing taxes to pay for unjustified salary increases, and creating less democratic government by undermining the power of elected politicians.[5]

Educational historian Wayne J. Urban examined in historical perspective this problem of why teachers are motivated to join unions. In his study of teacher unionism in the Progressive Era, Urban found that although teachers claimed they formed unions to improve public education and benefit the students, in fact they organized for more pay, better benefits like pensions and tenure, and advancement based on seniority. According to Urban, organized teachers and reformers had different objectives. "Teachers sought policies and procedures which would secure benefits and improve working conditions while reformers sought changes which would ameliorate some problem in the schools."[6] From this study, and in subsequent publications, Urban concludes that teachers' economic motives were and are dominant in the aspirations of teachers' unions.[7]

Other scholars have argued that the early years of teacher unionism were a golden era of reform but that the CTU and later generations of teachers were more conservative and self-interested. The introduction of higher teacher qualifications in the early decades of the twentieth century produced a new middle-class workforce. By the 1920s, public school teachers left street politics behind in favor of personal rewards and pure and simple unionism. Red baiting and professionalism further destroyed radical teacher activity and led teachers' unions to become narrow economic organizations. The AFT, a reform organization in its early years, moved to embrace bread-and-butter unionism by the 1960s.[8]

All these views make important contributions to the debate surrounding the nature of teacher unionism, but they distort the picture through over-simplification and systemization. There is a persistent tradition, although a minority one, in the history of teacher unionism in which teachers sought to use unions as vehicles to reform the school system and the wider society.

Female leaders of teachers' unions in the Progressive Era from Atlanta to Chicago to Minnesota were committed to women's suffrage and social reform. They took an active part in the community and sought to transform the public schools so they provided an equitable and high-quality education for all children.[9] Teachers in the New York Teachers League, founded in 1913, and its successor the New York Teachers Union advocated an overhaul of the school system and looked to the wider community to help them achieve their goals. In the 1930s, the New York union collaborated with parents to remove racist textbooks from the classrooms, promoted the study of African American history and culture, and campaigned for better school facilities.[10] In the 1960s, feminists and black activists in the AFT sought to introduce new teaching methods and curriculum and make common cause with the social movements of the era.[11] Historian Steve Golin, in his study of striking Newark, New Jersey, public school teachers in the early 1970s, found that the teachers "wanted to make more money *and* improve the schools."[12] At the turn of the twenty-first century, the Teacher Union Reform Network, a group of teachers' locals across the country, promotes reform of the public school system.[13]

Self-interest and social reform are not only both evident in the history of teacher unionism but represent an ever-present dualism that has characterized, and continues to characterize, the life of the schoolteacher and the activities of teachers' unions. Like other workers, teachers believed they deserved to make a comfortable living for themselves and their families, but, caring deeply about their profession and their students, they often had a broader range of concerns. At times, public school teachers noted that smaller class sizes, better teacher training and teaching methods, improved school equipment and facilities, increased funding for education, special education programs for needy students, and greater teacher input into curriculum would help the teachers and the students. The life of the student outside the classroom, and issues in the wider community, could not be completely ignored by the teacher if he or she wanted to make the job of a teacher more satisfying and easier to perform. The policies of local and national governments, racism, and the students' living conditions influenced the educational experience of students and classroom teachers. Therefore, each teacher and teachers' union faced the dilemma of whether to concentrate solely on issues of self-interest or to advocate reform of the school system. Sometimes, this tension has produced conflict for dominance within the union between those individuals and groups most attracted to bread-and-butter unionism and those most drawn to social reform, and teachers have been swayed toward one position or the other.

Traditional demands of higher salary and improved benefits dominate the activities of teachers' unions at most times and in most places, but in some periods a number of teachers have embraced reform. Scholars need to chart the twists and turns in these positions within the context of larger social, political, and economic developments. Therefore this book integrates the story of Chicago teacher unionism into the broader history of the Great Depression, World War II, the McCarthy era, and the tumultuous 1960s, eras that profoundly shaped the activities of Chicago schoolteachers. In periods of political and social upheaval, such as the 1930s and 1960s, more teachers wanted to use the union as a vehicle for social reform while others still argued that the proper role of a teachers' union was to fight for better wages and conditions. Those public school teachers who sought to improve the system of public education did not agree on exactly what, or how, improvements should be made. Which teachers supported reform and which ones opposed it? What kind of reforms did public school teachers want and what obstacles did social reformers face? What impact did they have on the schools? These are all questions this study seeks to answer.

The teacher unionism that emerged in Chicago in the early years of the twentieth century was not the same as the teachers' union that prospered in the 1960s. Earlier in the century, teachers' unions including the CTF and the CTU embraced a form of what I term "professional unionism," which eschewed strikes and collective bargaining to address their demands. Instead, they allied with local labor federations, built alliances with middle-class reform groups and community organizations, lobbied politicians, used the legal system, petitioned the Board of Education, and promoted professional growth and social activities. In the 1940s and 1950s, the CTU and other teachers' unions moved away from community politics and professional development and sought gains in salary, benefits, and working conditions through the adoption of collective bargaining laws. By the 1960s, the teachers became less dependent on parents, students, and the general public and forced the Board of Education to unilaterally adopt a traditional form of union prevalent in the private sector that focused on collective bargaining and negotiation of binding contracts between the employers and the union. Why did teachers' unions shift their focus from professional unionism to embrace a form of unionism prevalent in the private sector to satisfy their demands?[14]

Schoolteachers influenced Chicago public education and the politics of the city in a variety of ways. Through their close relationship with Chicago civic organizations, the labor movement, and city and state politicians, teachers curbed some of the excesses of the Chicago Democratic political machine, attained equal pay for female and African American teachers, influenced the allocation of funding for public education and teachers' salaries, protected academic freedom from Cold War excesses, acquired the right of collective bargaining, and helped to reform the schools to meet several of the demands of some sections of the black community. Yet a hostile and resilient Chicago political machine, a membership divided by gender and race, and powerful business and conservative organizations restrained the teachers' attempts to improve teachers' salaries and working conditions and the quality of the Chicago public school system.

Gender crucially influenced the occupation of teaching, job satisfaction, union militancy, and attitudes toward reform.[15] With two-thirds of the teaching workforce female, teacher unionism was firmly located in the context of women's work and women's struggles to enhance the status and rewards of teaching. For most of this century, boards of education denied female teachers equal pay with men, the right to marry, and access to leadership positions in the schools. In Chicago, female elementary school teachers used the union as a vehicle to campaign for equal pay with high school teachers. Both men and women sought the rewards of professionalism, but in the early years of the century women were the driving force behind social reform. Partly because women were more satisfied with their earnings and status, had fewer family responsibilities, and showed greater commitment to children's education, they were more likely to seek reform than men. By the 1960s, however, differences between the demands of men and women became much less pronounced.[16]

This book pays particular attention to the role of schoolteachers in challenging the racial discrimination that blighted the Chicago school system and the teachers' relationship with the Chicago civil rights movement. This book starts with the premise that race has played a major role in shaping the history of American urban education, and it highlights the racialized thinking and practices of public school teachers. The CTU was formed mainly by white teachers, many the sons and daughters of European immigrants, but as more African Americans entered the teaching force after World War II, the union was severely divided along racial lines. By the 1960s, African American teachers challenged their white colleagues to help black teachers achieve social and economic equality within the union and the school system. African American teachers, overwhelmingly employed as substitute teachers in Chicago's schools, campaigned for equal pay and status with their full-time white colleagues. Furthermore, many black teachers wanted the union to focus on improving the quality of the segregated schools, while most white teachers continued to campaign for available revenue to be spent on teachers' wages. Black teachers, parents, and students joined together in an alliance that forced the CTU and the Board of Education to fundamentally reform the union and the public school system.[17]

An analysis of the impact of teachers' labor activities permits a greater understanding of the development of public education. The practice of education has always been the result of tumultuous struggles and compromises between politicians, business, labor unions, and community organizations. A detailed study of events in Chicago shows how each of these has fought to shape schooling to suit their interests. Even though the school administration and state and local politicians played decisive roles in limiting the choices of public school teachers, many innovations in the Chicago public schools were the direct result of unionized teachers and their reform allies. They brought about changes to public education and to local politics that still benefit Chicago teachers today, but because of the obstacles they faced and the decisions they made, unionized teachers left many problems unresolved.

1

The Formation of the Chicago Teachers Union, 1929–1937

The 1930s was a pivotal decade for American workers and the labor movement in the private sector of the economy, but for public school teachers and other workers in the local, state, and federal government, the decade proved less dramatic. Thousands of industrial workers engaged in strikes and sit-down stoppages during the Great Depression, and union membership rose from 3.6 million in 1930 to 9 million in 1940 to reach more than a third of non-agricultural workers. Men and women built permanent labor organizations and the federal government passed legislation that has sustained the private sector labor movement until today. With few exceptions, however, public school teachers remained at their posts, and the membership of the American Federation of Teachers (AFT) embraced less than 4 percent of teachers throughout the decade. Labor legislation that helped private sector employees organize and bargain with their employers excluded schoolteachers and other workers in the public sector, and school boards across the nation ignored most teachers' unions and suppressed others. Those teachers who joined unions remained divided in separate men's and women's and high school and elementary teachers' locals.[1]

Chicago was one of the only cities during the Great Depression where public school teachers actively challenged the policies of school authorities and built a united teachers' organization, the Chicago Teachers Union (CTU). Although divided by gender, ethnicity, and religion and between lower paid elementary and higher paid high school teachers, still more than two-thirds of the teachers joined the CTU, making it the largest teachers' union in the country. A number of factors explain the exceptional rise of teacher unionism in Chicago. The politically controlled Chicago public school system faced near bankruptcy just as the Great Depression approached. Teachers faced pay cuts and months without pay. Many teachers believed they alone stood as the protectors of a system of public education that business and political elites had abandoned. The existence of a strong private sector labor movement, a tradition of teacher unionism in Chicago dating back to the Chicago Teachers Federation (CTF), and the acceptance of labor by the Democratic political machine and its supporters in the school administration, help explain why teacher unionism flourished more in Chicago than elsewhere.

The Growth of Chicago's System of Public Education

In the nineteenth century, Chicago emerged as the major commercial, financial, and manufacturing center of the Midwest. Connected to the major agricultural and industrial areas of the country by the Great Lakes and an extensive network of rivers and canals, and later by a modern railway and road system, the city blossomed as the commercial gateway to the West. A diversified economy including garment factories, steel works, and sprawling stockyards helped make Chicago a major industrial city. Supplemented with migration from the rural Midwest and the southern states and a huge influx of immigrants from eastern and southern Europe, the population of Chicago grew from less than 5,000 in 1840 to 1.7 million in 1900 and to nearly 3.4 million in 1930, making Chicago the second largest city in the nation after New York.[2] (See Table 1.)

As Chicago expanded on the banks of Lake Michigan, the city's system of public education enrolled more of its children and acquired greater responsibilities. As with many other U.S. cities, an increase in the population and the introduction of anti–child labor and compulsory education laws led to a greater demand for schooling in general, and for high schools in particular. Public school enrollment in the United States doubled from approximately 12.7 million in 1890 to 25.6 million in 1930, and high school attendance increased more than twentyfold from 200,000 to 4.4 million during the same period. In 1890 the Chicago public schools enrolled fewer than 140,000 pupils, but by 1930 this figure had increased to more than 440,000. Fewer than 3,000 pupils enrolled in twelve Chicago high schools in 1890, but by 1930 this number had risen to more than 100,000 pupils attending fifty-one high schools in the city (see Table 1). The Board of Education employed fewer than 3,000 schoolteachers in 1890, but by 1930 the figure had risen to nearly 14,000 (see Table 2). By the mid 1920s, the Board of Education employed more than 15,000 people in an array of technical schools, night schools, elementary schools, junior high schools, senior high schools, and schools for those with disabilities. As the largest employer in the city, the public schools accounted for the biggest portion of Chicago's public expenditures.[3]

In the early twentieth century, reforming politicians and professional elites reorganized the Chicago public schools and, like other school districts across the nation, placed them under the control of education and business experts. Even though individual states, rather than the federal government, have had fiscal and regulatory responsibilities for U.S. public education since its emergence in the nineteenth century, states delegated the main responsibility for running public education to local, often poorly organized and politically controlled school districts. As urban school systems grew in size and became more important in the life of the nation, progressive reformers called for their reorganization. After a campaign for reform in Illinois, the state legislature in Springfield passed the Otis Bill in 1917, which officially put public education policy in Chicago under the control of a central Board of Education. Under the new law, the mayor, with the approval of the city council, appointed the eleven-member board. Board members, who served five-year terms, appointed a school superintendent, an attorney, and a business manager. The

Table 1. Chicago Population and Public School Enrollment, 1840–1930

Year	Total Population	Elementary	High Schools	Junior Colleges	Overall Attendance
1840	4,470	317			317
1850	29,963	1,919			1,919
1860	112,172	6,539	312		6,851
1870	298,977	27,342	602		38,939
1880	503,185	58,519	1,043		59,562
1890	1,099,850	131,341	2,825		135,541 (A)
1900	1,698,575	215,660	10,201		255,718 (A)
1910	2,185,283	257,620	17,781		301,172 (A)
1920	2,701,705	291,678	36,433	491	393,918 (A)
1930	3,376,438	326,000 (B)	103,851 (B)	3,374	444,816 (A)

Sources: Mary J. Herrick, *The Chicago Schools: A Social and Political History* (Beverly Hills, Calif., Sage, 1971), 403. (A) This number includes evening, summer, and special students not included in regular day schools. (B) In 1924 the Board of Education established junior high schools in Chicago. The figures for 1930 include the seventh and eighth grades in elementary school and the ninth grade in high school. In 1931 there were 41,568 pupils enrolled in twenty-seven junior high schools and 100,856 pupils enrolled in twenty-four senior high schools George D. Strayer et al., *Report of the Survey of the Schools of Chicago, Illinois,* Volume 2 (New York: Bureau of Publications, Teachers College, Columbia University, 1932), 148.

Table 2. Teachers in the Chicago Public Schools, 1840–1930

Year	Elementary Teachers	High School Teachers	College Teachers	Total Teachers
1840	4			4
1850	21			21
1860	126	9		135
1870	515	22		537
1880	901	33		958 (A)
1890	2,591	120		2,711
1900	5,104	306	20	5,806 (A)
1910	5,800	640	33	6,390 (A)
1920	7,398	1,342	38	8,778
1930	10,171 (B)	3,208 (B)	209	13,688

(A) This number includes teachers in special kinds of work, not in regular classrooms. (B) Junior high school teachers included with elementary school teachers. Source: Mary J. Herrick, The Chicago Schools: A Social and Political History (Beverly Hills, Calif., Sage, 1971), 406.

Board of Education set its own budget, which then had to be approved by the city council. Although in theory the Chicago Board of Education remained independent of the mayor's office, in reality city politicians controlled the board and used the schools to further their political and economic interests. In the late 1920s, George Counts, prominent education expert, noted that the mayor's power to appoint the members of the Board of Education has "bound the school system to the city hall and has subordinated the interests of education to the vagaries and vicissitudes of partisan politics. It has fostered the tradition that board members are creatures of the mayor and must either do his bidding or resign."[4]

At no time was this political control of Chicago public education more apparent than under the regime of Republican mayor William H. Thompson. Mayor of the city from 1915 to 1923 and again from 1927 to 1931, Thompson had connections with organized crime and presided over some of the worst political corruption in Chicago's history. "The Council was wrecked, the administrative services looted, the election machinery captured, and vicious hands reached out for the schools and the courts," Charles E. Merriam, a former reforming mayoral candidate, complained during the mayor's first term of office.[5] Subsequently, the mayor appointed associates to the Board of Education who granted contracts for school construction and equipment to business groups that had direct links to city politicians. Land owned by the Board of Education in the expensive downtown area was leased to business friends, including the Chicago Tribune newspaper, in long lease agreements for nominal rent. In the late 1920s, three thousand school employees, including janitors, lunchroom workers, and school clerks, gained employment through political connections.[6] Consequently, in 1931 Columbia University professor George Strayer found in his survey of the Chicago system of public education that the non-educational operating costs of Chicago schools were higher than those in all other major cities. Chicago spent 12.9 percent of its educational budget on the operation of its plant, while Detroit spent 11.4 percent, Cleveland 10 percent, Philadelphia 7.5 percent, and New York 5.9 percent. Maintenance costs in Chicago constituted 5 percent of its annual budget, while in Cleveland the figure was 4.8 percent, in Detroit 3.8 percent, in Philadelphia 3.3 percent, and in New York 3 percent.[7]

The growth in school attendance and the prolific spending of the Chicago Board of Education led to financial difficulties for the school system. The Chicago school budget rose from less than $17 million in 1915 to more than $56 million in 1925 and to $79 million in 1930. Throughout this period, the Chicago Board of Education partly financed the budget through deficit spending. Rather than base its budget on the amount of taxes already collected, it sold tax anticipation warrants, bonds that were redeemable from the tax levies of the following year, to the banks at high rates of interests to obtain more money for the present budget. As tax money for the following year was always higher than for the current year, and bank interest on tax anticipation warrants mounted yearly, the system resulted in progressively greater debt for the Board of Education.[8]

The public school infrastructure in Chicago showed little signs of benefiting from these huge expenditures. George Strayer's 1931 survey of Chicago's public schools found 11 "buildings so inferior and so inadequate in every respect" that they should have been abandoned. Strayer described 86 schools as only slightly better, 153 as "decidedly below approved standards of educational adequacy" that needed substantial repairs, 52 as in fairly satisfactory condition, 64 as in satisfactory condition, and only 11 as "very satisfactory" that required "little or no alteration."[9] More than 50 percent of Chicago's schools were more than thirty years old and 27 percent more than forty years old. In contrast, in 1930 only a third of the 600 schools in New York City were more than thirty years old.[10]

Chicago's Public School Teachers

On the eve of the Great Depression, public school teaching in Chicago and other U.S. cities was a female-dominated occupation. In 1870, women made up about 60 percent of American schoolteachers; by 1900 the figure had risen to nearly 80 percent and by 1930 83.5 percent of teachers in the United States were women.[11] A strict sexual division of labor operated in the schools. The vast majority of elementary school teachers were women while the majority of men worked in the high schools. While 86 percent of the 14,000 Chicago teachers were women in 1930, women constituted 95 percent of the elementary school teachers, 80 percent of the junior high school teachers, and 62 percent of the senior high school teachers. In general, women high school teachers tended to teach liberal arts subjects, while men teachers taught science, vocational arts, and physical education. Whereas the overwhelming majority of teachers were women, principals and other senior school administrators tended to be men. While 186 of the Chicago principals were men, 178 were women, and most of the female principals worked in the elementary schools.[12]

Cultural traditions and the policies of school administrators account for the high preponderance of women schoolteachers. Historically, women identified more with the concerns of the home and family and, by extension, the education of children. From an early age, many girls were encouraged by parents and schoolteachers to enter teaching because it was a respectable and reasonably well-paid occupation. Many considered teaching the ideal profession for women before marriage and as an extension of women's natural mothering role. In turn, well-groomed independent female teachers stood as career examples to ambitious students in their classrooms. Limited opportunities open to women combined with the increase in the number of women graduating from college influenced the number of women choosing teaching. School authorities often preferred women teachers for their supposed moral influence, patience, nurturing ability, submission to authority, and willingness to work for less pay than men.[13]

Teaching was not only a women's profession, but a single women's profession. Teaching attracted those women who chose to remain single and many women left the classroom after they married or when they had children. In the nineteenth century, public school systems, including Chicago's, introduced rules that required women teachers to resign from their posts if they married. School administrators argued that married women teachers could not cope with family and professional responsibilities and therefore expected women to remain single, devoted to their vocation, and dedicated to their students. Rural schools enforced marriage rules to a greater degree than did urban systems. In 1930 only about 18 percent of women teachers in the United States were married, while in Chicago, where there was "no evidence of any discrimination against marriage in the existing administrative practices" according to George Strayer, 24.5 percent of women teachers were married.[14]

If gender played a large part in determining the makeup and inequalities of the Chicago teaching force, so too did race. With few other opportunities, teaching was the most popular occupation among African American college-educated women. More than half of black college graduates became schoolteachers in 1910.[15] African Americans, who first migrated in large numbers from the southern states to Chicago and other northern cities during World War I, constituted 6.9 percent of the city's population in 1930 but only 2.3 percent of public school teachers. Along with other northern cities with growing black populations such as Philadelphia, Boston, and New York, Chicago oversaw a rigidly segregated school system. Students living in racially segregated neighborhoods attended their local schools while the board assigned African American teachers to overcrowded black schools that offered inferior facilities compared to those offered to whites in the surrounding neighborhoods.[16]

Black teachers also enjoyed fewer career prospects than did white teachers. With only two black high schools in the city, DuSable and Wendell Phillips, the vast majority of black teachers worked in elementary schools even if they were trained for better-paying high school work. Out of 321 black teachers who worked in the Chicago public school system in 1934, 285 of them taught in the elementary schools. With fewer opportunities for African American high school teachers, many qualified teachers from the South had to work as substitutes or take other jobs in Chicago until teaching positions opened up for them. Few African Americans reached the position of school principal. Maudelle Bousfield became the first black principal of a Chicago elementary school in 1928 and the first black high school principal in 1939.[17]

Overwhelmingly white and female, the teaching staff further reflected the fact that Chicago was a city of immigrants. As in many major U.S. cities, a majority of Chicago schoolteachers originated from immigrant, and disproportionately Irish, families. In 1900, 61.1 percent of Chicago schoolteachers came from immigrant families and 27 percent from Irish immigrants.[18] In the 1930s Chicago teachers were more likely to be of native stock, but, reflecting the ethnic change in the city, those from immigrant families were beginning to originate from eastern Europe. In a survey of four hundred students at the Chicago Normal School undertaken in 1931, approximately 65 percent had native-born parents. The majority of these named Ireland, then Germany, then England as the land of their ancestors, and a few named Poland, Slovakia, and France. Most of the 35 percent with foreign-born parents came from British, Russian, German, Polish, Czechoslovakian, Rumanian, and Swedish families.[19]

The ethnically diverse teaching force was further divided between Catholics and Protestants.[20] Since the arrival of Irish Catholics to Chicago in the nineteenth century, many Protestants had exhibited strong anti-Catholicism. Anglo-Americans invariably regarded the Catholic Church as authoritarian and Catholics as unpatriotic because their allegiance was to the Church in Rome. The growth of the Catholic school system in Chicago and the Catholic Church's lack of support for public education led Protestants to believe that Catholics were set on undermining the public education system. In the twentieth century, the issue of Prohibition, the rise to prominence of Irish Catholics in Chicago politics, and the movement of Catholic teachers into the public schools further engendered native Protestant resentment. Continuing into the 1930s, many Protestants continued to believe that the Roman Catholic Church and Catholic teachers were intent on undermining public education in Chicago, but in general religious and ethnic antagonism was not as acute as earlier in the century.[21]

Chicago public school teachers came from a variety of social backgrounds. A number of studies have shown that in the first decades of the twentieth century American public school teachers were the sons and daughters of farming families.[22] In Chicago, older teachers, who joined the public school system earlier in the century when Chicago and its public schools were growing rapidly, were more likely to be from rural areas, while younger teachers were more likely to be born in Chicago. Reflecting this, more than 70 percent of students at the Chicago Normal School in 1931 were born in Chicago.[23] Historian Marjorie Murphy suggests that in the early years of the twentieth century, Chicago schoolteachers came increasingly from "high white-collar" backgrounds. In 1880, 15.4 percent of Chicago public school teachers originated from "high white-collar homes," but in 1900, 27.2 percent of Chicago teachers did. At the same time, the proportion of teachers from "blue-collar" families declined from 47.7 percent to 35.6 percent and by "1910 the decline in blue-collar origins became pronounced."[24] At the same time, the class origins of elementary school and high school teachers differed. In the early 1930s, teachers from white-collar homes were more likely to work in the high schools, while elementary school teaching remained the greater choice of those from blue-collar families.[25]

Differences in pay, prestige, and working conditions distinguished elementary school teachers from high school teachers. The mostly female elementary school teachers received lower pay than their high school counterparts because school authorities had always believed that women needed less money than the predominantly male high school teachers. High school teaching was also believed to be more academically challenging than teaching in the lower grades, and high school teachers therefore had to attain superior educational credentials than elementary school teachers. Chicago Board of Education rules dictated that elementary school teachers had to attain post–high school normal school training while the high school teacher had to gain a college bachelor's degree. Chicago elementary school teachers were paid in nine yearly steps from $1,500 to $2,500, depending on experience, while high school teachers were paid in ten steps from $2,000 to $3,800.[26] Elementary school teachers endured larger classes than their high school counterparts. In 1930, Chicago elementary school teachers had an average of forty-six pupils per class, junior high school teachers thirty-five pupils, and senior high school teachers twenty-nine pupils.[27]

Although elementary school and high school teachers experienced different working conditions and salaries, with their position of authority over children, their security of employment, and their cleaner working environments, all schoolteachers enjoyed better working lives than most blue-collar workers. While management maintained close control over the working lives of industrial workers, teachers held considerable command over the pace and organization of their work. Their terms of employment guaranteed Chicago teachers a standard salary schedule of forty paid weeks, ten paid holidays, and ten paid sick days. The Illinois state legislature granted Chicago teachers the security of a pension, tenure, and stated criteria for promotion, benefits that most other workers who faced the insecurity of periodic unemployment and arbitrary treatment from management only dreamed about.[28] The average annual earnings for full-time employees in the United States was $1,405 in 1929, but the median salary for Chicago elementary school teachers was $2,505, for junior high teachers $2,757, and for senior high school teachers $3,366, pay which allowed many teachers to enjoy a relatively comfortable standard of living including vacations abroad.[29] Finally, while industrial workers often toiled for long hours in intellectually unrewarding work, teachers invariably loved the subject they taught and gained satisfaction from performing a valuable public service.

Since the early twentieth century, normal schools (teacher training colleges), boards of education, and professional journals described teachers as professionals and expected them to adopt certain attitudes and behavior that further distinguished them from other workers. Normal schools emphasized character development such as virtuous behavior, dedication to work, and obedience to supervisors. Teacher training textbooks portrayed teaching as an exceptional and noble profession in which, as one author claimed, "monetary consideration is secondary. Unselfishness is one of its prime principles. Altruism is the prevailing spirit." As members of this noble profession, teachers were told by the textbooks to maintain their dignity and not call attention to themselves.[30] The National Education Association (NEA) code of ethics concurred that a teacher "should avoid controversies which may tend to decrease his value as a teacher. . . . Members of the teaching profession should dignify their calling in every way. . . . A teacher's own life should show that education does ennoble."[31] To reflect this status, school boards instructed their teachers to maintain high standards of personal appearance. Writing in *The Chicago Schools Journal,* a Board of Education publication, Peter Dykema, a professor at Teachers College, Columbia University, told his readers that a teacher should be "a woman who is attractive, [and] well dressed [and] a man who is well groomed and carries himself well."[32]

Public school teachers internalized these ideas of social superiority associated with professional status. They saw themselves as people with superior educational skills who had raised themselves above the manual working class. Bessie Slutsky, a Chicago high school teacher, recalled that before the Depression, "the idea that teaching was a noble profession, free and immune from the cares of a more sordid world, was still prevalent in the minds of many teachers. As teachers, they felt that they had to maintain a professional dignity, had to be blameless and subservient, and had to be neutral to social, economic, and political matters." Teachers "believed that their professional dignity and self respect required that they keep aloof from any organization affiliated with labor. As teachers, they felt that their problems were different—that they were more concerned with ideals than just a job."[33] John Vieg, who conducted a survey of Chicago government in the early 1930s, found that "teachers, trying to maintain their socio-economic status by identifying themselves with the professional class, frequently look with disdain upon their brother public servants in the employ of the city or the county."[34] As a result, as teachers' union pioneer Margaret Haley noted about teaching in the early twentieth century, "[o]ne of the few compensations of teaching in that time seemed to be a teacher's consciousness of a certain social superiority over her non-teaching neighbors."[35]

By the late 1920s, however, it had become clear to many teachers that although they attained higher pay and status than many industrial or unskilled workers, they fared poorly when compared to other established professions.

In 1930, while the maximum yearly salary for any Chicago teacher was $3,800, the average annual earnings of doctors was $5,000, of lawyers $4,500, and of dentists and engineers $4,000. Even a janitor in the Chicago public schools, whose starting pay stood at $1,540 a year, was paid more than the elementary school teacher, who started at $1,500 a year.[36] As a profession dominated by women, teaching had not gained the public respect that other professions enjoyed. The association of teaching with "women's work," at a time when professions were dominated by men, helped to ensure that teaching was not recognized as a real profession.[37] "The present status of the American schoolteacher is that of a wage-slave, an employee of the school board and the superintendent," writer Upton Sinclair observed in 1924. "[I]t is not the status of a free citizen nor of a professional expert."[38] Similarly, sociologist Willard Waller suggested in the early 1930s that the "teacher in our culture has always been among the persons of little importance, and his place has not changed for the better in the last few decades."[39]

Professionalism further failed to deliver on the promise that teachers could attain autonomy at the workplace. Like highly skilled craft workers, teachers prided themselves on their skills and expected to make independent judgments on the best way to teach their students. More importantly, teachers cared about what they taught and whom they taught and wanted to create a caring environment where learning could flourish. Instead, in the early years of the century, school administrators sought greater regulation and supervision of teachers' work.[40] "There is a marked tendency for organization, division of labor, and systems of rules to render teaching more perfunctory than it would otherwise be," concluded George Strayer in his survey on Chicago schools.[41] School administrators treated teachers as hired workers and refused to bring them into the decision-making process or to allow them the independence to do their work. In 1924, Chicago school superintendent William McAndrew abolished the teacher councils that allowed teachers' representatives to offer their views on school policy. The superintendent also placed greater emphasis on teachers' attendance and punctuality and instituted classroom observations to give efficiency ratings to teachers each semester. Although teacher committees made suggestions for textbook purchases, principals often ignored their views and chose textbooks from an approved Board of Education list.[42]

Although teachers enjoyed longer vacations and shorter workdays than most blue-collar workers, they often had to work into the evenings and on weekends. In an article in the *American Teacher* published in 1927, Chicago teacher C. L. Vestal listed in more than fifty lines of text the amount of non-instructional work required of teachers. The teachers had to grade work and record grades, make out report cards for each pupil, write scholarship forms, and pursue many other clerical activities.[43] The number of pupils assigned to each teacher in Chicago made this particularly difficult. While the North Central Association of Colleges and Secondary Schools recommended teacher loads of 150 pupils per day as normal and 160 as a maximum, the typical teaching load in the early 1930s was 224 students in the junior high schools and 177 in the senior high schools of Chicago.[44] In addition, schoolteachers led a number of after-school student clubs including subject clubs, vocation clubs, hobby clubs, health and efficiency clubs, social clubs, civic clubs, service clubs, and athletic associations. Outside the schools, the teachers participated in a further variety of cultural and educational organizations.[45]

The poor working conditions of many teachers in the inner-city schools of Chicago further belied the professional status of teachers. Teachers in poor neighborhoods were often exposed to diseases and illnesses that the children brought to school. In the 1920s, as the school population increased, more teachers were instructing illiterate, badly behaved children, some without a full grasp of the English language. Textbooks and other classroom materials were invariably old and inadequate. Teachers labored in cheerless buildings with poorly stocked or non-existent libraries, inadequate toilet facilities, and few playgrounds. Although some schools, especially the newer ones, were more than adequate, others had classrooms that were often poorly lit, poorly heated, and poorly ventilated. The dreary classrooms included little more than chalkboards, a map or a wall chart, desks, and a wastepaper basket. Commenting on the décor of the Chicago classrooms, George Strayer commented, "Too many city classrooms still resemble enlarged prison cells and in too many bad taste is rampant."[46]

The identification of teaching with women's work further devalued the precarious social status of male teachers. Because "teaching has been identified as a feminine profession," historian Richard Hofstadter remarked, "it does not offer men the stature of a fully legitimate male role. . . . The boys grow up thinking of men teachers as somewhat effeminate and treat them with a curious mixture of genteel deference (of the sort due to women) and hearty male condescension."[47] Sociologist Willard Waller also found that male teachers gained little respect from other men. "It has been said that no woman and no Negro is ever fully admitted to the white man's world," he observed. "Possibly we should add men teachers to the list of the excluded."[48] The social status of male teachers further declined over the early years of the twentieth century as the high school became much less of a male preserve.

In 1900, women constituted less than 50 percent of the Chicago high school teachers, but thirty years later, 80 percent of the junior high school teachers and 62 percent of the senior high school teachers were women.[49] G. Stanley Hall, psychologist and leading figure in the NEA, noted that the "progressive feminization of secondary education works its subtle demoralization on the male teachers," rendering "the profession less attractive to manly men of large caliber and of sound fiber."[50] In the early years of the century, more pay for high school teachers compensated men for this lack of social status, but by the late 1920s high school teacher's wages increasingly resembled those in the elementary schools.

Teachers identified themselves as professionals with a higher status than blue-collar workers, but by the late 1920s, both male and female public school teachers voiced the view that professionalism had delivered less than it had promised. Professionalism may have been intended as an ideology that elevated teachers' status, but the teachers' desire for adequate salary, better working conditions, control over their teaching, and respect for the service they performed all remained unfulfilled. In April 1927, schoolteacher Marian Lyons wrote that teachers "owed it to their professional self-respect" to oppose higher class sizes, standardized tests, and "mass instruction and mechanization." The introduction of new tests, she continued, "seems to many teachers a deliberate attempt to secure order by mechanizing instruction, reducing the teacher to an automaton, and the pupil to a memory machine." "Do educated people," she asked, "do their best at a work which has definite spiritual aspects when they feel that they are being driven?" Teachers, "as professional workers," objected to the practice of double daily registration to check on absent teachers.[51] In October 1925, teachers at Schurz High School objected to tighter controls on timekeeping of teachers. The teachers believed that it "allies teaching to a job in which tools are dropped at the blowing of a whistle, takes away the rights and joy of service, levels professional pride and will lead to disastrous results."[52] Significantly, in March 1928, the newly formed Elementary Teachers Union (ETU) claimed that it stood for the "freeing of teachers from the increasingly intolerable burden of red tape and clerical work for what should be their main function, teaching, through the simplification of records and procedure, and the placing of transferable clerical work in the hands of clerks."[53]

Overall, Chicago public school teachers had to overcome many hurdles to form a united union and improve their lives. The vast majority of teachers were women, who were traditionally less likely to join unions than men, many came from farming or white-collar backgrounds that traditionally espoused individualism rather than collectivism, and the majority identified themselves as professionals who sought higher social status. Schoolteachers had a large degree of individual responsibility, which further hindered collectivity. The teaching force also suffered from ethnic, gender, and religious rivalries and divisions between elementary school and high school teachers, which had to be overcome to form a teachers' union.

Teachers in Chicago, however, were hardly the most privileged section of society. Although increasingly from white-collar families, Chicago teachers were not in general from highly advantaged backgrounds, and most remained more firmly rooted in working-class families than teachers outside the big cities. They labored with inadequate financial rewards under a hierarchical structure in the schools and increasingly saw that the reality of their working lives was in conflict with the rhetoric of professionalism. Under the impact of the Great Depression, the public schools and their teachers faced the greatest crisis in their history as money ran out and teachers faced financial ruin. In a strong union town like Chicago, with a long tradition of teacher unionism, teachers again turned to labor organization.

Teacher Unionism

Chicago was the center of teacher unionism since women elementary school teachers formed the Chicago Teachers Federation (CTF) in 1897. The organization sought higher teachers' salaries, demanded job security through pensions and tenure, equal pay and promotion, and sought a greater say in classroom management and school policy. The CTF also pursued wider political goals. Under the leadership of Irish Americans Margaret Haley and Catharine Goggin, the CTF sought a reappraisal of the tax system that allowed corporations to pay few taxes, wanted to increase and protect the financial resources of the schools, advocated women's suffrage, and campaigned for progressive politicians. In November 1902, the four-thousand-member CTF affiliated with the Chicago Federation of Labor (CFL), the municipal affiliate of the American Federation of Labor (AFL), becoming the first group of teachers to affiliate with a local labor federation.[54]

Margaret Haley, whose rural Irish American upbringing was replicated by so many other Chicago schoolteachers, dominated the early years of teacher unionism in Chicago. Haley was born in November 1861, some fifty miles southwest of Chicago, to an Irish mother and an Irish Canadian father. Her father Michael was a farmer, owner of a small stonecutting business, politician, and member of the Knights of Labor. Like most other women teachers,

Haley never married. She started teaching in rural Illinois in 1877 at the age of sixteen and in 1882 moved to Chicago and taught in an elementary school near the stockyards in the South Side until she left the classroom in 1900 to become a full-time business agent for the CTF. Haley tirelessly campaigned for women's suffrage, independence for Ireland, and municipal reform. After her colleague Catharine Goggin died in a car crash in 1916, Haley increasingly ran the CTF as her own domain, and she was domineering and reluctant to work with others.[55]

When the school system increased in size, high school teachers formed their own unions, which reflected gender differences in the workforce. In early 1912, Herbert Miller, a charter member of the CTF, and other male teachers formed the Chicago Federation of Men Teachers, later renamed the Men Teachers Union (MTU). In response to the men's decision to unionize, in 1914 women high school teachers organized a separate union, the Federation of Women High School Teachers (FWHST). With comparatively few high school teachers in the public school system, the two unions had barely two hundred members apiece at the end of World War I.[56]

Chicago public school teachers played a major role in promoting a nationwide teachers' organization. In response to Chicago teachers' call for a national union of teachers, eight locals formed the AFT in April 1916, making Chicago its first headquarters. Charles Stillman of the Chicago Federation of Men Teachers became the first president of the AFT, a position he retained until 1923. Throughout the period up to the 1960s, big city locals, particularly in Atlanta, Chicago, and New York City, remained the backbone of the AFT.

The success of teacher unionism in Chicago was due in no small part to the fact that the city had one of the largest and at times the most militant and most progressive labor movements in the nation. The CFL, to which the CTF affiliated, was a progressive organization that included women and immigrant workers. Led by Irishman John Fitzpatrick, the CFL had formed close relations with socialists and other political radicals to help the CFL in their organizing drives among building workers, packinghouse workers, and women garment workers. The reform agenda adopted by the CFL encompassed greater public control over business, more equal taxation, adoption of protective labor legislation, and attainment of collective bargaining rights with employers. The CFL opposed World War I and supported Irish independence from Britain.[57] Against the wishes of AFL president Samuel Gompers, in the early 1920s Fitzpatrick was a leading light in the formation of the Farmer Labor Party, the most successful attempt by the labor movement to form an independent political party in the twentieth century. After the Farmer Labor Party experiment had all but ended by the mid 1920s, Fitzpatrick and the CFL turned away from radical politics and concentrated on bread-and-butter unionism and on building contacts with Chicago politicians.[58] With the CFL as its organizational center, organized labor grew in strength and gained wide acceptance in Chicago. In 1903–04 the CFL embraced more than 245,000 members, more than half the city's labor force.[59] At the time, Chicago "could possibly challenge London for the title, trade union capital of the world," labor historian David Montgomery insists.[60]

In this milieu of labor organizing, it is little wonder that many schoolteachers turned to unionism. According to labor historian James Barrett, a "working-man or -woman in Chicago in 1904, then, was surrounded by a *labor ethos*. His or her neighbors were union people, and the values of the labor movement—class solidarity, industrial militancy, and a certain pride in being a part of the movement—are important influences in daily life."[61] Teachers from Irish, British, and German working-class families had strong traditions of unionism and participated in the same cultural, religious, and political organizations as other union members. Their fathers and mothers, brothers and sisters, and husbands and wives were often union members. Those who migrated from rural areas could not fail to be impressed with a union movement that seemed an accepted part of city life. Teachers served on CFL committees, taught in CFL classes, and spoke on the CFL radio station. Furthermore, the close proximity of strong private sector unions showed the effectiveness of unions and further reduced anti-union attitudes among public school teachers.[62]

Chicago boasted a strong progressive middle-class reform movement, which further assisted teachers' unions in Chicago. Middle-class reformers such as Jane Addams from Hull House and Mary McDowell from the University of Chicago Settlement House adopted the concerns of organized labor.[63] Organizations such as the Chicago Woman's Club and the Woman's City Club supported the CTF and its campaign for reform of the Chicago public schools. Many teachers held membership in these organizations and attended Board of Education hearings, council meetings, and sessions of the state legislature to support anti–child labor laws, compulsory school attendance legislation, and greater funding for public education.[64] Affiliated with the CFL and progressive reform movements, teachers helped bridge the gap between the workers' movement and middle-class reformers. The Women's Trade Union League (WTUL), formed in 1903, proved particularly important in cementing an alliance between teachers, labor, and middle-class reformers. The WTUL set out to organize women into unions, to establish workers' education programs, and to support legislation for shorter hours and protection for women workers. Mary McDowell of the University of Chicago Settlement House became the first president of the Chicago branch of the WTUL in 1904. The organization was one in which teachers and middle-class reformers like Jane Addams, Mary McDowell, and Margaret Dreier Robins and labor leaders like Agnes Nestor of the International Glove Workers Union worked together. The CFL and the WTUL ran the Chicago Labor College, which relied upon the efforts of schoolteachers.[65]

While social and political conditions in Chicago encouraged the unionization of public school teachers, teachers' unions periodically faced enormous opposition from employers, politicians, and local government officials who condemned labor unions in general and public sector unions in particular. Teachers, it was commonly believed, should be selfless and not put their own needs ahead of their students. Women teachers, in particular, were expected to maintain proper decorum and to refrain from demonstrating or striking. Most objections to public sector unions rested on the idea that teachers' unions were irreconcilable with the sovereignty of government. In a representative democracy, presidents, governors, mayors, and judges argued, the public schools belonged to all the people who controlled the schools through their elected representatives and their appointees. For public officials to recognize public sector unions, bargain over wages and conditions, or to allow them to strike, would require school administrators to share decision-making authority with unelected people and violate the sovereignty of the government and the democratic will of the people.[66] "Public servants are in the service of the public as a whole," suggested an editorial in the *Chicago Daily News* in 1915; "they should not declare exclusive allegiance to any one group of citizens however numerous or strong."[67]

The World War I years witnessed a concerted nationwide attempt to destroy the fledgling teachers' unions by politicians and boards of education. Backed by business elites, newspapers, and local politicians, the Chicago Board of Education president Jacob M. Loeb issued the Loeb Rule in 1915, declaring teachers' unions to be "inimical to proper discipline, prejudicial to the efficiency of the teaching force, and detrimental to the welfare of the school system" and prohibiting public school teachers from joining labor unions.[68] Loeb stated that the CTF "is a curse to the school system. In a large municipality as this there is no need for lady labor sluggers."[69] Invoking the Loeb Rule in 1916, the board refused to re-employ sixty-eight teachers, most of them CTF members. In return for the reinstatement of the teachers, the CTF disaffiliated from the CFL and the AFT in May 1917, thus breaking all formal links with organized labor.[70]

Reaction against public sector unions intensified further during the red scare of 1919–20. Threatened by the Bolshevik Revolution and a postwar strike wave, conservative groups and politicians turned against radicals and critics of the American economic and political system. After a strike by Boston police in September 1919, local governments across the country enacted laws against public sector unions, including teachers' unions, and broke up those in existence.[71] In the anti-union open shop climate of the 1920s, organized labor in the public and private sector faced employer opposition, and AFL membership declined from nearly five million in 1919 to less than three million in 1933. School superintendents encouraged and often cajoled their employees to leave the AFT and join the NEA. By 1930 the AFT had only 7,000 members while the NEA had 172,000.[72]

The teachers' unions that survived differed sharply from private sector unions. While the private sector labor unions relied on more adversarial tactics such as striking to satisfy their demands, teachers emphasized lobbying, the use of the legal system, and accommodation with school administrators. Teachers aligned with labor federations to use their connections to local politicians and their influence in lobbying the state legislature. The AFT had a no-strike policy, which it maintained until the 1960s. Teachers' unions sought to raise salaries and improve working conditions by "'contacts'—personal access to officials and other persons on places of power who might give us information or set in motion steps toward attainment of our objectives," the MTU suggested.[73] The teachers' unions presented their demands for better working conditions, tenure, pension rights, and higher wages as necessary for successful teaching and an efficiently run school system. To achieve the gains that went with professional status, the AFT locals sought to convince school administrators and the general public that unionism and professionalism were compatible projects. Any action that could damage the responsible image of the unions endangered the partnership and the possibility of attaining professional status.[74]

By the mid-1920s, the Chicago Board of Education had become more accepting of teachers' unions. Prompted by a new mayor, the Board of Education rescinded the Loeb Rule in the early 1920s and allowed teachers to join labor organizations. After William McAndrew's tenure as Chicago school superintendent ended in 1927, an even closer relationship was built between the unions and the new superintendent William Bogan and board president Wallace Caldwell. The two men attended banquets and meetings of the MTU, the FWHST, the Elementary Teachers Union (ETU), and the newly formed Playground Teachers Union (PTU).[75] In 1930, the four AFT unions in Chicago jointly declared that "the superintendent and the Board of Education recognize the importance of the work being done by the Teachers' Unions, and afford them every consideration."[76]

Internal divisions among schoolteachers influenced the type of teacher organizations that operated in Chicago on the eve of the Great Depression. The MTU and FWHST sought to maintain the pay differentials of high school teachers over elementary school teachers, while Margaret Haley's CTF and the ETU wanted greater parity for elementary school teachers. Ethnic and religious divisions also permeated the teachers' unions and played a large part in interunion disputes. The CTF membership was predominantly Irish Catholic, while the memberships of the MTU, the FWHST, and the ETU were, initially at least, more likely to be Protestant and of British and central and northern European origin.[77]

In the 1920s, the MTU and the FWHST, the largest AFT locals in Chicago, developed different views and policies regarding the role of a teachers' union in the life of the city. Assuming the mantle of the reforming CTF and playing a larger role in the reform movements in the city, the FWHST supported legislation that would establish a minimum wage, reduce women's working hours, and raise the compulsory school age. They participated in the work of other organizations such as the Political Equality League, the Women's Trade Union League, and women's groups such as the Cook County Federation of Women's Clubs, and they taught classes in workers education colleges. The opposition to the more left-wing-inclined leaders of the FWHST by the conservative heads of the MTU led to open disputes at AFT conferences. The MTU showed a greater willingness to yield to the Board of Education, and many of the union's leading members became principals in the school system. By the early 1930s, the FWHST looked upon the leaders of the MTU with "slight disdain because of a belief that they follow an unnecessarily timorous course when confronted with a conflict involving higher authorities in the school system."[78]

Many of the differences between the MTU and the FWHST were influenced by gender. Both men and women public school teachers were concerned with bread-and-butter issues like teachers' salaries and working conditions, but the women teachers seemed more inclined than the men toward school reform and community politics. In the Progressive Era and beyond, women proved to be the most consistent and most active social reformers in general and educational reformers in particular.[79] Accommodating the prevailing views of gender difference, women saw the education of children and, by extension, the reform of public education as part of women's sphere of interest. Whether it was in the Parent Teacher Associations (PTA), or the women's groups that played a leading role in educational reform, women in general took more interest in improving the public education system than did men.[80]

Men teachers showed a greater willingness than their female counterparts to fight for immediate monetary gains rather than school reform. More likely than women to be married, male teachers usually had to carry larger financial burdens, and the wages and status of male teachers were lower than those of other male professionals even though the wages and status of women teachers were higher than those of other women. The MTU leaders often complained about low turnout at union meetings, the lack of willing candidates for union office, and the inability to increase membership, but in the years following World War I, William T. McCoy, then president of the MTU, wrote to Charles Stillman crediting the rise in membership of the MTU to "the salary situation," which "has put heart into lots of wobblers."[81] Even during the Depression, the MTU concentrated its efforts on salary issues, while the FWHST devoted more of its time to educational and professional issues.[82]

By the eve of the Great Depression, the teachers' unions in Chicago remained deeply divided. If ethnic and religious differences between groups of teachers had declined, a residue of personal animosity, the desire of union leaders to maintain positions of prestige, and competition for members meant that there was a lack of unity between the CTF and the AFT-affiliated union leaders. Mary Herrick, president of the FWHST, recalled years later that she found Margaret Haley "impossible to get along with" and that Haley had an "unwillingness to cooperate in any activity she could not control."[83] To Haley, Herrick was "a cheap little nincompoop" and Agnes Clohesy, leader of the ETU, "a deliberate rascal. . . . She was a personal promoter of herself. She'd walk over her dead relatives and dead friends to get to a place."[84] The disunity, squabbling, and ineffectiveness of the existing organizations made it difficult to attract new members. The combined membership of the teachers' unions in 1929 was only about 10 percent of the teaching force.[85] It would take the deprivations of the Great Depression and a new generation of leaders to unite the still divided Chicago teachers' unions and create the largest teachers' union in the country.

The Great Depression

The financial problems of the corrupt, bloated Chicago public education system escalated on the eve of the Great Depression, and the resulting payless paydays for teachers provided the preconditions for the establishment of the CTU. The amount and type of funding states provided for school districts varied from state to state. The Illinois legislature assured that Chicago, compared to other big cities, was exceptionally dependent on a local property tax as a source of funds for its public schools. While more than 90 percent of revenue for public schools came from the property tax in Chicago, only 30 percent came from the same source in New York.[86] A further 3 percent of Chicago's income came from rent and income from school lands, and only 6 percent came directly from the state. Consequently, Illinois ranked thirty-ninth in the nation in state funding for education.[87]

Additionally, local politicians and assessors throughout the 1920s failed to tax many major property holders and large corporations. Between 1915 and 1925, as Chicago's population increased by 28 percent and there was unprecedented new construction in the city worth some $200 million a year, the official assessed valuation of property increased by only $29 million per annum.[88] Beginning in the summer of 1926, Margaret Haley's CTF set out to reform the tax structure. The CTF lobbying prompted the Illinois State Tax Commission to investigate the state's tax system in May 1928 and order a complete reassessment of Cook County property. But taxes could not be collected until the assessment was finally completed in April 1930, and even after the county resumed the collection of taxes, a group called the Association of Real Estate Taxpayers campaigned against the tax commission's reassessment and withheld tax payments until the Illinois Supreme Court ruled against them in April 1932.[89]

The economic problems of the Great Depression added further difficulties to the ability of Chicagoans to pay taxes to finance the Chicago school system. From 1929 to 1933, the U.S. gross national product fell from $103 billion to $56 billion and unemployment rose from 3.2 percent of the workforce to 25 percent.[90] Thousands of midwesterners migrated to Chicago in search of work, and temporary shelters dotted some of the major downtown streets and parks. In October 1932, almost half of Chicago's workforce was unemployed, and with 100,000 on welfare rolls, the city's relief expenditure increased from $11 million in 1931 to $35 million in 1932. Those holding jobs found their wages reduced; as late as 1940 average weekly wages were lower than they had been in 1929.[91] Consequently, many homeowners were unable to pay all their back taxes. As a result of the reassessment, the tax "strike," and the effects of the Depression, millions of dollars in Chicago taxes went uncollected between 1928 and 1932. The tax delinquency rate in Depression-era Chicago was nearly five times that of New York City.[92]

To add to their problems, the Chicago Board of Education faced pressure from the business community to cut public education expenditures. As the economic crisis deepened in the early 1930s, a host of local and national organizations formed to promote the curtailment of public expenditure in general and spending on public schooling in particular.[93] A group of Chicago's leading bankers, merchants, and industrialists formed the Citizen's Committee on Public Expenditures (CCPE) in February 1932 with the intention of curtailing the cost of public education. Fred W. Sargent, CCPE secretary and president of the Chicago and Northwestern Railroad, declared, "To some extent, the banks have shown themselves willing to be guided by us [and] . . . they have shown that they positively will not lend money for any municipal function which does not have our active support."[94] As the banks' income declined due to failures on mortgages and loans, and owning several million dollars worth of tax anticipation warrants, the banks were eager to redeem their warrants by urging retrenchment. Supported by the *Chicago Tribune,* which campaigned for cuts in "fads and frills," the CCPE pressured the Board of Education to cut its expenditure by declaring that the banks would not buy any more tax warrants from the Board of Education. Without the financial support of the banks, the Board of Education had no option but to obey the CCPE. The CCPE had "taken charge for the people of the people's affairs," Sargent declared. "Chicago has actually had a revolution," bemoaned Robert C. Moore, secretary of the Illinois State Teachers Association. "The officers and boards elected by the people no longer function independently of the dictation of the small, self-appointed oligarchy."[95]

Anton Cermak, the Democratic mayor elected in April 1931, assisted the CCPE in its retrenchment efforts. Born in Bohemia in 1873, Cermak was first elected to the City Council in 1909. In the 1920s, Cermak united the Democratic Party in Cook County and won over the immigrant and anti-prohibition vote in the 1931 mayoral election. In public the mayor chased tax delinquents, opened his doors to the teachers' organizations, and expressed concern at the deterioration of the public school system. Behind the scenes, he consolidated the Democratic control of Chicago politics and helped create a political machine that took complete control of all governmental agencies of the city. As long as the number of school janitors and other public employees who had close ties with the Democratic Party machine were protected, he was prepared to work with the CCPE in pressing the board to cut expenditures. Fred W. Sargent observed in 1933: "Since March, 1932, Chicago has been steadily achieving a sharp reduction in the operating costs of its government through the cooperation of its various officials with an extra-legal body of which I am the general chairman. . . . Our committee found its power in the genuine eagerness of most of the officials to cooperate." Consequently, after a series of meetings between the CCPE and the Board of Education in July 1932, the board cut $15 million from the proposed $90 million budget and slashed a further $4.5 million the following January.[96] On February 15, 1933, Cermak was shot while riding with President-elect Franklin Roosevelt in Florida, and he died from his wounds on March 6.

After Cermak's death, the Chicago City Council selected Edward J. Kelly, chief engineer of the Sanitary District, to replace Cermak as mayor and sort out the public school system's finances. Between May and July, Kelly gained complete control of the Board of Education by appointing seven new members to the eleven-member board, including his close friend coal dealer James B. McCahey as board president.[97] On July 12, 1933, as Chicago welcomed the Century of Progress Exposition, Kelly and the Chicago Board of Education announced the last round of education cuts. Board members voted to fire 1,400 teachers—10 percent of the total workforce—increase the teaching load of high school teachers from six to seven classes a day, shorten the school year by a month, require the elementary principals to supervise two schools instead of one, cut the number of kindergartens by half, abolish the junior high school system and transfer the students to the elementary schools, discontinue the city's junior college, and drop or curtail several other services. The board's decisions represented, according to *The Nation*, "the most destructive blow at primary and secondary education in the annals of any American city." George Frederick Zook, new U.S. commissioner of education, described the cuts in Chicago as "a return to the dark ages in education."[98]

Although public school teachers elsewhere faced non-payment of salaries, the sequence of events, beginning with the tax reassessment order of the Illinois State Tax Commission in 1928, spelled special hardship for Chicago teachers. The Chicago teachers faced greater pay cuts and more payless paydays than most other Chicago public sector workers as the financially troubled Board of Education blamed the banks for pressuring them to cut their budget. At the same time, janitors and other school workers, unlike the tenured but organizationally weak and divided teachers, had the protection of machine politicians. Between January 1931 and May 1933, the 14,000 Chicago schoolteachers received their monthly salary on time on only three occasions. By May 1933, the board owed teachers six months of salary. The Board of Education paid the teachers in "scrip" or tax-anticipation warrants, which teachers then had to sell to merchants or banks, often for less than face value. Beginning in 1932 the school board shortened the school year by one month, effectively cutting the salaries of the teachers by 23.5 percent. In the eighteen largest cities in the nation, only Cincinnati and Jersey City had larger cuts in salaries than Chicago, and only Portland cut its school term as much.[99] A survey of 6,315 Chicago schoolteachers taken in early 1932 found that 3,488 teachers had outstanding accounts for rent, 4,137 for clothing, 2,256 for food, and 1,034 for fuel. Teachers, sometimes the only one in the family with a job, had more than 20,000 people "wholly" or "practically" dependent on them. In the survey, 2,767 teachers reported that they lived in homes where unemployment was a problem.[100] As a consequence of the financial hardship, the *Nation* reported in May 1933, "[h]omes have been lost. Families have suffered undernourishment, even actual hunger. Their life insurance cashed in, their savings gone, some teachers have been driven to panhandling after school hours to get food." One Chicago teacher committed suicide due to the financial pressure.[101]

If financial problems caused enormous difficulties for Chicago teachers, so too did deteriorating conditions within the classrooms. As unemployment increased in the city and fewer jobs became available, more students stayed in school, and enrollment went up, especially in high schools. Predictably, class sizes increased and working conditions worsened. Teaching became more difficult as students often turned up for school undernourished and unfit to partake in classroom activities. "If a girl in my class begins to grow thin and turns an ever paler face toward me, more than human sympathy requires me to know why. It is my job," suggested one Depression-era Chicago high school teacher. "If a boy—a normally well behaved and sensitive lad of fifteen—is transformed into an ill-tempered daydreamer, I can sometimes read the answer in the patches on his clothing. In these stern years when I look searchingly into the eyes of a student, often it is as revealing as if I had peered through the window of a Chicago home."[102]

Despite pay cuts and payless paydays, most Chicago public school teachers proved unwilling to strike.[103] With few public funds available, striking was not necessarily an effective way to collect their back pay, and teachers had few other options but to carry on working in the hope of being paid. Chicago teachers believed they should not sacrifice their pupils' education or add to their misery by taking a strike action. "We [were] determined on one thing," commented one Chicago teacher. "We were not going to hurt the children. We went on teaching, whether we were paid or not." The teachers' vocal concern for the needs of their students was not simply a public relations exercise but was accompanied by action. To alleviate the suffering of the Depression, teachers organized committees within schools to collect and distribute money and clothing to the poorer students and served breakfast to hungry children. During the school year of 1930–31, the teachers of Chicago contributed more than $112,000 for food and clothing for their students.[104] Yet teachers agonized because they could not contribute more to student financial welfare. "One of the hardest things, however, is the fact that we simply haven't the money with which to give hungry children lunches as we have done before," claimed Agnes Clohesy, president of the ETU. "Even now we do it when we have the cash. To see children hungry under our very eyes is unbearable."[105] In the end, the teachers proved willing to relinquish at least some of their pay and restrain from striking to keep the school system afloat. "Although we have suffered a great deal, suffered terribly," one teacher declared, "the large body of Chicago teachers will not desert the Chicago schools."[106]

Teachers' Unions in the Great Depression

From 1929, as teachers' salaries began to arrive late, the teachers' unions maintained a philosophy of professional responsibility and sought a nonconfrontational solution to the crisis. The AFT unions generally relied on relieving the distress of their members, educating the public about the crisis, and pressuring elected officials. The unions placed an emphasis on routine publicity efforts, writing letters to representatives in state government and occasionally taking legal action. In particular, the unions wanted the Illinois General Assembly to increase the state's contribution to the Chicago school budget. The Illinois legislature, dominated by Republican downstate representatives, however, was reluctant to bail out Chicago Democratic officials they considered corrupt and wasteful.[107]

The teachers' unions began a new phase of agitation in the autumn of 1931 when they appealed to liberal middle-class reform organizations for assistance. With a common interest in promoting public education, teachers gained the support of reformers and women's groups. Since their personal appeals to politicians had gained no concrete results, the teachers' unions and their reform allies planned mass meetings and petitions and sent delegates to Springfield to confront state politicians directly. In the autumn of 1931, a petition signed by more than 14,000 teachers and other employees called on the board to sell tax-anticipation warrants to obtain income. After the board threatened to close the schools in December 1931, more than 26,000 people attended an AFT protest meeting. Meanwhile, the major teacher organizations presented a petition with more than 900,000 signatures to the Illinois General Assembly calling for an increase in the state's contribution to the

Chicago schools' budget and to keep the schools open. The schools stayed open but no regular pay for the teachers was forthcoming.[108]

A strategy that appealed to public opinion to pressure political representatives only gained limited success. Ninety percent of school income derived from property taxes, but those residents without children and those who sent their children to Catholic schools, more than one-fourth of the school-age population in Chicago during the Depression, were reluctant to see a raise in property tax to support Chicago public education.[109] Moreover, the wider dispersal of property ownership since the beginning of the century made a larger section of the population increasingly reluctant to support higher property taxes to fund public schools. In 1907, 16.3 percent of Chicago families owned a home. By 1930, the figure had nearly doubled to 31.1 percent.[110] On the other hand, in other cities like Detroit, where funding for public education was not as dependent on the property tax and where far fewer of the population attended Catholic schools, the public schools maintained broader popular support.[111] Unwilling to accept a raise in taxes, many Chicago citizens were won over to the need for reduction in school expenditures as a better alternative to closing the schools.

The public also had a limited sympathy for the payless teachers, who were perceived as privileged. During the Depression, working women in general, and working married women in particular, faced employment discrimination and the charge that they were taking the jobs of married men with families to support. For some, women teachers working without families or for extra income needed less pay. An NEA survey undertaken in 1931 found that only 23 percent of school districts hired married women as new teachers and only 37 percent retained women teachers if they married.[112] "It should be borne in mind that the Chicago teaching staff is dominated by women," journalist Howard R. Smith announced in support of his claim that teachers did not deserve too much pity. "Here are some pertinent facts: Of the 14,000 teachers, 12,000 are women. Of the 12,000 women teachers, 3,000 are married women."[113] In downtown Chicago, as groups of teachers demonstrated against their lack of pay, a motorist opened his door and shouted, "Go get a husband!"[114]

Despite some public hostility, Chicago teachers received at least limited support from the ranks of organized labor in the city. The cutbacks in teachers' pay in the early 1930s were greeted with a strong attack from John Fitzpatrick and the CFL, with which the Chicago teachers' unions were affiliated. The delegates to the CFL's annual conference in 1932 passed a special resolution denouncing the CCPE for its extralegal role in dictating education expenditures. Fitzpatrick often appeared with teachers' union leaders on public platforms and the teachers' unions were given free time on the CFL radio station, WCFL. Yet CFL leaders were unprepared to offer effective resistance to the economy drives of the board or to give organizational support to the teachers' unions. Because of corruption and patronage, the school janitorial and maintenance workers, who were part of the powerful building services unions in the CFL, were never subject to pay cuts as large as the weak and divided teachers, nor were they paid irregularly. Likewise, unionized construction workers gained employment and higher wages because of the excess money the board spent on school building. The powerful janitors and builders were unwilling to upset the politicians at the risk of losing the benefits their members received. In July 1933, the CFL condemned superintendent William J. Bogan for calling for cuts in the maintenance staff, which had already "contributed until it hurt." Throughout the crisis, the CFL offered largely verbal support to the teachers of Chicago.[115]

Without any concerted support from organized labor, the leaders of the teachers' unions continued to counsel patience and restraint. "Any demonstration on the part of teachers at this time may seriously interfere with payment of salaries in cash," stated Agnes Clohesy, ETU president, in March 1932.[116] The following year, MTU president C. L. Vestal also warned against teachers taking any "ill-considered action." "There must never be the appearance of insubordination on the part of teachers," the FWHST made clear. Accordingly, on the initiative of their unions, the teachers continued to sign petitions and write letters to their political representatives. Yet a strategy that stressed responsibility had been remarkably unsuccessful. As James A. Meade, another MTU leader, complained in early 1933: "Our faithfulness and modesty and our respect for established authority have been rewarded by starvation, by loss of home, by loss of credit, by insults added to injury."[117]

The unions' failure to obtain their members' pay prompted at least some teachers to explore new approaches. Many began to see the weak and divided position of the unions as the main reason for lack of success in the dispute. Accordingly, between 1931 and 1933, ordinary teachers founded a number of temporary groups to unify their ranks and to actively pursue their demands. In November 1931, the South Side Teachers organized a number of mass meetings, publicity campaigns, and voting drives, and appealed without success to various teachers' unions to cooperate in framing a legislative program.[118] Three more rank-and-file teachers' organizations emerged in 1932: The Civic Education Association of Chicago, initially organized by teachers from Senn High School on the North Side, aimed "to bring all of the teachers of Chicago, organized and unorganized, into one effective unit." The Chicago Teacher

Voter Association set out with the sole aim of campaigning for politicians sympathetic to the teachers' plight. The South Side Teachers called a city-wide meeting of teachers in October 1932, which established the All-City Delegates Group to carry on its founders' work.[119] The South Side Teachers called for a boycott of stores, hotels, and other businesses that had participated in the tax strike.[120]

This new activism stemmed from the financial problems that teachers faced, but also from the feeling that the teachers, who had been promised the status and pay of professionals, had been let down by the school authorities and the community. As professionals and public servants, teachers would not strike. In turn, teachers believed they possessed certain rights and wanted to be treated with dignity by supervisors, parents, and students. They thought they should be financially looked after by the community and not be subject to the vagaries of politicians and businessmen. Repeatedly, Chicago teachers voiced the concern that they were not getting the recognition they deserved for the important work they were doing. In other parts of the country, teachers worked with boards of education to oppose business-backed education cuts, but the Chicago board, businessmen, and politicians colluded against teachers. Consequently, school superintendent William Bogan noted: "One serious cause for the unhappiness of the teachers is the growing suspicion that they and their work are not appreciated. The public in general appears to be apathetic. Some sections are hostile."[121]

Teachers began to express the idea that they were defending democracy and the public education system from self-serving business and political elites. Reflecting a general public optimism with the promise of education, teachers viewed the schools as avenues for social mobility and bulwarks of a more democratic society. The recent growth of the high school system, which promised countless working-class children greater opportunities, contributed to this idealism among teachers. As guardians of these democratic institutions, teachers were reluctant to forsake them or their students. Schoolteacher C. L. Vestal called "for the protection and advancement of those values upon which a tolerable life for us all depends. The public schools are the most important custodians of those values."[122] At the annual meeting of the Chicago Division of the Illinois State Teachers Association in November 1931, five hundred teachers unanimously adopted a resolution that "[t]he schools are the best investment of the nation and bring returns out of all proportion to the money spent on them. They must be safeguarded most carefully in times like the present in order that false or harmful economies may not be allowed to creep onto educational practice."[123] Many teachers believed there was a nationwide plot by people of power and wealth to cripple public education and to restrict schooling to those who could afford it. In June 1932, Harry Tate, president of the Chicago Teacher Voter Association, told a meeting of three thousand teachers in Grant Park that the schools were "the last bulwark protecting the American democracy." The "present apathy of officials to the plight of the teachers was part of a concerted movement to eliminate free public high school education," he charged.[124] Another Chicago teacher believed that the CCPE "is our enemy. . . . There is no possible doubt of their intention; they are attempting to starve the teaching force into submission to their program and to cripple the city's educational system. They would like to reduce public education in Chicago to the three R's."[125]

If the payless paydays convinced many teachers that politicians were corrupt and that business was trying to cripple the system of public education, how far did this translate into criticism of the American economic and political order? One teacher believed that the situation was "planting seeds fit for Russia! They are turning their most faithful, strongest allies for instilling respect for government and good obedience to authority (the teachers) into communists or worse! How in God's name, can we respect and uphold any institution that treats us as we have been treated?"[126] The truth was far less dramatic. Despite the overwhelming obstacles they confronted, few teachers proffered any broader critique of American capitalism. During the payless paydays, teachers merely condemned individual bankers and politicians, not the economic and political system itself. As Chicago schoolteacher David Davis wrote of teachers' politics in May 1932: "As he looked out over the business enterprises of his small community, roamed the hills and fields along the rivers of his small area, he imbibed the feeling of a glorious country under a satisfactory arrangement. . . . No, communism makes no appeal to him. In him there flows too much the milk of American kindness and individual freedom." However, as Davis continues, his colleagues were disturbed by the failings of capitalism and the way teachers were "referred to as tax waster, tax spender, tax eater." He concluded: "Of desire to subvert capitalism there is little, and to revolutionize our form of government there is none; but of suspicion and distrust of capitalists there may be much."[127]

By March 1933, the teachers, owed more than six months' pay, were demoralized by poverty, disgusted by their treatment, and disenchanted with the union leaders' passive strategies. On March 17, MTU president C. L. Vestal wrote that "the leaders of the teacher organizations wish to do their part to keep our common boat on an even keel in spite of the storm, but the rank and file are becoming even harder to quiet. . . . [T]hey are putting more and more pressure on their leaders to 'do something.'" Still, the leaders of the AFT and the CTF continued to plead with the Board of Education and acting mayor Francis J. Corr, chosen by the city council as temporary mayor after Mayor Cermak was killed, for cash payments and to counsel patience and restraint to the teachers.[128] An editorial in the NEA Journal in 1933 exclaimed, "When America's great crisis is a story in the pages of history, there will be a significant chapter devoted to the unfailing sacrifice of the Chicago teachers, who are now carrying on under almost inconceivable difficulties, far beyond the point which might fairly be considered the limit of human endurance."[129] Facing financial ruin, and with the union leaders unable to deliver on their promises, teachers turned to more militant methods and to new unofficial leaders who emerged from their own ranks.

The Volunteer Emergency Committee

The final news that drove many teachers into unprecedented direct action centered not around protecting the schools from business and political elites but the more self-interested issue of pay. On Friday, March 17, 1933, the Chicago Herald and Examiner reported that janitors had secretly received a $5.00 a month pay raise in January, before teachers had received a 15 percent pay cut. On the following Monday, acting mayor Corr announced that all city employees except schoolteachers would receive some pay. Teachers would not be paid because he had no legal power to sign the tax warrants the board issued to the teachers in lieu of cash. In response to the news, a group of teachers constituting themselves as the Volunteer Emergency Committee (VEC) organized a mass demonstration attended by hundreds of teachers at City Hall to demand their pay. For the next four months, thousands of angry teachers regularly stormed Board of Education and city council meetings. The VEC was unconcerned with the professional goals of the teachers' union leadership and made no other demand than "through mass action" to attain regular pay for the teachers.[130]

Reflecting the influence of gender differences on teachers' aspirations, the VEC was organized and led by men. A self-appointed central committee of four high school male teachers made plans concerning the time and places of the demonstrations and communicated the details to other teachers through a grapevine system. Although initiated by male teachers, the VEC drew support from women teachers and became active in pursuing alliances with parents and students to address the teachers' demands. To many parents, the VEC was the only group willing to militantly defend the education system from the political and business elites. To the students, their trusted and dedicated teachers now needed their support.[131] Consequently, the VEC organized parades of tens of thousands, which often met at the appropriately named Liberty Square, at the corner of Congress and Michigan in Grant Park, and marched on Loop banks demanding that they buy tax warrants from the Board of Education.[132]

The undisputed leader of the VEC was a high school teacher named John M. Fewkes, a tall, muscular man who personified the young angry male high school teacher during the pay dispute. Born on February 19, 1901, in Loma, Colorado, Fewkes began work as a Chicago schoolteacher in 1921. He became a physical education teacher in Tilden Technical High School on the South Side in 1925, joined the MTU in 1928, and became a regular attendee at meetings. An unsuccessful candidate for the Progressive Party against the existing leadership in the May 1932 union elections, by the following year he had become "the most powerful and widely recognized leader among the teachers." He informed the City Council in March 1933 that "[t]his is an emergency and whether it is legal or not legal, we need cash, cash that belongs to us for salaries that we have earned." The contrast between the man *Time* magazine called "the John L. Lewis of the teaching profession" and the timid, passive union leaders could not have been starker.[133] Margaret Haley described him as a "zealot . . . that type that carried people off their feet by emotionalism . . . a fine specimen of physical manhood, well built, and he has a demeanor that is impressive."[134]

Although militant in their demands, John Fewkes and the VEC were not politically radical. Although he had been called "a radical," Fewkes made it clear that in reality he was "holding in line many teachers who wanted to far exceed present demonstrations." He was part of a new generation of teachers, many from outside the city, who cared little for the splits that had been in the unions before. A deeply patriotic and religious man, Fewkes voiced no political demands. The VEC rebuffed the support of the Communist Party, inscribing its banners with "Communists Not Welcome," and a law and order committee of blue-shirted physical education instructors who marshaled its demonstrations kept away communists and other radicals. Fewkes was careful not to become too critical or distance himself too much from the leaders of the MTU. In the spring of 1933, when the Board of Education threatened MTU leader James Meade with dismissal after a fiery speech on the radio, Fewkes led a successful march to the board offices to have him reinstated.[135]

The VEC campaign drew support from many students who joined the teachers' marches and demonstrations. As many as 50,000 pupils from West

Side and South Side schools went on strike on April 5 to protest the delay in the payment of teachers' salaries. During the day, police were called to stop student disturbances and to control a student demonstration that descended on the home of acting mayor Corr. A number of teachers in various schools staged a one-day strike by reporting themselves sick. In some schools, those teachers who turned up for the day walked out with their students. On the following day, thousands of students struck in other schools across the city. There was, according to a *Chicago Daily News* reporter, "an endemic series of strikes, demonstrations and disorder in protest to the delay in the payment of teachers' salaries." It was, according to *Time,* the "biggest and most exciting school strike Chicago had ever seen."[136] The following week, student delegates from across the city voted against a general strike in the high schools but in favor of petitioning the city council for payment of teachers. The Student Committee on Education organized demonstrations, often led by high school bands, and cooperated with teachers in petitioning the mayor.[137]

Stopping short of advocating a strike, the VEC organized a number of sensational events to publicize the plight of the teachers and to collect their pay. On April 8, teachers interrupted the official flag-raising ceremony at the Century of Progress Exposition in Grant Park. Carrying banners that read "Chicago, the Wonder City, Has 14,000 Unpaid School-Teachers," protesters heckled the assembled dignitaries, prompting exposition officials to cancel the flag raising that day. The VEC also organized boycotts of stores, hotels, and other businesses that were still tax delinquent, arranged personal calls on tax strikers to pressure them into paying their taxes, and sponsored a series of parades and demonstrations involving parents and students. In response to plans for a huge downtown demonstration on April 15, the Chicago Board of Education rushed checks for seven days' salary—approximately $1,600,000—to the schools and directed teachers to pick them up on the day of the demonstration. That maneuver did not halt the demonstration: some 20,000 teachers, pupils, and parents led by John Fewkes marched down Michigan Avenue to the banks, demanding payment of eight months' back salaries to the teachers.[138]

Teacher demonstrations eventually reached a violent climax on April 24, the first day of spring vacation, when five thousand teachers gathered in Grant Park in the downtown business area. The crowd split into five columns and marched in different directions to the five large banks that had refused to buy tax warrants: First National Bank, Harris Trust and Savings Bank, City National Bank, Northern Trust Bank, and Continental Illinois Bank. Inside the banks, teachers threw ink on the walls, tipped over desks, and broke windows.

Surrounded by teachers shouting "Pay us! Pay us!" the bank executives had to call for the police to remove the teachers.[139] On the following Wednesday more than three thousand male teachers armed with schoolbooks again confronted the bankers, invading the Chicago Title and Trust Company, breaking windows, and ransacking the building. Mounted police clubbed the teachers as they hurled books at the police and their horses. Reports indicated that several teachers and police were injured in the fighting.[140]

The bad nationwide publicity, coming just as the Century of Progress Exposition was opening in the city, forced Mayor Kelly and the banks to meet the VEC and ask it to cancel its protests and, in return, obtain the overdue money for the teachers. Subsequently, Fewkes and the other VEC leaders held a series of meetings with Mayor Kelly, Governor Henry Horner, and the heads of the five major Chicago banks, who promised to purchase warrants to pay the teachers. On Saturday, May 13, as 15,000 teachers assembled in Grant Park ready to raid the banks once more, Fewkes told those present that the teachers would receive nearly four months' pay in cash. Five months salary remained outstanding, however.[141] On June 9, the final day of the spring term, five thousand teachers, parents, and students fought with police as they protested in downtown Chicago against the bankers, the CCPE, and the politicians. In July, angry teachers stormed Grant Park and tore down the "Century of Progress" flag, and two hundred teachers led by Fewkes marched from city hall to the NEA annual meeting to protest their lack of pay.[142] In response to criticism voiced by union leaders, Fewkes observed, "Parading may be looked upon as unethical for members of our profession. . . . But we found it the only effective means of dealing with the local situation. We intend to continue these demonstrations until our teachers are paid in full."[143]

The VEC's actions and the final round of education cuts announced by the Board of Education on July 12, 1933 (which resulted in the firing of 1,400 teachers and further cutbacks in education services), convinced union leaders previously hostile to the VEC that they had to work together. A group of eight teachers' organizations, including the CTF, the MTU, the ETU, and the FWHST, formed the Steering Committee of Teacher Welfare Organizations to coordinate their efforts against the cuts. On July 16, representatives from the teachers' unions and about forty civic groups formed the Citizens Save Our Schools Committee, later renamed the Citizens Schools Committee (CSC) to coordinate a campaign against the board's attacks on education.[144] The CSC followed the same strategy the teachers' unions had in their struggle over teachers' pay: holding public meetings, sending petitions to city hall, and urging its members to write to the federal government. In the first four months after the board's announcement, the CSC distributed nearly two million leaflets, organized more than 125 neighborhood meetings, started legal proceedings against the Board of Education to withdraw the cuts, and collected 350,000 signatures on a petition to immediately rescind the cuts.[145]

The rank-and-file action that had culminated so spectacularly in the formation of the VEC and the demonstrations of the spring of 1933 evaporated after the formation of the CSC. Consequently, the campaign against the cuts was formulated and led by the teachers' unions in the CSC. Fewkes and other VEC leaders joined the CSC in July 1933 at the invitation of union leaders. To cooperate and maintain harmony with the union leaders in the CSC, Fewkes and the VEC refrained from organizing any independent action. The payment of four months' salary in May and June 1933, and regular pay, rendered the teachers' situation more tolerable and kept them from further militant action. In October 1933, the MTU agreed to collect $5 from each member to aid those who had lost their jobs. Unemployed teachers were given other jobs. By the end of 1934, almost 900 of the 1,400 teachers sacked had been reassigned to new positions.[146]

During 1933, the petitions and deputations of the CSC produced some real, if limited, successes. When the new school term started in September, the Board of Education instituted few of the proposed cuts in physical education, music, and the arts. Teachers taught an average of six classes rather than the seven proposed. The board later quietly rescinded other cutbacks. Within a year, they restored junior colleges, and principals returned to supervising one school each instead of two. By September 1935, the board had reassigned all the teachers dismissed in July 1933. Starting in 1937, the administration had lengthened the school term and by 1940 had restored it to forty weeks.[147]

Teachers finally received the back pay the Board of Education owed them only after the intervention of the federal government. In May 1934, the U.S. House of Representatives passed an amendment to a Senate bill allowing the Reconstruction Finance Corporation to loan money to the schools. The federal government loaned Chicago $22,300,000 in exchange for school land as security, enabling the teachers to receive all of their back salary in August 1934. This was the first time the federal government had loaned money to a branch of local government for operating expenses.[148]

Formation of the Chicago Teachers Union

The school crisis of 1929–34 drastically changed the attitude of many teachers about Chicago politics. Those who thought their professional skills and service would be rewarded by school authorities and that they should keep away from mass action saw that their thinking was erroneous. One teacher, Edith Smith, commented in 1934 that "there are things I won't forget easily. . . . Few of us are the sweet, complacent, non-thinking 100 percenters that we used to be. Our eyes have been opened. . . . After four years of learning that bankers are our worst enemies, that politicians are interested in votes and power only and use the city's children merely as pawns in their selfish game, that we can depend on no one but ourselves, we cannot be restored to our previous complacency."[149] Schoolteachers found themselves payless with many people in the community unsympathetic to their needs. John Vieg suggested in his 1938 study of the Chicago schools that there had been a "fluctuating militancy of the teaching personnel and their dawning real-ization of the fact that, despite their habiliments and their belonging to a 'profession,' they are workers."[150] One Chicago teacher stated that she was "prepared to serve, but also prepared to fight."[151]

The payless paydays further convinced many Chicago teachers that they could not protect their jobs or maintain their standard of living except through a strong, unified teachers' union. Earlier in the century, teachers formed unions that reflected gender and ethnic divisions in the workforce and differences in pay and status between those who labored in elementary schools and those in high schools. Some of these ethnic and religious differ-ences may have declined, but they had not disappeared. Men and women and elementary school and high school teachers all faced economic problems and deteriorating working conditions, but serious differences in pay and status remained. The Great Depression and the success of the VEC, however, con-vinced many teachers that they needed to unite into one union. "One of the greatest contributions that the VEC has made to the teachers of Chicago has been to demonstrate the power that they can exert when unified in any com-mon task," Fewkes asserted.[152] High school teacher Bessie Slutsky concurred. The teachers "realized that they could not protect their jobs or maintain their standard of living commensurate with the requirements of their profession and social status, save through a strong all-inclusive teacher organization," she believed.[153] Hence, a new generation of teachers who were buoyed by their success in organizing the VEC and other temporary organizations sought the amalgamation of the existing teachers' unions.[154]

Unification proved possible in Chicago because the city saw little of the political factionalism that divided teachers elsewhere. The FWHST was more reluctant than the MTU to amalgamate into one union because the former had traditionally supported left-wing causes while the latter was a bread-

and-butter union. However, the FWHST became convinced of the possibility of unity by the shared opinions of all the union leaders on the major political issues of the day: namely the threat of a takeover of the AFT by the communist-led New York local and opposition to AFT affiliation with the newly formed Committee (later Congress) of Industrial Organizations (CIO). The CIO, formed in November 1935 by John L. Lewis, president of the United Mine Workers of America, and other dissident AFL union leaders, sought to organize across industrial lines all the unorganized, including those the AFL had been reluctant to organize: blacks, women, and the unskilled. All the Chicago leaders agreed that they should remain linked to the CFL, which remained politically powerful in the city, rather than join the CIO, which had no council and few affiliates in Chicago. Hence, Chicago saw none of the political factionalism between communists and liberals that divided the New York teachers. Indeed, by uniting into one union, the leaders of the Chicago teachers knew they could dominate the national AFT and oppose the communist unions of New York. Thus delegates to the AFT convention from the four Chicago unions met in July 1937 and unanimously agreed to vote against affiliation with the CIO.[155]

In May 1937, Fewkes became president of the MTU on a platform advocating amalgamation of all Chicago teachers' unions. The following October, the five thousand members of the four existing AFT affiliates, the Men Teachers Union, the Federation of Women High School Teachers, the Elementary Teachers Union, and the Playground Teachers Union, merged to form the Chicago Teachers Union, Local No. 1 of the AFT, with John Fewkes as first president. The new CTU experienced a huge increase in its membership, which a contemporary commentator likened to a "tidal wave."[156] By September 1938, the CTU claimed 8,500 members, making it the largest teachers' union in the country. Approximately two-thirds of Chicago public school teachers were CTU members; not until 1960 did another teachers' union in a large city secure a majority of those eligible for membership. Chicago was the first major city in America to achieve a united teachers' union; every other major city still had competing men's and women's and elementary school and high school teachers' unions.[157] It was clear to Anton Johannsen, vice president of the CFL, that "whatever may have been the private opinion in the past about teachers and their so-called dignity, not to identify themselves with the labor movement, has apparently completely disappeared."[158]

For a variety of reasons, however, up to a third of Chicago public school teachers refused to join the CTU. Some teachers clung to the notion that union membership was "unprofessional." The newly instituted Association of

Chicago Teachers (ACT), which opposed affiliation with labor on the grounds that it was unprofessional, had approximately six hundred members in the summer of 1939.[159] Many elderly, mostly Irish American, elementary teachers refused to join the CTU and remained loyal to Margaret Haley's CTF. Haley declared that she objected to merging with the other teachers' unions because the CTU included principals as members and would be dominated by high school teachers, who would not be willing to attend to the special problems of elementary school teachers. Reflecting its aging elementary school membership, the CTF concentrated its efforts on obtaining equal salaries for elementary school and high school teachers and improving the teachers' pension. The number of elementary school teachers that stayed with the CTF is difficult to determine, but the figure was possibly between one and two thousand. While in October 1938, 3,230 high school teachers (73 percent of all high school teachers) had joined the CTU, 4,375 elementary teachers (just 51.3 percent of all elementary school teachers) had joined.[160]

If the payless paydays and other problems in the school system proved vital to unification and to CTU growth, so too did the nationwide upsurge in union organizing in the 1930s. The deprivations of the Depression and prolabor federal legislation—in particular Section 7(a) of the National Industrial Recovery Act of 1933 and the National Labor Relations Act of 1935, known as the Wagner Act—encouraged many American workers to join unions and engage in militant action. In the ensuing upheaval, a general strike paralyzed San Francisco in the summer of 1934 and more than 350,000 textile workers were involved in a nationwide strike that shut down mills from Maine to Alabama. Autoworkers sat down in their factories in General Motors plants in Cleveland, Ohio, and Flint, Michigan, in the winter of 1936–37, forcing their employers to recognize the CIO-affiliated United Auto Workers (UAW) union. After their victory, a wave of strikes spread throughout the country. In Chicago, the main targets for Lewis and the CIO were the notoriously anti-union packinghouse and steel industries. To organize these industries, the CIO set up the Packinghouse Workers Organizing Committee (PWOC) and Steel Workers Organizing Committee (SWOC), both of which waged successful campaigns. Subsequently, the CIO gained recognition in the rubber, oil, electronics, and textile industries. Altogether, between 1933 and 1940, union membership in the United States grew from 2.8 million to nearly 9 million.[161]

Although the Wagner Act, which established collective bargaining rights for workers, did not apply to the public sector, it gave unions legitimacy through the governmental seal of approval, and CTU supporters capitalized on President Franklin Roosevelt's recognition of labor to recruit new members. CTU president John Fewkes told a teachers' meeting in April 1937 that "you have a right to organize. . . . The Wagner Act has convinced the United States of America that the president and our judicial bodies are going to back any decent labor movement. . . . Who dares to attack us for organizing a union? . . . they have the president of the United States of America against them."[162] As Chicago schoolteacher Elsa Ponselle recalled: "Everybody was heart and soul in the unions those days. Somebody said, 'Why not a teachers' union?' And why not?" New AFT locals were formed across the country and AFT membership rose from 7,000 in 1930 to 30,000 in 1940.[163]

This nationwide upsurge in unionism cannot alone account for the spectacular growth of the CTU. Public sector unions were excluded from the Wagner Act, and prejudice against them remained stronger than against unions in the private sector. A poll published in August 1937 found that 74 percent of those asked believed that government employees should not be able to join labor unions. Yet, another poll taken in the same month found that 76 percent of respondents were in favor of labor unions and only 24 percent against.[164] The prevailing prejudice against public sector unions, and especially industrial action by government workers, was expressed in 1937 by President Franklin Roosevelt: "Since their own services have to do with the functioning of the government, a strike of public employees manifests nothing less than an attempt on their part to prevent or obstruct the operations of government until their demands are satisfied. Such actions, looking toward the paralysis of government by those who have sworn to support it, is unthinkable and intolerable."[165] Although blue-collar public sector unions, such as postal workers and public works departments, had been active for some time, white-collar unionism in the public sector was relatively new. The American Federation of State, County and Municipal Employees (AFSCME), formed by white-collar workers in 1932, received its charter from the AFL in October 1936 but had barely 13,000 members by the following year.[166] Although teachers nationwide faced deprivation during the Depression, the vast majority of them remained unorganized, and growth was confined to a few larger cities. While two-thirds of the public school teachers in Chicago were CTU members, less than 4 percent of the national teaching force joined a union in the 1930s.

The CTU was particularly successful in gaining members because the city remained a strong union town with a tradition of teacher unionism, which reduced the anti-union policies of politicians and education board members. The CFL comprised about 293,000 members in 1929 and by the end of the 1930s the combined CFL and CIO membership in Chicago stood at about 393,000, or more than a quarter of the workforce.[167] Teachers who wanted to join the new union faced relatively little opposition from Chicago politicians and the Board of Education, and they enjoyed the protection of tenure. With tenure, contracts were no longer renewed annually, teachers could only be dismissed under certain conditions, and teachers had the right to appeal adverse decisions. After the state legislature passed the Otis Law (strengthening teacher tenure in 1917 and making it more difficult to dismiss teachers), the Board of Education rescinded the Loeb Rule, and authorities tolerated teachers' unions in Chicago. Mayor Kelly and the Democratic machine sought the support of John Fitzpatrick and the CFL and did not want to oppose a CFL-affiliated union, so machine supporters in the schools avoided conflict with the CTU. Although Chicago schools superintendent William Johnson initially banned the CTU from distributing literature in the schools and from holding union meetings on school premises, Mayor Kelly instructed Johnson to end his token opposition to the union.[168] Subsequently, the board allowed the CTU to operate in the schools, gave Fewkes a leave of absence for his time as union president, and allowed union delegates time off to attend conferences.[169]

Conclusion

"When America's great crisis is a story in the pages of history, there will be a significant chapter devoted to the unfailing sacrifice of the Chicago teachers," an editorial in the *NEA Journal* proclaimed in 1933.[170] Yet the historical significance and legacy of the Depression-era events in Chicago is found not in the financial hardships the teachers endured, but in the militancy they exhibited and the teachers' union they forged. For three decades, Chicago public school teachers were divided into quarreling unions that sought to gain professional status through non-militant activity. Faced with payless paydays, a new leadership emerged and teachers took to the streets demanding salaries and the respect they deserved. "This, to anyone even slightly familiar with the usual character and demeanor of the average American teacher, was indeed something new under the sun," recalled teacher Emma Levitt.[171]

While Chicago public school teachers were devoted to the public school system, and many began to believe that they alone were the protectors of a system of public education that those in power had abandoned, the issue that finally led to the formation of the VEC, and the ultimate consolidation of the teachers' unions in Chicago, was the issue of pay. Reflecting gender differences over the importance of bread-and-butter demands or social reform, the VEC was formed by male teachers who made no other demand than to obtain payment for the teachers. The VEC appealed to all Chicago teachers, long promised the rewards of professionalism, who were concerned with obtaining economic remuneration and in the process retaining their dignity. The demands that brought Chicago's teachers' unions together—teachers' desire for adequate salary and for dignity and respect that professionalism promised—remained. The gap between the idealized image and the actual status of teachers is crucial to an understanding of teacher militancy and the future trajectory of the CTU.

With no legal right to bargain with the school administrators, the CTU remained vulnerable to the vagaries of local politicians and overly dependent on the CFL. Most importantly, as Chicago teachers formed the CTU, they confronted a political machine that was gaining even greater control over the public schools. The union faced a critical choice: forge an alliance with reform organizations that would challenge the machine and change the city's politics and public schools or align with the machine and concentrate on issues of salary. The road taken would determine the character of public education in Chicago for years to come.

2

Struggling for an Identity,
1937–1941

Liberal reformers greeted the formation of the Chicago Teachers Union with widespread enthusiasm, believing that it heralded a new era in the city's system of public education and politics. University of Chicago professor, reforming Chicago alderman, and later U.S. senator Paul H. Douglas called the amalgamation "one of the most encouraging things that has happened in the city in recent years." Thomas E. Benner, dean of the School of Education at the University of Illinois, suggested that the formation of the CTU was "an important step towards democracy in the educative service." Public school teachers elsewhere looked to the CTU for guidance and inspiration. The CTU received visits from leaders of other locals and invitations from teachers, some as far away as England, for the union to explain the reasons for its success and to outline their program.[1]

Within the CTU leadership and rank and file, there was no clear agreement on which policies the union should pursue. Some, such as the new union executive secretary Kermit Eby, sought to align his organization with liberal elements in the city, play a major role in Chicago politics, and reform the public school system. Others, such as CTU president John Fewkes, showed less interest in political and educational reform and wanted the union to focus on salary restoration and achieving better working conditions. All teachers demanded a restoration of the pay that had been cut during the payless paydays of the early 1930s, but how far would they support the wider political demands of Kermit Eby? Drawing lessons from the business and political corruption that had caused the cash crisis in the public schools and inspired by the impulses that informed the larger upsurge of labor in that decade and the ideas of progressive educationalists, many Chicago teachers paid great attention to the need to reform the public school system. In effect, these teachers fashioned their own vision of public education that challenged the running of the existing Chicago public schools system. They demanded consultation with school authorities over decisions that affected their teaching, called for the end of political control of the schools, and sought the introduction of a school curriculum that addressed the political and social problems of the day. To satisfy their demands, public school teachers looked to the Chicago Federation of Labor (CFL) for support, became involved in electoral politics, and allied with civic organizations and liberal and progressive elements in the city.

Even if teachers began to think more about political and educational reform, the CTU's mobilization occurred amid increasing political control of the city's schools as Mayor Edward Kelly built one of the most powerful political organizations in U.S. history. At the same time, an increasingly conservative climate in the city and the nation confronted the newly formed union. The issue of public education threatened the stability of the Chicago Democratic machine, but by the end of the decade, the reform impulse was blunted and the schools remained even more firmly under the rule of politicians. Rather than openly challenge the Democratic organization as Kermit Eby suggested, John Fewkes and many of the schoolteachers began to compromise with Kelly's machine to satisfy bread-and-butter demands.

Mayor Kelly and the Democratic Machine

Mayor Edward J. Kelly and the Democratic Party consolidated their control over Chicago politics and public education in the mid 1930s. Kelly, elected mayor three times between 1933 and 1947, and Patrick Nash, head of the Cook County Democratic Party until his death in 1943, built what historian Roger Biles called "the most powerful—and probably the most famous—political machine in the nation." The Kelly-Nash machine had excellent organizational skills, faced weak political opposition, and enjoyed public support from the popularity of President Franklin D. Roosevelt's New Deal.[2] Reflecting on Kelly's success in reducing Chicago's debt and keeping taxes down, the *New York Times* commented in 1935 that the mayor had "turned one of the most ill-governed of cities into one of the best-governed." In his first contested mayoral election of 1935, Kelly carried all fifty wards and 799,060 votes, 75.3 percent of those cast, to his Republican opponent Emil C. Wetten's 167,106 votes. The Kelly-Nash machine seemed unassailable.[3]

Chicago had had a long history of political interference in the public school system, but the problem escalated after Kelly became mayor. As a reward for political services, Mayor Kelly had appointed seven new members to the eleven-member Board of Education in 1933, including his close friend James B. McCahey as board president. The board members were self-made small businessmen who had little previous experience in educational matters, and most neither lived in Chicago nor sent their children to the city's schools. After the death of school superintendent William J. Bogan in March 1936, the board appointed assistant superintendent William H. Johnson as the new superintendent of the Chicago public schools. While Bogan had maintained his independence from the board and Chicago politicians, Johnson was closely aligned with the Democratic machine and its supporters in the school administration.[4]

To Mayor Kelly and Patrick Nash, the schools were a vital source of political patronage. The non-instructional departments were quickly filled with patronage appointments, but the degree to which the education department could replace those already employed as teachers was tempered by teachers' tenure. To overcome this obstacle, Superintendent Johnson issued temporary teaching certificates to political contacts. The number of temporary teaching appointments in the Chicago schools jumped from 176 in 1937 to 234 in 1938 and to 434 in 1939. In 1940, the Education Committee of the City Club of Chicago reported that since 1937 "the use of temporary appointments has increased alarmingly to the point where it threatens to nullify the whole merit system which the Otis Law attempted to establish."[5] Superintendent Johnson and the board also appointed political friends to the administration and faculty of the Chicago Teachers College, formally known as the Chicago Normal School. Those favored by the political machine gained admission to the college as students, and the Board of Education only employed teachers who graduated from the college.[6] Finally, the Board of Education began to employ politically favored principals by manipulating the principals' exams overseen by Superintendent Johnson and two of his appointees.[7]

The Board of Education practiced widespread favoritism in the granting of contracts for school construction and equipment. The board assigned more than twenty books written solely or jointly by Superintendent Johnson in fields, as an NEA report later declared, "in which Dr. Johnson has not taught and has not been trained or prepared and is not recognized as an authority." The Chicago schools began to receive sports and candy shop supplies from a newly designated board source at higher prices than they had paid before. In 1939–40, Chicago was fourteenth out of the fifteen largest cities on the amount per pupil it spent on instruction and first in amount per pupil it spent on operation of plant.[8]

As patronage and corruption raised Chicago's educational costs, city politicians sought to keep property taxes down, and state politicians sought to limit educational expenditures. Both the rural-dominated Illinois legislature and Governor Henry Horner remained reluctant to increase the state's contribution to education to bail out corrupt Chicago politicians. In 1936 the Kelly-Nash machine supported Democrat Herman Bundesen for governor, but Horner won the nomination and was re-elected, making it even harder to obtain funding from the Illinois capital. Each time a measure was introduced in the state General Assembly to increase funding for Chicago public education, influential groups such as the Civic Federation, the Chicago Real Estate Board, and the Better Government Association fought the legislation on the grounds that it would be paid for with higher taxes. Thus during the 1930s, the Illinois General Assembly failed to pass an income tax, or to even raise a general sales tax, to finance the cash-strapped Chicago public schools. In 1936 Illinois ranked thirty-sixth out of forty-eight states in state contributions to public schools.[9]

With the Kelly-Nash machine unwilling to raise property taxes, Illinois politicians reluctant to increase the state's share of education funding, and the Board of Education using its resources to increase patronage, Chicago public school teachers continued to suffer. At the beginning of 1937, Chicago high school teachers had the eighth lowest maximum salary and the fifth lowest minimum salary in twenty-one of the largest U.S. cities, and the Chicago elementary school teachers had the second lowest maximum salary and the seventh lowest minimum salary. In eleven of the fifteen largest cities, public school teachers had had their rates of pay restored to pre-Depression levels. In the remaining four, Cleveland teachers had suffered a pay cut of 4 percent, St. Louis 6 percent, and Los Angeles 10 percent, while Chicago teachers had suffered a pay cut of 23.5 percent (see Table 3). In Chicago, the employees of the City of Chicago Sanitary District had had all their pay cut restored, those working for the Park District and Cook County were still cut only 7.5 percent, and the First Preserve District employees still had their pay cut 6.25 percent.[10] (See Table 4.)

Superintendent Johnson imposed his own ideas on the education department of the school system. More than anything else, the aggressive and domineering Johnson wanted to maintain sole control of the educational policy of the schools, and he sought no input from teachers and had no intention of even meeting, let alone negotiating with, the newly formed CTU. The central

Table 3. Salary Range of U.S. Teachers on February 1, 1937

City	High School Teachers Maximum	High School Teachers Minimum	City	Elementary School Teachers Maximum	Elementary School Teachers Minimum
Newark, N.J.	4600	2200	New York	3830	1608
New York	4500	2148	Newark, N.J.	3600	1500
Pittsburgh	3800	1800	Pittsburgh	3200	1200
St. Louis	3760	1400	Jersey City	2890	1190
Boston	3744	1728	Detroit	2800	1500
Jersey City	3510	1870	Rochester	2700	1200
Rochester	3350	1600	Washington D.C.	2600	1400
Milwaukee	3300	1400	San Francisco	2580	1500
San Francisco	3204	2004	St. Louis	2538	1100
Philadelphia	3200	1800	Cleveland	2448	1020
Washington D.C.	3200	1800	Cincinnati	2435	974
Cleveland	3060	1275	Philadelphia	2400	1200
Baltimore	3000	1500	Boston	2400	1248
CHICAGO	**2907**	**1377**	Milwaukee	2400	1200
Louisville	2850	935	Louisville	2400	765
Los Angeles	2840	1660	Los Angeles	2280	1300
Detroit	2800	1700	Baltimore	2200	1200
Seattle	2484	1462	Seattle	2116	1200
Cincinnati	2435	974	Portland	2000	1040
Portland	2000	1280	**CHICAGO**	**1912**	**1147**
Minneapolis	1986	926	Minneapolis	1721	705

Actual salaries with Chicago salaries cut 23.5 percent. *Source: Chicago's Schools* (March 1937), 1–3.

Table 4. Pay Restoration in the Chicago Area, 1937

	Maximum Cut	Present Cut
City of Chicago	21	0
Sanitary District	10	0
Public Library Board	27	0
First Preserve District	12.5	6.25
Cook County	15	7.5
Park District	20	7.5
Board of Education	23.5	21.8

Source: CTU Weekly News Bulletin, November 26, 1937, 1.

office of the Board of Education increasingly told teachers what to teach and supplied all the textbooks without input from those who had to use them.[11]

In order to implement its own patronage program, the board tried to silence its critics within the schools. Teachers who opposed the board's policies found themselves demoted or transferred. In March 1937, former Men Teachers Union leader William T. McCoy was demoted from the position of principal at Bowen High School to the principal of Beidler Elementary School, with drop in salary of some $800 a year. The same year, Johnson charged two teachers at the Chicago Teachers College with "disloyalty" and demoted them to high school positions. Superintendent Johnson ran a "ruthless administration that brooks no criticism" and presided over a "reign of terror" which frightened teachers into "hapless silence," commented the *Chicago Daily Times*.[12] In November 1939, Johnson supporters took over the Chicago Principals Club, and thereafter, the club, which had been one of Johnson's most vociferous opponents, frequently had the superintendent and the Board of Education as honored guests at its functions. A former executive of the Principals Club claimed, "The organization has deteriorated from a club dedicated to guarding the best interests of the school children to one whose members lick the boots of Supt. William H. Johnson in the hope that they may gain personal advancement."[13]

In its formative years, the CTU faced a resurgent conservatism. Business groups such as the National Association of Manufacturers and the U.S. Chamber of Commerce feared that poorly paid radical teachers indoctrinated students in what they considered the antibusiness plans of the Roosevelt government. Across America, conservative politicians, business groups, and patriotic organizations campaigned for the schools to instill a commitment to American political institutions and to inculcate the values of free enterprise.[14] In 1937 the American Civil Liberties Union declared that "it is hazardous in most communities for teachers to discuss in the classroom, and often outside, one or another of the subjects of communism, Soviet Russia, pacifism, trade unions, public ownership of industry, free trade, government regulation of industry, dishonest banking, civil liberties for radicals, racial equality, birth control, and sex hygiene."[15] By August 1935, twenty-two states and the District of Columbia had laws that required public school teachers to take an oath to support the U.S. Constitution. Twelve of these states had passed their laws since 1931.[16]

Chicago conservatives orchestrated their own campaign against the teaching of radical ideas in the public schools. "I am convinced there is considerable communism in the Chicago school system," Chicago school board trustee Charles Fry declared. Chicago Democratic representative William J. Connors agreed: "I don't think Communism has gone far in our state school system, but I do know that in Chicago the teachers have been subjected to the most vicious sort of undermining tactics by those who would overthrow our form of government. In their extremity, some of the teachers have given more heed to Communistic talk than they would if they were being paid regularly. I was amazed to learn that, in a recent teachers meeting in the city hall, there was objection to singing of the national anthem, although it was sung." In December 1937, Elmer J. Schnackenberg, minority leader of the lower house of the Illinois General Assembly, demanded the "purging" of "un-American instructors" from Illinois schools, claiming they were "poisoning the impressionable minds" of students. During 1934, the Hearst newspapers in Chicago, backed by Governor Horner, Mayor Kelly, and the Board of Education, campaigned for the enactment into law of loyalty oaths for Illinois schoolteachers. The communist teachers must be "rooted out like germs of pollution and disease," Hearst's *Chicago Herald and Examiner* proclaimed. In April 1935 the Illinois house of representatives passed loyalty oath bill 226, but the legislation was blocked in the senate two months later.[17]

Chicago, like other U.S. cities, certainly had a number of committed and active communists within the public schools. Chicago was the birthplace of the U.S. Communist Party in 1919, and in the fall of 1931 there were approximately two thousand party members in the city, a number which grew to more than three thousand in 1934.[18] During the Popular Front period of the mid-1930s, when the Communist Party allied with liberals and socialists and espoused reform, communist supporters in the Chicago public schools were firm advocates of the unification of teachers' unions. Once the teachers formed the CTU, communists called, unsuccessfully, for the union's affiliation with the left-leaning Congress of Industrial Organizations (CIO).[19]

Overall, few communist teachers operated in the Chicago public schools. Although many communists played leading roles in the CIO and the unionization of industrial workers in Chicago during the 1930s, the leaders of the teachers' unions shunned communist support. Opponents of communism were hard-pressed to find radical teachers in Chicago. In 1934, Elizabeth Dilling published a book titled *Red Network: A Who's Who and Handbook of Radicalism for Patriots,* which listed 460 organizations and well over a thousand individuals as suspected radicals in Chicago. The only teachers included in the list were Charles Stillman and Lillian Herstein, both of whom strongly opposed communism.[20] There was "a communist cell within the Chicago Teachers Union," John Fewkes recalled, "but it never had any influence to speak of and has just been a sort of loyal opposition."[21]

Chicago's public school teachers included fewer communists in their ranks than many other trades and industries in the city. Chicago Federation of Labor president John Fitzpatrick had made great efforts to remove communists from the CFL since the early 1920s, and the anticommunism of Fitzpatrick prevailed in the CFL during the 1930s. As Robert W. Iversen argued in his study of communism in the public schools: "When the Communists moved their national headquarters from Chicago that year [1923], they ceased to have any effective role in Chicago unionism."[22] Probably because of the opposition of Fitzpatrick, the Communist Party in Depression-era Chicago was more interested in working in the CIO and particularly in the stockyards and the steel industry.[23] Most importantly, as many studies have found, communists were disproportionately Jewish, immigrants from eastern and southern Europe, and African American, groups not represented in any strength among Chicago public school teachers. Chicago teachers, mostly native born of Irish, British, and German stock, came from communities with long traditions of unionism but not communism. Thus, while the CTU included few communist members and remained the center of anticommunist activity in the AFT, the four-thousand-strong New York teachers' union probably had close to a thousand Communist Party activists in its ranks before its expulsion from the AFT in 1941.[24]

The Politics of Teacher Unionism

Alongside John Fewkes, the most influential figure in the CTU was the newly appointed full-time executive secretary Kermit Eby. Born on September 21, 1903, in St. Joseph County, Indiana, Eby became a teacher in his home state after leaving school, a Brethren minister in 1927, and a student of international relations at the University of Chicago from 1929 to 1931. He then assumed the position of a high school teacher in Ann Arbor, Michigan, and helped organize the first teachers' union in the town. A member of the Michigan Socialist Party, he befriended autoworkers' leader Walter Reuther, helped to organize the autoworkers union, and participated in the sit-down strikes that led to the union's recognition. In 1936 he was suspended from his school by the board of education for his union activities and for corrupting the children with his beliefs. Recommended to the CTU by former alderman and progressive reformer Charles Merriam, he leapt at the chance to put his political ideas into action and became the union's spokesman in August 1937.[25]

Eby and Fewkes had different visions for the role the new union would play in Chicago politics. Eby was deeply committed to Christian socialism. Imbued with the ideas of rank-and-file activism that he saw in Michigan, he envisioned a teachers' union that would identify with the concerns of other workers and work in a coalition with left, liberal, and community organizations to reform the Chicago political system and improve the schools. The union, he argued, must "perpetuate the idealism that made Jane Addams the glory of Chicago" and should "develop teachers with a professional pride and social outlook" who would take an active role in the politics of the city. For Eby, teachers must "take part in the people's struggles and to grow roots in the community."[26] According to Eby, "[t]eachers cannot be secure in an unhealthy community. Teaching should be more than just a job, and a teacher organization more than just a pressure group." A teachers' union should be "an avenue for the achievement of a healthier community."[27]Believing that the CTU should be built on democratic participation of every member, he recommended periodic turnover in union policymaking positions and the payment to union representatives of the same wages as their members.[28]

In contrast, Fewkes focused on delivering better pay and improved working conditions to his members and on centralizing union decision making. Despite his brief moment of militancy with the VEC, Fewkes turned out to be a cautious leader who opted for compromise before conflict. He was less concerned with union democracy and community politics than was Eby. Unions, he maintained, were not agents of social change. They could provide good wages and better working conditions, but they could not fundamentally change Chicago politics or improve the lives of students outside the classroom. Fewkes further believed that the centralized leadership of the VEC was a major part of its success and wanted the new union to be controlled by full-time officers who made all the major decisions. While other founders of the union had wanted membership meetings to ratify CTU policy, Fewkes used his prestige to create a policymaking delegate assembly, the house of representatives, consisting of some 160 members. He wanted a "few people who are going to direct the actions of the group and that those people should have the opportunity to go ahead and do things; that they should not have to go back to the organization."[29]

This dispute between Fewkes and Eby over the direction of the CTU was nothing new to teacher unionism in Chicago or elsewhere. This schism was evident within the CTF between Margaret Haley, who supported reform, and many rank-and-file members who argued that the CTF should concentrate on improving teachers' pensions and tenure.[30] This conflict re-emerged between the bread-and-butter-oriented MTU and the more reformist FWHST. Once teachers formed the CTU, it was inevitable that this tension would resurface as the new union decided on policy and strategy. In 1930s Chicago, however, both Fewkes and Eby initially agreed that the Democratic political machine had to be confronted if teachers were to receive their pay. Therefore, the conflict between the two was initially submerged as they both sought to form alliances that would oppose the policies of the Democrats and their supporters on the Board of Education.

Whether they supported the reformist views of Eby or the bread-and-butter ideas of Fewkes, Chicago public school teachers showed enormous enthusiasm for the new union. Out of a claimed membership of 6,500, 3,500 teachers waited in line for an hour to attend the formal launching of the CTU on October 28, 1937. Approximately 80 percent of the membership voted in the first elections for CTU officers in December 1937 even though the offices of president and other leading positions were unopposed. After a long day's work in the classroom, many teachers who lived and worked the length and breadth of the city played an active role in the life of the union. From the formation of the CTU to the outbreak of World War II, more than six hundred teachers engaged in union committees or as CTU representatives, hundreds of schoolteachers regularly paid to attend union study classes, thousands participated in social activities, and the three-thousand-seat Chicago Auditorium was frequently packed as teachers came to listen to a variety of CTU speakers discussing a myriad of topics.[31]

The widespread enthusiasm Chicago schoolteachers showed for the CTU reflected a change in their political and social views and can be ascertained from Arthur Kornhauser's Chicago Attitude Survey, taken in 1937. Kornhauser, an associate professor of business psychology at the University of Chicago, asked two thousand people from seventeen occupations a number of questions to understand the differences in outlook between social classes. In the survey, the opinions of Chicago schoolteachers stood much closer to those of manual workers than to other "professional" groups such as engineers, lawyers, and physicians. In all positions, teachers were decidedly liberal and often the most liberal in the survey. Reflecting the attitude of teachers toward cost-cutting groups like the Citizens' Committee on Public Expenditures (CCPE), 88 percent of the schoolteachers in the survey believed that "wealthy businessmen have too much influence in running the affairs of the nation." Also, 67 percent of schoolteachers declared themselves in favor of the New Deal and 80 percent believed that "the government should aim at making peoples' wealth and incomes more nearly equal." Reflecting the unfair treatment teachers received during the payless paydays, 75 percent of the teachers replied "no" to the question, "Do you think that working people in general get fair treatment and fair play?" This was the second lowest number of "no" answers to this particular question in the survey.[32]

Schoolteachers voiced many concerns shared by other workers during the 1930s. In general, many workers in the United States were inclined to a "moral capitalism" in which they and their children would have a chance at social mobility and a greater share of the national income. Workers sought to gain a voice in their working lives, to be treated with respect by employers, and gain greater job security. Reflecting this, teachers sought economic security with the reversal of the 23.5 percent salary cut, better working conditions in terms of smaller classes and less bureaucratic clerical work, and dignified treatment from the school authorities.[33]

Many Chicago public school teachers drew on other impulses to fashion their own vision of public education and challenge the existing Chicago public school system. Progressive educators and in particular the so-called "social reconstructionists," a group of intellectuals who became convinced during the economic depression of the early 1930s that schoolteachers and public education should take a lead in constructing a fairer society, influenced the views of many Chicago schoolteachers. In numerous speeches, books, articles, and journals such as *Social Frontier* and *Progressive Education,* George Counts, John Childs, John Dewey, Goodwin Watson, and other Progressive educators who were active in the AFT had argued that teachers should join labor unions and spark the labor movement to push for educational reform. Most famously, George Counts argued in his 1932 pamphlet *Dare the Schools Build a New Social Order?* that schoolteachers should impose on their students the view that economic resources should be distributed more equally. Outside the classrooms, Counts urged teachers to join labor unions and campaign for educational reform and the democratization of society. Counts argued that "teachers, if they could increase sufficiently their stock of courage, intelligence and vision, might become a social force of some magnitude. Through powerful organizations they might at least reach the public conscience and come to exercise a larger measure of control over the schools than hitherto. To the extent that they are permitted to fashion the curriculum and the procedures of the school they will definitely and positively influence the social attitudes, ideals and behavior of the coming generation."[34]

Through strong personal connections, social reconstructionists influenced the thinking of the Chicago teachers. Chicago had long been a major center of educational reform. Francis Parker, principal of Cook County Normal School; John Dewey, professor at the University of Chicago Laboratory School; and Ella Flagg Young, superintendent of the Chicago public schools from 1909 to 1915, all played prominent roles in Progressive education. Former University of Chicago professor George Counts corresponded with CTU leaders and spoke at union meetings, and the union supported Counts when he successfully ran for president of the AFT in 1939. Progressives John De Boer, director of student teaching at the Chicago Teachers College, and George E. Axtelle and William W. Wattenberg, both from the School of Education at Northwestern University, joined the CTU and published articles in the union publications. Various other Progressive educational theorists appeared on CTU platforms and on weekly CTU radio programs. The *Chicago Union Teacher* and the *American Teacher* published numerous articles by and about the social reconstructionists, and teachers actively participated in Progressive Education Association conventions.[35]

The views of some Chicago teachers were further influenced by the growth of fascism in Europe and the supposed threat of fascism at home. As the Depression continued and fascism spread from Italy to Germany and then to Spain, some Americans felt that the conditions were ripe for fascism to take hold at home. Schoolteachers believed that unelected groups who dictated education policy and threatened teachers' academic freedom endangered both public education and U.S. democracy.[36] Lillian Herstein, for example, declared, "We still have for the most part our civil liberties. That does not mean, however, that Fascism cannot get a foothold in America and use the public schools as its instrument."[37] CTU leader Mary Herrick concluded in 1935 that "[t]he danger from Fascism is greater than that from Communism, and both can be defeated by independent, clear thinking, idealistic American citizens."[38]

The most important demand of the Chicago schoolteachers was stopping the interference in public education by local corrupt politicians and business groups. The payless paydays reaffirmed to many Chicago schoolteachers that educational experts should run the schools, not politicians and business-people who were using the schools for their own ends. "Chicago teachers are convinced that there are unseen political and economic powers which control Chicago government and education, powers which are definitely anti-social in their attitudes toward education," noted a CTU publication. "Likewise, they feel that there are many areas in Chicago politics that need cleaning up and that the time has come for teachers to be a major force for reform in the community."[39] Kermit Eby declared to a meeting of three thousand cheering Chicago schoolteachers in 1938, "Let every teacher unite with parents and civic groups throughout the city for political action. The time has come for Chicago to clean its Augean stables. Together with the public we can restore the morale of the teachers, discredit the politicians who have usurped the educators' position, and preserve the democracy we cherish."[40] As schools superintendent William Johnson promoted politically connected teachers to the positions of principal and gave temporary teaching certificates to less-qualified but better-connected teachers, the union campaigned for the appointment and promotion of teachers on merit, not on the patronage of politicians. In addition, teachers demanded that school finance should not be controlled by bankers or other business leaders but by elected state and federal legislators, and they wanted to increase the state's and the federal government's financial contribution to the Chicago schools and rely less on the local property tax.[41]

Public school teachers also sought a greater say in school policy and rejected Superintendent Johnson's authoritarian approach to school administration. Teachers wanted to be consulted about curriculum, class size, and policies that affected their working lives. One of the first resolutions adopted by the CTU house of representatives called upon the school authorities to "provide channels for teacher participation in shaping educational policies according to principles consonant with democratic education."[42] According to union activist Edna Siebert, the teachers wanted "an opportunity to help develop educational standards and ideals. Union teachers believe in the principle that it is the teachers' responsibility to help formulate educational policy. They are willing to cooperate in the administration of their schools, but they maintain they should have an opportunity to suggest and advocate such changes in the school system as seem to be improvements."[43] As an organization, the CTU sought to influence school policy by undertaking research, publishing reports, and giving this information to the school administration and interested community organizations. Democratic participation in decision making also meant the right of the CTU to negotiate for its members and to have at least some say in public education policy. For the remaining years of the decade, the CTU leaders tried, sometimes successfully but more often not, to discuss school problems with the school administrators.[44]

Although teachers wanted more input in school policy, neither the CTU nor teachers elsewhere made a concerted effort to achieve collective bargaining rights with the Board of Education. Labor unions in the private sector thrived during the late 1930s, but teachers' unions still faced opposition from the general public, school administrators, and the government.[45] Congress excluded public school teachers and other public sector employees from the National Labor Relations Act of 1935, which granted collective bargaining rights to labor unions in the private sector. "All government employees should realize that the process of collective bargaining, as usually understood, cannot be transplanted into the public service," wrote President Franklin Roosevelt in August 1937. "It has its distinct and insurmountable limitations when applied to public personnel management. The very nature and purposes of government make it impossible for administrative officials to represent fully or to bind the employer in mutual discussions with government employee organizations," he asserted. "The employer is the whole people, who speak by means of laws enacted by their representatives in Congress."[46] It was only in 1959 that Wisconsin became the first state to pass a law that granted municipal employees, including teachers, the right to join a union and to collective bargaining, and it was not until the 1960s that the CTU achieved collective bargaining rights with the Board of Education.

If collective bargaining rights for teachers seemed beyond the realm of possibility, teachers still demanded greater control over what they taught in the classroom. Chicago teachers declared that they wanted a public education system in which teachers were free to experiment in the classroom and to pursue their work without the interference of supervisors, administrators, or politicians. One of the central planks of the union was the demand for academic freedom and for adequate tenure to protect teachers from arbitrary dismissal. Lillian Herstein insisted that "teachers must be absolutely free to discuss frankly and thoroughly all current, political, social and scientific questions [and] express their approval or disapproval of any government policies." For the good of the children and their "spiritual and intellectual development," teachers "must expose them to all points of view, orthodox and unorthodox, so that they may learn how to think for themselves in the presence of real situations and conflicting ideas."[47] Kermit Eby argued that the formation of the union meant a chance for teachers to have "free speech on political and social matters without the loss of job."[48]

But the desire to control their own teaching had been undermined by the increase in enrollment and class sizes during the Depression and by the management policies of Superintendent Johnson, which had made teaching in the Chicago public schools much more difficult. "Education as now infesting the educational plant of Chicago is based on the wrong principles or else the buildings are not designed for it," argued one teacher. "Pupils and teachers alike gypsy from one room to another like parts on the conveyor belt in an automobile plant."[49] Another teacher complained that administrators were "assigning teacher and class to a corner of the lunch room for science, or accounting or stenographic work, where the clatter of dishes and the loud voices of the lunch room assistants may add to the general unfitness of the milieu. The basis of the difficulty is the inability of our school authorities to provide adequate space and suitable equipment for the Education of Children." These conditions, the teacher concluded, "make teaching a farce and learning impossible."[50]

Like the progressive educational theorists, some schoolteachers expressed a desire to use public schooling to revitalize the American liberal tradition and establish a more democratic society. While business groups and newspapers such as the *Chicago Tribune* campaigned for a restrictions in the liberal arts curriculum, schoolteachers held that the safeguarding of liberty required the expansion of the so-called "fads and frills" and the widest diffusion of knowledge throughout society. A female teacher argued that without a broader conception of public education, there would be a "small class who possess or control most of the wealth, who have a monopoly on most the cultural advantages, who thru their influence determine the political, economic and social policies of the nation. At the other extreme there will be a very large submerged class who will have comparatively little of the comforts or luxuries of life, whose education will be stripped of all so-called fads and frills." By contrast, she suggested, the "progressive development of society" can only be achieved "by expanding our present education and giving an ever broader and more liberalizing kind of education to the masses of the people."[51] Using the language of the social reconstructionists, Lillian Herstein argued that public schools should be "instrumental in bringing about a more just social order by peaceful methods."[52] Chicago schoolteachers, surrounded by corrupt politicians and interfering big business at home and creeping fascism abroad, saw themselves as defenders of free institutions that could only be maintained with educated citizens. High school teacher Wanda Taeschner, chair of the AFT National Educational Policies Committee, used her national platform to urge teachers' unions to "extend and enrich democratic education and to widen educational opportunity."[53]

As the reform era of the 1930s opened up greater opportunities for questioning U.S. society, some Chicago teachers at least surreptitiously adapted the school curriculum and pushed at the boundaries of acceptable classroom instruction. Although under scrutiny from politicians and pressure groups, once the classroom door was closed teachers had a large degree of autonomy. Schoolteacher Edith Smith revealed that she passed on what she had learned about politicians and business leaders to her pupils: "they have heard some remarks about the present Chicago city administration that would burn the ears of our dignitaries." As a result, the students "are doing some thinking of their own about profit versus service and 'wider distribution of the nation's wealth.'"[54] As fascism spread in Europe, some Chicago teachers wanted an emphasis in the curriculum on world affairs and on the political, social, and economic structure of society. "It is the task of the schools to interpret the world and its problems to the boys and girls of America in order that a citizenry is developed capable of solving the problems of unemployment, social prejudice, poverty and war," argued Ethel Parker, editor of the CTU paper, in 1938.[55]

The interest of teachers in developing a curriculum that dealt with social and political problems was apparent in a survey undertaken in October 1939. A CTU committee surveyed 213 members to find out what issues the membership wanted to learn more about in the CTU-run study classes. The survey listed forty-two possible topics for study from which the teachers could make their choices. As well as the topics of "book reviews" and "pensions," the teachers' most popular choices included "propaganda analysis," "progressive methods," and "international issues." All these topics were part of political developments at home and abroad that could form the core of a socially concerned curriculum.[56]

Many schoolteachers voiced concern not only with what was taught, but the way it was taught. In reaction to lecturing and rote learning, which was still prominent in classrooms across the nation, some Chicago teachers insisted that teachers act as guides to students' learning. Influenced by Progressive education, they espoused the idea that the classroom should not be autocratic or based on rigid discipline but should promote initiative, open-mindedness, and self-confidence in children. "Teachers should be encouraged to experiment, within their respective fields, in both educational matter and class-room procedures in which each pupil has a necessary part," the Education Committee of the CTU believed.[57] One high school teacher, Hayne Leavell, declared that he and his fellow teachers were in a "struggle to achieve more democracy in our way of classroom life." He preferred a "self-governing class" in which the students learn "under leaders elected by themselves, while I serve as coach."[58] High school teacher Wilson Boetticher suggested, "If the student is allowed an active share, under teacher guidance, not dominance, in class and school organization, the Social Studies class has begun to answer the demand that something be done to provide training in citizenship that will carry on after formal schooling is over."[59]

Just like their male colleagues, women wanted restoration of pay, better working conditions, a say in school policy, and autonomy in the classroom, but they also voiced their own demands. At a time when some educational experts wanted to tempt men back into teaching by paying them more than women, elementary teachers, more than 90 percent of whom were women, sought economic equality in the form of a single salary schedule that gave elementary school and high school teachers the same pay. In addition, as many school boards dismissed or refused to hire married women teachers on the grounds that they did not need the money, women insisted on the right of married women to teach. In particular, they sought maternity leave so that married women would find it easier to return to work, and they protested legislation that sought to prohibit the right of married teachers to keep their jobs. The CTU supported state legislation prohibiting school boards from using marriage as reason for the dismissal of women teachers and forbidding the employment of married women whose husbands earned more than $1,500 a year.[60]

Women schoolteachers played an active role in the Chicago union. In the first CTU elections in 1937, all the main offices except the president were filled by women, including the positions of vice president, recording secretary, financial secretary, treasurer, and all six regional vice presidents. Out of twenty-six elected officers, nineteen were women. In the schools, women dominated the ranks of elected union delegates. A report from March 1938 showed that only one out of twenty union delegates was a man. Between 1938 and 1941, approximately two-thirds of the CTU delegates to the AFT conventions were women. In New York and Gary, Indiana, the other major locals in the AFT, women made up only 40 percent of their delegations.[61]

Former Federation of Women High School Teachers (FWHST) leaders Mary J. Herrick and Lillian Herstein brought the tradition of women's social reform with them as they played prominent roles in the early years of the CTU. Both women had a long history of involvement in the labor movement, a strong commitment to racial equality and working women's issues, and experience in a variety of community organizations. Herrick, a social science teacher, had been president of the FWHST from 1933 to the organization's demise in 1937. Then, at the age of forty-two, she became first vice president of the CTU with responsibilities for high schools. Like Fewkes, Herrick was a member of the Disciples of Christ, a liberal Protestant denomination that stressed egalitarianism. She provided the organizational experience and labor and political contacts that John Fewkes needed to build the new union. From 1935 to 1940, Herrick served as AFT vice president and was instrumental in building the nationwide influence of the CTU.[62]

While Mary Herrick was a quietly spoken, behind-the-scenes administrator, Herstein, nine years her senior, was a fiery street speaker and veteran of political conflicts. In 1937, *Life* magazine described the fifty-year-old Herstein as "the most important woman in the American labor movement." She joined the FWHST in 1916 and remained for twenty-five years the only woman on the executive board of the CFL. She taught English at Crane Junior College on the west side of the city and became a leading advocate for workers' education. During the 1920s and 1930s, she was an instructor in workers' education at the University of Chicago, the University of Wisconsin, and Bryn Mawr College. Herstein also helped form the Farmer Labor Party, which had been organized in 1920 by the CFL, and in 1932 she ran unsuccessfully for Congress in Illinois. In 1936, a strong advocate of old age pensions and unemployment insurance and convinced by the New Deal policies of Franklin Roosevelt, Herstein directed the Speakers Bureau of Labor's Non Partisan League, an organization that supported the re-election of Roosevelt as president.[63]

To further encourage women to join the union, the union initiated a program of social and cultural activities. Thousands of teachers attended tea parties, card parties, and style shows in various parts of the city, and the union organized picnics and summer outings to the country, golf tournaments, dances, operettas, luncheons, and movie shows. The CTU ran its own bowling league, which attracted more than five hundred bowlers in thirty-six teams from different schools by 1939. The union also gave a much-needed outlet for talented teachers in the arts. The union had its own dance group, theater group, writers group, orchestra, choral group, and glee club. In preference to traditional male-orientated sports like football and baseball, the CTU promoted the more genteel sports of golf, tennis, ping-pong, bowling, and softball.[64]

From its inception, the CTU, as much as any other predominantly white educational association or even teachers' union, promoted the demands of its black members. While labor unions helped African Americans as much as if not more than most organizations, they were often guilty of reflecting society's racist ideas. With few exceptions, for generations many labor unions had excluded or discriminated against black workers, and most African American workers either ignored unions or forged their own. It was only during the late 1930s, with the development of the more inclusive CIO, that union leaders placed more emphasis on promoting racial equality. With a left cadre of activists and organizing in the non-union unskilled sectors of the economy, the CIO unions actively recruited black workers, who in turn joined unions in greater numbers.[65]

Although some of the CTU's leading founders such as Kermit Eby and Lillian Herstein wanted the organization to promote racial justice, none took as much interest in the project as Mary Herrick. She taught in the South Side in the all-black Wendell Phillips High School between 1928 and 1935 and then at Jean Baptiste Pointe DuSable High School from 1935 until her retirement in 1961. As part of her M.A. in political science at the University of Chicago, Herrick chose to write her thesis on "Negro Employees of the Chicago Board of Education," for which she examined the political patronage that led to the segregated pattern of employment in the schools. Aside from her union work, Mary Herrick encouraged her black students. Alice Blair, former deputy superintendent of the Chicago Public Schools, commented that Herrick "constantly made me believe that I was worthwhile, that I could achieve, and I could make a contribution not only to my family but to my race." A colleague of Herrick's at DuSable High School remembered that she "went in to her own pocket to help get some of these kids into college and to pay their tuition . . . she went above and beyond the call of duty in the help she gave those black students." She was a "sincere and a great teacher."[66]

While many labor unions North and South barred black members or relegated them to segregated locals, Chicago's teachers' unions neither excluded nor isolated African Americans. Teachers chose some blacks to become union delegates and officers. Clarence Lee, a teacher at Wendell Phillips High School, was a member of the organization's house of representatives from 1939 to 1948 and served on the executive board from 1942 to 1948. With African American teachers allowed to teach only in all-black, overcrowded, and underfunded schools in the "Black Belt" on the city's South Side, Lee beseeched his black colleagues to join and participate in the union to obtain equality. In the few months after its founding, the CTU study classes, radio programs, and publications featured African American speakers such as A. Philip Randolph, head of the Brotherhood of Sleeping Car Porters, and leaders of the Chicago Urban League, who discussed issues such as organizing black workers and racial discrimination in housing, jobs, and schooling.[67]

Yet the issue of race played only a small part in the activities of teacher unionists in Chicago. While espousing racial equality, the CTU did little in practical terms to challenge racial discrimination in the hiring of black teachers, the assignment of black teachers away from white schools, or the unequal segregated system of education. White teachers, the overwhelming majority of the union membership, remained unconcerned with the problems of their black colleagues or black schools. The black teachers, of whom only a few hundred at best were union members, were too few to put pressure on the union to tackle racial issues. It would require a growth in the number of African American teachers, the movement of African Americans beyond the Black Belt, and an active civil rights movement to bring about change in later decades.

Community Alliances

To achieve its aims, the union set out to forge links with local civic groups. Unlike teachers in New York City, who were tainted with communism, and unions in the private sector, whose strikes were often opposed by middle-class reform organizations, the CTU had strong liberal credentials, a no-strike policy, and common interests with reform organizations. Both the teachers and the civic groups sought reform of the funding for the Chicago system of public education, the removal of political influence in the schools, and the return of teachers' pay. The CTU set up a public relations committee to cooperate with civic, labor, and religious groups in the city in order to sway public opinion, support legislation and put electoral pressure on the Democratic politicians.[68]

Urged on by Kermit Eby, large numbers of teachers played an active role in the Citizens Save Our Schools Committee, later the Citizens Schools Committee (CSC), founded in July 1933 to oppose the educational cuts. The CSC produced its own journal, *Chicago's Schools,* and dispatched speakers to every part of the city. Teachers spoke at its meetings and constituted the bulk of the membership, as much as 90 percent of the approximately five-thousand-member committee in 1934. Between 1938 and 1947 the CTU contributed about $3,000 per year to the CSC, or more than a third of the union's average yearly expenditure.[69]

The teachers also maintained strong relations with other influential civic organizations. Charlotte Carr, the head of Hull House, became a regular speaker at CTU events, and union representatives attended meetings at the settlement house.[70] The CTU affiliated with the Women's Trade Union League (WTUL), and Lillian Herstein and Genevieve Souther of the CTU served on the executive board of the Chicago WTUL.[71] Other groups such as the Chicago Women's Club, the Women's City Club, and the League of Women Voters remained supportive of the CTU. Mary Herrick became chair of the Cook County Federation of Women's Clubs during the Depression. John Fewkes, Kermit Eby, and Mary Herrick, all committed Christians, were particularly important in attaining the support of Chicago churches.[72]

Parent Teacher Associations (PTAs) joined with other civic groups in aiding the CTU. These predominantly white middle-class organizations had seen a spectacular growth in membership during the Great Depression. Before the education cuts of the early 1930s, PTAs worked at the level of the local school, concentrated on social events and support for school functions, and did not concern themselves with school policies. Under the impact of growing high school attendance and the payless paydays, the PTAs reluctantly became more politically active and interested in the running and financing of public schools. During the payless paydays, the Illinois Congress of Parents and Teachers cooperated with the teachers in opposing the education cuts, and Holland Flagler, president of the Illinois Congress of Parents and Teachers, became the first president of the CSC. Most of their actions were carried on at the local level, where the PTAs petitioned their legislators to gain more money for the schools and the teachers.[73]

The union engaged in an unprecedented campaign to shift the ideological debate surrounding Chicago education and politics. Union members on the publicity committee issued daily press releases and distributed a weekly paper, a monthly magazine, and other publications to civic groups, local newspapers, university and school libraries, ministers, and educators. From its inception, the CTU sponsored a weekly radio series over WCFL, the CFL radio station, and administered a speakers bureau that sent out representatives to speak at hundreds of meetings of PTAs, women's clubs, unions, educational conferences and conventions, civic organizations, and schools of education.[74]

The alliance with community organizations and union propaganda proved important in the CTUs ideological war with the Kelly-Nash machine, but it was the economic strength and political connections of the CFL that the CTU hoped would put direct pressure on the Board of Education. "[E]very major issue the Union undertook required the assistance of the Chicago Federation of Labor," argued high school teacher Bessie Slutsky in the early 1940s. At the end of the 1930s, CFL membership stood at about 330,000. The CTU was the second largest local in the CFL, and teachers' leader Lillian Herstein played a prominent role in the federations' executive board. CFL leaders appeared at CTU meetings and allowed the union to broadcast a weekly radio series on its radio station WCFL. Moreover, the CFL was the most powerful affiliate of the Illinois State Federation of Labor, whose main work was lobbying for legislation in the state legislature at Springfield.[75]

Most important, by the mid 1930s the Kelly-Nash machine had formalized a working agreement with the CFL. The formation of the CIO in 1935 pushed the CFL to the right and into the arms of Mayor Kelly. While Lewis launched an organizing drive in the mass-production industries, including meatpacking and steel in Chicago, the AFL, with its historic focus on the skilled worker, bitterly opposed the CIO. In June 1937, under orders from AFL president William Green, Fitzpatrick disaffiliated all the CIO unions, which included the more left-wing unions in the CFL. The more conservative affiliates that remained within the weakened CFL became more accommodating to the Democratic machine.[76]

But Mayor Kelly and the Democratic machine cemented a close relationship with the newly organized CIO in the city as well. After the Memorial
Day massacre of May 1937 at the Republican Steel plant, when police opened
fire and killed ten CIO picketers and wounded more than eighty others, Kelly
made a concerted effort to appease the CIO. The following year the mayor
pressured Armour, the large packinghouse company, to recognize the CIO.
In return for the non-interference of police in future picketing and strikes
and the appointment of union officials to municipal bodies, the CIO supported Kelly in the 1939 mayoral elections.[77]

The alliance between the CFL and the Kelly machine proved beneficial to
both parties. The mayor consulted with the CFL leadership on various political appointments, including those on the Board of Education. Charles W.
Fry, president of the Machinists Union and appointed to the board in 1933,
and his successor, pipe fitters leader Wilson Frankland, consistently voted
with the other board members. The political machine protected the jobs and
high wages of city employees, including school janitors. In 1939 Kelly used
his influence in the state senate to defeat the Lantz bill, a measure forbidding
sit-down strikes, secondary boycotts, and mass picketing. In return, the CFL
endorsed Democratic candidates at election time and kept peaceful industrial
relations that enabled Kelly to consolidate and strengthen his power.[78]

At a time when politicians and school administrators frowned upon political activism by teachers and other public workers, the CTU became directly involved in electoral politics. In 1939–40 the U.S. Congress passed the
Hatch Act, which banned public employees from running for office in federal
elections.[79] Yet the CTU rejected this non-political stance, campaigning for
liberal reformer Paul H. Douglas, a professor of economics at the University
of Chicago, in his successful election as alderman of the 5th Ward in 1939.
John Fewkes, Mary Herrick, and Lillian Herstein headed the campaign and
used it to highlight the situation of the teachers in the schools. Subsequently,
Douglas, a CTU member, became one of its staunchest allies and often the
only alderman to vote against Mayor Kelly in the City Council. Later the
CTU supported Douglas in his campaign to become U.S. senator and Adlai
Stevenson in his effort to become the governor of Illinois.[80]

Unable to support either Kelly or his main Democratic opponent Tom
Courtney in the 1939 mayoral election, the CTU attempted to run its own
mayoral candidate. The CTU, along with progressives Charles E. Merriam and
Paul H. Douglas, urged Harold L. Ickes, secretary of the interior in Franklin
Roosevelt's first cabinet and a former Chicago lawyer, to run for mayor as an
independent Democrat. The CTU believed that Ickes would act as a rally-

ing point for all those who wanted reform of the city. In November 1938, the CTU executive committee sent John Fewkes to Washington, D.C., to urge Ickes to run for the Democratic nomination. After talking to Ickes, Fewkes visited William Green, president of the AFL, and asked him to encourage other Chicago unions to support Ickes' candidacy. Partly because a statute prohibited anyone who had not lived in the city for at least a year before the election from running for mayor, and partly because he was committed to his work in the nation's capital, Ickes chose not to run.[81]

Union leaders instructed their members to vote for candidates friendly to the teachers' cause. The CTU committee on political information sent questionnaires on teachers concerns to all candidates for alderman, congress, and the state legislature. The union asked the candidates whether they would urge the school board to decrease class sizes, restore teachers' pay, support collective bargaining, and uphold the merit system. The union tabulated this information and the votes of sitting candidates on bills supported by the union and published the results in the CTU paper. The CTU dispatched teachers to interview candidates for ward committeeman and asked if they would refrain from using political influence to hire or promote teachers.[82]

The growing influence of the CTU forced candidates for political office in Chicago to take account of the unions' concerns. Republican ward committeeman Raymond J. Peacock, candidate for county assessor, based his campaign around the corruption of the Kelly-Nash machine and "the plight of the teachers." He stood for the restoration of teachers' pay, protection of teachers' tenure, restoration of the ten-month school year, support for the teachers' union as a bargaining agent in matters concerning welfare of teachers, and appointment of new school trustees and superintendent.[83] Prospective and sitting aldermen attended CSC meetings to show their concern for public education. In April 1940, the six candidates for governor and the four for state's attorney spoke at a CTU membership meeting. Each candidate supported the teachers' position of getting politics out of education, increasing teachers' salaries, and naming a new board of education.[84]

Results

The CTU had some successes with their strategy, particularly in persuading the board to restore teachers' pay. In June 1937, Fewkes and other teachers staged a two-hour sit-down in the office of board president James McCahey demanding the restoration of pay, but McCahey refused to see them. After Fewkes threatened to send hundreds of teachers to the Board of Education every week, McCahey reluctantly met with representatives of the teachers.[85] As Margaret Haley recalled, "McCahey faced the probable event of a recurrence of the Marching Periods of 1933. Such a recurrence would be even more serious than it had been then for the reason that the Fewkes crowd had, as Fewkes had said, a more powerful backing, and for the added reason that the public was more radically minded than it had been in the earlier period. Something had to be done—and done fast—to break the growing power of the Fewkes Union."[86] On July 28, 1937, the Board of Education announced its first partial restoration of teachers' pay by adding four days to the beginning of the 1937–38 school year.[87] In the summer and fall of 1937, at the request of the CTU, thousands of church leaders, politicians, and voters in Chicago sent letters to Mayor Kelly, Governor Horner, and the members of the Board of Education requesting the restoration of pay. In January 1938, the Board of Education added an additional six days to the school year.[88]

While Chicago schoolteachers made some headway in restoring pay, the CTU had less success in opposing patronage in the school system. The CTU supported three high-profile court cases, which dominated newspaper headlines from 1937 to 1939, to publicize the issue of patronage. In one case, William T. McCoy was ousted as principal at Bowen High School in March 1937 because he had requested the transfer of a close friend of James McCahey's sister. In the other two cases involving Raymond M. Cook on the one hand and Hiram B. Loomis and Russell L. Wise on the other, the plaintiffs alleged that the 1936 principals' exam was fixed in favor of those with political connections. Although the CTU lost these cases, they generated enormous publicity and made clear to the public that the schools were in the grip of political control.[89] In December 1940 the Board of Education appointed an independent Board of Examiners chosen from the heads of universities to control the oral part of the principals' exam and the entrance exam to the Chicago Teachers College. It was a minor victory and one that eased but did not end the problem of patronage.[90]

The ending of political patronage remained elusive, but the CTU played a part in helping to stop the spread of vocational educational programs and of further patronage. On November 10, 1937, Chicago newspapers reported that the Board of Education was going to switch from 80 percent emphasis on academic subjects to 80 percent vocational subjects in the Chicago high schools. The board would replace more than half of the 4,338 high school teachers with vocational education instructors. To save money, Superintendent Johnson announced, only temporary appointees were to be named for teaching positions in the academic subjects. The plan would have allowed

Johnson to replace half the high school teaching force with political appointees. Mayor Kelly supported the vocational plan as "a great idea." The following day, a committee of the school board left for a two-week inspection tour of the San Francisco and Los Angeles trade schools.[91]

Concerned about the replacement of teachers with patronage-controlled temporary teachers and the decline in the academic curriculum, the CTU set out to stop the introduction of the vocational plan. Kermit Eby called the plan "fascist." Fewkes warned: "The change from the fundamental assumption of American education that schools shall train for citizenship, to the idea that they should train children for obedient and unquestioning participation in a fixed industrial order, strikes at the heart of Americanism." With the newspapers publicizing the opposition to the plan, and the CFL making deputations to the mayor's office, Kelly called a meeting with Superintendent Johnson and representatives from the CFL, the IFL, and the CTU. Political observers believed that the mayor, "having his hands full with the Democratic factional fight, apparently decided that the Johnson plan was arousing too much heat, and that something ought to be done about it. So the union leaders were invited to step up." Johnson blamed the newspapers for misrepresenting his views and denied that there was ever any such plan. Accordingly, the *Chicago Herald and Examiner* front-page headline declared that "Unions Win Protest on Schools, Vocational Plan Revised; Ban Politics."[92]

The 1939 Mayoral Election

As the 1939 mayoral election approached, both the CTU and the Kelly-Nash machine faced problems. For the CTU, the machine was still firmly in place, teachers' pay had not been fully restored, and there was little increased spending on education. Although the machine politicians were formidable opponents for the union, the 1939 mayoral election was going to be a more difficult contest for Kelly than the 1935 election had been. After the Memorial Day massacre of May 1937, Kelly was concerned about losing support in some of the core working-class constituencies. In contrast to 1935, the mayor faced stronger opponents as Republicans were joined by reform-minded independents, and Tom Courtney, the major contender for the Democratic nomination, gained the support of Governor Horner.

The issue of the public schools dominated the 1939 mayoral election campaign. The CTU, its allies, and newspapers highlighted the political control and deteriorating conditions in the schools, and these issues became among the most debated of the campaign. In response to the publicity, all four candidates in the primary election, including Mayor Kelly, promised to eliminate politics from the school administration. The strength of the school issue, and of the CTU, was confirmed on February 6, 1939, when, in an unprecedented meeting, all four mayoral candidates appeared before more than three thousand CTU members.[93]

With Kelly facing possible electoral defeat, the mayor directed the Board of Education to make concessions to John Fewkes. As the mayoral elections approached, the board added another five days to the school year and Kelly set up a citizens' advisory committee on schools and agreed to consult it about future appointments to the board. In return, the CTU leadership stopped its criticism of Kelly and remained neutral during the election. On March 3, 1939, Fewkes congratulated Kelly for his victory in the primary elections, and in reply Kelly thanked Fewkes for the "generous helpfulness which your organization accorded me in the primary campaign."[94]

The main promise Kelly gave the teachers in return for their acquiescence was that his supporters would introduce a bill in the state legislature to increase the pegged levy for education and restore the teachers' salaries. In May, after Kelly had safely won the mayoral election, a bill to increase the pegged levy in Chicago from $48 million to $52 million, sponsored by the CTU and supported by Kelly-Nash but opposed by tax-cutting groups, was introduced in the senate. Union leaders and members lobbied hard on the bill's behalf. Legislators, the *Chicago Tribune* reported, "Have been bombarded with letters, telegrams and telephone and personal calls from teachers."[95] The bill passed. "As evidence of the power wielded by the lobby," the *Chicago Daily News* declared, "this bill, unpopular with legislators because of the tax increase, went through the senate without debate last week, although most of the votes for it had to come from downstate senators." As a result, the Board of Education finally restored the school term to its pre-Depression level of ten months in January 1940, but the teachers still did not have all their salaries restored.[96]

The Board of Education, under orders from Mayor Kelly, made other concessions to the teachers. Mayor Kelly ordered Superintendent Johnson to restore Raymond M. Cook to the faculty of the Chicago Teachers College. Moreover, the *Chicago Daily News* reported, "Most recent of the groups to feel the sweetness and light is the Chicago Teachers Union, sharply critical and generally ignored by the school administration in the past, but now virtually recognized as the bargaining agency for the educational staff employees."[97] While women teachers in other school districts were fired for marrying, as a result of negotiations between the Board of Education and the CTU, the board agreed to revise the maternity leave ruling. Previously, teachers who went on maternity leave went to the bottom of the unassigned list of teachers when they returned to work, but the new ruling guaranteed that teachers on maternity leave would have their positions open for two years.[98]

Failure

Once Kelly had been safely re-elected and Superintendent Johnson reappointed in April 1940, the board turned against the CTU. Superintendent Johnson refused to negotiate with the CTU and ignored the union's pleas for meetings. On some occasions union leaders would turn up for a rescheduled meeting to find the superintendent not in his office. Relations between the board and the CTU leaders deteriorated even further. In December 1940, Fewkes told a meeting of the Ridge Citizens Schools Committee that he had received death threats from McCahey. "McCahey told me that if I did not get rid of Kermit Eby, executive secretary of our union and foe of the McCahey-Johnson gang, he would have us both blasted out of the city," revealed Fewkes.[99] McCahey denied making the threat but said of Fewkes: "I won't even let him come into my office. Both he and Mr. Eby are persona non grata around here. I don't have anything to do with either of them." Kelly's supporters offered inducements and threats to the husbands of the leaders of the PTAs to make their wives end the campaign against the board, and school principals denied the PTA the right to meet in school buildings.[100] The board pressured PTA groups to cancel meetings attended by union officials or else school supplies would be curtailed. School district superintendents were ordered to attend talks union officials gave to PTA meetings and report back to Superintendent Johnson. Political appointees who worked as school clerks and principals reported to the Board of Education on union activities at the schools, advised members not to attend union meetings, and pressured union delegates not to distribute union literature.[101]

The Chicago teachers proved unable to achieve most of their major goals because the union and reform groups in the city had underestimated the extent to which the Democratic machine was able to consolidate and extend its electoral support. African Americans, workers, and the sons and daughters of immigrants had forged a Democratic coalition in Chicago and the nation as a whole.[102] The Kelly-Nash machine, the beneficiaries of the new political alignment, had control over hundreds of departments and thousands of appointments throughout the Chicago region, and through patronage and the popularity of the New Deal, the Democrats were able to keep the support of Chicago's citizens The electorate, increasingly homeowners and parents of children who attended Catholic schools, often expressed support for Mayor Kelly's stance on low property taxes. Kelly and fellow Catholic McCahey gained further support from Catholics, who by the late 1930s made up more than half the population of Chicago.[103]

By the end of the 1930s, the public not only supported the Democrats, but were also less concerned with educational matters. Public education had recovered from the worst days of retrenchment as the schools stayed open and the teachers continued working. Indeed, in 1940 an NEA national survey found that 85 percent of people thought education had improved in the last few years.[104] Jesse H. Newlon, professor of education at Teachers' College, Columbia University, and a member of the Strayer team that surveyed the Chicago public schools in the early 1930s, told a meeting of the Chicago Women's Club in October 1937 that little had changed in the conditions in Chicago schools. He blamed not just politicians but also the citizens of Chicago. "Public interest in schools means good schools," he noted. "If the schools of Chicago are not all they should be the responsibility rests with the people. It is a sad but incontrovertible fact that the people get what they deserve, not what they need."[105]

As the electoral base of the Democrats remained secure throughout the 1930s, the powerful business community in the city made no attempt to oppose the Kelly-Nash machine. Since the activities of the CCPE in the early years of the Depression, business leaders who sent their children to private schools had little interest in saving public education. As long as the police and fire services were protected, the wealthy in Chicago supported the low-tax policies of the mayor. The *Chicago Tribune,* by far the most influential newspaper in the city, and the banking community, which gained much from tax anticipation warrants in the depths of the Depression, remained silent about the condition of the public schools under the control of the Democratic machine.[106]

If the business community remained supportive of the Kelly-Nash machine, its counterpart in organized labor provided more backing to Kelly's regime and further hindered the CTUs campaigns. CFL president John Fitzpatrick successfully intervened with the mayor when Superintendent Johnson banned the CTU from operating in the schools and refused to meet with the union. Besides that, however, the CTU benefited little from the CFL's agreement with Mayor Kelly. The CFL was willing to mediate between Kelly and the CTU, but it would not openly criticize Kelly or campaign for the end of patronage in the schools. While the most powerful affiliates of the CFL, the long-established building and municipal unions, gained jobs through patronage and higher salaries, the CTU, which embraced a smaller portion of CFL membership, had to accept its junior position in the federation. In July 1939, for example, John Fitzpatrick criticized the CTU for allowing its member Robert English to use the CTU name on a petition by the striking CIO workers at the William Randolph Hearst papers. Fitzpatrick informed Fewkes that he should "secure a retraction or repudiation on the part of your member in this connection, or that your union repudiate him." To make sure the CTU got the point, Fitzpatrick told Fewkes: "You may not know that we have had to expel two Teachers locals for refusal to be loyal to the American Federation of Labor and the Chicago Federation of Labor in this matter." English refused to retract his support, so the CTU renounced his actions and claimed they were carried on without the knowledge or authorization of the union.[107]

The increasing conservatism and undemocratic positions of John Fitzpatrick and the CFL alienated some of their left-wing and most active supporters. As chairman of the CFL Schools Committee and member of the executive board of the CFL, Lillian Herstein became a close friend of John Fitzpatrick. She was also active with Fitzpatrick in the Farmer Labor Party and supported him when he stood for mayor. In 1938, however, Herstein opposed John Fitzpatrick when he refused to allow an Evanston teachers' union delegate, George Axtelle, to take his seat on the CFL because he supported a CIO-inclined union, the American Newspaper Guild. She was further dismayed when Fitzpatrick expelled from the CFL the Adult Education Teachers of Chicago, a group of Works Project (Program) Administration (WPA) adult education teachers Herstein had helped organize when she became one of the leaders of the WPA adult education program in Chicago.[108]

Although external factors contributed to the CTU's failures, the Chicago schoolteachers who joined the union in the 1930s failed to build on the activism they exhibited during the early days of the Great Depression. Although many teachers became active in the union, most simply paid their membership dues and used the CTU's credit and legal services. Many teachers did not want their union to prioritize social reform or to become involved in wide-ranging community and political matters, but to concentrate on restoring their pay. Kermit Eby recalled one occasion when a delegation from the union came into his office to see him and "reminded me that I was employed to represent their economic and job interests before the Board of Education and before the public, not to reform the school system nor to concern myself with teaching methods." He believed that "[h]e who would understand union administration must understand the pragmatism which governs the behavior of its leaders, a bread-and-butter philosophy which springs from the rank and file."[109]

As the Board of Education paid teachers regularly and rescinded much of their salary cut, teachers became less interested in wider educational reform. While other workers faced unemployment during the Depression, Chicago public school teachers saw their standard of living improve due to deflation and their salary scale, which guaranteed them a pay raise every year. Indeed, many teachers, because of their long service, had reached the maximum on the salary scale.[110] Other teachers gave in to patronage politics. A CTU delegate from Spry School informed Edna Siebert, membership chairman of the CTU, that one teacher had not renewed her union membership and "changed her affections for political reasons. I understand that the Superintendent assigned her son on a temporary certificate to Normal College as a substitute."[111] Political appointees did not want to rock the boat against their political masters and threaten their secure and relatively well-paying jobs.

When the original excitement began to abate and the machine extended its control over the schools, the fledging union had problems keeping the interest of those schoolteachers who supported reform. Overwhelmed by the day-to-day task of teaching in difficult circumstances, most teachers had little time to retain a commitment to activism or continue to be involved in union affairs. As the Kelly-Nash machine strengthened its hold on power, those who initially supported reform saw enormous obstacles in their way, and few successes. With enthusiasm for reform beginning to wane, the union had trouble maintaining its membership. Rather than climb to ten thousand members as the union leaders had hoped it would, by 1940 union membership had slipped to fewer than seven thousand, 56 percent of the teaching corps. Many overworked teachers had simply given up.[112]

Faced with these obstacles, John Fewkes and other union leaders showed a willingness to cooperate and compromise with the Board of Education. The 1939 mayoral election agreement proved to Fewkes that concessions could be wrung from Kelly and the Board of Education if they concentrated on regaining pay and dropped their criticisms of the Kelly regime. Increasingly, Fewkes believed that rather than continue to fight the political machine through public pressure, the CTU should follow the example of the building unions and seek political patronage through the CFL. Others like Kermit Eby opposed the Kelly-Nash machine and advocated an alliance between the teachers and the wider community. While Mary Herrick, the behind-the-scenes organizer and co-worker with Fewkes in the AFT, gravitated toward Fewkes, the more outspoken and forceful Lillian Herstein moved toward

Eby.[113] As part of the turn toward compromise, Fewkes began to assume more control over the union. In January 1940, Herstein resigned from the CTU's executive board, accusing Fewkes of failing to consult with the rest of the leadership or to assign her to union committees.[114]

Dissatisfaction with Fewkes's increasingly bureaucratic procedures was apparent in the campaign led by Fewkes and Herrick that sought to expel the communist-dominated New York and Pennsylvania locals from the AFT. After complaints from New York teachers and a campaign by conservative newspapers, the AFT organized a referendum of its membership in spring 1941 to decide whether to revoke the charters of the locals. Consequently, before the referendum the CTU urged the membership to vote for revocation and organized a mass meeting at which no opponents of expulsion were invited to speak. In reply, more than six hundred members of the CTU signed petitions asking for a membership meeting at which the leaders of the communist-leaning locals could put their case, and Communist Party supporters in Chicago worked with other leftists to oppose expulsion.[115] The petitions were less a sign of procommunism among the teachers than a rank-and-file revolt against the bureaucratic and undemocratic procedures in the CTU. In response to the petitions, the CTU hired Orchestra Hall for a membership meeting on April 14 in which the president of the New York local debated the issue with the leaders of the CTU. Subsequently, the referendum declared overwhelmingly for revocation and the AFT expelled the locals.[116]

Conclusion

The events immediately following the formation of the CTU confirm the existence of a long-standing and persistent tension between bread-and-butter unionism and reform unionism in the history of teachers' unions. Within the CTU, the two orientations became associated with the two leading members of the new organization: John Fewkes and Kermit Eby. Fewkes, the guiding force behind the newly established CTU, believed that the main function of a teachers' union was to gain higher wages and better working conditions for its members. When Eby became the first secretary of the CTU, he suggested that the most important role for the union was not increasing the teachers' wages but reforming the Chicago political system and improving the education system. In the economic and political crisis that enveloped the Chicago public schools, many teachers gravitated toward reform, believing that their problems could only be solved with the democratization of the city's politics.

By the end of the decade, the Chicago teachers' desire for reform had begun to wane, and many, including CTU president John Fewkes, looked to accommodation with the Chicago Democratic machine. Mayor Edward Kelly had managed to sustain the support of the electorate, grow closer to the CFL, and quiet criticism from middle-class reform groups. Neither the Illinois legislature nor homeowners, many of whom sent their children to Catholic schools, nor business organizations wanted to increase funding for the public schools. As long as the leadership of the CFL and the public was supportive of Mayor Kelly and the Board of Education and the CTU was unable to build a city-wide reform movement, the teachers had little chance of fulfilling their aim of removing political control from the schools.

Even though the Democratic machine remained in power and public school teachers still endured a salary cut and suffered forced transfers and demotions, the union had achieved some successes. The CTU established links with middle-class reform groups, educational experts, and liberal politicians that would sustain them in years to come. Through political alignments and lobbying, the CTU helped to restore the ten-month school year, rescind wage cuts, and bring corruption to public attention. Most importantly, for the first time in any major city in the United States, public school teachers were able to build a lasting united teachers' union that included a majority of the workforce. The concrete achievements of the CTU may have been few in the 1930s, but the establishment of the union laid the foundation for future victories.

3

World War II, Accommodation, and the Struggle for Equal Pay, 1941–1947

The Chicago public school teachers and the rest of the nation were thrown into turmoil on December 7, 1941, when the Japanese attacked Pearl Harbor. After the United States entered World War II, both the public education system and the labor movement played a major role in the home front and were, in turn, fundamentally affected by the war. The former ended the war in a position of financial crisis while the latter continued to grow in numbers and influence. How did the war affect Chicago public school teachers and their union? What role did they play in the war effort and how did it affect the attempts of Kermit Eby and others to pursue educational and political reform? As the Democratic machine consolidated its control over the public schools, the CTU leadership accommodated the Board of Education. School administrators, with the backing of the union leadership, removed many of the reformist teachers from the schools and intimidated into submission those who remained. The teachers' social reformism of the 1930s, which had already waned, virtually disappeared during the war years, to be replaced by an increased emphasis on bread-and-butter demands.

Wartime disruptions particularly led to profound changes in the behavior and expectations of women public school teachers. Economic deprivation, greater work opportunities for women in other industries, and nationwide concerns for the rights of women workers led elementary school teachers to demand equal pay with high school teachers in the form of a single salary schedule. By demanding a pay scale that used experience and educational credentials as the sole criteria for rewards, Chicago elementary school teachers proclaimed the need for a public education system in which the work of men and women and elementary and high school teachers would be equally valued. Through its connections with organized labor and a new alliance forged with the political machine, the CTU was able to go some way to winning one of the first single salary pay campaigns in the country. In response, men teachers rebelled against the single salary schedule. The CTU, wishing to keep the union together, halted its equal pay campaign, demanded wage raises for all teachers, and joined in the most militant period of teacher protests the nation had yet seen. For the first time, teachers began to call for collective bargaining rights, which would eventually fundamentally change the orientation of the union and the public school system.

The CTU and World War II

After he had completed his two terms as union president in the spring of 1941, CTU rules forced John Fewkes to step down from his full-time position. In the ensuing elections, Fewkes was succeeded by high school teacher Ira S. Turley, a former secretary and vice president of the Men Teachers Union who supported the bread-and-butter unionism espoused by Fewkes. Although he retired from the CTU presidency, Fewkes still maintained a strong influence in union affairs. He was elected AFT vice president in 1942 and AFT president in 1943, a post he had to quit when he relocated to Washington, D.C., to work for the War Production Board. As president and vice president of the AFT, Fewkes maintained his headquarters in Chicago, advised Turley and the other CTU leaders, and continued to serve on many important union committees.

On December 9, 1941, two days after the Japanese attack on Pearl Harbor, Ira Turley and the CTU pledged complete support to the federal government in the prosecution of the war and offered Chicago mayor Edward Kelly the services of the union. Kelly, who had become regional coordinator of civilian defense, turned over a number of Chicago high schools to the National Defense Training Program, which prepared thousands of men and women for work in the defense industries. He further allowed the U.S. Navy to transform the newly opened Chicago Vocational School and the Wright Junior College into navy training centers. During the war, Kelly used other school buildings as selective service and rationing registration centers, while staff and students collected scrap metal and grew food in the so-called victory gardens on school grounds. To help in the war effort, the Board of Education reversed its longstanding practice of rarely meeting with CTU representatives and held regular meetings with the union leaders to discuss the war mobilization of the school system. Ira Turley became a member of the Board of Education Committee for the Sale of Defense (later War) Bonds, which promoted the sale of bonds among Chicago public school teachers. To boost morale, in June 1942 the CTU cooperated with the Board of Education in staging a Flag Day Sunday parade of 400,000 people, which stretched for fifty miles through the streets of Chicago.[1]

While patriotism and antifascism motivated teachers and CTU leaders alike to support the war, the hostilities offered the leadership of the union the opportunity to gain wider acceptance among the general public. Teacher unionism had long been under attack from conservative pressure groups, but since the late 1930s, when the *Saturday Evening Post* first sensationalized communist control of the AFT, the CTU and other AFT locals spent much of their time deflecting accusations of communism and lack of patriotism. After CTU leaders John Fewkes and Mary Herrick led a successful campaign to expel the communist-dominated New York and Pennsylvania locals from the AFT in 1941, Fewkes declared, "I feel the American Federation of Teachers now has a real opportunity to grow rapidly since its Americanism can no longer be questioned."[2] To the CTU leaders, patriotism during the war was the best way to further undermine the communist and "un-American" tag that threatened teacher unionism. "It is good public relations for teachers to be able to show the public the extent of their contributions. . . . We want to be able to prove to all and sundry that we have done our share," an editorial in the CTU newspaper declared in 1944.[3]

Even though gaining public support for teachers' unions was important to Turley and Fewkes, the wartime emergency gave the union leaders the more important opportunity to reach an accommodation with the Board of Education. Turley, backed by Fewkes, suggested that the best hope for teachers to rescind the remaining pay cut and improve teachers' working conditions lay in remaining on friendly terms with Mayor Kelly and his supporters in the school administration. As a result, the CTU increasingly acted as an auxiliary to the Kelly administration in its wartime activities and spent less time criticizing the Board of Education's corrupt practices and more time promoting the war effort. The CTU used its weekly radio broadcast on WCFL, the Chicago Federation of Labor (CFL) radio station, to call for greater efforts by schoolteachers in pursuing the war. The CTU turned over its publications, study classes, and annual educational conferences to promoting the war effort and boosting wartime morale. The CTU leaders, with the backing of the board, urged members to de-emphasize criticism of U.S. social and economic institutions in the classroom and replace censure with patriotic assertions. Ira Turley declared that teachers "will be asked to sacrifice more and more time and money to promote the war effort. We must do it and do it gladly." By September 1944, the CTU had invested $12,000 of its reserves in war bonds and sent communications and gifts to its members in the armed forces. The union sent the proceeds of CTU social activities, including the card party and style show, to the general fund of the United Service Organization (USO).[4]

Chicago schoolteachers and the CTU played a major role in home front activities. By the end of 1943, more than five hundred CTU members had enlisted in the armed forces. Hundreds of other schoolteachers regularly spent their summer vacations working in defense industries. Lester Brown, Chicago-area war manpower director, estimated that five hundred Chicago teachers worked in war plants during the summer of 1944 alone. The CTU organized a unit of the American Red Cross and hundreds of teachers volunteered to be trained as nurse's aides. Many public school teachers helped Mayor Kelly's office with draft registration, rationing programs, war bond distribution, and salvage collection. John Fewkes worked with the War Production Board in Washington, D.C., and fellow activist Lillian Herstein served as a consultant to the board on problems relating to women workers. Overall, a CTU survey found that during the war approximately one-third of its members participated in civilian defense, nearly half worked for the CTU Red Cross unit, and nearly a third reported working on other war-related activities such as lecturing on gas defense, first aid and water safety, working on draft and ration boards, participating in the medical corps, and volunteering at the Chicago Service Men's Center.[5]

The Chicago teachers' contribution helped Chicago become one of the foremost supporters of the war. Chicago collected more salvage and sold more war bonds than any other city. War bonds sold through the public schools during the war exceeded $40 million and through the payroll totaled more than $50 million. After the war, Mayor Kelly received the Award of Merit, the U.S. Army's highest award to a civilian, recognizing his and Chicago's services to the war effort.[6] As Harry C. McKinsie, district superintendent of high schools, observed at the end of the war, the teachers "were the unseen generals, the unsung heroes and heroines of all these drives and competitions."[7]

Accommodation

With the war still raging and the mayoral elections of spring 1943 drawing near, school superintendent William Johnson and the Board of Education made a concerted effort to intimidate into submission the most vocal critics of their policies among the school staff. An NEA investigation of the Chicago schools undertaken between November 1944 and May 1945 noted that "in most of the buildings there is located at least one individual who promptly reports to the downtown office teachers' conversations or conduct that they deem to indicate a lack of submission to the current administration." The report revealed that teachers felt "'[l]oyal' school employees are rewarded; critical ones are punished."[8] In December of 1942, Johnson demoted school principal Butler Laughlin, supporter of Kermit Eby and outspoken critic of the board, transferring him from Lindblom High School to the smaller Harper High School.[9] A whole group of liberal CTU teachers, including union activist Lillian Herstein (before she left for work with the War Production Board), were affected when the Board of Education abolished the Department of Lectures for the junior colleges and dismissed 115 teachers in the summer of 1942. The following summer the board dismissed twenty-one faculty members of the Chicago Teachers College and transferred twenty-one others. Progressive educator John De Boer, director of student teaching at Chicago Teachers College since 1931, was transferred from Chicago Teachers College to Herzl Junior College in 1944.[10]

In addition to intimidating the opposition, it is likely that political appointees of the Democratic machine infiltrated the CTU. Superintendent Johnson increasingly controlled appointments to the Chicago public schools by the use of temporary teaching certificates and through control of the Chicago Teachers College. Johnson mandated that only graduates of the college could become elementary school teachers in the Chicago public schools and that only Chicago elementary school teachers could take the high school teachers' exam. These political appointees joined the CTU and played a role in the union's activities. As a *Chicago Daily News* editorial noted in January 1943, "the McCahey-Johnson regime, by a process of combined infiltration and terror, is just now engaged in an effort to inject its authority into the affairs of the Chicago Teachers Union, with a view to stifling in future all independent criticism from that source."[11] The NEA report undertaken in the winter of 1944 and 1945 found that the school administration had made "a studied plan" to "seek the control of teachers organizations either by extending favors to leaders, by attempting to divide the organizations, by members of the machine penetrating into the organizations, or by the actual capturing of its offices in elections."[12]

While some of the most vocal critics of the political machine faced transfers and demotions, the CTU leadership made a deal with Superintendent Johnson. Turley and his supporters pledged to end their criticism of the board's activities and remain neutral in the upcoming mayoral election; in return the board promised to rescind teachers' pay cuts, listen favorably to future CTU wage demands, and protect Turley and his supporters in the school system.[13] Consequently, while the transfer of Butler Laughlin was denounced by civic groups and met by a walkout of five hundred of his students with placards reading "Why Must Politicians Interfere With Our Education?" the CTU executive committee did not even discuss the matter.[14] In August 1943, after the Board of Education had dismissed twenty-one faculty members of the Chicago Teachers College, one of the teachers voiced dismay because they "can be dismissed or transferred without a concerted and immediate public protest on the part of the union." With the CTU making no complaint, a group of the dismissed teachers decided to take their case to various educational and professional organizations. One teacher, Stuart Brent from the Chicago Teachers College, asserted that the CTU is a "company union" and that "the union has sold out."[15] In October 1942, Ira Turley invited school superintendent Johnson to be a guest of the union at the CTU annual card party and style show, and the following January the CTU gave $1,300 to Mayor Kelly's pet project, the Chicago Service Men's Center. While the CSC supported Kelly's opponent George B. McKibbon in the 1943 mayoral election, the CTU remained neutral and did not make the schools an election issue. Nor did the CTU oppose the reappointment of James McCahey as board president in May 1943 or William Johnson as superintendent of schools in April 1944, while the CSC opposed both.[16]

While the CTU's stance in favor of the war was generally replicated by labor organizations elsewhere, the unwillingness of the CTU to defend its members was not. In response to patriotic appeals, AFT locals supported the war effort and the labor movement adopted a no-strike pledge for the duration of the war. But while the CTU left its members to face victimization and intimidation alone, other unions used the courts and government agencies to protect their members' rights and argue vociferously for greater wage increases. Many on the shop floor ignored their leaders' pleas to maintain labor peace. Strike levels rose through the early years of the war so that in 1944 there were nearly five thousand strikes involving more than two million workers, the most stoppages in U.S. history up to that point, and the following year saw some 3.5 million workers on strike.[17] Some teachers joined in the strike activity. In 1942 teachers in Yellow Springs, Ohio, walked out because the Board of Education there refused to support the teachers over a discipline case in a school. Teachers in Rankin, Pennsylvania, staged a sit-down strike to receive a salary increase in February 1943. In April 1944 in Pontiac, Michigan, teachers went on strike for a week for a $20 pay raise, and the following month in nearby Flint, Michigan, the site of the famous auto sit-down strikes of the 1930s, all thirty-five public schools were closed after teachers struck demanding a raise and the employment of clerical staff so they could devote more time to teaching. Altogether some two thousand teachers engaged in twelve work stoppages during the war years.[18]

As part of the deal between the Chicago Board of Education and the CTU leadership, the union dismissed its executive secretary, Kermit Eby. Eby became increasingly independent of the leadership and remained a strong vocal critic of the board and city politicians. At the AFT conference held in Gary, Indiana, in August 1942, Eby, against the wishes of the CTU leadership, supported George T. Guernsey, editor of the *American Teacher*, whom the AFT leadership dismissed because of his alleged sympathy for the communist-leaning eastern locals. In response to this and other indiscretions, the CTU executive board suspended Eby in January 1943 and in February voted 19-10 to recommend his dismissal to the union house of representatives. Subsequently, the house narrowly voted 89-79 to terminate Eby's contract.[19] As the *Chicago Sun* claimed, the sacking "climaxes a constantly growing row between Eby on one side and Turley, McCahey and board adherents on the other." Margaret Heineman, a member of the Board of Education, "hinted there might have been a connection between Eby's suspension and a desire on the part of union members to please the school administration." Kermit Eby called his sacking "a victory for the forces hoping to remove the Chicago Teachers Union as an obstacle to the dictatorship of the McCahey-Johnson school policies."[20]

After Turley removed the troublesome Eby, the board kept its side of the bargain. In January 1943 the Board of Education restored the final part of the teachers' pay that had been cut during the Depression. Cordial letters began to be exchanged between Mayor Kelly, Superintendent Johnson, and the CTU leaders. Kelly agreed to union requests to repair some unsafe roads outside schools and to tighten up police security at schools that had experienced violent pupil behavior. The union leadership declared, "In recent months there have been some signs that your officers are succeeding slowly in building a practical approach to honorable negotiation with our employers on the basis of what is fair and reasonable."[21]

While teachers were relieved to finally see their salaries restored, many CTU members rebelled against the actions of the union leadership. In January 1943, the CTU executive board received a petition signed by nearly five hundred schoolteachers asking for a referendum on the Kermit Eby case. Nearly a third of the executive board and half of the house of representatives voted against expulsion.[22] Many union members, parents, and civic organizations wrote to local newspapers condemning the sacking of Eby. One teacher believed Eby was fired because he was "fearless and direct in his criticism of [the board's] rape of the public schools." The teacher warned that "there is a union election this spring and the 8,000 teachers in the union are becoming aroused at the sellout to the McCahey-Johnson crowd; hence the attempt of Turley and the other officers to make it appear as if the war between the union and the spoilsmen were still going on. It's a phony war." Another teacher believed that Eby's "efforts did more to reconcile the civic organizations to labor affiliation for teachers than those of any other person."[23]

Although many teachers objected to Eby's firing, many others cared little for Eby or his politics. One indignant teacher wrote to Ira Turley in 1942 criticizing the "fellow-travelers of the communists" who spoke at study class meetings. Voicing the views of many, he declared that the "union does not need to provide recreations for its members. . . . Reasonable salaries and decent working conditions—these are the things that most of the teachers want."[24] After his sacking, Eby concurred with these thoughts. In early 1944 he complained that teachers "avoid the responsibility of making the decisions" and they consequently "support a dictatorial school administration, a paternalistic principal, and a union which exalts the 'leader' principle." Eby "discovered that many of the teachers were not too interested [in community issues] and preferred to go about their daily tasks of checking in and checking out unmolested by greater concerns. For them the union was little more than an office at 509 S. Wabash which had no relation to their daily work . . . as one teacher told me 'Wasn't I being paid to look after their interests, not to run around.'"[25]

For many of those teachers who initially supported Eby, the crusading days of the 1930s had lost their appeal. With the political machine extending its rule over the public schools, the calls for academic freedom and the end of political control of the schools seemed further away than ever. Many politically appointed teachers would not support Eby's radical ideas because they did not want to upset their political masters and threaten their secure jobs. The CSC claimed that "[t]oo many Chicago teachers have lost sight of the goal. Teaching is just a rather dreary job measured by pay days—a hard job with much drudgery in which they take little pride."[26] In addition, although Eby had supporters in the union, he had failed to build any kind of organizational base that would sustain him or his political views. In contrast,

Fewkes and Turley had control over the union newspaper and finances and used them to bolster their own positions.

The enormous effort the Chicago schoolteachers put into supporting the war meant that many of them had even less time and inclination to stay active in union affairs. With gasoline strictly rationed and public transportation restricted, the union curtailed its cultural and social activities due to poor attendance. Time-consuming defense work also took precedence over union committee work. The union's newspaper reported that at a CTU membership meeting held in May 1942, "many members had to be absent because they were taking first aid courses, serving as minute men, or helping in various kinds of civilian defense work." The teachers' role in the CSC also weakened. In 1940 there were five thousand members in the CSC, 90 percent of them teachers, but by 1947 CSC membership had dropped to twelve hundred, less than half of them teachers.[27]

The firing of Eby and the accommodation of Turley virtually put an end to the conflict over the unions' aims and strategy that had been apparent in the union since its formation in 1937. Eby, Lillian Herstein, and their supporters who sought greater rank-and-file control of the union and promoted a major union role in liberal and progressive movements had been removed, left, or silenced. Turley, Fewkes, and the other union leaders wanted to concentrate the unions' resources upon purely economic issues. Rather than seek community support for the teachers' cause, Fewkes and Turley sought greater cooperation with the Board of Education. With the ousting of Eby and the resignation of Herstein, the CTU concentrated virtually all its efforts on gaining benefits for teachers through affiliation with the CFL and the support of the Democratic political machine.

Single Salary Schedule

The elimination of left-wing reformers did not usher in uniformity of opinion in the CTU's ranks. A rank-and-file challenge to the CTU leadership exploded during the war over elementary school teachers' demand for a single salary schedule, or equal pay with high school teachers. Chicago elementary school teachers were paid in nine yearly steps from $1,500 to $2,500, depending on experience, for a five-hour day, while high school teachers were paid in ten steps from $2,000 to $3,800 for a six-hour day.[28] The origins of the equal pay campaign lay in the changes in general thinking about the relative value of elementary school and high school teaching. In the first three decades of the twentieth century, the demand for high schools increased as more children stayed on in school beyond the elementary grades. While public school enrollment doubled to 25.6 million between 1890 and 1930, high school enrollment increased more than twenty times to 4.4 million. As school enrollment rose, the high school took on a more comprehensive and less elitist outlook. Psychologists suggested that elementary school teaching was as important for children as was high school teaching. As a result, many boards of education began to question the idea that elementary school teaching required significantly less preparatory training than high school teaching. In Chicago, the Board of Education raised educational requirements for new elementary school teachers, first to three years of college in 1930, then to four years in 1938.[29]

In recognition of these changes, the demand for a single salary schedule first emanated from elementary school teachers and some enlightened educators in the early 1920s. In 1921 the NEA adopted a resolution in favor of a single salary schedule. The single salary, prominent education experts declared in the early 1930s, recognized that the teaching of elementary school children was of equal importance as the teaching of high school youth and that the preparation time was equal. Furthermore, they argued, a single salary schedule would persuade elementary school teachers to remain as elementary school teachers rather than seek better-paying high school jobs. In smaller towns, where teachers were previously paid individually with no uniform salary schedules at all, single salaries began to be introduced. By 1931, 22 percent of school systems used the single salary schedule, and in 1941 it was 31 percent. In larger cities, where separate salary schedules had long been in operation, there was resistance to any change that would increase costs. Indeed, rather than a single salary schedule, an increasing number of school districts sought to attract more men into teaching by introducing schedules that paid men more than women. Only in 1943 did the first city with a population of more than 500,000—Detroit—adopt the single salary scale.[30]

Although the single salary schedule had long been a goal of the CFT and the AFT, it was only during the labor upsurge of the 1930s that elementary school teachers began a concerted campaign for equal pay in Chicago. In November 1930 the Chicago Division of the Illinois State Teachers Association, a lobbying organization dominated by elementary school teachers, went on record approving the single salary schedule. Because of the wholesale deprivations of the payless paydays of the 1930s, attacks on married women teachers' right to work, and calls for more men in the profession, teachers' demands for a single salary schedule stalled. Grateful simply to have a job and with all teachers facing a salary cut, campaigning for equal pay seemed unrealistic. A 1936 NEA report concluded: "There appears to be less emphasis on the issue of the single-salary schedule in recent discussions of salaries than was to be noted a decade ago." Once the country was out of the depths of the Depression, however, the demand for a single salary schedule arose again. In November 1937, the Chicago Division of the Illinois State Teachers Association again adopted a resolution in favor of a single salary schedule. From the late 1930s, the CTF petitioned the Board of Education demanding a single salary schedule.[31]

By arguing for a single salary, the women elementary school teachers declared that they had the same aptitude and character as male high school teachers. They actively challenged their unequal position within the workforce and demanded not just equal pay for the same job but equal pay for women's work in the form of elementary school teaching. By gaining a single salary schedule, teachers in the elementary schools would acquire higher status and the skills of women's work would be as equally valued as men's work, ideas that did not gain wider acceptance until the 1970s.[32]

A possible reason for this renewed demand for equal pay was the changing social composition of the elementary school teaching force. In the early part of the century, women schoolteachers were overwhelmingly young and single and most left their work or were forced to leave by school administrators when they married or had children. Partly due to the Depression, by the late 1930s more women teachers stayed in the profession after marriage and many returned after child rearing. As a result, women elementary school teachers were more likely to be married, older, and more experienced than they were earlier in the century, and they were increasingly interested in having a long-term career outside the home. Less than 1 percent of Chicago elementary school teachers had fewer than six years of teaching experience and only 22 percent had less than four years of college. These more committed elementary school teachers likely felt they were entitled to greater rewards than their younger colleagues of yesteryear and were more inclined to seek them.[33]

Teacher shortages and greater employment opportunities for women during the war bolstered elementary school teachers' ability to press their demands. When millions of men joined the armed services, vacancies in other higher-paying occupations became available to women as never before. More women entered the labor force as the government and employers encouraged women to take jobs traditionally held by men. With the number of single women exhausted in the early years of the war, employers recruited married women in unprecedented numbers. The number of employed women, mostly married, increased from 14.6 million in 1941 to 19.3 million in 1944, and represented 36 percent of the workforce. In Chicago, more than 300,000 women filled jobs left by men who entered the military. The War Manpower Commission designated Chicago a Group 1 city because of the critical job shortage, and the civilian defense volunteers knocked on people's houses pleading for women to go to work.[34] Rather than face dismissal for marrying, women teachers now enjoyed job security. One Chicago elementary teacher told an interviewer during the war that she would not enter teaching again because "[m]ore interesting fields are open to women now."[35]

While increased job opportunities raised the expectations of women teachers, so too did the challenges to pay differentials undertaken elsewhere. Even if the rhetoric was stronger than the reality, government agencies, employers, and unions became supporters of equal pay for equal work. In 1942 the National War Labor Board established the principle of equal pay for women who did the same work as men and the National Association of Manufacturers supported the demand. Women activists prodded the labor movement to move away from the traditional demands of a family wage for men and protective legislation for women, in which the man would earn enough to support his family, and toward campaigning for equal pay for women. Union leaders, fearing that employers would use cheap women workers to replace men or erode male workers' standards, often supported higher pay for women. The United Autoworkers (UAW) established a Women's Bureau and together with the United Electrical Workers (UEW) pursued equal pay cases through the machinery of the War Labor Board.[36]

The rising cost of living during World War II contributed to the upsurge among Chicago elementary school teachers. The federal government estimated that living costs rose 33 percent during the war, but the AFL and the CIO estimated that it was nearer to 50 percent. In addition, in 1939 the government, under the Public Salary Tax Act, for the first time required public school teachers to pay federal income tax, and in January 1943 the U.S. government introduced the Revenue Act, which imposed a 5 percent victory tax levy on every worker. Chicago schoolteachers suffered greater economic hardships than almost any other group. The Board of Education cut the pay of teachers by 10 percent to pay for "voluntary" subscriptions for defense bonds. Chicago teachers had had no raise in salary since 1922 and had suffered a 23.5 percent pay cut during the Depression that was not fully restored until January 1943. As the lowest paid, elementary school teachers suffered the most. An NEA report from 1943 showed that the median salary of Chicago elementary school teachers ranked seventeenth out of nineteen cities studied. Based on the elementary school maximum of $2,500 set in

1922, the real wages of an elementary school teacher fell from $2,821 in 1940 to $2,504 in 1942. The War Labor Board set the maximum salaries of Chicago accounting clerks, traffic clerks, carpenters, and electricians in June 1943 at between $2,745 and $3,120, while the maximum pay for Chicago elementary school teachers remained at $2,500.[37] "Those in the lower salary brackets have passed beyond the stage where they merely had no margin of saving to the place where they can purchase War Bonds and pay the Victory and Income tax only by heavy personal sacrifice," one schoolteacher declared in December 1943.[38]

The CTU was reluctant to campaign for a single salary schedule. Many high school teachers in Chicago opposed the call for a single salary, claiming that the requirement that high school teachers had to have a master's degree, and elementary school teaching only a bachelor's degree, demonstrated to them that high school teaching was more difficult than elementary school teaching. CTF leader Frances Kenney noted in her visit to a number of schools that the high school teachers objected to the CTF because of their support for a single salary. "The single salary schedule of the Union is one of the very sore points, particularly in the high schools. . . . Definitely they are opposed to it."[39] In effect, if the union supported the single salary too strongly, the issue would divide the union.

Although the CTU leadership was disinclined to campaign for equal pay, the existence of the CTF as a rival for the affections of elementary school teachers bought pressure to bear on the CTU leadership. It is notable that Margaret Haley resurrected the idea of a single salary as the CTU was being formed and organized petitions of elementary school teachers to obtain a single salary schedule. As long as its main rival campaigned for the single salary while the CTU did not, it was in danger of losing elementary school teachers as members. For example, after Haley reported in the CTF journal, the *Bulletin,* in 1937 that the CTU leaders did not want a single salary schedule, many elementary school teachers refused to join the new union. One teacher declared that "a great many people had been affected [by the CTF *Bulletin*] and that one school which had intended coming into the Union one hundred per cent as soon as the charter was issued and not one teacher from that school came in." Another teacher also "mentioned a school where the delegate is not keeping the union members because of that bulletin."[40] The CTF had declined in size and influence since its heyday in the early years of the century and since the death of Margaret Haley in January 1939, but it still remained a rival to the CTU for the loyalty of the elementary school teachers who made up nearly two-thirds of the teacher workforce. The remaining CTF leaders believed the CTU was its main competitor for members, and it became more critical of the CTU and drew closer to the Board of Education.

From the outset in 1937, the CTU went on record favoring a single salary schedule for equal service and qualification. To attract elementary school teachers and forestall the influence of the CTF, the CTU had to go some way to accepting the elementary school teachers' demands for equal pay. Rather than seek the immediate implementation of equal pay, the CTU proposed only that the elementary school teachers' nine-year salary schedule with a maximum of $2,500 should be increased to include an additional tenth year of $2,625. Recognizing the difference in the length of the school day between elementary school and high school teachers, the union proposed that eventually the elementary school teacher should receive five-sixths of the high school teachers' pay with the same number of years of service. While the war was on, however, the CTU leadership made little effort to achieve even these modest aims. It merely appeared before public meetings of the Board of Education and pleaded unsuccessfully for a tenth step on the elementary school teachers' salary scale.[41]

Opposition to the CTU leadership coalesced for the first time in the 1943 elections for union officers. In the three previous CTU elections for president, the only candidates for leadership positions were an official slate recommended by the CTU policymaking body. In 1943, an opposition slate led by elementary school teacher Susan Scully, a member of the CTU executive board, was put forward by membership petition. Scully ran for president of the union on a platform of calling for the democratization of the CTU and a single salary schedule. In the end, Scully gained 48.2 percent of the vote and, although she lost, her slate won three of the twelve contested places.[42]

Responding to its CTF rival and hoping to appease the majority of its elementary school members, the CTU leadership made a more concerted effort to obtain the single salary schedule. The union no longer simply called for a tenth year on the elementary school teachers' pay scales, but actively campaign for the immediate implementation of the single salary schedule. Subsequently, the CTU leaders launched a campaign to achieve that goal, enlisting the support of rank-and-file schoolteachers, labor unions affiliated with the CFL, various civic groups, and individual PTAs. In January 1944, it presented its plan for a single salary to the Board of Education, claiming that the teaching of elementary school children was as important as the teaching of high school youth and that a single salary schedule would persuade elementary school teachers to remain as elementary school teachers rather than seek higher-paying high school positions. Representatives from the

Citizens Schools Committee, the Chicago Women's Club, several PTAs, and other civic organizations appeared at the meeting to support the CTU.[43]

Chicago in the early 1940s seemed the most unlikely of places for a successful wage campaign by public school teachers. The drive had to be waged against the advice of the government and the National War Labor Board, which aimed to curb wage increases. The concept of equal pay for men and women was not universally accepted. The Chicago teachers had to confront a Board of Education that was far more likely to spend its limited income on the war effort, on buying overly expensive school equipment from political friends, or on rewarding other school workers, such as janitors, who had gained their jobs through political patronage, rather than on the teachers who had long opposed their rule. As one elementary school teacher cautioned a group of fellow teachers in December 1942, "there is a tremendous pressure on the Board to use some of its funds for other workers besides the teachers."[44]

While other boards of education across the country began to introduce single salary schedules because the demand for military and civilian manpower created teacher shortages in the elementary schools, this was not the case in Chicago. From 1940 to 1945, the number of elementary school teachers employed by the Chicago public schools fell about 10 percent, and the number of high school teachers fell 13 percent. Yet there was no shortage of elementary school teachers in Chicago because a fall in the birth rate, a rise in Catholic school attendance, and the migration of families to the suburbs led to a decline in school enrollment.[45] (See Table 5.) By the end of the war, enrollment at the Chicago Teachers College had declined to a third of its prewar enrollment because thousands of certified graduates still waited to be assigned. By 1948, not all graduates of the class of 1940 had yet been appointed to teaching positions.[46] As a result, the board used surplus teachers for special services and in some cases for reducing the size of classes.[47] "The ratio of pupils to teachers in both elementary grades 1–6 and high schools, is lower in Chicago than in most of the cities from which data on the subject were obtained," a report into class sizes in eleven major school systems announced in 1946.[48]

Although there was little sign of a teacher shortage in the elementary schools, conditions in Chicago ultimately proved favorable to the CTU and the adoption of the single salary schedule. The Board of Education cared little about the relative distribution of school finance between elementary school and high school teachers and was in a strong position to pay the single salary schedule because of savings due to the decline in school enrollments. Therefore, it benefited the board to make some move on equal pay and appease its

Table 5. Student Enrollment and Teachers in Chicago Public Schools, 1940–45

Year	Elementary Students	Elementary School Teachers	High School Students	High School Teachers
1940	318,445	8,174	144,671	4,674
1941	311,023	7,768	135,295	4,583
1942	302,502	7,742	126,762	4,538
1943	293,110	7,605	117,435	4,458
1944	283,984	7,487	116,111	4,086
1945	279,030	7,371	115,715	4,066

Sources: Chicago Board of Education, *1950 Facts and Figures,* page 11 for students and *Board of Education Proceedings,* 1939–1945 for teachers.

newfound friends in the CTU leadership. In January 1944 the school board adopted the principle of the single salary, giving an increase of $125 per step to the elementary school teachers' schedule while giving no increase to high school teachers. It shortened the pay schedule of high school teachers by one year to nine years, the same as the elementary school teachers. Under pressure from elementary school teachers, the CTU executive pressed for further movement toward the adoption of a single salary schedule.[49]

Men Schoolteachers Revolt

After completing his two terms of office, Ira Turley stepped down from his position as CTU president in May 1945, just as the war in Europe was coming to a close. The new president, Arthur W. Walz, a former union vice president and high school teacher, was a supporter of Fewkes and the increasingly narrow vision that came to dominate the union's policies in the 1940s. Eschewing any wider political role, Walz asserted, "Members of new locals should understand that Labor Unions do not attempt to operate business or government. They are set up to protect their members."[50]

While the country's need for women workers during the war led to calls for equal pay and sympathy for women's concerns, the focus shifted to the needs of the returning men as the war came to a close. After the war, employers, unions, and government agencies no longer saw the need to discuss comparable worth and equal pay. Government officials, business owners, and popular journals urged women, particularly married women, to leave their jobs and return to the home. In movies, radio programs, and magazines, models of independent women became less prominent, replaced by images of housewives, the celebration of domesticity, the family wage, and traditional values. Psychiatrists, psychologists, and child experts emphasized women's nurturing abilities and the role of women in the family. Thousands of women left manufacturing jobs and female employment fell sharply after the war as the employment of returning servicemen was highlighted.[51]

Arthur Walz took over the reins of the union at a time of growing revolt among high school teachers over low wages and the union's strategy of prioritizing the elementary school teachers' campaign for equal pay. Just like elementary school teachers, high school teachers paid federal income tax for the first time in 1939, contributed their share of the victory tax in 1943, and faced rising living costs during the war. But the Board of Education's adoption of the first stage of a single salary schedule in January 1944 meant that elementary school teachers gained a $125 raise in pay while the high school teachers received nothing. The following year, wages for high school and elementary school teachers remained stagnant. In November 1945, the high school teachers in the CTU house of representatives voiced "persistent objections and dissatisfaction" to the union's policy of seeking a $400 increase for high school teachers and between $452 and $875 for elementary school teachers over a four-year period. In response to the protests, the house unanimously adopted a resolution that the four-year program should be adopted in its entirety in January 1946. The Board of Education rejected the CTU request but announced a further movement toward equal pay with a $225 raise for elementary school teachers and $150 for high school teachers.[52] Many high school teachers objected and voted with their feet. In 1946, 308 Chicago elementary school teachers resigned from the public school system, but this fell to 270 in 1947. In contrast, 85 high school teachers left in 1946, but this rose to 120 the following year.[53]

The greatest opposition to the single salary schedule among the high school teachers came from the men. In December 1945 the CTU newspaper reported that "[f]or the past weeks there has been a steadily increasing unrest among men high school teachers in connection with the salary program that has been adopted by the Union."[54] Men teachers in general faced greater financial burdens than their female colleagues. A study of 336 CTU members undertaken in 1946 found that only 32 percent of the women were married but 91 percent of the men were. Men had more dependents than women and undertook more additional paid work. Some 51.4 percent of the men high school teachers reported having jobs in addition to teaching, while only 7.8 percent of women high school teachers had additional employment.[55]

As women moved toward equal pay, male teachers voiced resentment at their relative decline in pay and status. For many men teachers the only way to maintain some semblance of masculine status in a low-paying, female-dominated profession was to maintain higher pay than the female elementary school teachers. A single salary, which implied that women's work was as important as men's, threatened the status of male teachers. The men's opposition to the single salary schedule and to their low pay spread to a general dissatisfaction with teaching. A 1946 survey undertaken in Chicago found that nearly 80 percent of both elementary and high school women teachers remained satisfied with their choice of profession, while only 65 percent of men declared their satisfaction.[56]

In January 1947, Henry G. Borchardt, a chemistry teacher at Chicago Vocational School, wrote an article in *Life* magazine that exemplified the thinking of many men teachers. Borchardt argued that the public did not give men teachers respect because they worked in a low-paying profession dominated by women. According to Borchardt, the public was contemptuous of men teachers because of their low earnings and "visibly uneasy with them because they are supposed to know more than the average man." Many of the men he met "were afraid that I would correct their grammar and be shocked at their swearing. Another said, 'Aw, he'd just be a wet blanket on everything' . . . too goody-goody for them."[57] Borchardt and other male teachers resurrected the idea prevalent in the prewar years that a female-dominated school had detrimental effects on the education of students. In September 1930, Robert E. Jones, a professor at the Massachusetts Institute of Technology, declared that women had "emasculated the public-school system" and insisted that "[o]ur boys and girls have not been taught to think. . . . They come to the age of maturity ignorant of and uninterested in the principles of ethics, government, science, and society, and unable to criticize them in any but the most superficial way. . . . The faults I have been speaking of are the faults of women teachers."[58] More than fifteen years later Henry Borchardt suggested that women teachers caused juvenile delinquency since they were unable to deal with discipline, and that the status of the profession had declined as more women had gone into teaching during the war and replaced high school men teachers. Looking to the future, he believed "that a matriarchy is developing in the U.S. It will come full circle in a few years when education is handed over almost entirely to women." Rather than equal pay, Borchardt wanted to raise the salaries of men teachers above those of women to encourage more men to enter the teaching profession.[59]

These views took organizational expression in late 1946 when a group of Chicago high school teachers formed the Men Teachers Club (MTC), which quickly attracted more than eight hundred male high school teachers. Claiming to be the only teacher organization that considered the welfare of men, the MTC asserted that the CTU was "women ridden." The dominance of women teachers was hurting the pay and status of the profession and leading to declining educational standards.[60] The MTC declared "our respect for education is pretty well summed up in the fact that it has become women's work. To the American Indian that meant the lowest, meanest kind of slavish toil. . . . Women have always been willing to take half their pay in praise, gratitude, and other intangibles."[61]

The group advocated special compensation for men teachers, believing that "as heads of families" men needed more pay than women. According to MTC president Herschel Scott, more than a third of the men teachers had quit the Chicago schools because "men can no longer afford to teach in the Chicago schools." Schools needed to attract men by increasing their salary because "[f] or the sciences, industrial and vocational subjects, and competitive athletics you must have men. Also you must have them as school administrators for the best of reasons, but the fact that women prefer to work under men supervisors is reason enough." Paraphrasing the noted psychiatrist Dr. Edward Strecker, Scott added that "the emasculation of public school faculties has gone much too far. He wants to know why 95% of the school problem cases are boys. How do you answer that?" On October 9, 1946, three representatives of the newly formed group appeared before the Board of Education to demand a 30 percent pay raise for men teachers only and a separate salary schedule for men and women teachers. Subsequently, after the board rejected the increase for men teachers, the MTC threatened to strike.[62]

Even though the MTC gained the support of many men teachers, others opposed it. Supporting a general raise for all teachers, the CTU objected to the men's demands. Some high school teachers believed that elementary school teachers deserved pay parity and others objected to paying wages on the basis of gender. A petition from Phillips High School came out against the MTC demands. "[I]t is the considered opinion of the undersigned *men and women teachers* of the School that the acceptance by the Board of such a policy would run counter to the long established policy of '*equal pay for equal work*,' would create dissension and dissatisfaction in the teaching ranks, and would be an undemocratic and retrogressive step . . . there is no scientific basis for asserting that one sex is of more value to the educational field than another, nor any sound economic basis that only men are heads of families."[63]

The CTU responded decisively, condemning the MTC for its decision to strike and instructing its members not to respect MTC picket lines. Since its formation, the union had championed the principle, if not always the practice, of a single salary schedule, and it had supported the right of married women to teach. In addition, toward the end of the war the CTU and other labor unions supported the right of equal pay for equal work. The CTU opposed the idea of a larger raise for men because the "principle of equal pay for equal service is fundamental in our democracy. The high quality of women's service in our schools cannot be questioned."[64] The CTU backed Mary Anderson, director of the U.S. Women's Bureau of the Department of Labor, who promoted the first of a series of equal pay bills in Congress in 1945. While reformers would have to wait until 1963 before Congress passed an Equal Pay Act, at the state level the campaign was more successful. In 1940 only two states had equal pay legislation, but by 1963, twenty-two states had adopted some form of equal pay measures. The CTU supported the Equal Pay for Equal Work legislation in the Illinois General Assembly, which was finally passed by the Illinois state legislature in 1947.[65]

Postwar Militancy

The call for a single salary schedule from women teachers and the anger of male teachers at their declining status became intertwined with a nationwide upsurge of all workers brought on by economic and social changes during World War II. Union membership reached 14.5 million after the war, an all-time high of 35 percent of the labor force. Cancellation of military orders and reductions in the length of the workweek brought unemployment and a reduction in pay for workers across the nation. At the same time, the lifting of price controls in the summer of 1946 produced spiraling inflation. Consequently, the final years of the war and the immediate postwar years saw a renewed wave of worker militancy. In 1945, 3,470,000 workers became involved in strikes that cost employers thirty-eight million days of lost production. Half a million steelworkers struck in January 1946 followed by electrical, rubber, auto, and packinghouse workers. Altogether in 1946, 4,600,000 workers struck, losing 116 million days of production, the single most strike-torn year in U.S. history. In 1947, 2,170,000 workers struck, losing 34.6 million days.[66] Chicago workers participated in this wave of militancy. Strikes in steel, meatpacking, and railways, and at International Harvester and American Telephone and Telegraph, swept through the city between early 1946 and the spring of 1947.[67]

The immediate postwar years saw the largest teachers' strike wave in U.S. history. The most dramatic postwar strikes occurred in Minnesota and New York. In November and December 1946, 1,160 teachers in St. Paul, Minnesota, walked off the job to demand an increase in the school budget. The strike, the first by an AFT local, closed its seventy-seven schools for a month and resulted in a $1,000 a year increase for the teachers.[68] In February 1947, 2,400 teachers in Buffalo, New York, struck and closed all the city's ninety-eight public schools, turning away 72,000 children in the biggest teachers' strike the United States had yet seen. Pupils wrote, "Give Teachers a Raise" and "We Don't Want Scabs" on the blackboards in the empty classrooms, and some students joined the picket lines. After the mayor offered raises averaging $525 a year, the teachers ended the week-long walkout.[69] Altogether, some fifty-seven strikes took place between 1946 and 1949, while only twelve had occurred between 1940 and 1945. Teachers in "more than 100 communities were talking of strike votes," reported *Life* magazine in March 1947. Two out of three respondents to an AFT questionnaire expressed the desire to repeal the no-strike policy.[70]

The AFT, which had adopted a no-strike policy shortly after it was founded, had trouble responding to the upsurge. Independent groups and affiliates of the CIO and NEA, not the AFT, instigated the strikes. At the local level, some AFT officials became much more supportive. The president of the Illinois State Federation of Teachers (ISFT), for example, told his fellow teachers in November 1946: "I say to you exploited underdogs of our economy, rise up in unified action in every local federation and in a righteous fury demand just salaries."[71]

The crisis in public education contributed to the dissatisfaction of the teachers. Spending on schools declined during the war as states put available funds in service of the war effort. "Teachers Pay—A National Disgrace," declared *Readers Digest* in October 1945. "Our schools need better teachers and our teachers need much better pay," *Life* magazine concluded in September 1946. It was "an unspeakable disgrace," it continued, that some schools would not open for the new school year because they could not find teachers. Poor wages and bad working conditions, the *Saturday Evening Post* added that same year, prodded teachers to leave the profession.[72]

Like other workers, Chicago public school teachers saw their living and working conditions decline during the war. With a maximum salary of $2,312.60 for Chicago elementary school teachers in 1941 and $2,850 in 1946, their purchasing power fell $186.50. A high school teacher's maximum salary rose from $3,515 in 1941 to $3,950 in 1946, but the teacher's purchasing power fell by $568.30.[73] (See Table 6.) While teachers used to be attracted to the profession by work-free Saturdays and a pension, by the end of World War II most occupations enjoyed a five-day week, and the Social Security Act of 1935 gave most other workers pension rights.[74] Chicago teachers further complained that conditions in the schools hindered the educational process. "How can teachers teach democracy to children when they themselves have no opportunity to take part in any decisions as to school policy and are not permitted to make any suggestions of any sort?" According to a 1946 survey, 68 percent of teachers complained of too much clerical work, 62 percent of a collapse of standards due to no-failure policies, 57.7 percent of no time for marking papers, 48.2 percent of interruption from the school office by phone or messenger, and 47.3 percent of no opportunities for helping individual students.[75]

In the postwar years, teachers increasingly voiced disillusionment with the job of teaching and the lack of community support. One Chicago teacher complained of "lack of appreciation by the public," and another believed the public to be "utterly thankless."[76] Having had their faith in public education battered by cost-cutting politicians and an uncaring public, they now took more interest in economic remuneration. Teaching "has become just a job, a means of earning a livelihood," observed Benjamin Fine in his nationwide study of the schools undertaken after World War II. "Gone are the joys of serving society, of assuming responsibility for growing young minds. The pioneering spirit has gone out of teaching."[77] Chicago teacher Mrs. Sakelson concurred. She noted that "in my building are union members and the only thing that means anything is to make money and if it takes a strike, they will go out. The teachers who are coming out of our own normal school have no regard for any professional ethics. But I certainly say that the younger ones have no idea of professional ethics or, for that matter, much professional responsibility."[78]

While many teachers had been reluctant to partake in militant activity during the Depression, after World War II teachers had fewer inhibitions, different perceptions, and better employment opportunities elsewhere. Those who had kept their jobs during the Depression felt lucky to be employed,

Table 6. Decline in Chicago Public School Teachers' Pay, 1941 to 1946

	Maximum Salary 1941	Maximum Salary 1946	Dollar Loss in Purchasing Power
Elementary School Teachers	$2312.60	$2850.00	$186.50
High School Teachers	$3515.00	$3950.00	$568.30

Source: E. F. Gibney, "The Public School Teacher in a Metropolis," (Ph.D. diss., Northwestern University, 1947), 278.

acted cautiously, and refused to strike. With a shortage of teachers after World War II, many public school teachers were more confident and proved less willing to accept their low pay and deteriorating working conditions. Teachers felt angry that they were in a low-paying and low-status profession, but they did not have the fear of the Depression-era teachers.

Chicago was caught up in this rising militancy. After the Board of Education's budget hearing in January 1946, the CTU reported, "Protests from local units concerning the salary allocations. . . . Elementary teachers protested their continued inadequate salaries; high school and college teachers protested the discriminatory salary raises and the inconsistency of granting them smaller salary increases than were granted the groups both above and below them." High school and elementary school teachers petitioned the CTU leaders to take action to achieve salary increases. While the male teachers in the high schools generally urged an across-the-board raise, the petitions from female teachers in elementary schools urged the union to take action to implement the single salary schedule. One petition from schoolteacher Mildred Lynch at Arnold School claimed that she polled twenty-seven union members, of whom twenty-five "were not satisfied . . . with the new salary schedule for Elementary teachers in relation to the single salary schedule." The CTU studied the strike question and concluded that the Chicago union was not bound by the AFT rule barring walkouts. However, because "teachers' services are rendered not to employers, whose profits could be cut, but to children, a POSITIVE program was deemed a more effective means for gaining teacher and public support."[79]

Most importantly, because of this postwar militancy, the CTU and other teachers' unions changed their general orientation from professional unionism to one more focused on traditional unionism by seeking the right to bargain with the Board of Education. Although school boards were under no legal obligation to bargain with teachers, during the war some made agreements with their local unions and set a precedent for teachers in other school systems. East St. Louis, Illinois, teachers won the first bargaining election ever held in Illinois in 1944, and the Cicero, Illinois, Council of the West Suburban Teachers Union signed the first collective bargaining agreement with the local education board in the same year. Subsequently, union teachers negotiated agreements in Anaconda-Butte, Montana, and La Crosse, Wisconsin.[80] In 1946, after teachers in Norwalk, Pennsylvania, struck to achieve collective bargaining rights, the school board signed an agreement recognizing the Norwalk Teachers Association as the sole bargaining agent for its members.[81]

As public sector employment and unionism mushroomed, other government workers joined the call for collective bargaining rights. Because of the increasing demand for public sector services, nearly six million people worked for federal, state, and local governments in 1947. To take advantage of the growth in the number of government workers, in the spring of 1946 two CIO unions, United Federal Workers of America (UFWA) and the State, County and Municipal Workers of America (SCMWA), merged to form the United Public Workers of America (UPWA). With a membership of more than 100,000, the UPWA claimed to be the largest public employees' union in the country. Its main AFL-affiliated rival, the American Federation of State, County and Municipal Employees (AFSCME), organized in October 1936, claimed 100,000 members by March 1946. By the following year, about 600,000 public sector workers were affiliated with the AFL or the CIO unions. With increased membership, these government employee labor organizations lobbied Congress for collective bargaining laws. Ultimately, however, the main piece of legislation they supported, the Rhodes-Johnston bill, failed to become law.[82]

Chicago teachers and their union began to demand collective bargaining rights too. Chicago teachers sent petitions to the CTU urging the union to take action to achieve bargaining rights with the Board of Education, and, in response, the CTU leadership made a concerted effort to educate themselves and the membership about the practicalities of collective bargaining. The union enlisted the support of the University of Chicago's Industrial Relations Center and the Illinois State Federation of Teachers to train teachers in bargaining techniques.[83] The CTU prodded the Illinois State Federation of Labor to support legislation in the Illinois assembly that would grant public sector unions the right to bargain with their employers. John Fewkes made frequent visits to Springfield to lobby legislators, but the CTU was unable to convince the Illinois state assembly to pass the legislation. In 1945 a senate bill giving public sector employers the right to enter into collective bargaining agreements with representatives of their employees passed the General Assembly, but it was vetoed by Republican governor Dwight Green. From 1947 to the mid-1950s, the ISFT tried unsuccessfully to introduce legislation at the General Assembly at Springfield to permit public bodies, including school boards, to make collective bargaining agreements with their employees.[84]

Nevertheless, to appease both the men and the women, the union pressed for both the full implementation of the single salary schedule and a large raise for the high school teachers. At the January 1947 budget hearing, the CTU demanded a wage increase of $350 to $480 for high school teachers and from $500 to $1,150 for elementary school teachers. The Board of Education made the second giant step toward the adoption of the single salary schedule when it approved the salary schedules proposed by the CTU with few exceptions, including the use of a ten-step schedule rather than the CTU's proposed eight steps. Elementary school teachers and high school teachers obtained the same pay based on hourly rate, but the high school teachers continued to work six hours a day while the elementary school teachers worked five hours. The single salary schedule had been practically achieved and the raise in pay for high school teachers dissuaded the Men Teachers Club from striking.[85]

The union was able to maintain the support of its members and avoid a damaging split; henceforth the MTC declined in influence. Inadvertently, the MTC helped to change the focus of the CTU campaign from a demand for a single salary schedule to a raise for all public school teachers. Soon after the events of 1947, the MTC merged with another men's union, the Schoolmen of Boston, to form the American Schoolmen's Association. The newly formed organization blamed the "feminist groups and teacher organizations dominated by women" who have bitterly opposed higher wages for men teachers. They declared that equal pay is "part of the Communist creed of 'equal pay for everyone.'" By 1952, Chicago and Boston, the two cities with strong men teachers' unions, remained the only two cities with a population more than 500,000 that had not adopted a full single salary schedule of equal pay and equal hours of work. By 1947, 64 percent of school districts used the single salary schedule, and in 1951 it was 97 percent. The Board of Education finally established the single salary schedule, the same pay for elementary school and high school teachers, in January 1954.[86]

Conclusion

The war had a notable impact on gender relations in the public schools. The living costs of Chicago's elementary school teachers rose during the war and dramatically altered the expectations of women teachers as greater opportunities opened up for women outside the teaching profession. In one of the first major campaigns for the single salary schedule, these teachers, mostly women, managed to pressure the Board of Education into introducing the first step of a single, and equal, salary schedule for both elementary school and high school teachers. At the end of the war, however, men teachers rebelled against the pay raise for women and prodded the union into considering their case. The threat of internal dissension forced the CTU leaders to pursue a relatively successful campaign for pay raises for all teachers, but it curtailed the campaign for equal pay.

The story of the CTU struggle over the single salary scale dovetails nicely with a number of studies that have argued that union women in the years before the modern feminist movement promoted labor solidarity along with their own gender-specific concerns. This "labor feminism" in the Chicago public schools and in other industries and professions was rooted in trade unionism, worker education, community organizing, and legislative lobbying. As Dorothy Sue Cobble, for example, argues, the definition of feminism needs to be expanded to include these "union feminists" who sought economic advancement through collective union power and not simply individual social mobility.[87] Indeed, historians have all but ignored the conflict over the single salary schedule even though it was one of most successful struggles by women workers to achieve equal pay.[88]

The World War II years saw other significant changes in the CTU. Unlike private sector workers, Chicago public school teachers during the war had no right to negotiate a bargaining agreement with employers and had to either confront the Democratic machine or seek accommodation to satisfy their demands. Union leaders and most teachers chose good relations with the school board rather than conflict, and the decision to support the Democratic machine achieved some concrete results. In return for removing Kermit Eby and acquiescing to continued political control of the schools, the board restored teachers' pay to pre-Depression levels, and a pay raise for all teachers had been achieved by the war's end.

The postwar teacher militancy prompted the CTU to make the most profound change in its orientation by advocating collective bargaining rights. By doing this, they moved away from the professional model of teacher unionism, which focused on lobbying to meet the teachers' demands, to one modeled on traditional industrial union strategies. Reflecting the cautious approach of the union leadership and the teachers, Fewkes and the CTU leadership sought to introduce legislation into the state capital of Springfield rather than pressure the Chicago Board of Education into unilaterally granting bargaining rights. The following decade would see little advance in the campaign for collective bargaining, but the union was now set on a course that would eventually fundamentally change the orientation of the union, the public school system, and the lives of schoolteachers.

4

The Cold War in the
Chicago Public Schools,
1947–1957

The decade after World War II proved difficult for the American public school system, teachers, and teachers' unions. Rapid population growth led to bulging enrollments in urban school systems, but the federal government refused to increase funding for education. A red scare brought on by the developing Cold War sought to limit academic freedom and political dissent and promote conformist attitudes in the classroom. While many private sector workers enjoyed collective bargaining rights with employers under the Wagner Act, public sector employees had to accept the dictates of unchecked management. The wave of teacher militancy that had engulfed the country in the aftermath of World War II subsided and the number of teacher' strikes declined dramatically. The AFT leadership condemned communism in the public schools, retreated from political engagement, and concentrated on bread-and-butter issues.[1]

How much was Chicago in accord with this national picture? What impact did the conservative climate of the 1950s, and in particular the red scare, have on the Chicago public schools and their teachers? In Chicago, events proved less demoralizing for teachers and their unions, as conditions in the school system improved rather than worsened over the decade. After a concerted campaign against Mayor Edward Kelly and the Board of Education by reform movements in Chicago, Kelly declined to seek re-election in 1947 and all his leading supporters in the public school administration resigned. A new mayor, school superintendent, and board president promised to provide the Chicago public school teachers the rewards of professionalism they had long hoped for: higher pay, better working conditions, and a greater say in school policy. In the midst of all this, the CTU sustained the support of teachers as it espoused liberal anticommunism and went some way in defending Chicago schoolteachers and the public school curriculum from conservative attack.

The Fall of the Kelly-Nash Machine

The political fortunes of Chicago teachers improved dramatically in 1947. The one issue that had shaken the Democratic machine during the 1930s, the deteriorating state of the Chicago public school system, came back to haunt Mayor Kelly as the war came to an end. In 1944, various reform groups in Chicago had asked the National Education Association (NEA) to investigate the administration of the Chicago public school system. The NEA's report, published in May 1945, created a storm of controversy as it exposed the extent to which city politicians had used the public schools for their own ends. The report found that the faculty of the Chicago Teachers College, and temporary teachers in the public schools, had attained their positions through political connections. The board had transferred to other schools or demoted teachers who opposed the McCahey regime and had controlled teachers' organizations either by extending favors to their leaders or by capturing offices in elections. Finally, the NEA reported that serious financial irregularities plagued the schools. The commission called for thorough action by the Illinois governor and legislature and warned that if these practices continued there would be "a progressive degeneration of the Chicago schools which will mark and handicap them for many years."[2]

The report galvanized opposition to Mayor Kelly and his school administrators. In January 1946, the NEA expelled school superintendent William Johnson from the organization for unethical conduct. A City Council committee investigation made up of Kelly supporters, which denied all the allegations in the NEA report, could not stop the furor. In March 1946, the North Central Association of Schools and Colleges, the school accrediting agency, warned that it would withdraw accreditation to the Chicago schools unless a new Board of Education was established.[3] Buoyed by the report, a number of newspapers and community groups turned their ire on the Kelly regime. The *Chicago Sun,* which had opposed the Kelly regime since the paper was first published in 1941, splashed revelations from the NEA report across its front pages. The Church Federation of Chicago, representing 1,200 churches with 400,000 members, called for the resignation of the Board of Education. Subsequently, Parent Teacher Associations (PTAs), the Citizens Schools Committee (CSC), and other civic groups organized mass meetings in halls and churches across the city.[4] A number of civic groups formed the All-Chicago Emergency Committee of Schools in July 1946 and sent a 50,000–signature petition to Mayor Kelly demanding the resignation of the Board of Education.[5]

Under pressure to act, Mayor Kelly responded to the NEA report in April 1946. He appointed an advisory committee of six university presidents, led by Illinois Institute of Technology president Henry T. Heald, to investigate the entire school system. The Heald Report, issued in June 1946, recommended that Superintendent Johnson resign, that Kelly appointees be removed from the Board of Education, and that the mayor create a committee to make nominations to fill the vacant board positions. Superintendent Johnson resigned the day the report was published, and by September, four members of the eleven-member board joined him in tendering their resignations, and the terms of two others expired. On the recommendations of the Heald Report, Mayor Kelly set up the Commission on School Board Nominations, which filled the vacancies with reforming board members. Finally, in December 1946 Mayor Kelly announced that he would not run for re-election, and board president James McCahey declared that he would retire when his term expired in April 1947.[6]

The CTU played a small part in the final demise of Mayor Kelly and his supporters in the public schools. Locked in a political deal with the Board of Education since the start of U.S. involvement in the war, the CTU was conspicuously absent from the list of organizations that had asked the NEA to investigate the schools in 1944. The content of the NEA report exposed the unions' lack of opposition to the Board of Education. Indeed, the NEA knowingly undertook the study and used the findings to expose the inactivity of the CTU, the largest local of the NEA's main rival the AFT. Only after the investigation was underway did the CTU agree to cooperate with the NEA, and the union leadership played no role in the community-wide effort to remove Johnson and McCahey after the report's publication.[7]

Although the CTU contributed little to the end of the McCahey and Johnson regime, many public school teachers made significant contributions to the cause of reform. As an organization, the CTU and its predecessors had kept political control of the public school system before the public eye for nearly a decade, and in the process they made machine control of the schools more difficult to operate, publicized its injustices, and rendered it illegitimate to a number of Chicagoans. Most of the revelations in the NEA report had been previously unearthed and widely publicized by the union.[8] Moreover, many union activists bypassed their union's leadership and campaigned for the removal of Kelly and his allies. Edward E. Keener, president of the Chicago Division of the Illinois Education Association and a union activist, was one of those who initially approached the NEA to make a study of the public schools. In the forefront of the campaign to remove the mayor and his supporters were those who had aligned themselves with Kermit Eby during his fight to avoid dismissal from his post as union secretary. Former CTU executive members Lillian Herstein and Butler Laughlin, principal of Harper High School and the man whose wartime demotion Turley and the CTU executive board had ignored, spoke on many anti-McCahey platforms.[9]

After Edward Kelly had pledged not to run for re-election in 1947, the Democratic Party candidate, reformer Martin H. Kennelly, was elected as mayor and initiated a new era in the Chicago public school system. Democrats chose Kennelly because he was a businessman and had little previous direct connections with the Democratic Party and Chicago politics.[10] Like Kelly, Kennelly was an Irish American born in the Bridgeport neighborhood on the South Side, but unlike his predecessor, Kennelly had little desire to run a patronage-fueled political machine. William B. Traynor, vice president of Swift and Company, replaced James McCahey as board president. Some of Kelly's appointees, including Bernard Majewski, board member since 1936 and vice president under McCahey, refused to resign from the Board of Education. Reform-minded citizens, however, made up the majority of Kennelly's new appointees to the board.[11]

In July 1947, Herold G. Hunt, from Kansas City, took over the new and more powerful position of general superintendent, created when the state legislature revised the Otis Law. Believing that the board's direct management of the school system and control of the school superintendent was the major cause of the corruption, the legislation eliminated the position of business manager and gave the general superintendent greater independence and authority over all school matters, not just the education department. Hunt promised to keep the schools free of political control and guaranteed appointment and promotion on merit. The Chicago Teachers College became independent of the political machine and teachers no longer depended on political connections to gain employment. Hunt replaced non-teaching patronage appointees with exam-qualified civil servants, and within two years patronage in the schools had virtually ended. "Thus for the first time in Chicago's history," political scientist William J. Grimshaw suggests, "the school system was operating in its entirety independently of the city's political system."[12] In complete contrast to Johnson's authoritarian managerial approach, Hunt expressed a willingness to cooperate and obtain agreement with others on running the Chicago public school system. The new general superintendent decentralized decision making, gave more classroom autonomy to teachers, allowed committees of principals and teachers to choose textbooks, and consulted civic groups on important school issues. According to the CSC, a new "refreshed atmosphere" and "spirit of democracy" now pervaded the schools.[13]

As part of his policy of openness and inclusiveness, General Superintendent Hunt made a special effort to cooperate with the CTU. As CTU leader Mary Herrick recalled, "No Superintendent of schools had ever been welcomed to Chicago with such warm offers of cooperation as was Herold C. Hunt. . . . The relation of Superintendent Hunt with the Teachers' Union was probably warmer than with any other group."[14] To show his willingness to break with the past, Hunt appointed union members and foes of the old regime to major jobs in his administration.[15]

The CTU Threatens to Strike

As the Chicago public schools welcomed a new administration, the CTU saw another change in leadership in May 1947 when Arthur Walz stepped aside to allow John Fewkes to return as CTU president. Fewkes, who had relocated to Washington, D.C., as chief of the Industrial Safety Section of the War Production Board in 1943, returned to teaching physical education at Tilden High School at the war's end, and he received 64 percent of the vote in the May 1947 CTU presidential election. With the end of the Kelly regime, many of those who opposed political control of the schools and the CTU's eagerness to accommodate those in power now applauded Fewkes's willingness to work with the new school administration. In November 1950, the union house of representatives amended the CTU constitution and removed the restriction that the president could succeed himself only once. Altogether, the Chicago teachers elected Fewkes nine more times and he remained president until June 1966.[16]

Immediately after his return to the CTU presidency, Fewkes had to address a crisis over teachers' pay. Because of the lack of funds, the pay raise that the Board of Education had awarded the teachers in January 1947 had still not been put fully into effect by the year's end. The union demanded that the raise be fully implemented in the 1948 budget. As an indication of the changed climate in the school system, the new general superintendent, Herold Hunt, the Board of Education, and Mayor Kennelly all supported the teachers' demands for a wage raise and the board adopted the union's salary proposal on January 20, 1948. To pay the increase in salary, however, the City Council had to approve a raise in the property tax rate. The Democratic-controlled City Council, not wanting to be responsible for increasing taxes and reluctant to fund a public education system they could no longer staff with patronage employees, blocked the pay raise, claiming insufficient funds.[17]

The publicity generated by the NEA report made the wider community more aware of the inadequacies of the Chicago public schools, and the community showed greater support for the teachers. The Chicago Region of the Illinois Congress of Parents and Teachers surveyed its members on whether the teachers' salary demands should be met. Some school PTAs offered to lend up to $2,000 to teachers if it became necessary to strike, and others offered to serve hot meals to pickets at their school.[18] The CTU obtained a million signatures for a petition to Illinois governor Dwight Green in December 1947 urging him to call a special session of the state legislature to raise the State Distributive Fund to subsidize the teachers' wage demands. As a Republican, Green refused to bow to the public pressure, insisting that the Chicago Democrats raise their own money through an increase in the property tax.[19]

With the news that the City Council had blocked the pay raise, teachers and especially the men in the high schools erupted in fury. Herschel Scott, leader of the Men Teachers Club (MTC), declared that at his school, "[w]e have voted solidly not to turn a wheel until the first pay checks are out." As hundreds of other Chicago schoolteachers staged sit-down strikes in their classrooms, thousands of students left their classes and went home. At Tilden High School more than fifty teachers sat in at the principal's office and classes had to be stopped.[20] Some condemned the striking teachers as unprofessional. Lillian Herstein replied, "that is a throwback to the attitude which prevailed when I entered the teaching profession thirty years ago. But it most assuredly is not an attitude consistent with the needs and urgencies of 1948."[21]

After the City Council refused to grant the teachers' pay raise, the teachers—for the first time in their history—voted nine to one to strike if the City Council refused to approve the board's budget and delayed payment further. The strike was in violation of the AFT's no-strike policy. Most importantly, for the first time, the Board of Education and the mayor stayed on the side of the teachers. Reluctantly, the council voted to increase taxes, approved the budget, and averted the strike.[22]

The support General Superintendent Herold Hunt and the Board of Education gave the CTU for its wage claim further cemented cooperation between the public school administrators, the union, and the teachers. Public opinion had played an important part in getting the levy passed, but the backing of Hunt and Mayor Kennelly was crucial. The lesson many teachers drew from the dispute was that Hunt had achieved what community protest had failed to do. This confirmed to Fewkes and many doubters in the union leadership that the strategy of cooperation with the Board of Education was the correct one. After the teachers received their pay raise, Fewkes told the delegates that the "finest of relationships between the Union and the school administration have been established and will continue to be maintained."[23] Fewkes sought to depend less on the public for support and more on building a strong relationship with General Superintendent Hunt and eschewing the last vestiges of community politics. By the end of the 1940s it was clear that the CTU political action committee, which had led the campaign against Mayor Kelly with such fervor in the 1930s, was dormant.[24] With a cooperative mayor, superintendent, and Board of Education, CTU leaders believed that "[i]n this city, prospects for progress are the brightest in two generations."[25]

The installation of a more sympathetic schools superintendent and Board of Education helped to remove any sense of urgency from the CTU campaign for collective bargaining rights. On the one hand, the support of the superintendent and the Board of Education for the CTU wage claim in 1948 cemented cooperation between them and the union and lessened the haste, if not the need, for collective bargaining. Apart from the unsuccessful lobbying efforts of Fewkes and the Illinois State Federation of Teachers (ISFT) in the General Assembly in Springfield, the Chicago public school teachers waged no mass campaign to attain collective bargaining rights. Opposed by the Republican-dominated assembly, the Chicago Civic Federation, and the Taxpayers Federation, all the bills were defeated. On the other hand, for all their openness to cooperation, neither Herold Hunt nor the Board of Education wanted to lose managerial prerogatives to the CTU by instituting collective bargaining. Instead of bargaining rights, Hunt set up "teachers councils" in 1949, which were made up of delegates elected by teachers, who would act as advisors to the mayor. The union opposed the councils until they collapsed in 1953.[26]

Chicago public school teachers emerged from the events of January 1948 more united than they had ever been before. The internal strife within the union over the adoption of the single salary schedule had ended with the establishment of equal hourly pay for all teachers, and the demands of the men teachers had subsided with a substantial raise in pay. In addition, the willingness of the CTU leadership to strike extinguished many teachers' criticism of the CTU leadership, raised Fewkes's prestige among teachers, and drew the members and leaders closer together. High school teacher Sherman Cook declared after they had won the pay raise in January 1948 that "[p]erhaps even more than the raise, we should be thankful for the way the schools (and teachers) have been raised in the public's estimation." Another high school teacher, Gertrude Hardt, suggested that "teachers can never be used as political footballs again, which in turn has given us teachers renewed faith and courage in our forward march."[27] CTU membership, which had declined from 61 percent of teachers in 1938 to 52 percent in 1947, rose again to nearly 60 percent by 1948. Significantly, after Fewkes was elected in May 1947 there were no opposition candidates to either him or the other official candidates until 1958.[28]

The position of the CTU solidified further as the main rivals to the union faded after the war. The Men Teachers Club membership fell from more than eight hundred in 1946 to two hundred in 1950 and the organization had disbanded by the early 1950s.[29] After Margaret Haley's death, many members of the Chicago Teachers Federation (CTF) joined the CTU and, without the charismatic figure of Haley, those that remained dissolved into factional splits, and the CTF played a small part in the political life of the city. Led by Frances M. Kenney, most of the members of the CTF, who were older Irish American teachers, continued to enjoy the CTF's social events and the group's insurance and credit union. Reflecting the concerns of its aging membership, the CTF concentrated its energies on improving teachers' pensions and social security. By 1950, the CTF had only three hundred members. Frances Kenney died in 1968 and the CTF disbanded.[30]

Even though the union and the school administration moved closer together, teachers' salaries and the schools they worked in did not change for the better. In 1949, the year following the threatened strike, the board rejected the CTU's wage demands, claiming a lack of funds. With each subsequent budget, the board gave nominal increases to the teachers, far less than the CTU had proposed at budget meetings. Between 1945 and 1953, the minimum monthly pay for a Chicago elementary school teacher rose from $135.42 to $250 and from $200 to $288.33 for a high school teacher. During the same period, the monthly pay of a stenographer had risen from $168.90 to $290.30, a painter from $182.00 to $476.60, and an electrician from $197.60 to $396 per month.[31] Without increased financial help from the state or the federal government, the school infrastructure showed little signs of improvement. Indeed, in 1951, 38 percent of Chicago public schools had been built before 1900 and only 13 percent since 1930.[32]

By the mid-1950s, however, salaries and benefits had improved and when compared to the Depression or the early postwar period had advanced dramatically. As school enrollment increased and teachers were in short supply, the school board had to offer higher salaries to attract and hold teachers. Pay rose from a minimum of $3,400 and maximum of $6,650 in 1954 to $5,000 and $8,500 in 1960. Paid sick leave increased from five days in the early postwar period to ten days in 1955, and the accumulative sick leave total was increased from fifteen days to 120 days in 1960.[33] As political scientist Paul Peterson discovered, the pay and benefits of Chicago public school teachers increased more than other occupations from 1955 onwards.[34] Furthermore, Chicago public school teachers enjoyed the full payment of their salaries and regular paydays, which they had not had between 1930 and 1943, and elementary school teachers, the majority of the workforce, benefited from equal pay with high school teachers.

In addition to increases in salaries, Chicago public school teachers had much else to be grateful for. The fear and corruption imposed by Mayor Kelly and the Democratic machine in the schools was replaced by respect and cooperation from General Superintendent Hunt. Appointments and promotions to principal or school administrator depended more on merit and less on connections with the political machine. Summary demotion and the transfer of teachers to other schools if they displeased those in power ended. Superintendent Hunt consulted teachers on curriculum and textbook selection.[35] Even though schools were aging, class sizes stabilized. Average elementary school class size in Chicago fell from 39.6 in 1947 to 37.2 in 1956 and rose only slightly from 30.7 to 31.5 in the high schools.[36]

Postwar Political and Economic Changes

Dramatic changes in the post–World War II political climate confronted teachers and their unions. Republicans, victorious in the midterm congressional elections of 1946, now controlled both houses of Congress for the first time since 1930. Seeking to halt further reforms and roll back the gains of the New Deal, the Republican-dominated Congress rejected national health insurance, which most Western European allies had already adopted. Overriding President Truman's veto, Congress passed the Labor Management Relations Act (the Taft-Hartley Act) in June 1947, which revised the 1935 Wagner Act and prohibited secondary boycotts, banned the closed shop, and permitted state "right to work" laws.[37] In Illinois, Republicans controlled the state senate throughout the 1940s and 1950s, usually dominated the house, and ended Democrat Adlai Stevenson's reign as governor in 1953 with the election of Republican William Stratton.

A further rightward shift in the nation occurred as the Cold War developed and anticommunism came to dominate U.S. domestic politics. After World War II, Soviet-style regimes' rapid takeover of Eastern Europe precipitated an attack on the Communist Party as a threat to national security. In March 1947, President Harry Truman issued Executive Order 9835, which called for investigations of all federal employees to uncover evidence of subversive behavior. In 1949, the government indicted and jailed the Communist Party's leadership under the Smith Act, which made it a crime to advocate or to belong to an organization calling for the overthrow of the government by force. In 1950, Congress passed the McCarran Internal Security Act, which required communists and "communist front" organizations to register with the U.S. Attorney General. The House Un-American Activities Committee (HUAC), founded in the late 1930s, investigated "communist subversion," most sensationally in Hollywood where left-leaning actors, directors, and writers were allegedly spreading communist messages through their movies.[38] The 1947 Taft-Hartley Act required union officials to sign a non-communist oath. The Congress of Industrial Organizations (CIO) in 1949 and 1950 expelled eleven of its affiliates that had substantial communist leadership or influence.[39]

In this climate of conservative ascendancy, conservative groups, often using anticommunist rhetoric, formed a broad coalition that campaigned against federal interference in public education. Republicans in Congress, concerned with the threat of government control over the economy and society, had little intention of transferring local control of education to a federal bureaucracy. Taxpayers groups, the U.S. Chamber of Commerce, and the National Association of Manufacturers wanted to avoid higher taxes, Catholic organizations opposed legislation that funded only public education and ignored parochial schools, and southern politicians would not accept federal funding bills that mandated an equal share for racially segregated schools. Indeed, in 1944 conservative Republican senator William Langer attached an amendment to a bill denying aid to segregated schools, knowing the bill would face certain defeat in Congress. Some business groups and taxpayers associations used anticommunism to oppose federal funding for education. The Catholic Church condemned the public schools for their communist teachers and the AFT and NEA for their alleged communist sympathies. Catholic archbishops, the Catholic press, and parishioners condemned those who supported federal funding for public schools for their "atheistic communism" and as "Communists, materialists, agnostics and secularists bent on the frustration of freedom of education."[40] In October 1951, AFT leader Selma Borchardt reluctantly announced that "no Congress for some time to come will enact any bills to provide general federal aid for education." She was proved right. Substantial federal aid for education in the Elementary and Secondary Education Act (ESEA) only passed Congress in April 1965, long after the red scare had receded, Lyndon Johnson had won a landslide victory in the 1964 presidential election, and the Democrats controlled both houses of Congress.[41]

Organized labor and public sector unions in particular came under attack in this conservative mood. The postwar strike wave, the largest in the nation's history, had led politicians and employers to suggest that labor was out of control and threatened postwar economic recovery. The threat of communist-leaning unions among government workers particularly worried politicians. More than six million federal employees were subjected to loyalty and security checks under presidents Truman and Eisenhower. In July 1946, after the formation of the communist-leaning UPWA, Congress passed Public Law 419, which required federal employees to sign an affidavit declaring they would not become a member of any organization that advocated strikes. The Taft-Hartley Act of 1947 included a provision, Section 305, which made it unlawful for federal sector workers to strike, at the threat of dismissal. In 1955, Congress introduced the more draconian Public Law 330, which made it a felony for federal employees to strike or to belong to an organization that asserted the right to strike.[42] After 2,400 teachers in Buffalo, New York, struck in February 1947, the New York state legislature passed the Condon-Wadlin Act, which called for the dismissal of striking public sector workers. After the war, nine states enacted no-strike laws for public employees.[43] Frightened by legislation and a hostile political climate, public sector workers, including schoolteachers, became less willing to militantly campaign for their demands. While nearly 12,000 teachers engaged in forty-eight work stoppages between 1946 and 1948, in the next six years only 7,400 teachers took part in thirty-three stoppages.[44]

Anticommunism in Chicago

While working conditions in the public schools improved and teachers' salaries showed steady progress, the major problem Chicago public school teachers faced revolved around academic freedom. At a time of heightened international tensions during the early years of the Cold War, many Americans began to believe that a cadre of communist teachers was intent on instilling pro-Soviet sentiments in the nation's children. Older organizations, like the American Legion and the Daughters of the American Revolution, were joined by new conservative groups in the anticommunist crusade. The American Education Society, founded in 1938, sought to "Keep American Schools American" and fought against radical teachers. The National Council for American Education (NCAE), established by Allen Zoll after World War II, attacked public schools for their alleged communist influence while it promoted the use of private schools. The NCAE claimed to want the "eradication of Marxism and collectivism from our schools and national life."[45] These groups had substantial support. A national opinion poll from September 1949 showed that 73 percent of those asked opposed Communist Party members teaching in the schools and only 15 percent approved. A poll taken four years later found that 66 percent thought that even former Communist Party members should not be allowed to teach in colleges and universities.[46] Bowing to pressure, in 1948 the AFT voted against allowing communists to teach and in 1949 the NEA barred communists from membership in the organization and urged that they be denied employment in the public schools.

Spurred on by conservative pressure groups, the U.S. Congress turned its attention to removing communist influence in the classroom. Starting in the early 1950s, the Senate Internal Security Subcommittee (SISS), chaired by Senator Pat McCarran, conducted hearings into subversive influence in the education system that lasted for more than three years. The HUAC, under new chairman Harold H. Velde, also examined communist influence in public education. Former communists, such as New York teacher Bella Dodd, appeared in front of the SISS and the HUAC to expose links between teachers' unions and the Communist Party and describe alleged communist influence in the schools. By July 1953, more than a hundred schoolteachers had been suspended or dismissed for non-cooperation with congressional committees. Thousands of others lived in fear of being called in front of a committee or being condemned for subversive teaching.[47]

The anticommunist crusade against public school teachers had much success at the local level. In 1949 the New York state legislature passed the Feinberg Law, which required the New York State Board of Regents to draw up a list of "subversive organizations" in which membership would mean dismissal from the public schools. Consequently, between 1953 and 1958, thirty-three New York public school teachers were dismissed and another 283 resigned when threatened with investigation. Many teachers in schools and universities were required to take loyalty oaths. In 1954, three years after the Pennsylvania legislature had passed a loyalty oath, twenty-six teachers were fired because they refused to discuss their past political activities. In 1957, only seventeen states did not require teachers to take an oath of some kind.[48]

In the conservative climate of the postwar years, the nation saw a wholesale attack on the Progressive education movement. The Sons of the American Revolution, for example, argued that Progressive education had a detrimental impact on teaching methods and called for a return to the three R's and an end to "fads and frills." Allen Zoll and the NCAE alleged that Progressive education promoted socialism. Others joined in the assault. Dr. Ernest Cadman Colwell, president of the University of Chicago, suggested in 1950 that "the American public school system is a failure. . . . College freshmen are increasingly illiterate year by year, unable to read or think."[49] Newspapers printed articles on the detrimental effects of Progressive education on the school system. In 1953, University of Illinois history professor Arthur Bestor published *Educational Wastelands: The Retreat from Learning in Our Public Schools,* an influential book which criticized the public school curriculum and called for a return to traditional teaching methods and subjects. Between 1949 and 1953, leading academics sponsored by the Conference of American Small Business Organizations (CASBO) established the *Educational Reviewer* to oppose Progressive educators and Marxist influence on school textbooks. Under the attack, in 1955 the Progressive Education Association disbanded and two years later *Progressive Education* suspended publication.[50]

Chicagoans could not hide from the prying eyes of the red baiters. In Chicago, as elsewhere, politicians, conservative pressure groups, and city newspapers set out to expose communist subversion and attack liberal causes. While anticommunism in Chicago did not claim the national headlines, many individuals lost their jobs and left and liberal causes suffered. Investigated by HUAC, a number of left-leaning labor unions such as the United Public Workers and the United Packinghouse Workers of America found it difficult to prosper in the city. Chicago aldermen, the local press, and white resident associations accused the Chicago Housing Authority and its head, Elizabeth Wood, of communism for allocating public housing to black families in previously white neighborhoods.[51]

The tone of postwar anticommunist activity in Chicago was set by the Illinois legislature. After lobbying by the American Legion, the Illinois state assembly created the Seditious Activities Investigation Commission, otherwise known as the Broyles Commission (after its chairman, Republican senator Paul Broyles) in 1947, to probe communist influence in the state. The committee included five members of the senate, five members of the house, and five citizens, including two past commanders of the American Legion. Under Senator Broyles, a former commander of the American Legion, the committee reported that the education system was the most vulnerable to communist penetration.[52] In 1949, the commission held hearings to investigate the political activities of professors at the University of Chicago, but with the faculty defended by university chancellor Robert Hutchins, the hearings accomplished little. Most damning for the Chicago public schools, the commission report stated that teachers "in certain high schools in the city of Chicago, are ardent followers of subversive movements."[53] The truth was far less spectacular. Even Bernard Majewski, Chicago Board of Education member and chief proponent of anticommunism, estimated in the early 1950s that communists made up "not over 1 per cent" of board employees.[54]

Taking their cue from the Broyles Commission, Chicago anticommunists singled out the public schools for attack. The *Chicago Tribune* condemned communist teaching and campaigned for the removal of liberal textbooks from the public schools. In 1947, the *Tribune* launched an exposé of more than fifty school textbooks that the newspaper claimed were pro-union and pro–New Deal. The books, the paper admitted, were not used in the Chicago schools, but the article gave a warning to administrators and teachers that its textbooks and school materials could be sensationally scrutinized for their liberal content.[55] On June 1, 1949, Senators Roland V. Libonati and William Knox introduced a bill in the state senate requiring the state superintendent of schools to examine textbooks for materials "antagonistic to the ideals" of the American form of government. A textbook committee was formed with the powers to examine all school civics textbooks and give their approval.[56]

The part of the Chicago schools' curriculum that came under most scrutiny from conservative watchdogs was the civics course. After the American Legion protested the teaching of procommunist doctrine in the Chicago high schools, in 1948, General Superintendent Herold Hunt appointed a committee of teachers, administrators, and representatives of citizens groups to revise the high school civics course. CTU leader Mary Herrick served as a committee member. The committee changed the course from one semester to a full year and outlined its curriculum revisions in a series of reports. The committee came under constant attack. The Broyles Commission report of 1949 stated that the Chicago high school teachers who taught the civics course were praising "foreign isms and philosophies of government." The *Chicago Tribune* campaigned for the removal of a series of books used in the course, including Frank A. Magruder's textbook *American Government,* Gavian, Gray, and Groves's *Our Changing Social Order,* and a book edited by former AFT president George Counts that had the ironic title *I Want to Be Like Stalin* but which condemned the Soviet Union.[57]

Hunt and the Board of Education bowed to the pressure. In early 1953, the textbook committee dropped the books from the approved list, and Hunt began consulting with conservative groups critical of the schools and appointed two conservative critics to the advisory committee on controversial subjects.[58] One of the appointees, an official of the Conference of American Small Business Organizations (CASBO), formed by Fred A. Virkus, announced "there isn't a decent civics textbook in Chicago. They're all tainted with statism, New Dealism, and socialism. Most of our teachers have been made unconsciously disloyal by the teachers' colleges."[59] In October 1950 Chicago Board of Education president William B. Traynor set up a committee to study ways to promote patriotism and combat communism in the schools.[60] All high school social studies, particularly civics and U.S. history, the Board Education informed teachers, had to show an "appreciation of the American government and way of life."[61] Instructional activities "are carried on in an atmosphere of patriotism," insisted Don C. Rogers, the assistant superintendent of schools, in 1954. "Chicago schools use carefully-selected textbooks . . . [which] present a wholesome picture of the American way of life in our democracy."[62] In the early 1960s, Robert Havighurst, in his survey of the Chicago public schools, found that school libraries had acquired a "plethora of anti-Communist literature, infrequently, if at all, balanced by a kind or objective word about the Soviet system."[63]

In September 1948, Butler Laughlin, the new assistant superintendent for the Chicago public high schools, directed all civics teachers to incorporate into their course curriculum material from the *Congressional Record* that outlined the differences between "democracy" and "communism." To be sure that teachers understood the differences between the two political systems, Laughlin asserted that in the latter there is "limited toleration of religious teaching, ruthless suppression of political expression and freedom of speech, strict control of the press, state control of education, and no freedom from unreasonable search and seizure." Communism, he concluded, offered "lower educational standards, poorer working conditions, a poorer educational system and generally more limited life than democracy" in America. Over the next few years school administrators like Laughlin would continue to try to mold the public school curriculum to fit a new and more conservative political climate.[64]

Under pressure from the media, politicians, and government agencies, Hunt acted against alleged communist influence among Chicago public school teachers. In June 1949, the Board of Examiners recommended Ira H. Latimer, executive director of the Chicago civil liberties committee, for a certificate to teach in Chicago public grade schools, but the Board of Education, on Hunt's recommendation, overturned the decision.[65] The following June, Ira Latimer's wife Imogene, a probationary teacher, was fired for unsatisfactory work.[66] In December 1949, Superintendent Hunt declared that Yolanda Hall, a graduate of the Chicago Teachers College and a self-confessed Communist Party member since 1939, would not be employed in the Chicago schools. He also announced that in the future all applicants for teaching jobs would be asked if they were communists.[67] Subsequently, the Chicago Board of Examiners invited candidates for teaching jobs to declare their membership in "subversive" organizations and denied certification to some individuals on political grounds.[68]

While showing little sympathy for communists or other radicals, Hunt leapt to the defense of teachers whom he thought had been unfairly accused of communist sympathies. In the spring of 1948, the *Chicago Herald American* printed statements from students at Senn High School that accused fifty-eight-year-old civics teacher Emilie Noack of instructing her students on how to become communists. Noack, a teacher at Senn since 1924 and self-styled liberal and Roosevelt supporter, denied the allegations. Pupils and colleagues at Senn petitioned on her behalf and the faculty urged the union to defend her. In response, Hunt investigated the matter and came out in support of Noack, who remained in the schools.[69]

Anticommunists spread fear in the schools as they continued to target even the most conservative of teachers for comments allegedly made in the classroom. In December 1951, the *Chicago Tribune* printed an article that alleged that there was "socialist bias in high schools." David A. Shewfelt, a student at Amundsen High School, wrote to the *Tribune* that "[h]istory and civics classes are dominated by socialistically inclined teachers . . . and the conservative ones are pushed out of the department." He further alleged that "[i]n our school the civics teacher told her class that our country needed socialism, it is bound to come and therefore we should prepare ourselves for it." Fellow student Arthur Renier, who had been instructed by his father to take notes of the teachers' comments, supported his story. The father produced an examination paper written by his son containing many marginal comments in the teacher's handwriting that "appear favorable to socialism or communism." The teacher, Edith Garriet, a member of the American Legion, denied she was in any way sympathetic toward socialism or communism and that the students took her remarks out of context. To prove her "innocence" she told the *Tribune* that she had pointed out to the students that "government interference in business is socialism," but that it did not "necessarily imply approval."[70]

Teachers faced further scrutiny from the Chicago Police Departments Subversive Unit, or "Red Squad," which started to investigate the political activities of all those who applied to or worked for the city, state, and county, and especially the Chicago public schools. In the 1940s and 1950s the Red Squads shared information with HUAC. Obtaining names from HUAC, the Red Squad investigated individuals and organizations suspected of communist sympathies, provided information to the committee, and appeared as clandestine witnesses at HUAC. Temporary teachers who had not obtained tenure and could easily be dismissed faced the most pressure. Either through informants, or by detectives following suspects, the Red Squad compiled files on teachers' political beliefs and passed them on to the Board of Education. When people applied for teaching positions, the board requested information from the Red Squads on their political views and activities.[71]

The Red Squads accused public school teachers of communist sympathies for a variety of reasons. They put one teacher under scrutiny because he worked as an instructor at a communist-run school during the war, another because he became a member of the Communist Political Association, and another for being executive director of the Chicago Council of American Soviet Friendship. Investigators accused members of the Progressive Party and the Independent Socialist League of being communists. Others came under suspicion because they subscribed to the *Daily Worker* or because they had parked their car in the vicinity of left-wing political meetings. Another teacher was under investigation because her husband had previously been a leading member of the Progressive Party in Chicago, and another was under scrutiny because she was active in Chicago Women for Peace.[72]

The red scare often turned into a black scare as the Red Squads put African Americans who supported civil rights under suspicion of communism. Conservative anticommunists argued that few racial problems plagued the United States and that communists who advocated racial equality were stirring up trouble. African Americans who advocated civil rights, they charged, fell for communist propaganda and helped America's enemies. The Red Squads suspected one teacher of communist sympathies because she worked as a clerk for the NAACP. One school employee notified the Red Squads that a temporary teacher may have been a communist because she took "an anti-White outlook and states that there is no such thing as democracy because of the treatment of Negroes in this country." At DuSable High School, where Mary Herrick taught, investigators put no fewer than sixteen teachers under suspicion for communist beliefs, the majority of them African American.[73]

Margaret Burroughs, the famed artist and founder of the DuSable Museum of African American History in Chicago, was one black teacher at DuSable High School whom the Red Squads investigated because she participated with communists in a number of political activities. Burroughs consistently spoke to the rest of the high school's faculty about racial injustice and attended civil rights meetings and demonstrations. Consequently, in 1952 the Board of Education summoned Burroughs to its downtown office to discuss her political views. The committee wanted her to provide them names of communist-inclined teachers, which she refused to do. Afraid that she would get into further trouble, Burroughs took a yearlong sabbatical leave from teaching and went with her family to Mexico to study painting.[74]

African American teacher Barbara Sizemore faced accusations of communism in the early 1950s from a white principal who believed black teachers were "unpatriotic." The principal at Shoop Elementary School on the South Side initially led the teachers and students on a military-style march around the school each morning before the communal singing of the Star-Spangled Banner. After the school debating society argued the pros and cons of communism, however, the principal reported Sizemore, the faculty sponsor of the society, to the Board of Education. The board instructed Sizemore to bring her lesson plans to a meeting downtown. The board dismissed the charges of procommunism against Sizemore but passed her name on to the FBI, who investigated her activities and those of her family for the next few years.[75]

The Red Squads drew on a network of students, teachers, and principals to gather information on teachers. In June 1953 a principal informed the Red Squads that a number of pupils had complained that a substitute teacher "praised Communism at every opportunity." The Red Squads interviewed five students who claimed that the teacher stated, "If it wasn't for Communism Russia would not have become as strong as it is now. Russia doesn't want war. Russia is a peaceful nation." In February 1956 a principal of a Chicago high school informed the Board of Examiners, which renewed the teaching certificates of substitute teachers, that a substitute history teacher had made statements to his pupils which "pertained to the disposition of the Tokyo Rose case, and also to the matter of taking an oath to become a teacher." As a result, the principal informed the board, he "left certain doubts in the minds of the young people . . . I do not believe that [he] should ever substitute . . . as long as the aforementioned doubts persist."[76]

Sometimes Red Squad investigators put pressure on members of the Board of Examiners not to employ suspected communists. In March 1951, investigators interviewed an examiner about an alleged communist teacher working in the schools. The investigators informed the examiner that the teacher was "identified with a number of Communist-front associations and has entertained at a function sponsored by the Communist Party." The examiner told the interviewer that "a very influential Negro politician was sponsoring" the teacher for a job with the Board of Education. Under pressure, the examiner became "extremely flustered" but was described by the investigator as acting "innocently" in employing her.[77]

The CTU and Liberal Anticommunism

The CTU and other liberal organizations faced a difficult decision on how to respond to the red scare. During the Depression years of the 1930s, the American left, including communists, socialists, progressives, and liberals, sometimes united in opposition to conservatism and fascism. They agreed on government regulation of the economy, more equal distribution of wealth, support of the labor movement, and backing for New Deal legislation. After the Nazi-Soviet pact of August 1939 and once the Cold War began, however, the left fragmented. Liberals and conservatives agreed that the Soviet Union and its supporters in the United States posed a threat to the nation and suggested that communists were not holders of legitimate political positions but conspirators in aid of a foreign power. As historian Mary Sperling McAuliffe argues, a "new liberalism" emerged that condemned totalitarianism (both fascist and communist), supported Cold War military defense, and embraced patriotism. Liberal politicians such as Minnesota senator Hubert Humphrey and Illinois governor and Democratic presidential candidate Adlai Stevenson joined in the anticommunist campaigns. Groups such as the American Civil Liberties Union (ACLU), split between old radicals and new liberals, expelled communists from leadership positions, sidestepped controversial issues, and spent much of its time and energy on internal disputes over communism.[78] The CIO expelled left-led affiliated unions in 1949 and 1950.

In many ways, the CTU had taken a "new liberal" position long before the start of the Cold War. The CTU had strongly opposed communist influence in the AFT in the late 1930s, and the socialist left within the CTU leadership, such as Kermit Eby and Lillian Herstein, had played no role in union affairs since the early years of the war. Thus, while the CTU faced few criticisms from anticommunists because of its record of opposing communism and its outward show of patriotism, the Citizens Schools Committee (CSC), the main community organization that supported reform in the schools, suffered constant attack in the anticommunist storm. Local newspapers accused CSC president John A. Lapp and the other leaders of the organization of being

communist sympathizers, and the Red Squads subjected the CSC to surveillance and investigation.[79]

John Fewkes and other CTU teachers opposed extreme anticommunism
but also were driven by fundamental moral and ideological disagreements
with communism. They saw the Soviet Union as a brutal totalitarian regime
and the Communist Party as an unscrupulous group willing to follow the dictates of a foreign power. In public and in private they voiced the opinion that
the party's intolerance of internal political debate and unwillingness to work
with other political parties made communism incompatible with democratic
principles. When John Fewkes found himself on the mailing list of the *Daily
Worker,* he wrote to the paper: "It is very apparent to any intelligent citizen
that the activities of the Communist Party are directly opposed to and in
conflict with the best interest of the people of the United States of America.
I am in no way in sympathy with any of your activities and will appreciate
having my name removed from your mailing list."[80] Also, Fewkes and many
other Chicago teachers were committed Christians who saw communism
as atheistic. "Communism," declared one CTU teacher, "conflicts with my
religious beliefs and with everything else that I hold dear."[81]

The anticommunism of the CTU leaders was not simply a principled response to what they perceived as the evils of communism, it was also a practical way to show to those in positions of power the respectability of teacher
unionism. Liberals eschewed any hint of communism, eager to prove their
loyalty to the nation and avoid the ire of the press and investigating committees. Even those who opposed McCarthyism made sure to condemn communism in more strident terms. John Fewkes recognized that the presence
of communists in the classroom or in the CTU would give conservatives
the opportunity to attack public education and teacher unionism. In 1949
Fewkes declared, "The increased heat in the cold war now in progress makes
it imperative that teachers in our public schools leave no doubt as to their
fundamental Americanism. I, for one, intend to stand up and be counted as
unalterably opposed to Communist-Fascist totalitarianism."[82]

The CTU defended the Chicago public school curriculum from the attacks of anticommunists while always pointing out their opposition to communism. While defending the public schools civics course, Mary Herrick
declared that "unscrupulous adventurers are exploiting the fears of the unin-
formed by organized attacks on ordinary school procedures, under the cloak
of patriotism." She upheld the "American tradition of freedom of speech and
thought, as that basic factor of our society most characteristic of our free
world and most unlike the Soviet thought-control." Yet she also defended the

civics course on grounds that it was not communist-influenced. "No proof is offered that the civics course is Communist. It is stated as a fact, with not the slightest substantiation."[83] Similarly, John Fewkes supported the adoption of George Counts's book *I Want to Be Like Stalin* in the civics course because opponents had misunderstood the content of the book, which criticized, rather than praised, communism.[84]

From this position of strength, the CTU resisted further attempts by conservative groups to scrutinize books that public school teachers used in the classroom. In June 1953, the union opposed a bill in the state legislature proposed by Republican senator John Meyer that sought to remove from schools books that were "antagonistic to or incompatible with the ideals and principles of the American constitutional form of government." Under the proposed bill, concerned citizens would be able write to the Illinois state superintendent of public education, who would then set up a committee to investigate the book. The committee would inform the Board of Education of its findings. The CTU declared that the bill was part of a "broadening assault on public schools" and would encourage "cranks and busybodies." Urging its members to write to its representatives in Springfield, the union concluded that the bill would "place unlimited authority in the hands of the Superintendent of Public Instruction, who, under its provisions, could dictate the textbooks to be used or not used in the schools throughout the state."[85]

Fewkes and the CTU leadership further defended the public schools from accusations of communist influence because they wanted to protect their ally General Superintendent Herold Hunt from those who sought to discredit him. Led by board member Bernard Majewski, the four remaining members of the Kelly-controlled Board of Education opposed Hunt because of his appointment of liberals in the school system, his unwillingness to indulge in patronage, and his liberal racial policies. Fewkes defended the schools from accusations of communism and accused "certain elements of the Democratic party who had their nose in the trough" of seeking to undermine the superintendent.[86] The campaign to oust Hunt finally succeeded in the spring of 1953 when he resigned his post and accepted a position at Harvard University.[87]

Because of its unquestioned record of anticommunism, the CTU remained in a strong position to defend the Chicago schoolteachers accused of communism and to uphold academic freedom. After the *Chicago Herald American* alleged that schoolteacher Emilie Noack made statements in the classroom in support of communism in the spring of 1948, the union quickly took her side. Fewkes suggested that she had "taught the children in her classes loyalty to their country and inspired in them an interest in improving our government." The CTU declared that the attack was "deeply resented by every teacher as an attack on academic freedom" and threatened to sue the *Chicago Herald American* unless they retracted their allegations. General Superintendent Hunt investigated the allegations and took no further action against Noack.[88] In April 1953, the union also defended a female teacher whose pupils had accused her of teaching "Communistic" ideas. "We have too many individuals who want to subject others to their ideas of what should be taught. They represent a few organizations with ideas as dangerous to America as communism," stated Fewkes.[89] In 1955, the CTU dedicated their educational conference to "Keeping the Schools Free" and opposed, unsuccessfully, the Board of Examiners' policy of making applicants for teaching positions declare their membership in organizations on the attorney general's subversive list.[90]

The union leadership followed the classic liberal Cold War stance of opposing communism and communists but seeking to protect the civil liberties of non-communists. In August 1952, the AFT conference voted overwhelmingly not to defend any teacher proved to be a communist, a stance the CTU supported. "The issue is not belief, but membership in a party whose legality is now quite questionable," Chicago schoolteacher Meyer Halushka stated.[91] Fewkes opposed any kind of loyalty oath because a "Communist wouldn't hesitate to lie in answering these questions, but they could trap an innocent teacher." Some years later, Fewkes commented that he was still in favor of expelling communists from unions and blacklisting any teacher who was a communist. "I personally believe that communists are detrimental to trade unions. . . . The education system in the United States of America which is for the purpose of educating individuals to existence in a democracy cannot possibly tolerate communist teaching in the schools," he suggested. The membership concurred. A survey of 171 CTU delegates taken in 1952 found that 75 percent believed that the union did a good job in opposing legislation against freedom of speech.[92]

While other teacher organizations, such as the CTF and the Chicago Principals Club, supported loyalty oaths for teachers to prohibit communists from working in the public schools, the CTU consistently opposed them. "You cannot preserve freedom by taking it away! You cannot preserve democracy by totalitarian means!" the union newspaper proclaimed in March 1949.[93] In May 1950, the CTU adopted a resolution that opposed loyalty oaths, and the following year it came out against the proposal of the Chicago City Council to force its employees to take such oaths.[94] The following March, Fewkes appeared before the Board of Education to denounce the board's loyalty oath proposal. Presenting his credentials as an anticommunist, Fewkes told the board he would continue to "wage an unrelenting war against Communist infiltration into the ranks of the Chicago Teachers Union, the American Federation of Teachers and the American Federation of Labor." He opposed the loyalty oath because the teachers had already "proven their loyalty," "sufficient safeguards against subversive activities already exist," and the amendment "will inject suspicion, distrust and hysteria into the school system." Because of the close relationship built up between the Board of Education, Herold Hunt, and John Fewkes, the board rejected the oath.[95]

Nevertheless, state politicians introduced loyalty oaths for public sector workers in Illinois. In the early 1950s, Paul Broyles, backed by the American Legion, unsuccessfully sponsored a series of bills in the Illinois legislature that sought to outlaw the Communist Party and to require loyalty oaths for government workers. In July 1955 the new Republican governor, William Stratton, signed a bill, effective on September 1, that forced public sector workers to take a loyalty oath.

The Illinois Broyles loyalty oath bill of July 1955 caused much consternation among the union leaders, but Fewkes always sought to obey the law. The Broyles bill was "anti-American . . . and clearly violates the Bill of Rights which is so fundamental to our American democracy," the *Chicago Union Teacher* declared in September 1953.[96] After the governor signed the loyalty oath law in July 1955, Fewkes relented and urged the teachers to comply. "Now that the state legislature has seen fit to pass the Broyles bill and the governor has signed it, teachers as good citizens will have to sign the oath."[97]

As a result of the anticommunist climate, fear grew among many teachers in the schools. Even though there were few communist teachers working in the Chicago public schools, in the postwar period communists were, not surprisingly, frightened to discuss their beliefs openly. Afraid they would not be employed by the public schools if they openly expressed their political affiliation, they had to lie to the Chicago Board of Examiners to gain certification in the public schools. Although they remained members of the Communist Party, they often denied they were communists and kept membership of the party secret even from their children. Many remained cautious in the classroom but continued political activity outside school hours.[98] "If you said the wrong thing to certain people they could report you as being communist affiliated . . . you had to be very careful," remembered one teacher who taught in Chicago in the early 1950s.[99] Many teachers became scared to teach anything that might be construed as controversial or radical, believing that students could misinterpret their activities, which might then be reported sensationally in the press or lead to their dismissal. The "dead weight of fear in the schools increases, and kills that spontaneity and honesty which have made our country move ahead in industry and human progress," Mary Herrick reported in 1953. "It approaches close to the worst forms of 'thought control' which is the most deadly characteristic of the Soviet dictatorship these self-styled patriots profess to oppose." The result has been to "induce fear and dishonest, cowering compliance in youth and teachers."[100] As the CTU concluded of communist accusations against teachers: "Such an experience cannot help but effect her health and efficiency in the classroom . . . the entire teaching body will experience of feeling of insecurity that will restrict individual initiative on the part of teachers and educational progress in our schools."[101]

In spite of this oppressive ideological climate, many schoolteachers managed to carry on teaching as they wished in the classroom. Chicago elementary school teacher Tommie Martin recalled that she knew little about communism and that anticommunism had no effect on her teaching.[102] Margaret Burroughs discussed black history with her students at DuSable High School, but when the principal walked past the door she would change to discuss more acceptable subjects, and when the principal had gone she would then return to her original subject.[103] In the lower-income schools, where many parents had less time or inclination to be concerned with the content of the curriculum, teachers were also able to teach much as they liked. In other schools the faculty, parents, and principal supported academic freedom and the teachers ignored the pressure to conform. "I just by-passed the curriculum as they had devised it and I had my own," concluded one teacher.[104]

Many teachers continued to oppose the adoption of loyalty laws and only signed under protest, while others found the laws to be unimportant. There was a deep period of contemplation among some teachers over whether to abide by the law or not. Some, such as Quakers, complained that it conflicted with their religious beliefs, others that it was an insult to question teachers' patriotism. The Communist Party teachers took the oath, saying it was more important to keep their jobs than it was to refuse to sign a loyalty oath.[105] For many teachers to sign a loyalty oath was a nuisance but not a big issue, and it made little difference to their teaching. "It was on the same level as the chest x-ray. It was just something you had to do to get the job," one Chicago public school teacher remembered. Another stated, "I had strong feelings about it, but then I said to myself 'rationalize it, what difference does it make. I'm going to do what I want to do anyway. I'm going to teach the way I want to teach anyhow.'"[106]

While the union leadership accepted, if reluctantly, the new law, some teachers decided to set up a legal test case in which some teachers would challenge the constitutionality of the law while others promised to pay for the legal action and contribute money to them if they were suspended from their jobs.[107] When school resumed in early September 1955, three Chicago public school teachers refused to sign the pledge: Shirley Lens, certified teacher of retarded children, and substitute teachers Albert Soglin and Sara Pickus. Speaking for the three of them, Soglin declared that "I cannot abandon the Bill of Rights by supporting the replacement of its principles and the search for truth by fear and conformity of opinion and behavior, condone a political test for a teaching position, or open the door to intimidation of teachers and educational organizations."[108] The American Civil Liberties Union (ACLU) filed a suit on behalf of Shirley Lens to restrain the school board from requiring teachers to sign loyalty affidavits, claiming the oath was unconstitutional, a position rejected by a district court in 1956. Finally, because she wanted to continue as a public school teacher, Lens, as well as Albert Soglin, signed the oath, but Sara Pickus still refused.[109]

By the second half of the 1950s, after it was apparent that communism was little threat to American society, the anticommunist surge began to subside. A combination of McCarthyism and growing disillusionment with communism contributed to the Communist Party's demise. The blacklisting of party members and the suppression of party leaders gave the party real problems. The revelations of Stalin's crimes by Khrushchev and the Soviet invasion of Hungary in 1956 turned many away from the party. Communist Party membership fell from 70,000 in 1945 to 12,000 in 1956, and after the invasion of Hungary, membership fell to 3,000 in 1958.[110] The Chicago Communist Party had dwindled to a dedicated few by the late 1950s. In 1954, Congress censured Senator Joseph McCarthy after he tried to indict the U.S. Army with charges of communist influence, and his outbursts subsided. The Supreme Court began to make decisions favorable to civil liberties. But the Chicago Police Department's Red Squads continued their activities until 1975 and the loyalty oath for teachers stayed on the statute book until 1983.

Conclusion

Throughout the 1950s, the Chicago public schools and many individual schoolteachers suffered because of anticommunist activity. Teachers had to careful about what they said and did in the classroom, and they had to take oaths to prove their loyalty. Some temporary and substitute teachers lost their jobs when their temporary certificates expired, and the board refused other qualified teachers permanent teaching positions. The open questioning that characterized much of the 1930s curriculum was replaced by one that put greater acceptance on celebrating American political and economic institutions. Overall, anticommunist persecution undermined teachers' autonomy in the classroom, reducing control over what they taught and limiting academic freedom.

Even though the Chicago public school system was under constant surveillance by anticommunists, the lives of public school teachers improved rather than worsened over the decade. The harassment some Chicago teachers faced was not as severe as teachers endured elsewhere. In New York and Pennsylvania, teachers were called before congressional panels, and hundreds either resigned before they appeared or were fired. In Chicago, few teachers lost their jobs and many continued to teach the way they wanted. In addition, the postwar years saw other major changes in Chicago politics and public education that compensated Chicago public school teachers for their plight. The Democratic machine's control of the public schools essentially ended as a community-wide campaign forced Mayor Kelly, his supporters on the Board of Education, and Superintendent Johnson to step down from their positions, and a new, more sympathetic school administration was installed. The public schools improved with less overt political corruption, and teachers enjoyed fairer treatment and decent salaries. Promotion was no longer dependent on political connections and the threat of arbitrary transfer was removed.

There was little change in the general orientation of the CTU in this period. It came out of World War II as a bread-and-butter organization committed to accommodation with school authorities and liberal anticommunism, and it continued on this path throughout the 1950s. With the end of the Kelly regime, many of those who opposed the CTU leadership because of its acquiescence to political control of the schools were now on the same side as Fewkes as he supported the new school administration.

The CTU was no bulwark against McCarthyism, but in the most trying of circumstances the union came out of the red scare with some credibility. The union made no attempt to defend communists or communist sympathizers from persecution, but few organizations, including the NEA or the AFT, were prepared to do so. To defend communist teachers would have alienated their members and drawn the wrath of politicians, school authorities and anticommunist organizations. Because of its record of anticommunism, the CTU was able to avoid media and political attacks. From this position of strength, the union defended non-communist schoolteachers accused of communism, supported greater academic freedom, opposed the introduction of loyalty oaths, and declared that professional teachers, not self-serving politicians, should devise school curriculum.

5

The Campaign for
Collective Bargaining Rights
and the Civil Rights Movement,
1957–1966

In 1958, folk singer Pete Seeger released a song, "Teacher's Blues," in which he lamented the economic position and erroneous thinking of public school teachers in the United States:

> Oh, teacher, teacher, why are you so poor?
> When it comes to unions, you're an amateur.
> Now, unions are for workers, but a teacher has prestige,
> Oh, unions are for workers, but a teacher has prestige.
> He can feed his kids on that old noblesse oblige.
> Now, prestige is fine, but so is bread and meat,
> Prestige is fine but so is bread and meat.
> What good is that white collar when you cannot eat?
> Yes, he wears a white collar, he's treated with respect,
> He wears a white collar, treated with respect;
> Financially, he's solid wrecked.
> Teacher, teacher, be a happy drudge."[1]

Within two years of the song's release, teachers began a campaign for collective bargaining rights that swept the nation, engulfing other public sector workers in its path, and changed the character of the labor movement and the administration of the public education system. Other public sector unions expanded in the 1960s, but none saw as much militancy as teachers' unions. "The U.S. teacher used to be afraid to smoke, chew, cuss or ask for a raise," *Time* magazine reported in 1963. "Now he denounces crowded classrooms, upbraids lawmakers, and goes on strike almost as readily as a dockworker. He even demands a say in things that school boards always considered their sole province. Teacher militancy is bursting out all over," the article concluded.[2] Membership in the American Federation of Teachers (AFT) grew from 59,000 in 1960 to 205,000 in 1970. National Education Association (NEA) membership stood at 714,000 in 1960, but after the NEA embraced collective bargaining in the 1960s its membership increased to 1,100,000 in 1970. In 1963, the AFT repealed its no-strike pledge and virtually every major city in the United States saw teacher walkouts, even though many of them were illegal and often resulted in the jailing of strikers. Between July 1960 and June 1974, the country experienced 1,017 teacher strikes involving 823,108 teachers costing 8,475,510 lost working days.[3] By the end of the 1970s, collective bargaining agreements covered 72 percent of public school teachers. Unions and administrators negotiated binding contracts, and public school teachers received salaries and benefits that they had only dreamed of before: paid vacation, medical insurance, and smaller class size.[4]

Chicago too saw a growing militancy that culminated in the Board of Education's recognizing the Chicago Teachers Union (CTU) as the sole bargaining agent for the schoolteachers in 1966 and the signing of a collective bargaining agreement. The momentum behind these sensational events was a new generation of public school teachers, influenced by the successes of collective bargaining in the private sector, who expressed growing dissatisfaction with their pay and working conditions and sought greater control over their teaching. As the Board of Education increasingly assigned new teachers to the less-desirable schools their older colleagues had fled, many disgruntled young teachers aligned with older radical teachers to demand collective bargaining rights for teachers to confront the central bureaucracy that was controlling their working lives.

As young and radical teachers campaigned for collective bargaining, they gained the support of the majority of teachers and eventually of Mayor Richard J. Daley, who felt threatened by a growing movement for civil rights for African Americans. This movement focused its attention on inequalities in employment and housing, but especially inequalities in public education, which were exacerbated as thousands of black families migrated from the rural South to the northern cities in a post–World War II second Great Migration. For northern blacks to acquire the quality education they demanded, they called on the Board of Education to dismantle the de facto segregation that condemned blacks to poorer schooling than whites. A minority of Chicago schoolteachers aligned with the civil rights movement, but most white teachers saw the civil rights movement and school integration as threats to teachers' classroom autonomy and working conditions. With the civil rights movement pressuring Mayor Daley to improve conditions for African Americans, the mayor ordered his supporters on the Board of Education to accede to the teachers' demands for collective bargaining rights.

Racial Segregation in the Chicago Public School System

Chicago experienced substantial racial transformation in the post–World War II years as black families migrated from the rural South to the urban North. In 1940, 277,731 African Americans lived in the city, making up 8.1 per cent of Chicago's population; by 1960, the figure had risen to 812,637, or 22.8 percent of the city's residents.[5] (See Table 7.) African Americans who came to Chicago entered a racially segregated city. Since World War I, when southern African Americans first migrated in large numbers to Chicago, whites had resisted the movement of blacks into their neighborhoods. Realtors, banks, and white residents combined to keep African Americans concentrated in the so-called Black Belt on the city's South Side. By the mid-1950s, as thousands of new black migrants entered these already impoverished areas and as new housing stock failed to meet the demand, the Black Belt became more crowded and blacks began to push out toward the surrounding white areas to gain access to better housing. After the U.S. Supreme Court struck down restrictive housing covenants in *Shelley v. Kraemer* in 1948, black families began to move to housing in previously white neighborhoods. As a result, the Black Belt on the South Side expanded and African Americans formed a so-called "second ghetto" on the city's West Side as blacks moved in to the area and whites rapidly migrated to the suburbs.[6]

A new mayor and a revitalized Democratic political machine was confronted with, and actively shaped, these changes in Chicago. Richard J. Daley defeated incumbent Martin H. Kennelly to gain the Democratic nomination for mayor in early 1955 and went on to beat the Republican candidate Robert Merriam in the mayoral election in April of that year. Daley, born the grandson of Irish immigrants in 1902 in the working-class neighborhood of Bridgeport in the South Side, was re-elected mayor five more times, serving until his death in December 1976. As both chairman of the Cook County Democratic Party and as mayor, he accrued enormous power. During his reign, Daley reignited a political machine that had lost influence under Kennelly and gained popular support by administering political patronage, guaranteeing efficient municipal services, and attracting new investment

Table 7. African American Population of Chicago, 1900–1970

Year	Total Population	African Americans	African Americans as Percentage of Total Population
1900	1,698,575	30,861	1.7
1910	2,185,283	44,103	2.0
1920	2,701,705	109,458	4.0
1930	3,376,438	233,903	6.9
1940	3,396,808	277,731	8.1
1950	3,620,962	492,265	13.5
1960	3,550,404	812,637	22.8
1970	3,362,947	1,102,620	32.7

Source: U.S. Census.

and jobs to Chicago. He supported the racial segregation that prevailed in his own South Side neighborhood and the rest of the city.[7]

The influx of black families with young children changed the racial composition of the Chicago public school system. Black enrollment climbed from 74,000 in 1950 to 250,000 in 1963, or from 21 percent to 47 percent of the total.[8] As more black students entered white neighborhoods and the public schools, many white families either fled to the suburbs or enrolled their children in parochial schools. In 1967, 43 percent of white children in the city attended parochial schools, but only 7 percent of black children did.[9]

By 1945, Chicago public schools had become so segregated that the president of the Chicago branch of the National Association for the Advancement of Colored People (NAACP) argued that they were "as much segregated as the schools in Savannah, Georgia, or Vicksburg, Mississippi."[10] A 1964 report confirmed this view, finding that 84 percent of blacks attended "black" schools, designated as 90 percent black enrollment, and 16 percent attended "white" or "integrated" schools, whereas 86 percent of whites enrolled in "white" schools and 14 percent in "black" or "integrated" schools.[11] The teaching force was also racially segregated. In 1964, only 4 percent of black teachers worked in "white" schools and until 1963 not one black principal worked in a "white" or "integrated" school.[12] "Chicago has the most segregated school system of any of the five [largest] cities," in the United States, concluded Gary Orfield in his nationwide study of school segregation undertaken in 1965.[13]

The Chicago public school system was not only racially segregated but also unequal. By the end of the 1950s, black schools suffered from greater overcrowding and offered inferior facilities compared to those of whites in the surrounding neighborhoods. In 1957, the average enrollment in predominantly white elementary schools in Chicago was 669 pupils, in "mixed" schools 947, and in black schools 1,275. Some white schools had underused classroom space while black schools worked on double-shift where half the students started their day early in the morning and the rest later in the day.[14] Although black schools had more underachieving students, the teachers had less time to give children individual attention than did teachers in white schools. These predominantly black schools were far more likely to be staffed by young, inexperienced, or uncertified substitute teachers, had a higher staff turnover than nearby white schools, and had more uncovered classes.[15]

Some Chicago Board of Education members advocated school integration, but most, bowing to the wishes of Mayor Daley, supported school segregation. For Daley and the Democratic Party, the movement of blacks into white neighborhoods threatened to push white residents, their electoral power base and a main source of the city's tax revenue, out of the city. Daley therefore continued to appoint members to the Board of Education who upheld segregation.[16] The Board of Education followed a policy of "neighborhood schools," whereby students could only attend their local school. This policy satisfied the demands of many parents to send their children to the nearest school, but it also restricted the attendance of black children to predominantly black schools and whites to white schools. With housing and neighborhoods racially segregated, this policy virtually guaranteed racially segregated schooling. To keep the schools segregated as the racial composition of neighborhoods changed, the board shifted school boundaries, issued transfers to white students in schools that had increasing numbers of black students, and built new schools and additions to existing schools.[17] A government report from 1966 found that "by far the greater part of the segregation in Chicago's public schools results from residential segregation combined with the Board's neighborhood school policy."[18] In April 1964, board member Raymond W. Pasnick, a United Steel Workers of America official and the only member of the Chicago Board of Education to consistently support school integration in the early 1960s, confirmed that "this board has deliberately imposed conditions and policies which have served to keep the two races in our school system apart and to discriminate against large segments of the racial minority."[19]

The new general superintendent of the Chicago public schools, Benjamin C. Willis, who replaced Herold Hunt after Hunt resigned in 1953, became a symbol to the black community of the white intransigence and racism that blighted the city and the public schools. Under Willis, the Chicago schools flourished. High enrollment forced the Board of Education to initiate a new school building program, and after public referendums approved a number of $50 million bond issues between 1953 and 1962, Chicago constructed 208 new elementary school buildings, thirteen high schools, a junior college, and a new teachers' college on the north side of the city, earning Willis the nickname "Ben the Builder." The number of teachers employed by the Board of Education increased from 14,000 in 1952 to nearly 25,000 in 1962 and student enrollment climbed from 414,400 to 531,608 (see Table 8). To pay for these changes, the Chicago public school budget increased from $158 million in 1953 to $388 million in 1966.[20] As a result of his record, Willis gained respect throughout the education world. He wrote numerous articles in professional and popular journals, was elected president of the American Association of School Administrators, was appointed by President Kennedy to a national education commission, and became chair of the Educational Policies Commission of the NEA. One college dean called Willis "practically peerless as a big-city school superintendent."[21]

The abrasive, self-confident, and unyielding Willis angered the black community by championing "neighborhood schooling" and by opposing the transfer of black pupils from overcrowded black schools to those in white

Table 8. Teachers and Student Enrollment in the Chicago Public Schools, 1952–70

Year	Number of Students	Number of Teachers
1952	414,400	13,988
1954	435,819	14,094
1956	464,062	16,508
1958	490,033	17,570
1960	513,092	20,912
1962	531,608	24,805
1964	566,873	
1966	588,004	22,343
1968	600,041	
1970	596,375	25,383

Source: Student enrollment from *Facts and Figures 1962–63* (Chicago, Board of Education), 18, *Facts and Figures 1971–72* (Chicago, Board of Education), 55, and number of teachers from Nicholas R. Cannella, *171 Years of Teaching in Chicago* (Chicago: CTU, 1987).

parts of the city. He refused to investigate or even recognize that segregation existed in Chicago or to find out how many empty classrooms existed in white schools while black schools suffered from overcrowding. The building program launched by Willis accentuated segregation by situating new schools in the overcrowded black areas rather than move the black students to nearby white schools. With the school building program unable to keep up with the demand created by black migration, the general superintendent rented temporary buildings and mobile classrooms, which opponents dubbed "Willis wagons." In 1960, more than 33,000 school children operated on double shifts, virtually all in black areas. The U.S. Commission on Civil Rights noted that in Chicago in 1962: "Timely measures might have desegregated substantial numbers of classrooms, if that were the primary object. The administration has made no effort to aid in integration; indeed, to the extent that it has recognized the existence of the problem, its policies have impeded rather than promoted integration."[22]

The Civil Rights Movement

Protests against segregated schooling in Chicago stretched back to the 1930s, but in the late 1950s African Americans started to build the largest civil rights movement in the North. Civil rights groups such as the NAACP, the Urban League, and the Congress of Racial Equality (CORE) published reports, sent deputations to the Board of Education, and issued press statements exposing the segregated nature of the school system and the inferior facilities offered to black children. At the same time, blacks began to organize pickets and sit-ins at overcrowded schools, particularly at ones that introduced Willis wagons. To rectify these problems, the civil rights groups demanded the building of new schools to end the overcrowding and called for better supplies and equipment, more modern facilities, and extended social services in black schools. In the short term, civil rights activists demanded the end of the neighborhood school policy so that black children could move from overcrowded schools to the better-equipped and underutilized white schools.[23]

In the summer of 1961, the NAACP launched "Operation Transfer," which urged black parents whose children attended overcrowded schools to enroll their children in nearby underused white schools. Although parents from more than a hundred black schools applied for transfers, General Superintendent Willis denied the requests. A group of parents backed by the NAACP then filed a suit in federal court, the *Webb v. Board of Education of the City of*

Chicago case, accusing the board of gerrymandering the school boundaries to create all-black schools. The case was suspended in the summer of 1963 after the Board of Education agreed in an out-of-court settlement to a thorough study of the school system that would locate and eliminate inequalities. The study, chaired by Philip Hauser, was published in 1964 but the board never implemented its recommendations.[24]

In 1963, as television broadcast nightly pictures of Bull Connor's dogs being set on civil rights demonstrators in Birmingham, Alabama, young activists re-energized the civil rights movement in the North. In July 1963, CORE members staged pickets and sit-downs at the Chicago Board of Education offices demanding immediate integration. The following month a group of CORE and NAACP members joined local parents and students to physically stop the building of mobile classrooms on the South Side. Protesters demanded a permanent new school building and the immediate transfer of black pupils to underused white schools. Police arrested more than 170 campaigners in a three-week period before the board finally agreed to stop the construction and move the mobile classrooms elsewhere. Similar protests by black parents spread to other schools when the students reopened in September.[25]

Increasingly, the Coordinating Council of Community Organizations (CCCO), an umbrella organization of more than twenty groups formed in 1962, led the civil rights movement in Chicago. Led by Edwin C. "Bill" Berry, head of the Chicago Urban League, the multiracial CCCO included new and established civil rights groups and religious, labor, and community organizations. Calling for the removal of school superintendent Benjamin Willis, the CCCO organized a one-day boycott of the Chicago schools. On October 22, 1963, "Freedom Day," nearly 225,000 students, virtually every black student in the city, supported the boycott. Thousands of these students attended "freedom schools" organized by the CCCO and staffed by ministers, college students, and retired teachers. On February 25, 1964, the CCCO organized a second school boycott in Chicago. Despite opposition from the Chicago NAACP and Chicago's black aldermen, 172,000 students did not turn up for school. The CCCO called for a third school boycott in June 1965. Even in the face of a court injunction obtained by the Board of Education, more than 100,000 students stayed away from school.[26]

Collective Bargaining

From the early twentieth century through the 1950s, collective bargaining rights eluded teachers' unions. Along with other public sector workers, they were excluded from the provisions of the National Labor Relations Act of 1935, which guaranteed bargaining rights to private sector workers. Since 1945, the CTU had unsuccessfully lobbied legislators in the state capital to pass a collective bargaining law covering teachers.[27] Without collective bargaining, the only avenue the CTU leaders had was to petition the Board of Education, make a short presentation at the board's annual public budget meeting, or personally appeal to individual board members or to the school superintendent. As CTU activist Ron Patterson declared, "it was a handshake deal . . . if anything was going to be done he would talk to the superintendent and if the superintendent said ok then they'd shake hands and that was it. If the superintendent said no there was no deal."[28]

Without collective bargaining, John Fewkes discouraged rank-and-file activism and promoted loyalty to the union leadership, which would deliver better salaries and working conditions to the teachers. Fewkes never tired of telling opponents that he had obtained the teachers their pay after the payless paydays of the 1930s and had united the feuding teachers into one union in 1937. The inspiration behind the communist purge of the AFT in the late 1930s, Fewkes condemned criticism as communist-inspired. He suggested that personal entreaty to the Board of Education and the school superintendent could improve pay and working conditions for teachers and that lobbying in Springfield would eventually bring a collective bargaining law. As CTU delegate Anthony Grosch remembered, "[a]nyone who has any ideas or criticisms or any kind of enlightenment values don't go over, or didn't go over, in the CPS or certainly not in the CTU. Fewkes . . . grew up in the Depression when teachers were paid in scrip . . . his vision of the union was loyalty of all the members and we'll work on improving your pay and working conditions, no disloyalty." Older teachers who had suffered in the Depression and the war acted reverentially toward Fewkes and the union leadership. Grosch remembered that when he first went to union meetings they were made up of "older people for whom the union was a kind of church."[29]

While spearheading a huge expansion program, general superintendent Benjamin Willis eschewed the cooperative style of his predecessor, aiming to control every detail of the school operation, stressing business efficiency and rule by professionals, and having little regard for teachers' autonomy or welfare. With the backing of the political machine, the business community, and the press, he refused to meet regularly with the CTU and PTAs and never seriously considered their recommendations.[30] The board deferred to his expertise. He controlled staff salaries, oversaw the examination and certification of teachers, and made appointments in the school administration. Willis gave his budget recommendations to the Board of Education to rubber stamp with only minimal time to consider the report.[31]

Teacher Dissatisfaction

As the city and its public schools went through social changes, Chicago public school teachers expressed growing discontent. In absolute terms, Chicago teachers' salaries and benefits had improved in the late 1950s as school enrollments increased and teachers were in short supply. Pay had risen from a minimum of $3,400 and maximum of $6,650 in 1954 to $5,000 and $8,500 respectively in 1960. The accumulative sick leave total had increased from fifteen days to 120 days in 1960 and to 180 days in 1963.[32] By the early 1960s, however, the pay and benefits of Chicago teachers no longer kept pace with those of teachers elsewhere. One report on Chicago teachers' salaries noted that "from 1962 to 1966 their salary increases were so small and so widely spaced that they did not even keep pace with the cost of living, to say nothing of maintaining parity with other sectors of the economy."[33] A comparison of Chicago teachers' salaries with the fourteen largest school districts in the United States showed that Chicago teachers' salaries remained "below the average for all cities prior to 1967."[34] In 1959, 56 percent of Chicago office employees and 58 percent of Chicago plant employees possessed medical insurance and 99 percent and 100 percent respectively enjoyed paid vacations.[35] Teachers had neither.

Teachers' salary expectations increased even more dramatically as the nation enjoyed unprecedented prosperity and teachers gained greater job security. Between 1946 and 1960, the U.S. gross national product leaped some 25 percent and median family income adjusted for inflation nearly doubled. The United States was the richest nation in the world as home ownership soared, most families drove at least one car, and nearly every household possessed television sets and owned an array of new consumer products.[36] Growing labor shortages in the public school system, job opportunities elsewhere, and a full employment economy further contributed to greater job security, more confidence, and a new spirit of militancy on the part of public school teachers in the 1960s. Teachers, especially women, enjoyed better career prospects and higher salaries in the expanding white-collar sector of the 1950s. Chicago public school teachers could also increasingly find employment in the Catholic school system. In 1950, lay teachers made up only 4 percent of the Catholic elementary school teaching staff in Chicago and 16 percent of high school teachers; by 1965, they made up 38 percent of elementary and 36 percent of high school teachers.[37] Suburban school systems, which offered their teachers higher salaries, smaller classes, and fewer student behavioral problems than their counterparts in Chicago, lured teachers away from the city and embittered those who stayed. Wanting to share in the general prosperity and with greater opportunities elsewhere, teachers proved less willing to accept their undesirable salaries.

Chicago public school teachers voiced further frustration with the increasing bureaucratization and centralization of decision making, which widened the distance between teachers and school administrators. One of the things "that teachers are particularly disturbed about is that teachers are rather ignored as individual human beings in this large system of ours," claimed teachers' union leader John Fewkes. "All too frequently a mathematical formula is applied in making changes in curriculum and program without regard to the human beings that are affected and teachers will find out through the newspapers that there is going to be a change in curricula that will affect their individual teaching job."[38] In January 1960, for example, General Superintendent Benjamin Willis eliminated home mechanics courses from seventy-eight schools and assigned the teachers elsewhere. The teachers were "shifted about from position to position without consultation or consideration," which "smacks of cattle being herded from pen to pen," Fewkes argued.[39] According to a study undertaken in the early 1960s, while 29 percent of elementary school teachers and 41 percent of Chicago high school teachers claimed that the chief source of their dissatisfaction with teaching was salaries, a full 46 percent of elementary school and 55 percent of high school teachers expressed discontent with the lack of channels for discussion and settlement of grievances.[40]

Teachers additionally believed that principals held too much power and, along with the central authorities, hindered innovation in the classroom. Since the late 1950s, reports, surveys, and conferences on improvements in curriculum and teaching methods created enormous enthusiasm among classroom teachers. Yet teachers encountered obstacles in the implementation of their plans. Elementary teacher Anna Anthony remembered: "There was a level of control that we could not buck because of the principal. Principals were like God and Goddesses during that time. . . . Why could we not contest decisions that were made by the principals?" Many of the principals stayed in the office all day, did not know the teachers by name, and expected the teachers and the students to blindly follow their orders. Anthony believed that the attitude of the principals "was a reflection of [Willis's] philosophy . . . we are in control, you do as you are told, if you don't like it you leave."[41]

Another teacher insisted, "In Chicago, the powers that be reject all innovation. Trying to win approval for a new program is like knocking your head against a stone wall. No matter how hard you try, there is no way you can make a dent in the wall."[42] Teachers wanted to limit the power of principals and school administrators to intrude on their classroom teaching.

According to a study by Robert Havighurst, teachers voiced the most discontent with the time they spent on non-teaching duties. As school enrollment increased dramatically, Willis insisted that teachers become more accountable to the school administration and take on greater responsibilities outside the classroom. Teachers often had little time for lunch break or class preparation because of the burden of duties. Havighurst's study found that 67 percent of elementary school and 79 percent of high school teachers claimed their chief source of dissatisfaction with their jobs was the amount of time spent on "record-keeping and other clerical duties."[43] As professionals, teachers expected to work in the classroom, not on what they considered demeaning duties that should not be their responsibilities. Chicago schoolteacher Ron Brown, for example, felt aggrieved that he was "being asked to do stupid things, hall monitor, lunchroom duties, things in that general category."[44] Chicago high school teacher Dorothy H. Miner complained in 1959: "If she is to give to the community the service for which she was trained—namely, the education of young people—her time and energy cannot be frittered away in pursuits that do not contribute to that purpose. Police work, bookkeeping, and money-changing are taking an ever-increasing slice of that time and energy."[45]

Teachers in Chicago, and across the nation, increasingly complained about violence and disruption from their students. In 1964, 45 percent of teachers polled in a nationwide survey, and 62 percent of those teachers with more than twenty years of teaching experience, believed that it was now more difficult to maintain discipline in the classroom than ever before.[46] In 1956–57 the Chicago Board of Education took fifteen cases of assault against teachers to court. In 1959–60 the board brought twenty cases to court, but in the six months between September 1963 and March 1964 they brought thirty-nine cases of assault against teachers to court.[47] But many other instances of assault did not reach the legal system. In a CTU survey of teacher safety and behavior problems carried out in the spring of 1961, 192 out of 374 CTU delegates reported severe behavior problems in their schools while another 152 reported that discipline and behavior are "daily but minor" problems in their schools. Another 71 reported that "a reasonable and prudent adult" would have reason to fear for their personal safety in and around their school."[48] On April 20, 1961, Josephine Keane became the first teacher murdered by a pupil in the Chicago public schools. Under the headline "The Trail of Terror in Chicago's Schools," the *Chicago Daily News* of March 6, 1964, claimed that "[t]housands of Chicago public school teachers work in circumstances of dread and danger. . . . It's getting so that teachers in some schools should draw combat pay."[49] A headline in the *Chicago American* of March 5, 1964, simply stated: "How to Spot a Teacher—Look for Cuts, Bruises."[50]

Teachers felt frustrated that public criticism of public education had reached unprecedented levels. During the 1950s, many complained that the public school system was failing, even if the explanations for its demise varied. Articles appeared in newspapers blaming Progressive teaching methods or badly prepared teachers for poorly educated children.[51] Teachers were now convinced that the school authorities and the wider community treated them unfairly and showed them a lack of respect. The teachers in the 1960s, however, were no longer willing to put up with complaining parents, and if they were, they wanted better financial compensation. More than thirty years after teachers expressed so much hope in public education, teachers were less willing than previously to bear the burden of society's problems, and they put more emphasis on gaining rewards for themselves and not their students, with whom they were often in open conflict. A national study of schoolteachers undertaken in 1967 noted, "Probably student discipline has become more of a problem, at least in urban areas. But in other matters— clerical work, class size, the degree to which teachers are made to perform subprofessional chores—there seems to have been a slight improvement. The point is," the report concluded, "that teachers today are much more concerned about these problems than before."[52] As CTU leader Mary Herrick succinctly put it, "teachers in Chicago and elsewhere now see no reason why they should continue to make up the difference between what the public demands of the schools and what the public pays to support them."[53]

It was the progress of the union movement in the private sector that inspired teachers to seek collective bargaining. After the passage of the Wagner Act in 1935, membership of labor organizations grew enormously, particularly in important sectors of the economy like steel and autos, so that by 1955, when the Congress of Industrial Organizations (CIO) and the American Federation of Labor (AFL) merged, membership was more than 30 percent of the workforce.[54] Thanks in part to the growth of labor unions, blue-collar workers enjoyed higher pay, greater job security, and unparalleled fringe benefits in terms of medical insurance and paid vacation. Teachers, who in the pre–World War II era benefited from greater rewards than private sector workers, had no legal protection for their efforts to unionize and were now losing their status above blue-collar workers. Many public school teachers had family members, friends, and neighbors in unions and were familiar with the gains the labor movement achieved through collective bargaining. In the 1960s, schoolteaching remained a profession of upward social mobility, with some 49 percent of Chicago elementary school teachers and 44 percent of high school teachers coming from the homes of manual workers, while only 26 percent of elementary school and 29 percent of high school teachers were the children of professional or managerial fathers.[55] Ron Patterson, the son of a CIO leader who started teaching in Chicago in 1954, claimed that teachers sought collective bargaining because "[w]e were looking at the other unions and they were doing pretty good."[56]

The Civil Rights Movement and Public School Teachers

White teachers increasingly complained about the growing civil rights movement in the city. Initially the movement focused on unequal school facilities and the policies of Benjamin Willis, but it soon turned to the activities of white teachers who remained in schools where there was an increasing black student population. In particular, black parents and civil rights activists complained that white teachers disciplined black students more often and more harshly than white students. While teachers punished white students for serious misbehavior such as violence or vandalism, they severely reprimanded black students for more trivial deeds such as talking in class and exhibiting a disrespectful attitude toward teachers. In Beale Elementary School on the South Side, for example, parents complained that the teachers beat the black students. Parents alleged that one teacher dragged a black boy into "the coat closet while administering a severe beating to the child." Other parents saw "a white teacher beating a Negro girl," and others charged that a black boy "was kicked in the eye by a teacher" and one "was beaten by a teacher and required medical attention." James Wagner, a black teacher who supported the parents' complaints, declared the principal "was a man who had no concern whatsoever for the people in that community. He had no concern for those children, and he still does not have that concern." The principal told the parents who complained that "[i]f you come here to tell me how to run my school or question my administration, I will dismiss you now." He called parents who objected to violence against their children "liars" and refused to see them. After a long campaign by blacks parents to remove him, in 1964 the Board of Education transferred the principal to an all-white school on the southwest side of the city.[57]

Undoubtedly, many Chicago public school teachers and principals exhibited the prevailing white racial ideas and brought them into the classroom. Many whites considered blacks to be more violent, less intelligent, and possessing lower morals than whites. A study of two black Chicago elementary schools undertaken in the summer of 1951 found that white teachers exhibited negative ideas about black students. White teachers called black students "niggers," "pickaninnies," and "trash" to their faces. One teacher thought black children were "more excitable," another that black children seemed "harder to handle" and had "low morals," and another that "Negroes have an inclination to theft." "It's terrible what some of our teachers say to the children," commented one teacher. "Negroes have to suffer under so much discrimination as it is." Many of the teachers at the school did not believe African American children could reach the scholastic level of white children and paid less attention to them.[58] Similarly, in the mid-1960s students at Crane High School on the West Side complained that teachers thought students at Crane were "too dumb to learn" and therefore "don't care what we do." One teacher at Crane concluded that "we have teachers who just don't like the kids here. . . . A small faction of teachers way down in the bottom of their hearts resents the fact that our student body is nearly all Negro."[59]

The negative view white teachers held of black students was accentuated by the fact that many of the teachers had achieved greater educational success than their parents and had little sympathy for underachieving black students.[60] Teachers came from stable families that had strong beliefs in the value of education and hard work, and they made the best of the educational opportunities available to them. Large numbers of Chicago schoolteachers came from Jewish and Irish households, two groups that particularly valued education. Many attended parochial schools and had little contact with African American students. With most whites unaware of the plight and aspirations of African Americans, these teachers, who had gained relatively high pay and status, drew further apart from the black students in the inner city schools, who they believed had little interest in learning.[61] As one teacher complained, "so many of our teachers come out of nice middle-class homes and they don't know anything about our kids. Our kids know more about life than they do."[62]

Some of these white teachers and principals were members of local communities that resisted black encroachment into their neighborhoods and saw the increasing enrollment of blacks into their previously all-white schools as the first step toward residential desegregation. White communities across the northern states feared that the movement of blacks into their neighborhoods would devalue their property and increase crime. Explaining the severe, often violent, prejudice white teachers displayed toward black students, one teacher suggested that other white teachers "have a built-in antagonism" to black students and are "protecting their property and homes, as they see it."[63] Most of the disputes between white teachers and black students occurred in the schools that were in the process of racial change, not those that had large, settled black communities. Joseph Rosen, principal of Howland Elementary School, highlighted the attitudes of the teachers in his racially changing school in 1961. When the student population changed from majority white to all-black enrollment, many of the teachers "fled as soon as they could." Those teachers that remained "were upset generally, for many had taught in the school for more than ten years, and the shifting of pupils in the school and community was too much for them. They often favored the whites they thought they understood and could trust much better than the others. Sometimes the comments teachers made brought distress to themselves and to the school, and discipline problems were the result of this open distaste for the new pupils." Of one teacher he said, "This teacher's intense apathy for the Negroes was known to me, as reflected by her comments in conversation, and in the number of discipline cases she sent to the office each day."[64]

While many white teachers "defended" their neighborhoods from racial integration, others sought transfers to the predominantly white schools to escape what they saw as the inevitable deterioration of working conditions. After a fully certified teacher had taught at a Chicago school for one year, he or she could apply to the board for a transfer to another school that had an opening. A study undertaken in the early 1960s found that teachers working in predominantly black schools of Chicago appeared far more likely to seek transfers than those in white schools. In District 1, where African Americans made up 3 percent of the school's pupils, only 1.5 percent of teachers requested transfers in the school year 1963–64, but in District 2, where 69 percent were black, 10.9 percent of the teachers asked for transfers in the same year.[65] Of course many teachers, both black and white, wanted to transfer from overcrowded schools that happened to be in the Black Belt to schools with better working conditions. However, a study undertaken in 1947–48 found that most applicants for transfer worked in schools with black students, and two-thirds of the applicants originated in mixed-race schools, which made up less than a third of the schools, suggesting that white teachers were fleeing changing schools.[66] One teacher revealed how teachers transferred out of the South Side black schools simply to move to schools with fewer black pupils. "I don't know what good it does these people to move anyhow. The

Negroes keep moving farther south so that they never really can get away from them anyhow," she commented in 1950.[67]

Many white teachers came to believe that the civil rights movement's demand for school integration threatened their working conditions. As disruptive behavior increased in the underprivileged neighborhoods and overcrowded schools, many white teachers associated African Americans and all-black schools with delinquency and violence against teachers. Every incident of violence or disruption by black pupils justified to many white teachers their decision to flee black schools and justified to those in white schools their opposition to integration. If the civil rights movement realized its demand for school desegregation, white teachers suggested, black students would enter white schools, which would inevitably lead to deteriorating working conditions for Chicago public school teachers. Moreover, a halt in teacher transfers, which the black community believed white teachers used to abandon black children and to maintain segregated schools, further threatened the working lives of teachers. Black parents believed that their children, like white children, deserved the best teachers, while the white teachers insisted that they reserved the right to teach where they wanted to teach.

White teachers also contended that the civil rights movement put at risk the teachers' long cherished demand for classroom autonomy. Teachers complained about unruly students and blamed parents for not instilling respect in their children, while the black parents and civil rights groups converged on the schools to condemn schoolteachers' attitudes and practices toward their children. Chicago teachers and school administrators agreed that professional educators should run schools with little parental intrusion. One female student at Chicago Teachers College commented in 1950 that "if I am the teacher the classroom is my domain and all parents keep out unless of course I call them in for some reason. Otherwise parents are strictly a nuisance."[68] Robert Havighurst in his study of Chicago public schools reported that "[a] number of principals and teachers feel that the civil rights movement has taken a form which makes it harder for them to work" in black schools. "We have to have the child identify with the school in a positive way," one principal argued. "But then you get people coming around, tearing down the schools, making these blanket accusations of inferior schools and inferior teachers. . . . It lowers [the teachers'] morale and it lowers the effectiveness of the school. . . . Why, I'd like some of those civil rights people to spend ten minutes in this office and handle the problems that I've handled."[69] After he was attacked by a gang of pupils from a nearby school, Edward D. Brady, white principal of Goethals Vocational Guidance and Education Center on the South Side, suggested that "this is at least partly the result of the unlawful demonstrations at the Board of Education and the continued abuse heaped on Dr. Willis." The children "get the idea that if one form of illegal behavior is alright, so are others."[70]

Because of this perceived threat, many white teachers defended General Superintendent Benjamin Willis and his policy of neighborhood schools, which held the line against school integration. When Willis temporarily resigned from his position in October 1963 because of conflict with the Board of Education, white teachers joined in the chorus of support for Willis. Teachers throughout the city, the *Chicago Tribune* reported, "were calling one another in a chain telephone operation" to "flood" the Board of Education and Mayor Daley with letters and telegrams supporting Willis and demanding that he rescind his resignation.[71] One teacher claimed that "the teachers who have worked under his guidance and direction know Dr. Willis has greatly improved Chicago's system." Another argued, "I know I speak for thousands of other teachers who believe in the wonderful results Supt. Willis has achieved, and who join me in asking Supt. Willis to continue this important leadership."[72] T. F. Connery, CTU high school functional vice president and teacher at Bowen High School on the southeast side, declared that "in the present controversy, which has caused Dr. Willis to submit his resignation, I back him up 100 per cent." Opponents leveled "false charges" against Willis, who "did more for the education of negro children than any other person in our history." Connery supported the neighborhood school policy and particularly criticized those groups who advocated the ending of teacher transfer rights. "LET US BE realistic and face the issue squarely," he opined. "How can teachers be expected to transfer from schools in a desirable district to those where the teachers are advised 'to sit in their locked autos until other teachers arrive so they can walk in pairs to the school from their parking spaces?'"[73] Bolstered by this, Willis withdrew his resignation.

The CTU and Civil Rights

During the 1950s and 1960s, the AFT was among the most progressive national unions. From its beginning the AFT had chartered segregated black and white locals in the South, but by the 1930s the organization campaigned for its white locals to join with the black ones. In August 1951, the AFT convention voted not to charter any new locals that practiced racial discrimination, and in 1957 the AFT expelled the segregated southern locals from the organization, losing some seven thousand members.[74] The federation filed briefs to the court that led to the *Brown v. Board of Education* U.S. Supreme Court decision in 1954 that outlawed segregation of public schools. In the 1960s, the AFT organized many teachers to participate in the freedom schools in the southern states.[75] In 1961, Herbert Hill, the NAACP's labor secretary and a strong critic of labor union racism, declared that "we have never hesitated to raise our voice in support of unions which are for racial equality. Such an example of demonstrated good faith and diligent application exists today in the American Federation of Teachers."[76]

At the local level, however, teachers' unions proved much less sympathetic toward the civil rights movement. The CTU, like most other AFT locals, played no part in its community's civil rights struggles. CTU president John Fewkes had little personal sympathy with the demands of the civil rights movement in Chicago, and he showed little enthusiasm in the 1950s for expelling segregated southern locals from the AFT. In December 1952, he proposed that the AFT executive council defer further discussion on the matter of submitting a referendum on expelling segregated locals.[77] At the annual AFT national convention in August 1956, Fewkes spoke against the expulsion of the segregated locals. Fifteen years earlier Fewkes had led the campaign to expel the communist locals from the organization, but now he suggested that "you cannot save any souls until you get the sinners into church or find some way in which to hold their interest long enough in order to preach the gospel to them."[78] With radicals Kermit Eby and Lillian Herstein no longer in the organization and the aging Mary Herrick spending much of the 1950s working for the AFT and growing increasingly supportive of Fewkes, few in the Chicago union leadership sought to promote the concerns of black teachers or the wider black community.[79] Unable to obtain higher wages for the teachers, in the 1950s Fewkes and his supporters positioned themselves as opponents of the demands of civil rights movement in the city, champions of school discipline, and supporters of harassed white teachers. CTU executive board member Meyer Weinberg recalled that the other board members were "devotees of segregation to the bitter end."[80] The union consistently refused to accept involuntary transfer of teachers from one school to another to racially balance the workforce, and it jealously guarded the right of teachers to voluntarily transfer to other schools.

Fewkes used every opportunity to deny that there was a deliberate policy of segregated schooling in Chicago, defended the neighborhood school policy, argued against transferring students, and remained silent on the issue of a segregated teaching force.[81] Unlike the United Packinghouse Workers and the United Auto Workers, the CTU did not take an active role in CCCO, never appeared at civil rights meetings, and exerted no pressure on Willis to integrate the schools.[82] While the United Federation of Teachers (UFT) in New York City supported school integration for years and expressed sympathy with a school boycott in 1964, the CTU showed no such support for the 1963 and 1964 school boycotts in Chicago.[83] In August 1963, Fewkes even defended mobile classrooms as "efficient and effective," declaring that "the mobiles were not intentionally used as a means of segregation."[84]

Fewkes's stance proved popular with the vast majority of the white union membership. In the early 1950s, a researcher found that while 75 percent of CTU school delegates believed that the union was doing a good job in defending free speech, fully 87 percent held that the union has sponsored an adequate civil rights program for teachers.[85] In his study of CTU activities, Barry Shapiro found that "anyone who tried to speak about school integration on the floor of the union House of Representatives in the early 1960s was actually hooted down." Unsurprisingly, Fewkes won every union election until his retirement in 1966.[86]

While refusing to speak out on school segregation, Fewkes and the CTU leadership condemned the actions of the civil rights movement. In September 1963, Fewkes, who had threatened to close the schools in 1933 and to strike in 1948, declared that a civil rights sit-in "interrupts the orderly process of children obtaining their fullest educational opportunities. It would be much more logical for the parents and other citizens to iron out their basic objections with the Board of Education. . . . Parents should discuss individual problems with the principal and the teachers without disrupting the orderly process of the education of their own and other peoples' children."[87] Rather than condemn school segregation, Fewkes suggested that "[c]ommunity organizations and parents have failed in many instances to give the teachers and the schools their support and help. In fact, the schools and the teachers have been charged with providing inferior educational opportunities for the children. This is a false and undermining statement. . . . parents must assume the obligation of instilling in their children a love of education, a respect for all duly constituted authority and an appreciation of the educational opportunities being provided them in the City of Chicago."[88] The CTU could not support the school boycotts because they would probably cause "the children to have some feeling of disrespect toward their schools and their teachers, and possibly a little bit more disciplinary problems when we come back to school after the strike," Fewkes claimed.[89] He refused to directly blame the October 1963 and February 1964 school boycotts for the increase in school violence, but he noted that "anything which disrupts the orderly process of education is bound to affect discipline in the schools."[90]

In addition to condemning civil rights protests, the CTU opposed the racial integration of the teaching force by upholding the right of seniority in teacher transfers. Under pressure from the civil rights movement, General Superintendent Benjamin Willis asked the Board of Education in April 1965 to make minor changes in the policy governing assignments and transfers of teachers. Teachers at schools with more than 90 percent assigned teachers would have some of their staff compulsorily transferred to other schools. Even though no high school and very few elementary schools fit this description, the CTU house of representatives gave the executive committee the power to call a strike if the policy was implemented, and the board quickly dropped the plan.[91] The following January, the CTU executive committee also disapproved of a racial head count of the teaching force authorized by the Board of Education because it might be used to set up racial quotas and lead to involuntary transfers of teachers.[92] In April 1966, the CTU house of representatives again threatened to strike if Willis went ahead with his plan to curtail voluntary teacher transfers.[93]

While ignoring the problems of racial segregation and discrimination, the CTU rigorously defended teachers and principals against violent attacks by pupils and parents. To highlight the problem of classroom violence, the CTU undertook studies, published numerous articles on the issue in the union newspaper, and sent letters and deputations to the Board of Education. Between 1955 and 1961, the CTU supported sixty-eight teachers in court cases, fifty-two of which concerned assaults on teachers. In 1960, the CTU pledged to support any teacher who found it "necessary to use force to compel compliance with the rules of the school or the direction of the teacher or in protecting themselves or students from assault."[94] The CTU turned over its 1961 education conference, entitled "Tomorrow's Exploding Schools," to the problem of school violence. In 1964, the CTU organized a special conference "to arouse the general public to the gravity of the problem of discipline in the Chicago public schools and to plan a program that will protect teachers and other school personnel from assaults by students, parents, and intruders."[95] After a teacher was found not guilty of striking a twelve-year-old student, the CTU and AFT vice president, John Desmond, announced that the union would file false arrest charges on behalf of teachers found not guilty of accusations brought by parents.[96] Rather than blame racism or the poor condition of the segregated schools for discipline problems,

Fewkes highlighted "parental and adult delinquency" and lack of security in the schools.[97] While the editor of the *Chicago Sun-Times* blamed "poverty, slums, neglect, discrimination, ignorance, [and] mistrust" as causes of school violence, Eileen Shannon, editor of the *Chicago Union Teacher* declared, "[s] hould not indifferent parents who are unfamiliar with discipline take a major share of the responsibility? Violence is indeed a symptom, but should not people who urge boycotts and similar disobedience of law also take another large share of blame for the outbreaks of violence?"[98] As black parents called for the removal of uncaring principals and racist teachers, Fewkes and the house of representative supported the teaching staff.[99]

Generational Conflict

Many historians argue that male high school teachers were the driving force behind the campaign for collective bargaining in the early 1960s because they expressed greater dissatisfaction with their conditions than their female colleagues did. Historian Wayne Urban suggests that "[t]here is little doubt that the teacher activism that developed in the early 1960s was largely a phenomenon that originated in the ranks of male high school teachers."[100] Stephen Cole argues that male high school teachers in New York, aggrieved over the introduction of a single salary schedule, were crucial in igniting teacher militancy. As both historians suggest, high school teachers had much to complain about. While in the past high school men had the psychological advantage of receiving higher pay than women elementary school teachers, the introduction of equal pay ended that. Now men teachers toiled for the same wage as the majority of the women in Chicago and elsewhere.[101] In an era that emphasized marrying young and husbands supporting stay-at-home wives, many male teachers in particular voiced anger that they could not fully enjoy this affluent lifestyle. Men were more likely than women to be married with greater family responsibilities and extra jobs. In 1963, 80.5 percent of men teachers were married, but only 62.3 percent of women teachers. According to a 1961 NEA research report, 47 percent of men teachers worked a second job during the school year and 60 percent during the summer months. "The typical man teaching in today's schools is both angry and impatient," the report suggested. "He thinks he is entitled to a better break in this era of two-car families and electric can openers, and he is. He is fed up with working nights, weekends, and holidays trying to make ends meet on a teacher's salary. He is tired of sacrificing his family for his profession."[102] Hence, while men constituted 14 percent of Chicago's elementary school teachers and 47 percent of high school teachers, 21 percent of elementary school teachers and 65 percent of high school teachers who expressed a "very unfavorable opinion of their present position" were men. Moreover, these angry men were a larger share of the teaching profession than they had been earlier in the century.[103] The number of male teachers in Chicago rose from 24 percent in 1958 to 29.5 percent in 1963.[104]

Yet the role that the dissatisfaction of male high school teachers played in the teacher militancy of the 1960s has been overstated. As more men entered teaching in the 1950s and teaching became less identified as women's work, the status of male teachers increased. With the rise in the school population and in the number of schools, male teachers also enjoyed more opportunities for promotion to principal or administrator. Indeed, a number of NEA surveys showed that male satisfaction with teaching was higher in the 1960s than it was in previous decades. In 1944, 45.3 percent of men expressed satisfaction with the job of teaching, 53.9 percent in 1956, 62 percent in 1961, and 63.3 percent in 1966.[105]

Teachers in the elementary schools, 86 percent of whom were women, faced worse working conditions than high school teachers, where the vast majority of men taught. In Chicago in the early 1960s, teachers in the elementary schools were more likely than high school teachers to be in the most overcrowded schools. In the early 1960s, the rise in the student population, the conflict between students and teachers, the worst scenes of violence, and the greater focus of the civil rights movement was found in the elementary schools, not in the high schools. Indicative of this, as Figure 9 shows, it was not high school teachers but elementary school teachers who were leaving the profession in greater numbers in the late 1950s and early 1960s.[106]

An often underestimated cause of the teacher militancy was generational discontent. Many of the most vociferous complaints about working conditions came from younger teachers who had entered the Chicago school system in increasing numbers as student enrollments soared. The huge expansion in the size of the Chicago teaching workforce meant an increase in the number of younger teachers. In 1958, 24 percent of Chicago teachers were under the age of thirty, in 1963 the figure was 27 percent, and in 1966 it was 29 percent.[107] Reflecting this influx of new teachers, in 1963–64, 32 percent of elementary school teachers and 33 percent of high school teachers had five or fewer years of teaching experience. With little teacher turnover and few vacancies in the stable schools in white neighborhoods, the Board of Education increasingly pursued a policy of assigning recently recruited young black and white teachers to the most overcrowded and difficult schools in

Figure 9. Resignations of Chicago Public School Teachers, 1955–66.

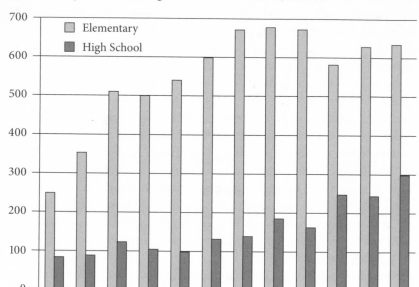

Sources: *Facts and Figures 1962–63,* 40; *Facts and Figures 1967,* 66; and *Facts and Figures 1969,* 66.

low-income neighborhoods. The "youngest and least experienced teachers tend to get the least desirable teaching assignments," Robert Havighurst found. While about 30 percent of Chicago elementary school teachers were thirty or younger, 40 percent of those in "lower class or slum" schools were in that age bracket. Likewise, 36 percent of high school teachers were thirty or younger, but 44 percent of that age group worked in "lower class or slum" schools. In 1963–64, the teachers in the "high status" schools had a median average of nineteen years of experience, but only four years in the "inner city schools." Havighurst even found that within these schools "the most difficult and unwanted courses are often assigned to new, inexperienced teachers."[108]

Young Chicago teachers, like many from their generation in the late 1950s and early 1960s, exuded a rebellious spirit and declining respect for authority, and they rejected the conformity and complacency of the older generation. *The Nation* called these teachers "a new breed . . . younger, better educated, with higher expectations. This 'new breed' will not accept lower wage rates and inferior working conditions in exchange for security of employment.

Nor will it settle merely for better wages; it demands a new status."[109] Nor were they willing to accept the cautious approach to gaining collective bargaining advocated by John Fewkes and CTU vice president John Desmond, both in their late fifties, who represented the ideas of an older generation. Quite simply, these young teachers coming of age during a period of affluence, low unemployment, and expansion of higher education had none of the fears of their parents' generation, which had experienced the upheavals and deprivations of the Great Depression and the Second World War. They brought youth and vitality to their profession and showed contempt for administrators, principals, and older colleagues. Reflecting both a sexist attitude toward women teachers but also a critique of the older generation, young Chicago high school teacher Robert J. Hoder blamed the "old-maid school teachers" who were "unaware of anything except their small, small world" for the lack of militancy among the teaching force.[110]

These young teachers wanted more freedom to introduce new teaching methods and greater classroom control from the prying eyes of principals. There was a generational feeling, whether on campus or in the workplace, that young people should have more influence over their own lives. Many of the conflicts and social movements of the era involved issues of participation in decision making, whether it was students seeking greater say in their universities, blacks seeking voting rights and control of their communities, or the New Left demanding participatory democracy.[111] While administrators expected obedience from their teachers, younger teachers demanded more classroom autonomy and the right to innovate and experiment with curriculum. Teacher Anthony Grosch, who began teaching at Jenner Elementary School at the age of twenty-six in 1962, felt the "frustration of young teachers who had similar yearnings to mine to be better professionals to make substantial changes in the school and the education of the children. . . . The administrative structure was indifferent." Young teachers were "not supported by the principals or the Board of Education in their endeavors to promote high quality education," Grosch believed.[112] As audio-visual technology, sophisticated science equipment, and new innovative curriculum models became available to teachers, older principals and teachers resisted new approaches and appeared out of touch to their younger colleagues. The older principals believed in more traditional ideas of authority and methods of teaching while the new teachers wanted more interaction and innovation in the classroom.[113] One teacher who entered teaching at the age of twenty-two remembered that at his first school the principal "did not believe in audio-visual or teachers manuals. So he took all the teachers manuals and all the audio-visual material, slides, films, and everything, and locked them and kept the key and locked them up from the teachers. . . . His philosophy was that a chalk board and piece of chalk is all a teacher needs."[114]

Many of these younger teachers voiced particular resentment that the Board of Education had assigned them to the most difficult schools in the system. As many as 19 percent of Chicago elementary school teachers and 15 percent of high school teachers with less than two years of experience voiced an unfavorable or very unfavorable view of their present position, while only 8 percent of elementary school teachers with more than sixteen years of experience and only 9 percent of high school teachers with similar service voiced unfavorable or very unfavorable views. Some expressed anger toward older teachers and others toward the students. One young female inner-city elementary teacher complained that "[t]here's no help for the new teacher. There were older teachers here when I came and they could have helped us through but they left." One newly assigned elementary school teacher exclaimed, "I don't know why I should be a warden. I don't know why I should have to spend most of my time just keeping the kids under control. Why, oh why can't I be a teacher?"[115]

Other young teachers, motivated by the conditions they saw in the poor schools, became sympathetic to the civil rights movement and made a conscious decision to teach in poorer black neighborhoods. In October 1965, a young, mostly white female faculty made common cause with the black community and the civil rights movement at Edward Jenner Elementary School at Cabrini-Green on the near North Side. Jenner, the city's largest elementary school with more than 2,500 pupils, had 96 percent black enrollment. After some teachers complained that principal Mildred Chuchut exhibited prejudice against black pupils and teachers, thirty members of the faculty sent a petition to the Board of Education claiming she was dictatorial and demanding her removal from the school. The local community formed the Concerned Parents of Jenner to support the teachers, and they further complained about inadequate school facilities. The Concerned Parents of Jenner staged a series of school boycotts, which students answered with absentee rates of up to 97 percent, and Martin Luther King, Jr., visited the school to demonstrate his support. Finally the Board of Education replaced the principal.[116]

Campaign for Collective Bargaining

The inability of the CTU to win collective bargaining rights and General Superintendent Benjamin Willis's refusal to address the teachers' problems led to growing discontent from some sections of the teaching force. As one teacher, Ken Brown, put it, "if the superintendent said no too often then okay you start talking real antagonism and that's when things started to change."[117] Opposition to the Fewkes approach first emerged in the late 1950s from groups of socialists, trade union militants, and civil rights activists who began to combine in different schools and in union meetings. With the worst excesses of the McCarthy era over, radicals became less frightened to openly voice their opinions. What united them was a desire for the union to improve teachers' lives in the classroom and to take an active role in demanding collective bargaining. As civil rights activist Timuel Black put it, they sought to "make the teachers' union a real union."[118]

African American teachers in Chicago carried on a tradition going back to the days of Reconstruction of trying to achieve quality education for black students both by their teaching in the classroom and by pursuing political changes outside the school. Many black teachers, attracted to teaching to educate and inspire their black students, promoted racial pride, had little truck with prevalent views of black racial intellectual inferiority, and blamed segregation for underperforming children. Black teachers dealt daily with the inequalities of the Chicago public schools and saw a generation of young black people handicapped by lack of equipment and supplies. They wanted their students to get equal treatment, equal opportunities, and equal access to school facilities and equipment. In Chicago, some black teachers became involved in the civil rights movement and tried to use the CTU as their vehicle to achieve greater equality.

Some CTU members emerged to become leading figures in the civil rights movement and the campaign for collective bargaining. Timuel D. Black first became active in teacher unionism in Gary, Indiana, in the mid 1950s. As a former pupil and friend of Mary Herrick, he returned to Chicago in 1956 to take over Herrick's job at DuSable High School while she was on leave and subsequently moved to Farragut School on the West Side. Black wanted the union to be a "tool to bring about social change and social justice." In February 1963, he stood unsuccessfully for alderman on the platform of ending segregation, and the following August he led the Chicago section of the March on Washington. He became president of the Chicago chapter of A. Philip Randolph's Negro American Labor Council (NALC), founded in Detroit in May 1960 by young black members of the AFL-CIO to fight for equality in the labor movement and to pressure companies to employ more African Americans. Joined by CTU leader Gerald Bullock, civil rights activist Al Raby, and local socialist party secretary Saul Mendelson, this organization played a major part in initiating and leading the struggle for integrating the public schools. It also sought to desegregate the Washburne Trade School, which, under the patronage of the skilled unions in the city, had an overwhelmingly white student population.[119]

Although many white teachers accepted ideas of black racial inferiority and sought to teach in schools with predominantly white students, there was no monolithic attitude on race on the part of the majority white teaching force. Radical civil rights activists, socialists, feminists, and others inspired by religious concerns rejected prevailing ideas on race and the need for segregated schools. In many of those schools that had an overwhelming majority of black students, the teaching force that refused to transfer remained committed to racial equality. All-black DuSable High School, for example, attracted white faculty members like CTU leader Mary Herrick, who had strong views on helping disadvantaged black children and who was beloved by both black teachers and students.[120] One African American elementary teacher remembered "excellent" relations between the white and black teachers in the black school in which she taught. "The people who decided to stay were very special in terms of wanting to work with the children," she recalled.[121]

Teachers in some neighborhoods proved more accepting of integration than others. In the historically liberal neighborhood of South Shore, adjoining Lake Michigan, many white teachers backed by community leaders proclaimed a strong commitment to integration. Those black families who moved into previously all-white South Shore mostly originated from the middle classes. They bought owner-occupied housing and the area remained racially mixed. The older teachers left and the younger ones who stayed or took their place committed themselves to achieving racial harmony.[122] Ken Brown, who started teaching general science in the Chicago public schools in 1959, explained that "I wanted to go to South Shore to help on the integration. At that time South Shore was Greek [and] Jewish. . . . When some of the black kids came in there was tension and difficulty and I wanted to smooth that out. My feeling was that this can be made to work. If it can work in any neighborhood South Shore was the neighborhood to do it." Most teachers in the school favored removing racist teachers. After one white teacher at South Shore made derogatory remarks about the black students, "the faculty were full square in favor of getting his arse out of the school," recalled Brown.[123] One black parent whose daughter was transferred along with other pupils from Hirsch School to South Shore in 1964 declared that "they were graciously welcomed by the teachers and the principal."[124]

Although the CTU as an organization did little in the civil rights movement, individual teachers and union members played leading roles in the
movement to integrate the schools. Since World War II, many Chicago teachers, black and white, male and female, became active in local civil rights
organizations such as the Urban League, CORE, and the NAACP. Schoolteacher Ethel Hilliard became president of the Chicago branch of the NAACP
women's auxiliary in 1941 and sat on the branch's executive committee.[125] The
Chicago NAACP education committee included schoolteachers Madeline
Morgan Morris and Faith Rich. Rich, a white teacher originally from Ver-
mont who joined the Chicago branch of the NAACP in 1942, worked as a
Chicago NAACP executive member and chair of the education committee
for several years. As head of an NAACP investigation, Rich published "De
Facto Segregation in the Chicago Public Schools" in the fall of 1957, which
exposed for the first time the extent of the racial inequalities in Chicago's
schools.[126] In February 1968, eight of the fifty-three delegates to the CCCO
were teachers. Church ministers, with eleven delegates, were the only occupation that had more representation among the CCCO.[127]

The first organized opposition to Fewkes's cautious approach emerged in
May 1958, when Meyer Weinberg stood as CTU presidential candidate in the
first contested union presidential election since 1947. Disillusioned with the
inactivity of the union on both teachers' welfare and civil rights, Weinberg
helped to organize the Independent Caucus as an opposition group within the
CTU. Born in New York in 1920 and raised in Chicago, Weinberg worked in
a defense plant during World War II, where he became a United Auto Workers (UAW) activist. After the war, Weinberg worked as a history teacher at
Wright Junior College in Chicago, joined the CTU, and was elected to the
executive board. Weinberg attracted to the Independent Caucus a group of
black and white activists who tried to tie the call for integrated schools with
a demand for collective bargaining, believing that a militant union leadership and collective bargaining would help to improve the conditions in the
schools, especially in the black neighborhoods.[128] Weinberg drew around him
militants such as William P. Moore, an African American physical education
teacher, high school teacher John J. Walsh, and Shirley Lens, the teacher at
the center of the Broyles oath controversy in the 1950s. Reminiscent of Kermit Eby in the 1930s, these militant individuals wanted to prove that public
schools could bring greater social equality. These young radicals convinced
other teachers that collective bargaining could help them achieve better pay,
eliminate non-teaching duties, improve working conditions, and lessen the

obtrusive power of school administrators. Nevertheless, Fewkes, who gained enormous support among white teachers who applauded his opposition to school integration, won the election with 75 percent of the vote.[129]

Despite the loss, Weinberg's campaign confirmed that pressure was building within the teaching force and the union for collective bargaining. Buoyed by the results, a number of union activists began to press the union leadership to take more action on pay and collective bargaining. In January 1959, after the board turned down a CTU request for a pay increase, the house of representatives voted with only one dissenting member (who instead advocated a strike) to organize a demonstration, the first teachers' march since the heady days of the 1930s. Subsequently, some eight thousand teachers marched to the Board of Education headquarters, but the board remained unmoved and passed the original budget two days later. When Weinberg ran again for president in the May 1960 union elections, the entire official slate was elected, but Fewkes's share of the vote fell from 75 percent to 64 percent.[130]

Weinberg spent much of the 1960s occupied with civil rights activities. Out of the Independent Caucus of the CTU emerged the Teachers for Integrated Schools (TFIS), formed in 1961. With William P. Moore as secretary, John J. Walsh as president, and Gertrude Berger as treasurer, TFIS affiliated with CCCO and at its peak had more than three hundred members. Starting in January 1963, they published their own journal, *Integrated Education*, which sought to connect with both the civil rights groups in Chicago and with other like-minded teachers in other cities. The TFIS campaigned for integrated schools and urged "teachers to take a leading role in community action for integration." Weinberg published a series of pioneering reports that revealed the extent of segregation in the Chicago public schools, and the TFIS subsequently played a leading role in the struggle to integrate the schools. TFIS supported the Freedom Day boycott of October 1963, taught at and supplied lesson plans for the freedom schools, and distributed 50,000 "Freedom Diplomas" to those who attended the schools.[131]

The campaign for collective bargaining gained further impetus as opposition to unions in general, and teachers' unions in particular, subsided. Opinion polls showed that more people supported public sector unions than ever before. A poll published in August 1937 found that 74 percent of those asked thought that government employees should not be able to join labor unions. By February 1959, only 43 percent of those polled opposed unions for public school teachers, and by November 1965, merely 28 percent believed that schoolteachers should not join unions.[132] The educational establishment too had become more accepting of teacher unionism. In January 1955, the

American School Board Journal, organ of the American Association of School Boards, cautioned against a "prejudiced attitude" toward unions and declared, "Unionization of workers is inevitable in these days, and employees in school systems can hardly avoid following the example of other workers in forming organizations which have affiliations with the nation-wide labor unions."[133] In 1959, Wisconsin became the first state to pass a law that granted municipal employees, including teachers, the right to join a union and to collective bargaining. By the end of the decade, AFT locals in Eau Claire, Wisconsin; Butte, Montana; Bremerton, Washington; Pawtucket, Rhode Island; and Cicero, Illinois, had some form of bargaining agreements.[134] A change was in the air in Illinois when the first collective bargaining bill since 1945 went for a vote in the legislature in 1959. The bill passed the Democratic-controlled house but died in a senate committee.[135]

The biggest impetus to collective bargaining came from New York City, the country's largest public school district. Under the leadership of David Selden and Albert Shanker, New York teachers organized the United Federation of Teachers (UFT), an AFT local, and launched a campaign to attain collective bargaining for New York City's 50,000 public school teachers. Complaining of low wages, few fringe benefits, large classes, and student unrest in the classroom, UFT president Charles Cogen threatened a teachers' strike in March 1960. In response, the New York Board of Education announced that it would allow a union election if 30 percent of the New York teaching staff requested one. With no sign of the agreement in sight, the UFT voted to strike. Although the Condon-Wadlin Act, passed in 1947, prohibited public sector strikes in New York state, more than five thousand teachers engaged in a one-day walkout on November 7, 1960, to demand a collective bargaining election. In response to the strike, in June 1961 Democratic mayor Robert F. Wagner, Jr., and the New York Board of Education authorized a collective bargaining election in which New York teachers overwhelmingly voted for collective bargaining rights. In another ballot in December of the same year, the New York teachers voted overwhelmingly to have the UFT as their sole bargaining agent. The ensuing agreement was the first collective bargaining agreement for public school teachers in a major U.S. city.[136]

In the following years teachers across the country, encouraged by the success of the New York teachers, struck to win bargaining rights. Between the New York strike and December 1965, the United States saw as many as sixteen strikes by public school teachers. In response to the wave of militancy, the AFT repealed its no-strike pledge in 1963. The upsurge in militancy also affected the NEA as it too endorsed collective bargaining and strikes. By early 1965, AFT locals had gained collective bargaining rights in Detroit, Cleveland, and Philadelphia.[137] In the 1960s, twenty-two states passed laws granting collective bargaining to local or state employees.[138]

The victory in New York had a profound impact on Chicago teachers. On the one hand, the membership grew increasingly dissatisfied with the CTU leadership and its collaborationist policy. On the other hand, the AFT engaged in a nationwide organizing effort and collective bargaining drive for the first time in its history, joining the AFL-CIO's Industrial Union Department for financial assistance. AFT president Charles Cogen visited Chicago to tell the CTU leaders "that the union ought to go ahead more strongly than it had been doing."[139] The "piling up" of grievances and "the fact that New York teachers and others have collective bargaining agreements," John Desmond declared in December 1963, has persuaded the CTU that "now is the time we should ask for collective bargaining ourselves."[140]

At the same time New York teachers were obtaining collective bargaining, the federal government gave public sector unions further legitimacy. In June 1961, President John F. Kennedy appointed a Task Force on Employee-Management Relations in the Federal Service, which led to Executive Order 10988. Just as section 7(a) of the National Industrial Recovery Act and the Wagner Act gave industrial unions encouragement in the 1930s, Executive Order No. 10988, issued by Kennedy in January 1962, gave support to public sector unions. The executive order did not allow federal employees the right to strike, but it granted them the right to organize and bargain over certain issues. Most states followed Kennedy's lead and gave comparable rights to local government employees.[141] Led by unions such as the American Federation of State, County and Municipal Employees (AFSCME), and the American Federation of Government Employees (AFGE), union membership among government workers increased more than tenfold, from less than 400,000 in 1955 to more than four million in the early 1970s.[142]

News of President Kennedy's executive order encouraged the CTU to abandon its goal of passing a collective bargaining bill in Springfield; instead it pressured the Board of Education to unilaterally grant bargaining rights to the teachers. "It is now time for the Board of Education to consider seriously setting up collective bargaining procedures with its employee groups," Fewkes declared. In January 1962, the CTU established the Collective Bargaining Planning Committee, which spent the following months obtaining the support of PTA groups, labor unions, and politicians. In 1963, the CTU presented a petition containing the signatures of more than 13,000 teachers to the Board of Education demanding collective bargaining, which the board subsequently rejected.[143]

Younger teachers turned to more militant methods than the CTU leaders did to satisfy their demands. Inspired by Albert Shanker and the successful campaign for collective bargaining in New York City, in September 1962 James Chiakulas, a twenty-two-year-old substitute teacher, formed the United Teachers Committee (UTC). Fellow teachers John Kotsakis and Jerome Winter joined Chiakulas as the main spokesmen for the UTC. The Chicago organization copied the name of the United Teachers Federation and obtained information, material, and resources from Shanker to use in the Chicago schools. At its peak, the UTC had about eight hundred dues-paying members, about twenty-five in the CTU house of representatives, an executive board, a downtown office, and its own newspaper. Working as an elementary school teacher, Chiakulas moved from school to school recruiting teachers into the UTC, and elementary school teachers made up the bulk of membership.[144] The son of a full-time AFL-CIO official, Chiakulas gathered around him civil rights activists such as Al Raby and Timuel Black, but mostly young teachers like John Kotsakis. Rather than embrace what they saw as controversial and divisive issues such as civil rights, the UTC concentrated all its energies on gaining collective bargaining. Chiakulas recalled that with some exceptions, "the old time teachers were neutral . . . middle-class, non-political, you could only appeal to them on the basis of economics and what was good for the children. If we could fight for smaller classes, if we could fight to maintain salaries so that we had a good element coming into teaching and if we could be treated fairly as professionals and have more discretion in the classroom." The UTC petitioned the union and used its influence in the house of representatives to push for greater action on collective bargaining, including a strike to meet their demands.[145]

Daley and Collective Bargaining

The CTU depended on the strength of organized labor to gain collective bargaining rights. Since the mid-1950s, the share of the workforce in the AFL-CIO had declined as the economy shifted from the traditional unionized manufacturing sector to the non-union service and white-collar sector. Employment in state and local government rose by 74 percent between 1951 and 1964 to reach 7.16 million, but only 1.5 million of these new workers joined labor unions. At the same time, white-collar employment rose by 27.7

percent between 1950 and 1960, but only 11 percent of them were in unions by 1964. With white-collar public sector work being the most rapidly expanding sector of the American labor force by the 1950s, the AFL-CIO had to make a concerted effort to recruit those workers, and teachers, as both public sector and white-collar workers, became the principal target of organized labor. After New York teachers' notable success in 1962, the AFL-CIO poured money into AFT organizing campaigns. Walter Reuther, president of the United Auto Workers and leader of the AFL-CIO Industrial Union Department, gave financial and organizational help to the teachers' unions.[146] The CTU received $500 per month for organizational material and the AFL-CIO provided two organizers. Reuther urged Mayor Daley to back the CTU's demands, and in February 1964 he came to Chicago to add his support by speaking at teacher rallies attended by thousands of teachers.

The Chicago Federation of Labor (CFL) followed the lead of the national organization in helping public sector workers to organize. After the New York teachers voted for collective bargaining in 1961, CFL head William Lee made the CTU his number one priority in the drive for public sector collective bargaining. In September 1961, public sector unions in Chicago established the Chicago–Cook County Council of Public Employees, with Fewkes as president, and it pressured the city council to grant collective bargaining rights to public workers. Ray Pasnick of the United Steel Workers of America, labor's representative on the Board of Education, consistently supported the CTU's demands.[147] CFL leader William Lee personally convinced Mayor Daley to declare his support for collective bargaining rights for teachers. Daley and the Democratic machine had traditionally opposed collective bargaining, which would regulate hiring, firing, and transfers and limit dependency on the machine and threaten its control of patronage jobs.[148]

By declaring for collective bargaining, Mayor Daley sought to retain the CFL's support and incorporate the CTU into the Democratic machine. As political scientist William Grimshaw points out, Daley hoped to get credit for aiding the teachers and gain the support of the electorate for maintaining industrial peace in the public schools, and also get the CTU to give consistent backing to the Democratic Party.[149] In April 1963, Daley threw his support behind unsuccessful state legislation that would have permitted collective bargaining for public employees. Henceforth, Mayor Daley urged the machine supporters on the Board of Education to bargain with the teachers without the aid of a collective bargaining law.[150]

Daley also became more supportive of the CTU to avoid conflict with the union and to concentrate all his energies on defeating the civil rights movement that threatened his power base. As the CTU prodded the mayor for collective bargaining rights, he came under escalating pressure from the civil rights movement, the largest in the North, to desegregate the schools. In the summer of 1963, civil rights activists staged sit-ins at the Board of Education and the office of General Superintendent Benjamin Willis. At the same time the Board of Education had to deal with the CCCO school boycotts in October 1963, the CTU was making its first demands for collective bargaining rights. In the middle of boycotts, sit-ins, and demonstrations, Daley wanted to alleviate his problems by removing the CTU's opposition to his Democratic machine. As political scientist Paul E. Peterson argued, "[i]n the midst of the great struggles surrounding Benjamin Willis, Daley could ill afford to have the CTU, still another political force within the educational arena, actively opposed to his policies."[151]

With the support of Mayor Daley, the Board of Education softened its stance on collective bargaining. In January 1964, the CTU house of representatives agreed to poll the membership on a strike if the Board of Education refused the union's demand for collective bargaining at the board meeting the following month. The CTU leadership opposed a strike. The following month, as the CCCO organized a second school boycott, the board granted the CTU collective bargaining rights but named both the CTU and the local affiliate of the NEA, the Chicago Division of the Illinois Education Association, as representatives of their members. Fewkes accepted the offer and withdrew the strike threat. Over the next few months Fewkes tried to persuade the Board of Education to hold an election to determine the sole representative of the teachers.[152]

Many teachers saw Fewkes's stance as a "sell-out" by the union and decried the union for lack of militancy. In May 1964, Thomas Connery ran against Fewkes in the CTU presidential election claiming that Fewkes was selling its members short by agreeing to an "obnoxious 'company-store' deal" with the board. Although Fewkes won by 5,116 to 2,639 votes, the results highlighted growing anger and impatience among Chicago schoolteachers at the leadership inaction.[153] In the next few months, dissidents in the union led by James Chiakulas and the United Teachers Committee picketed union meetings and petitioned the CTU leaders to strike for sole bargaining rights. Fewkes and CTU vice president John Desmond opposed a strike, believing that a strike might not gain the support of most teachers and claiming one was not needed as the union could obtain sole bargaining rights through negotiations with the board.[154]

In the summer of 1965, the local civil rights movement began to direct its attention much more on the role of Mayor Daley in maintaining not only segregated schools but discrimination in housing and employment. After the Board of Education renewed Superintendent Willis's contract, civil rights protests centered on City Hall rather than on the Board of Education. In June, the CCCO organized a third school boycott, and even in the face of a court injunction obtained by the Board of Education, more than 100,000 students stayed away from school; Al Raby, comedian Dick Gregory, and hundreds of demonstrators staged daily sit-ins at City Hall and were arrested in the streets. "The strategy in war is shoot the general and the troops will panic," argued journalist Jack Mabley. "Early in June Dick Gregory made it clear that Ben Willis was the objective in the first battle, but that Richard J. Daley was the target in the war." Daley now became symbolic of the "injustices tied to racism in the city as a whole."[155] At the same time, demonstrators picketed the home of Daley to demand Willis's resignation, and in July 1965, Martin Luther King, Jr., arrived in Chicago to put further pressure on Daley. King spent days speaking to crowds in the south and west sides of the city and led 15,000 marchers down State Street to the City Hall demanding better education, employment opportunities, and housing in the largest civil rights march the city had ever seen.[156] In the same month, the CCCO filed a complaint, prepared mainly by CTU member Meyer Weinberg, with the U.S. Office of Education charging that the Board of Education was in violation of Title VI of the Civil Rights Act of 1964 and it should therefore not receive any of the $30 million in federal aid due to it. In September 1965, U.S. commissioner of education Francis Keppel agreed to withhold federal funds from the Chicago schools, but under political pressure from Mayor Daley and President Lyndon B. Johnson, Keppel restored federal funding to Chicago within a week.[157]

In the midst of this civil rights activity, CTU activists continued their campaign to persuade the Board of Education to hold an election to determine the sole representative of the teachers. In June 1965, CTU full-timer Charles Skibbens and Richard J. Holland, a schoolteacher from Marshall High School, founded the Teachers Action Committee (TAC), which concentrated all its energies on pushing for collective bargaining rights in response to the timid leadership of Fewkes.[158] The TAC, a middle-of-the-road organization between the radical UTC and the conservative Fewkes, picked up support from the less politically active teachers and high school teachers ignored by the UTC. In September 1965, Charles Skibbens proposed a motion in the CTU house of representatives that teachers would strike unless the Board of Education set a date for the election to decide the teachers' representative in collective bargaining. The house voted to strike.[159]

With the CTU preparing to strike, the civil rights movement put further pressure on Mayor Daley. In the fall of 1965 a coalition of northern and southern civil rights groups with Martin Luther King, Jr., organized the Chicago Freedom Movement to end segregation and improve living conditions for inner-city blacks. In January 1966, King visited Chicago to dramatize the issue of poverty. Daley was particularly concerned about the bad publicity King might bring to Chicago, and in response he increased garbage collecting, street cleaning, and building inspections in poor areas.[160]

With pressure building on him, Mayor Daley finally encouraged the machine supporters on the Board of Education to grant the union's demand for a bargaining election. Board of Education member and Daley opponent Warren Bacon recalled that when the CTU threatened a strike in the fall of 1965, the board machine members "were adamant against granting the union the right of collective bargaining." But lobbying by Daley supporters proved effective: "Bill Lee, and one or two other top leaders very closely identified with the so-called 'power structure' of this city, were sent over to the board meeting, and those board members who were adamant against granting the union this right changed just like that," Bacon recalled.[161] Subsequently, the Board of Education relented and gave in to the union's demand. In an election held on May 27, 1966, the CTU won a landslide victory over the CTF and the Chicago Education Association. The board designated the CTU the sole representative of the Chicago public school teachers and proceeded to negotiate its first contract with the union. The following month, Benjamin Willis announced his resignation as superintendent, four months earlier than he had previously agreed.[162]

Conclusion

When thousands of teachers and other public sector workers gained collective bargaining rights in the 1960s, they participated in one of the major watersheds in labor history. The clear distinction between public and private sector workers, and the consequential belief that public sector bargaining undermined the sovereignty of government, had diminished. Lobbying of politicians, public relations campaigns, and alliances with community organizations now became less important to public sector workers. Public school teachers and other government workers now bargained and undertook industrial action just like private sector workers.

Although historians have been reluctant to do it, the campaign for collective bargaining in the 1960s must be incorporated into the larger narrative of the civil rights movement. The racial transformation Chicago experienced because of the second Great Migration, together with discrimination that the migrants encountered, led to overcrowded schools and worse working conditions for many Chicago teachers. The demands of the Chicago civil rights movement attracted some teachers who wanted to use collective bargaining to improve the segregated schools, but it appalled most, who felt that their working conditions were threatened by desegregation. With Mayor Daley amassing enormous power in his hands, it was to him that both civil rights activists and militant teachers turned to for solutions. Daley, under attack from the civil rights movement, appeased the CTU and granted the union sole negotiating rights with the Board of Education.

Once the union achieved collective bargaining rights, both the union and the civil rights movement in the city had changed dramatically. Through its negotiating rights, the CTU now had some say in how school revenue was spent and could justifiably take the credit or the blame for the public school system. The civil rights movement became more militant as improvements in black schools rather than integration became the major demand of many African Americans. These changes led to enormous conflict in the late 1960s but also to some major modifications in public education.

6

Teacher Power and Black Power Reform the Public Education System, 1966–1970

In May 1969, forty-one-year-old African American Chicago schoolteacher Roy Stell crossed a union picket line set up during the first official strike in CTU history and entered Calumet High School to teach his students. Stell, a CTU activist for fourteen years and a member of the union's policymaking body, was not alone; nearly half of Chicago's black public school teachers crossed union picket lines during the two-day walkout. Only three years after the CTU had triumphantly gained collective bargaining rights, Stell, a leading member of the civil rights organization Operation Breadbasket, and other black teachers who had joined the union to achieve higher wages, better working conditions, and quality education for their students, called for black teachers to leave their union and set up their own all-black labor organization.[1]

The stance of Roy Stell illustrates the problem virtually all big-city teachers' unions faced in the late 1960s as the civil rights movement entered its Black Power phase. In the campaign for collective bargaining, the CTU won the support of white and black teachers, but this fragile coalition fell apart in the late 1960s. While both black and white teachers asked their union to negotiate higher wages and better benefits, black teachers and black community activists increasingly wanted the union to use its new power to prod school authorities to improve the quality of education in the inner-city schools. Most famously, this conflict came to a head in New York City in the fall of 1968, when Albert Shanker and the United Federation of Teachers (UFT) called a city-wide strike in a conflict with the African American and Puerto Rican community–controlled schools in Ocean Hill–Brownsville. The predominantly white schoolteachers wanted to protect teachers' seniority rights and job security, whereas the residents of Ocean Hill–Brownsville sought more control over who would teach their children.[2]

The conflict at Ocean Hill–Brownsville has often obscured the fundamentally positive change black nationalism and teachers' unions have brought to public schooling. In many ways the conflict in New York proved to be more of an exception than the rule in teacher-community relations in the 1960s. In Chicago, like most other cities, politicians and the Board of Education proved unprepared to decentralize the school system and introduce community-controlled schools. While five years of civil rights activity had not brought integrated schools, when the CTU gained collective bargaining in 1966 and became a junior partner in the running of the public schools, black teachers, parents, and students joined together in an alliance that forced the union and the Board of Education to take on some of their demands and fundamentally change the union and the public school system.[3]

Chicago Public School System

After the departure of Benjamin Willis in the summer of 1966, the Chicago Board of Education appointed James F. Redmond as the general superintendent of the public schools. Born in Kansas City, Missouri, in 1915, Redmond, a white liberal who wanted school integration and more funding for the public schools, had previously worked in the Chicago public schools as assistant to General Superintendent Herold Hunt. He became school superintendent in New Orleans, a position he held from 1953 to 1961. Redmond, who exuded a calm and friendly manner and who the Chicago newspapers dubbed "Redmond the Conciliator" and "Gentlemen Jim," had to respond to both state and federal government pressure to integrate Chicago's schools. In 1963, the Illinois legislature had passed an amendment to the School Code of Illinois, known as the Armstrong Act, which required school boards to end school segregation.[4] After a U.S. Office of Education study noted the persistence of school segregation in Chicago, the federal agency threatened to withhold funds in January 1967.[5]

An inadequate and unfair system of school financing left the general superintendent with meager funds to improve the education system. Illinois, one of the wealthiest states in the nation, ranked forty-sixth in the country in the portion of state income spent on public schools in 1966. With schools still reliant on a local property tax, Chicago spent $614 to educate each high school student, New York City spent $800, and the wealthy Chicago suburb of Evanston spent $1,096.[6] Because suburban districts spent far more on their schooling, more affluent white families deserted the underfunded Chicago schools, moved to the suburbs, and enrolled their children in the suburban systems. This in turn compounded the problem of a shrinking tax base in the city. Unsurprisingly, an editorial in the *Chicago Sun-Times* argued that the union and the Board of Education "must fight and snarl over a meager pile of bones because the legislators had failed to insure adequate school financing."[7]

In response to the U.S. Office of Education's report, General Superintendent Redmond initiated the first real attempt to integrate the Chicago school system by announcing a busing plan in August 1967. Anticipating a backlash from the white community, the plan only called for the busing of black students, not white students, and only to schools in white areas with low black enrollment. To integrate the teaching force, Redmond proposed better pay for those teachers working in the inner city, the assignment of teachers to promote an equal balance of certified teachers in each school, and the restriction of teacher transfers. The plan also called for the creation of magnet schools to keep white middle-class families in Chicago.[8] The Board of Education, which remained committed to blocking integration, opposed the plan, but, under pressure from the U.S. Office of Education, reluctantly approved a pilot scheme. The board wanted to bus some one thousand black children in the overcrowded Austin neighborhood, on the West Side, and South Shore neighborhood, on the South Side, to white schools in the northwest and on the South Side.[9]

Standing on the plank of neighborhood schools, thousands of white residents and their political supporters in the Democratic Party protested the Board of Education plans. On January 10, 1968, 1,500 people turned up at a board meeting in what Mary Herrick described as "the most crowded and emotional session ever witnessed at a Board of Education meeting." Some politicians threatened to retaliate by opposing increased state funding for schools and passing laws to have board members elected. A petition opposing the busing plan quickly gathered 60,000 signatures.[10] In response to the uproar, in March 1968 the Board of Education refused to implement the original Redmond report, removed South Shore from the plan, and now called for voluntary, instead of compulsory, transfer of students in Austin. Before the children arrived, a firebomb exploded at one of the receiving schools, and with hundreds of white parents picketing the schools, the number of volunteers dwindled and the busing plan failed.[11] Subsequently, Board of Education member Jack Witkowsky declared in 1971: "Once in a while we would discuss the social benefits of integration, but never in my two years did we take a single major step designed to break up a system in which 90 percent of the black elementary pupils attend nearly all-black schools."[12] The persistence of residential segregation, white opposition, and lack of will on the part of the school administration had fatally wounded school integration in Chicago.

If school integration proved impossible because of the opposition of the white community and its supporters on the Board of Education, General Superintendent Redmond and Mayor Daley had more success in their efforts to increase the number of black school administrators and introduce African American studies classes into the curriculum. Changes in these areas appeased the civil rights movement without provoking the ire of white residents of the city. In 1964–65, blacks constituted only 3 percent of Chicago public school principals, 12.5 percent of district superintendents, and none of the six assistant superintendents.[13] By the beginning of the 1968 school year, blacks made up 6 percent of the principals, 18 percent of the district superintendents, and two of the eight assistant superintendents.[14] In contrast, the New York City public schools employed only six black principals and appointed their first black high school principal in 1968, and Newark, New Jersey, employed only one black principal in a school system with 78 percent non-white student enrollment.[15] Mayor Daley also appointed more black members to the Board of Education. In 1968 Carey Preston, secretary of the Chicago Urban League, joined Loraine Green and Warren Bacon to make three black members on the eleven-member Board of Education.[16] The Chicago public schools' curriculum department prepared Afro-American history courses, which began in the high schools in February 1968.[17]

Unlike his predecessor Benjamin Willis, who had maintained almost dictatorial control of the education system, Redmond made some move to decentralize school administration. Under Title III of the Elementary and Secondary Education Act of 1965 (ESEA), the board established the Woodlawn Experimental School Project in 1968, in which the Board of Education, the University of Chicago, and The Woodlawn Organization (TWO) jointly governed three schools. Yet Chicago's political machine and Board of Education never sanctioned the same degree of decentralization and community control found in New York City. Unlike the program introduced in Ocean Hill–Brownsville, New York City, for example, the leaders of the Woodlawn Project had no authority to transfer teachers unilaterally, and the board maintained ultimate control of the experiment. In the early 1970s, the U.S. Office of Education cut funding to the Woodlawn Project and the experiment came to an end.[18]

General Superintendent Redmond further engendered good will when he opened negotiations with the new CTU president John Desmond. Fewkes did not run for re-election as CTU president in 1966, but he supported his conservative ally, fifty-eight-year-old John Desmond, who defeated Charles Skibbens, the more radical Teachers Action Committee (TAC) candidate, by only 4,306 votes to 4,190.[19] Desmond was an Irish American Catholic and, like his predecessor Fewkes, a pragmatic, cautious leader who concentrated on winning larger salaries, more paid leave, and health insurance for his members. While the fiery Albert Shanker in New York invited confrontation, Desmond preferred negotiation over conflict.[20] To obtain higher wages for his members, Desmond maintained close relations with fellow Irish Americans Mayor Daley and General Superintendent Redmond, and he urged members to support Daley at election time.[21] The mayor, in turn, wanted to maintain stable working relations in the schools and avoid strikes, especially at a time when the civil rights movement opposed his views on integration.[22]

John Desmond proved much better at negotiating racial issues than his predecessor Fewkes and his fellow union leader in New York, Albert Shanker. In 1967 the CTU supported the Redmond desegregation plan and opposed legislation forbidding busing the following year.[23] John Desmond did not have the same determined and obstinate personality of Albert Shanker, and while Shanker and the UFT in New York proved hostile to community control and remained unwilling to compromise over the issue, the CTU expressed little opposition to the Woodlawn experiment. Desmond made sure to emphasize that violence in the schools was not a racial issue and that black teachers faced the biggest problems. In March 1968, the union organized a conference of academics and teachers to discuss racism in the teaching of U.S. history.[24]

For all the changes under Desmond, the CTU continued to prioritize the demands of white teachers at the expense of black teachers and students. Although some 60 percent of the students and more than a third of the teachers were African Americans, the CTU negotiating team included no black members. Jacqueline Wright, the union's recording secretary, and Glendis Hambrick, the union's treasurer, both elected in 1968, were the only major black members of the CTU leadership, and the three full-time paid union officers elected in 1968 were white.[25] Desmond blocked any attempt by the Board of Education to integrate the teaching force by opposing the involuntary transfer of teachers. This helped experienced white teachers, overwhelmingly certified and teaching in the better schools, who objected to compulsory transfers that would place them in the black schools, but it left black teachers and young and inexperienced white teachers in the segregated schools. Furthermore, the union put most of its emphasis on getting higher pay for teachers rather than educational improvements in the schools in the black community.[26]

From the time the CTU and the Board of Education negotiated their first contract in 1967, both sides adopted a narrow view of bargaining prevalent in the private sector, which restricted negotiating to wages and conditions rather than educational policy. With funding restricted, the leadership and most members believed that a labor union's first and foremost job was to provide teachers with a decent salary and then provide good working conditions. Consequently, Chicago public school teachers received benefits they had only dreamed of before. In 1967 the CTU obtained Christmas vacation pay (the first AFT local to do so), a $500 a year salary increase, fully paid medical insurance, two personal business days, a grievance procedure, and a duty-free lunch period. The first contract also addressed working conditions. The school board agreed to hire an extra 1,200 teacher aides to perform non-teaching duties (leaving more time for teachers to prepare for the classroom), added security protection in the schools, and reached an agreement on maximum class size. In the second bargaining contract the following year, the CTU gained paid spring vacation, a third personal day, severance pay, a preparation period for elementary school teachers (high school teachers already had one), and a $600 salary raise.[27]

In their negotiations with the Board of Education, the union showed little appreciation for the problems of African American teachers and refused to campaign for the certification of Full-time Basis Substitutes (FTBs). With many white Chicago teachers fleeing to the suburbs and school enrollment rising to unprecedented levels, the board introduced the FTB status so those teachers who had met state certification requirements but had not passed the Chicago Board of Education teacher certification examination could teach in the Chicago public schools. To keep costs down, the board increasingly relied on FTBs to do the same job as regular teachers but without the security of tenure, transfer privileges, the opportunity for promotion to the position of principal, and with lower pay than certified teachers. By 1963, about five thousand public school teachers, or a quarter of the workforce, worked as FTBs, and about 90 percent of them were black.[28]

Black substitute teachers in Chicago increasingly complained that the Board of Examiners that administered the Chicago Board of Education teacher certification examination deliberately discriminated against them. The National Educational Testing Service administered the written part of a two-part written and oral exam, but the Board of Examiners performed the oral exam, which became the main focus of accusations of discrimination. Black teachers believed they failed the oral exam not because of lack of knowledge about their chosen subject but because the Board of Examiners thought they had "unprofessional" black southern accents, were politically unsuitable, or exuded a confident manner deemed threatening to the white examiners. For example, Mamie Till Mobley, who became nationally known after her son, fourteen-year-old Emmett Till, was murdered in Mississippi in 1955, began teaching in the Chicago public schools in 1960; she believed she failed the oral exam because the Board of Examiners thought she was on an "ego trip."[29] Others claimed that examiners favored white teachers for certification because certification allowed teachers to transfer to other schools and the board wanted to keep black substitute teachers in black schools without the right of transfer to white schools.[30] Substitute teacher Tom Smith, for example, declared that the Board of Examiners limited the number of certified black teachers to stop "the horrid possibilities of Negroes teaching in lily-white schools."[31] Black teachers claimed discrimination in other school systems, but according to the journal *School Management*, "[c]ities most frequently cited for discriminatory testing practices are New York and Chicago."[32]

Many highly experienced and overqualified black teachers failed the Chicago teacher certification exam but still carried on teaching in the public school system. Harold Charles, who had worked as an assistant biochemist at the University of Chicago while he pursued a doctorate and was appointed chair of the science department at his school while still an FTB, failed the exam continuously.[33] John B. Mack twice passed the written exam but failed the oral exam even though he had taught in the New Orleans school system for six years before coming to Chicago in 1964, possessed a masters degree in library science, and earned thirty-six hours toward a Ph.D. Principal Jack H. Cantor of Stevenson School described Mack as a "person of rare talents who has carried on his work in a manner highly consistent with standards of excellence, imagination, creativity and ingenuity."[34]

For many black teachers, political and professional connections seemed the only way they could pass the certification exam. Only when his white principal wrote to the board on his behalf did Harold Charles gain certification.[35] After one African American teacher passed the written part of the exam but failed the oral part, her principal told her: "'Next time you take that exam you let me know and I'll see that you pass.' . . . I sure did pass the second time," she recalled. "I took the oral one when they asked me 'how do you like teaching' that was the only question they asked. . . . It was all fixed we understand that."[36] Another black teacher who twice failed the oral exam believed that a "plantation mentality" existed in the school system. "I was a black man and I demonstrated I was a man . . . not some wimp," he argued. After a white principal had used his personal connections in the administration, the teacher "laughed and joked" with the examiners and duly passed the exam. "My own ability or whatever meant nothing. Only when a good white man say 'let the nigger in.' . . . I appreciated what he did because he didn't have to do it but he shouldn't have had to do it," he concluded.[37]

The union leadership added to the problems of black teachers by excluding the FTBs from full membership of the union. The CTU designated FTBs associate members who paid full union dues and received full union benefits like other members but had less voice in union affairs. FTBs could only vote for eighteen delegates in the union's 220–member house of representatives and for one union vice president to represent them in the twenty-eight-strong executive board, and they had no vote in other union elections including the election for president. Fewkes and the other CTU leaders argued that to allow FTBs full voting rights in the CTU would lower the professional standing of the union.[38]

An organization called the Concerned FTBs protested the position of FTBs in the public school system. The Concerned FTBs, led by James B. McQuirter, Lonnie Hubbard, and Tom Smith, had some 1,300 members. They sent petitions to the Board of Education, organized demonstrations, and picketed the Board of Education and CTU meetings. The Concerned FTBs claimed that other school systems in the state only required teachers to pass the state exam and that teacher certification requirements were needlessly higher in Chicago than elsewhere. They further asserted that the Chicago Board of Education certification requirements were racially discriminatory, and they recommended that all FTBs who had met state certification requirements and served in the schools for at least two years should be automatically classified as regular teachers.[39] The Concerned FTBs also pushed for equal rights within the CTU and for the union to take up their case with the Board of Education. After an intense campaign by black teachers, a referendum of union members was held in March 1965 to determine if FTBs could become full-fledged union members. The substitutes' demand lost decisively by 5,217 to 2,275 votes.[40] Once he became union president, Desmond made some concessions to the FTBs. In November 1967 the CTU allowed FTBs to vote in union elections for the first time, but the union still refused to campaign for certification.

If the CTU, like many labor unions, neglected the demands of African Americans, teachers' unions in other cities made greater attempts to appease the black community. The UFT in New York City supported school integration for years, ran "freedom schools" staffed by teachers during its 1967 strike, and gave support to the wider civil rights movement. Whereas the CTU prioritized pay and demanded few school reforms in negotiations with the Board of Education, by 1968 the UFT had negotiated the inclusion of twenty schools under the More Effective Schools (MES) program, an AFT initiative launched in 1964, in which the board targeted inner-city schools for reduced class size, more teachers, and special services and programs involving nurses and social workers. The UFT also had achieved maximum class size of thirty-two in New York City's elementary schools and thirty-four in the high schools, while the CTU had only achieved a maximum class size of thirty-nine in elementary schools and thirty-six in high schools.[41]

The Black Community

Whereas the white community, the Board of Education, and the white teachers had halted any real change in the Chicago public schools, the black community had become more agitated and assertive. Many young urban blacks in the inner cities, particularly in the North, angrily criticized civil rights legislation for having little real impact on their lives and civil rights leaders for ignoring the problems of unemployment and poverty in the black ghettos. Blacks faced housing segregation, underfunded schools, job discrimination, discriminatory credit and mortgage practices, unequal treatment by the police and the courts, and the problem of organized gangs. In response to the slow pace of change and the seeming inability of civil rights legislation to tackle inner-city problems, a series of urban riots spread across the country. On August 11, 1964, the Watts district in Los Angeles erupted into violence. Within six days, thirty-four people were killed, more than eight hundred hospitalized, and more than four thousand arrested, and there was $45 million worth of property damaged.[42] The following year the country experienced eleven riots that lasted two days or more and twenty-five such riots in 1967.[43] On August 13, 1965, Chicago police arrested more than one hundred people and more than twenty suffered injuries on the city's West Side as black youths clashed with police after a fire truck from an all-white firehouse killed a black woman.[44] More seriously, in July 1966, four nights of rioting on the West Side began when youngsters who had turned on fire hydrants to escape the heat of a hot summer confronted police in the Lawndale area. In the ensuing disturbances, two died, more than eighty were injured, and more than five hundred arrested. The rioting only ended when 1,500 National Guard troops took to the streets.[45]

A new slogan, Black Power, first brought to national prominence in 1966 by Stokely Carmichael, head of the Student Nonviolent Coordinating Committee (SNCC), resonated with frustrated African Americans and became a rallying cry for young blacks. Black Power drew on a long tradition of black separatism and signified a resurgence of black nationalism in the black community not seen since the days of the Marcus Garvey movement of the 1920s. Using headline-grabbing rhetoric and antiwhite slogans, advocates of Black Power suggested that blacks should not integrate but separate from whites and should turn to self-defense rather than non-violence. Instead of trying to assimilate into white culture, nationalists suggested blacks should take pride in their own race and their own cultural achievements.[46] New and old black political organizations adopted various strains of Black Power. SNCC purged all whites from the group and H. Rap Brown, who took over from Stokely Carmichael as the leader of SNCC in 1967, changed the Nonviolent to National in the organization's name. Under new director Floyd McKissick, the Congress of Racial Equality (CORE) excluded whites from membership in 1967.[47] In October 1966, Bobby Seale and Huey P. Newton created the Black Panther Party for Self-Defense in Oakland, California, to oppose police brutality.[48]

The degree to which black people adopted Black Power or accepted its tenets varied enormously. Black Power leaders' support for Third World communist revolution and gunfights with police alienated many African Americans, while male posturing and association with violence held less interest for black women. Their policies, often couched in terms of the black community, were often dictatorial, romantic, and hostile to other black perspectives. Many African Americans recognized that with the language it used and the violence it condoned, Black Power inspired fear among many whites and opened up new divisions and confrontations along lines of race.[49] Yet Black Power also brought attention to racism and to the poverty in black neighborhoods and encouraged African Americans to take greater pride in themselves. The cultural influence of Black Power on young blacks was unquestioned. Many black youths stopped straightening their hair and let it grow into an Afro style, and some wore African-style clothes and adopted African-based names.[50]

Because of the influence of Black Power on young blacks, education became a main battleground of race relations in the late 1960s. Since the 1930s, black intellectuals and civil rights organizations often complained that art, civics, history, and literature textbooks ignored or denigrated African Americans. The Coordinating Council of Community Organizations (CCCO) believed that "[s]ocial studies textbooks in the Chicago Public School System treat the Negro as a lurking shadow in history, as a kind of fool or clown, or, more often, all but omit mention of the Negro because he has at once given more and received less than any minority group in the nation's history."[51] Black youths now joined this struggle and argued that schoolbooks, courses, and teachers should promote race pride by showing blacks in a positive light, by teaching the contributions of black people to the nation and the wider world, and by revising the way teachers treated such topics as slavery and the American Civil War. Rather than just integrate African Americans into the narrative, however, black activists now increasingly called for the teaching of separate African and African American art, literature, and history courses by black teachers.[52] Black college students from San Francisco to New York City disrupted classes to assert their demands.[53]

As the average age of black children rose in Chicago, the problem of inadequate schooling moved from the elementary schools to the high schools and from parents acting on behalf of their small children to older black students campaigning for quality education themselves. Those high schools with a rapidly increasing enrollment of black students but with predominantly white teachers and principals often saw violent conflict between teachers and students.[54] In September 1967, students fought with police outside Forrestville High School on Chicago's South Side during a rally to protest police brutality. Order was restored when police fired warning shots in the air and after twelve people were injured and fifty-four arrested.[55] More than three hundred students picketed Waller High School on the North Side in November 1967 demanding more black teachers, black history classes, and greater student input into school affairs.[56] A student strike was averted at Lindblom High School on the South Side in January 1968 only after the white principal rescinded an expulsion order against a black youth who swore at a teacher.[57] In April 1968, students at Hirsch High School on the South Side walked out of classes complaining about a dictatorial principal. The following day students at Parker High School left classes protesting conditions in the overcrowded school.[58]

Just as black youths began to take a greater interest in their education, black parents and activists turned their attention away from seeking school and faculty integration and toward an increased focus on the quality of public education. The violence displayed against Martin Luther King, Jr., in the white communities of Gage Park and Marquette Park in the summer of 1966, and the failure of the Board of Education to desegregate the schools in the face of whites who violently opposed school integration, horrified blacks and confirmed to most that they were safer staying in black neighborhoods and black schools. Under the further influence of Black Power, black civil rights groups such as CORE no longer advocated integration or even the transfer of black students from overcrowded black schools, but instead spoke about how the school system failed black students because it did not appreciate or address the special needs of low-income black children. The Coleman report, published in 1966, found that in nationwide standardized tests, "the average minority pupil scores distinctly lower on these tests at every level than the average white pupil." The gap between black and white pupils increased at each grade, which suggested that the "schools provide little opportunity for them to overcome this initial deficiency; in fact they fall farther behind the white majority in the development of several skills which are critical to making a living and participating fully in modern society."[59] Black schools, they argued, needed more funding than white schools to pay for smaller classes, remedial facilities, better supplies and equipment, more facilities such as lunchrooms and bathrooms, and extended social services to help children with learning difficulties. In November 1966, the CCCO and the Chicago chapter of CORE urged people to vote against a $25 million bond issue for school construction in a tax referendum because there was no assurance the money would be spent on black schools. In August 1967, the CCCO urged the Office of Education to withhold all federal funds from Chicago because they considered the board's proposals for desegregation inadequate.[60]

Groups of black parents and activists calling themselves Concerned Parents began to organize around improving their own local schools. They believed that white school principals and teachers and the white middle-class-controlled school board were insensitive to the needs of the local black communities. Whites could not be trusted to run individual schools in the best interests of the black pupils. Arguing that black teachers and principals exhibited more empathy for the plight of black children than did whites and acted as role models to black pupils, black parents no longer called for the transfer of experienced white teachers into black schools, but instead demanded the recruitment of more black teachers and principals. Black activists couched these demands for school improvements in terms of community control. White teachers, many living in communities other than where they taught and unable to build any rapport with black students or parents, came in for particular criticism. "We have too many educators who at 3:15 P.M. get in their autos and drive to the suburbs," Timuel Black declared. "They have no real kinship with the community and naturally the people feel hostile toward them. Furthermore, many of them believe that poor people are dumb and they don't get ahead because they don't want to get ahead."[61] Board of Education member Warren Bacon concurred. "The teachers do not have the attitude that all kids can learn. There is too much feeling that if a student has not learned, it is the fault of the student, not of the educational system." Patricia Smith, a student at Marshall High School, spoke of a teacher who told a black student with natural hair that "you're a dummy, you can't learn anything."[62]

While black parents continued to picket and boycott elementary schools complaining of overcrowding and inadequate facilities, increasingly the conflicts revolved around the removal of white principals from black schools. One of the first of these was in early 1966 when the Board of Education transferred the principal of Edward Jenner Elementary School, at Cabrini-Green on the near North Side, after the Concerned Parents of Jenner School staged a series of boycotts of the school.[63] In April 1967, Superintendent Redmond transferred the principal of Crispus Attucks Elementary School on the South Side after the parents demanded her removal. Often the black activists targeted the principals less for what they had done than because they were the most visible symbol of what the activists saw as the white power structure and the most vulnerable to pressure. A show of hands at a meeting of the Chicago Principals Club in March 1968 found that forty-two of those present had been threatened by local organizations.[64]

John Desmond and the CTU leadership aligned with the Board of Education and the white principals in these disputes, further angering many community activists. In March 1968, Eugene Richards, a white principal of Crown Elementary School on the city's West Side, claimed that three leaders of Concerned Parents of Crown had given him forty-eight hours to leave the school or else his safety could not be guaranteed. The group picketed the school and also called for the resignation of the white assistant principal, claiming the school was badly run and that the teachers beat the pupils. John Desmond and General Superintendent Redmond persuaded the principal to withdraw his transfer request.[65] Desmond claimed that "[t]he board of education must stand firm and not allow neighborhood pressure groups to control schools and threaten the lives of teachers and principals." After visiting the school and urging the principal to stay, Desmond argued, "If these tactics of harassment were successful at the Crown school, a series of similar charges would face principals and teachers throughout the west side."[66]

African American Teachers

Many black teachers were just as unsympathetic as white teachers to the demands of the radical black activists. Black teachers born and brought up in black middle-class neighborhoods of Chicago had achieved full-time certified status and were less likely to support school integration or teacher transfers. Many of them saw the new migrant students and FTBs from the southern states as unsophisticated, and they had less sympathy for those in the civil rights movement who suggested that racial discrimination and segregation caused black underachievement. As sociologist Franklin Frazier noted in the 1950s, "today many Negro teachers refuse identification with the Negro masses and look upon teaching primarily as a source of income. In many cases they have nothing but contempt for their Negro pupils."[67] Rather than support the militant methods of the students and black activists, they favored accommodating rather than antagonizing employers and politicians.[68]

Community control proved less than popular among some black teachers. "If, with radical groups, a teacher can be dismissed with any whim, then it could happen to anyone that the group doesn't like," an African American teacher feared. "In having black control, will the blacks set standards, determine subject matters, pay salaries, maintain schools, provide for supplies etc.? Do we trade slavery by whites for slavery by blacks?"[69] African American elementary school teacher Tommie Martin feared that if parents obtained more power to remove teachers, teachers may lose their job after an altercation with an unruly student. Martin also worried that it would take autonomy away from the professionals and give too much power to parents with neither the time nor the expertise to make major educational decisions such as choosing textbooks or selecting principals. "The teachers and the principals are the people who are trained to choose these textbooks and things," Martin asserted. The parents didn't "have any training or know anything about these textbooks, the budget and all this stuff. . . . Most of the parents who had jobs didn't have the time. . . . I don't know how they could choose a principal."[70]

Nevertheless, many black teachers joined with those black community activists who demanded fundamental change in the public education system. African American teachers believed in the potential of black children and promoted pride among black students. In November 1967, parents led a two-week student boycott after white principal Thomas Van Dam of all black Englewood High School transferred FTB black history teacher Owen Lawson because of "administrative incompetence." Parents and students claimed the principal dismissed Lawson because he emphasized black nationalist history in his classes and in lectures he delivered at the school's Afro-American history club. Whereas some students attended the "liberation schools" held at the local Methodist church, others picketed the principal's suburban home, demanding his resignation and Lawson's reinstatement.[71] Students from the

Afro-American Organization of Parker School, with the support of Concerned Teachers, staged walkouts in March and April 1968 demanding better school facilities, black studies in the curriculum, and a black principal.[72]

In addition to campaigning for better schools, in the late 1960s black schoolteachers, like other rank-and-file black workers across the nation, challenged the discriminatory practices of their white-controlled unions. To remove unsympathetic union leaders or to gain a say in the union, black workers set up national black caucuses in unions such as the United Steelworkers of America and the UAW. Others argued for all-black unions, and small independent black labor organizations emerged in the building trades and the care industry.[73] Still others saw all unions as bastions of white power that acted in their own self-interest. They argued that black workers should leave unions and set up "worker-community alliances" in which black workers would help to improve the services and lives of all black people.[74]

In Chicago, a number of newly formed teacher organizations sought to pressure the CTU to campaign on behalf of black teachers and the black schools. The Black Teachers Caucus (BTC), formed in 1966, was a black nationalist organization that tried to influence the policies of the CTU from within. Its leader, Bobby Wright, an elementary teacher at the South Side Bousfield School, was born in Alabama in 1934 and like many of his generation migrated to Chicago in the mid-1950s. Wright worked as a Chicago Transit Authority bus driver and a truant officer for the Board of Education at Crane school before becoming a certified elementary school teacher in January 1967. A friend described him as "fire and energy, thoroughly original, possessor of a monumental mind in a sea of lobotomized small thinkers."[75] Wright, a CTU delegate, gathered around him a group of other young black men, many of whom also had experiences of the civil rights movement in the South. The BTC organized independently of whites and opened membership to black teachers only."[76] In the 1968 CTU elections, the BTC called on black teachers to vote for black candidates regardless of the groups they represented.[77]

The BTC campaigned for improvements in the education of black students and the welfare of black teachers. They wanted more facilities and programs and smaller classes in black schools.[78] The BTC wanted the union to campaign for the inclusion of more blacks on the Board of Education, more black principals, and more certified black teachers. The BTC further claimed that only black teachers should be employed in black schools. "Every white person who has a job in the Black schools is denying a Black person a job. We cannot afford this. Therefore, the liberal white principals and teachers will leave along with all the rest," claimed Bobby Wright. "If they really want to help then they should go into Gage Park and on the Northwest side and tell those racists they are in favor of Black Self-Determination." Finally, the BTC wanted the immediate certification of all FTBs.[79]

Unlike the New York City African-American Teachers Association (ATA), which left the UFT in 1967, the BTC remained a vibrant part of the CTU. For ideological reasons, the BTC believed in both organized labor and the power of black teachers to achieve quality public education. Leading BTC member Robert Mason argued that "[a]s a Black teacher I still believe that the ultimate solution for better schools and teacher-employer relations is in the Chicago Teachers Union, and I am firmly convinced that the ultimate salvation of the Chicago Public Schools is in the Black teacher. . . . As a Black teacher I love the Chicago Teachers Union enough to criticize it fundamentally."[80] The BTC urged blacks to join the union so they could influence its direction and believed that only a black union leadership would take the concerns of black members seriously.[81] Robert Mason argued that he expected the CTU "to bring about fundamental changes in Black schools and I expect this organization to press with vigor in all areas of teacher welfare."[82] With blacks constituting a third of the Chicago teaching force, the BTC hoped that the CTU would take notice of the black teachers' demands. In contrast, black teachers constituted less than 10 percent of teachers in New York and the ATA saw less chance of influencing the UFT.[83]

The BTC took the lead in many school and community disputes. Robert Mason claimed that black teachers and the black community must join together to provide quality education. "Neither teachers nor parents have the power to bring about such changes by themselves. TOGETHER THEY CANNOT FAIL."[84] The BTC also helped to organize the Concerned Parents groups in the schools and became involved in other issues in the community such as housing and welfare.[85] Black teachers, like white teachers, however, wanted autonomy in the classroom and saw themselves, not the parents, as experts in the education process. They therefore wanted black parents to play a secondary role to teachers in the campaign for quality education. As one leader of the BTC put it in 1968: "The parents don't want to set the curriculum and make educational policy; they want their kids to learn. There's nothing black parents want more than education and they'll always do whatever the teacher says is necessary."[86]

While claiming to fight for the concerns of the black community as a whole, the BTC privileged the concerns of black men and alienated many black women teachers. African American men teachers purposely built the organizations to be led and dominated by black men.[87] "We felt that . . . black men got to come to the forefront. Black women had carried the fight for all these years and we got to come to the forefront and assume our responsibilities," remembered BTC treasurer Grady Jordan. BTC leaders wanted to reclaim the manhood that they believed the Board of Education and the CTU denied black teachers and black students. "Black children are now going to walk in dignity in affirmation of the manhood and selfhood of the entire Black race," declared BTC leader Robert Mason.[88] To restore their "manhood," blacks should stand up for their rights, be defiant and not servile, maintain pride in themselves, oppose paternalism, and become self-reliant. Additionally, however, BTC leaders believed that black men had to gain independence from women and reassert their authority. In order to attain "manhood," men had to be put into positions of power in the public school administration and in the union.[89]

The resentment of African American male teachers partly stemmed from the lack of status and social mobility that the teaching profession had promised but had not delivered. With openings in nursing, clerical, library, and social work, college-educated black women had more opportunities than college-educated black men in obtaining other professional jobs. As the black high school population increased after the Second World War, the Board of Education employed more black men, but fewer black men than black women passed the teachers certification or principals' exams. Because the board operated few black high schools in Chicago and high school teachers were disproportionately male, school administrators needed fewer black male teachers and principals. Examiners further considered black males troublesome and threatening, while they saw black women as more controllable and malleable.[90] The board appointed the first black woman as principal in Chicago in 1928, but they did not employ the first black male principal, Robert E. Lewis, until 1948, by which time six black women principals worked in the schools. By the 1960s, black women principals still out numbered men more than two to one.[91] Hence, black men teachers expressed anger that the certification exam prevented them from becoming certified teachers and principals and finally obtaining the upward social mobility they deserved.

But women could not be excluded from the BTC. One night as the group was meeting in Bobby Wright's basement, Mattie Hopkins, a teacher at Price Elementary School and member of the CTU house of representatives, "kicked the door open" and declared, "I hear you men are meeting down here and I'm coming in." Hopkins joined and became secretary of the group.[92] Hopkins, who was born in 1917 and received her degree from Tuskegee Institute in Alabama, taught in the southern states until 1951 and then in the Chicago schools from 1951 to her retirement in 1983. An Episcopalian and strong supporter of civil rights, she later became president of the Teachers Division of Operation Breadbasket.[93]

Other Chicago schoolteachers became active in Operation Breadbasket, formed in 1962 by the Southern Christian Leadership Conference in Atlanta to put "bread, money, and income into the baskets of black and poor people." The organization moved north to Chicago, led by Martin Luther King's aide Jesse Jackson, then a student at Chicago Theological Seminary. In 1967, King appointed Jackson the organization's national director. Initially, by calling for consumer boycotts, it sought to encourage companies to employ black workers, banks to give loans to black companies, and government to use black-owned businesses.[94] While the BTC was a new organization heavily influenced from the beginning by black nationalism, Operation Breadbasket remained a mainstream organization which evolved out of the earlier anti-Willis civil rights movement. After the decline of the CCCO, Operation Breadbasket replaced it as the main civil rights group in Chicago, mushrooming to incorporate a number of other issues affecting the black community and forming divisions for labor, ministers, teachers, and others. The Operation Breadbasket teacher division embraced about five hundred members and was led by high school history teacher Roy Stell, who sat on the CTU house of representatives, David Harrison, an elementary school teacher, and Harold Charles, a science teacher.[95]

The Teachers Committee for Quality Education (TCQE), led by civil rights activist Timuel Black, put further pressure on the CTU and the Board of Education. With five hundred members, the TCQE fought for FTB certification, a graduated state income tax to pay for education, and more black staff members in the public schools. Whereas the BTC espoused Black Power radicalism, the TCQE assumed a more moderate and reformist stance, appearing regularly before the Board of Education. In contrast to the BTC, the TCQE included white teachers and still held to the idea of integration as an ultimate goal. It believed that integration was not a necessary precondition for quality education, and for the moment Timuel Black fought for the improvement of black schools and proposed a central board of education and semiautonomous community boards to make day-to-day decisions. With the CTU unwilling to support the demands of black teachers, the TCQE used the courts and the Fair Employment Practices Commission to take up the cases of those FTBs who claimed discrimination in certification exams.[96]

Further pressure on the CTU leadership came from the Teachers Action

Committee (TAC), a caucus within the union. The TAC, formed toward the end of the Fewkes regime, initially concentrated on gaining collective bargaining rights for teachers and paid little attention to the problem of inner-city schools. Because of his active role in pushing for collective bargaining, the TAC candidate Charles Skibbens only narrowly lost to Desmond in the 1966 presidential elections. After the FTBs gained the right to vote in union elections, the TAC embraced the issue of the black teachers. To maintain the support of white teachers, the TAC remained opposed to a liberal teacher transfer policy. With its new position, the TAC embraced a large proportion of black members and younger white teachers who taught in black schools. All three main TAC candidates in the 1968 union elections worked in black schools. The TAC came to the position, under white elementary teacher John Kotsakis and African American Lester Davis of Highland High School, that the CTU should demand educational reform rather than aim for higher teacher salaries. Because the TAC was most concerned with gaining influence within the CTU, the organization made little effort to gain the support of the black community.[97]

The organizational focus of the new left white radicals was the Teachers for Radical Change in Education (TRCE), formed in early 1968 by Dick Kelly, a white substitute teacher at Hess Upper Grade Center. Other leaders were Heather Booth, wife of Paul Booth, former national secretary of the Students for a Democratic Society (SDS), and Ruth Shriman, member of the CTU house of representatives. TRCE was a militant group that wanted to unite all the teacher groups such as the BTC and the TAC and attracted old leftist activists such as Shirley Lens. They also supported student boycotts in the schools, black control of black schools, and immediate certification of FTBs. Many radical white teachers in the new left who believed in participatory democracy and became involved in the anti–Vietnam War and women's movement asked to be assigned to black schools. Most of its forty members taught in black schools, but others had no direct contact with the Chicago public schools. The TRCE wanted the CTU to concentrate its demands on educational issues and not on wage demands. It suggested that achieving equality education required fundamental change, not only in the union but in the larger society.[98]

As the young idealistic black teachers inspired by black nationalism clamored for the union to prioritize the issue of black schools and FTB certification, the 1968 contract confirmed to many that the union was more concerned with higher wages than with problems in the inner-city schools. In response to the demands of the black activists, the CTU requested an increase in the number of schools under the More Effective Schools (MES) program, reduction in class size in all schools, more teacher aides, and in-service training programs for teachers in inner-city schools. After the intervention of Mayor Daley averted a threatened strike that had been scheduled for early January, however, the union accepted a higher salary promise of $1,000 a year but with few of the other demands met. They gained some provisions, such as more teacher aides, workshops for inner-city teachers, and a pilot program for socially maladjusted students, but the agreement included few of their major requests for school improvements such as smaller class size or MES schools.[99] Most white teachers supported the stance of Desmond and the union leadership in prioritizing wages over educational improvements. Whereas Desmond narrowly won the 1966 union presidential election, in the spring of 1968, when TAC candidate Richard Holland ran against Desmond on the platform of support for inner-city schools, Desmond won by a two-to-one majority.[100]

FTB Strikes

Against this rising tide of black nationalism and union activism, the conflict between the union and the Board of Education on the one side and the black teachers and community activists on the other came to a head over the issue of FTB certification. While other school systems responded affirmatively to black disquiet over discriminatory teacher exams, the Chicago Board of Education refused to address the issue.[101] Even though blacks constituted more than 90 percent of the 5,500 FTBs employed by the Chicago public schools in April 1968, the Chicago Board of Education still refused to address the demands of the Concerned FTBs for automatic teacher certification after two years of work in the classroom. The union simply asked the Board of Education for salary adjustments for FTBs.[102]

At the same time, the arguments of the Concerned FTBs changed in response to heightened agitation in the black community. With black parents and students demanding more qualified black teachers in their schools, the Concerned FTBs made a special effort for the first time to gain the support of the black community. Concerned FTB leader James McQuirter argued that certification would make FTBs less transitory and help solve the problem of teacher turnover in black schools. Whether the tests proved discriminatory or not became less important to the Concerned FTBs than the fact that black teachers were doing the same jobs as white teachers for less pay. They argued that there seemed to be no correlation between test scores and teacher performance either in college or in the classroom. Failure in the Chicago exam did not result in being barred from teaching in the schools but only to teaching for less pay and benefits. By employing as FTBs those who had never taken or who had failed the certification exam, the Board of Education and the superintendent showed no confidence in the certification exams in determining the ability to teach. James McQuirter claimed that if the teachers who fail the exam "are good enough to stay in the system, they're good enough to get tenure." Now the Concerned FTBs claimed that not only was the oral part of the certification exam biased against black teachers, but the written exam was culturally biased against black candidates as well. According to McQuirter, the test makers based written exams on "white middle class values, so they automatically discriminate against blacks."[103]

There is much evidence to support the argument that the teachers' exams were biased against black teachers. White schoolteachers had an advantage because they had the same culture as those who designed and administered the teachers' exams. Even Morris Haimowitz, director of human relations for the Board of Education, admitted that the teacher certification tests should be overhauled because they "contain cultural elements that favor white teachers."[104] A study undertaken in 1973 confirmed the cultural bias of the written part of the National Teacher Examination. The researchers found that in the traditional test whites performed better but in another test with different questions blacks achieved higher results. They concluded that "whatever else this test may measure it has the potential of measuring a candidate's racial background with considerable accuracy."[105]

While black FTBs complained about the racism of the teacher certification exam, other teachers, both black and white, argued that the teacher exams, and the written part of the teacher certification exam in particular, were a true and accurate measurement of ability. According to many teachers, quality of preparation and the inferior education of blacks in the South explained differences in scores between racial groups. Many white teachers expressed resentment because black FTBs tried to end a certification process that they found perfectly fair. Some believed that they had "had to bust their asses" to pass the teachers certification exams and now black teachers wanted teaching jobs without taking the exam.[106] Some black teachers who had passed the certification exam also expressed opposition to automatic certification. Older black teachers had gained teacher certification and a secure, well-paying job at a time when fewer opportunities existed for African Americans.[107] "But why should standards be lowered for these people when we are trying to help our children," complained one black teacher. "If an FTB doesn't pass the examination, possibly he isn't ready."[108]

Unable to persuade the Board of Education to change the certification process or the union to fight for its demands, the Concerned FTBs turned to strike action to pursue their demands. Although the CTU met with the Concerned FTB leaders and asked them not to strike and many FTBs were scared to speak out because they had no job security, the Concerned FTBs staged three "sick-ins" in November 1967 during which some 1,300 teachers stayed at home.[109] In mid-January 1968, the Concerned FTBs initiated a two-week strike demanding Chicago teaching certificates after two years of satisfactory service. Mayor Daley and the Board of Education claimed they sympathized with the FTBs' demands but insisted that only the Illinois General Assembly could change rules governing teachers' certification. The CTU opposed the strike, but it gained the support of large numbers of certified black teachers. The Concerned FTBs claimed that two thousand, about a third of the FTBs, stayed out.[110]

The strike ended without winning any immediate change in certification, but after discussions with CTU president John Desmond, school superintendent James Redmond tried to appease the FTBs. In February 1968, Redmond announced that a one-time special certification examination, which would not include an oral component, would be given in the spring for those who had been FTBs for one year and received a favorable recommendation from their principal. The Concerned FTBs rejected the compromise and called for a boycott of the exam, arguing that on principle FTBs should automatically receive certification and, in practice, principals would give black and militant FTBs unfavorable recommendations.[111] A number of teachers filed a class action suit against the Board of Education claiming they were denied equal benefits for equal work and performance in violation of their rights to the equal protection of the law under the Fourteenth Amendment. On May 1, 1968, Judge Herbert L. Will denied the injunction and the May 4 exam went ahead, with 2,381 teachers taking the exam and only 714, less than a third, passing.[112] McQuirter claimed that the exam, in which a majority of whites passed but a majority of blacks failed, was fixed. The board claimed the unwillingness of the black teachers to properly study for the exam and the poor training given in the southern colleges explained the poor showing of black teachers.[113] The black teachers accused the CTU of colluding with the Board of Education in letting so many black teachers fail the special exam. The union refused to represent FTBs who complained of discrimination during the exam, creating greater resentment among black teachers. In effect, "the Chicago Teachers Union is not concerned with black teachers and therefore black children and that the Union like the examinations is unfair and becoming increasingly irrelevant to the black community," wrote Timuel Black.[114] In recognition of their frustration, Jim McQuirter subsequently formed the United Educational Employees, a black union of all school employees, and told black teachers to leave the CTU.

Student Revolt

Some Chicago students turned to violence after the death of Martin Luther King, Jr., on April 4, 1968, in Memphis. In the wake of the assassination, rioting and looting erupted in 125 cities, including Washington, D.C., and forty-six people were left dead.[115] The violence spilled over into the classroom. In Chicago, black students fought with white students and walked out of schools the day after King's assassination. On the West Side, students gathered at Garfield Park, then moved out to West Madison Street, the main commercial center, and erupted into rioting and looting and soon into sniper attacks on police. The west side of the city was engulfed in flames, and the rioters destroyed more than twenty blocks of West Madison Street. More than two thousand National Guard troops quelled the rioting and Mayor Daley ordered the police to "shoot to kill" arsonists and "shoot to maim" looters. Some eleven people were killed.[116]

The Chicago Riot Study Committee showed that conditions in the schools contributed to the riotous behavior. On Friday April 5, 1968, the day after the King's assassination, teachers and students in traditional black schools such as Forrestville, DuSable, Wendell Phillips, and Dunbar Vocational conducted classes as normal. In contrast, the students from those schools undergoing racial change participated in the riot. After interviewing teachers and students, the report found that a communication gap between the mostly white teachers and black students was a major cause of the riots. The report concluded that "had the administrators and faculty of all the black high schools established the rapport with students which some black schools had, school operations probably would have been successful on Friday, April 5."[117] The report recommended that "improvement of schools and educational programs in the ghetto is necessary to prevent student participation in future riot situations."[118]

In the weeks after King's assassination, further conflict involving black parents, students, and teachers ensued. In May 1968, forty-nine black teachers walked out of DuSable Upper Grade Center because the principal, Galeta Kaar, had aimed a racial slur at black teachers.[119] In the same month, more than half the pupils of five schools in the Altgeld Gardens district on the far

South Side boycotted schools when parents and teachers protested the treatment of BTC member Granville Neal, a third grade teacher at Carver Primary whom the board had transferred to another school. Neal claimed that before his transfer his evaluation had dropped from excellent to unsatisfactory by the white principal after a dispute over what should be included in a memorial service for Martin Luther King, Jr.[120] The *Chicago Daily Defender* noted that "[t]he threat of a black teacher revolt, which is just now beginning to make rumbling noises appears to be city-wide."[121]

The alliance between students, teachers, and parents and the desire for community control of the schools came together at Farragut High School on the West Side. Farragut was in many ways typical of the problems of inner-city schools. In the 1960s the school enrollment, but not the school administration, quickly changed from predominantly white to predominantly black. In 1968, 92 percent of the students and 50 percent of the faculty were black, but the principal and four assistant principals were white. Built in 1892, the school suffered from poor lighting, plaster peeling from the walls, broken clocks, and boarded-up windows. According to black critics, many of the white teachers appeared distressed to find black youths who "couldn't read" and "didn't know how to act in a classroom." They did not believe the black students could be taught, so they asked for transfers, turned up late for class, went absent, or read the newspaper in the class while the students played games. Even those teachers who wanted to teach had outdated books and little equipment. The white principal, Joseph Carroll, allegedly stayed in the office all day and did not even know the teachers by name, while gangs roamed the hallways fighting with other gangs or demanding protection money from the students. Not surprisingly, with little education going on and students afraid of the violence, the student absenteeism rates rose to 40 percent per day.[122]

During the summer of 1968, Harold Charles, chair of the science department of Farragut and staff coordinator for Operation Breadbasket, set out to remodel the school with the help of black teachers, students, and parents. Charles, a teacher at Farragut since 1963, took the ideas of community control and cultural nationalism seriously. Like many black teachers, Charles migrated from the South and became active in the civil rights movement. He was involved in The Woodlawn Organization (TWO) and marched with Martin Luther King, Jr., when he came to Chicago. After King's assassination, Charles followed his non-violent strategy and helped organize Operation Breadbasket in Chicago. Deeply affected by the death of King and the riots that left the area surrounding the school in burned-out ruins, Charles set out to enlist the support of other teachers, students, and parents to give the students hope, the chance of a college education, and a pride in their black culture. Charles organized the black teachers into the Farragut Black Teachers Association and enlisted the support of parents by visiting them in their homes and drawing up a list of improvements that needed to be brought to the school.[123]

When the school reopened in September, parents and teachers at Farragut issued a six-page "black manifesto" containing fourteen demands and a timetable for their imposition. The manifesto called for the employment of a black assistant principal chosen by the faculty, the introduction of a black studies curriculum, displays of positive black images in the school, black-owned business products in the schools, the employment of more black staff members, and improvement of facilitates such as gymnasium, auditorium, and laboratory facilities.[124] To "flex their muscles," Charles and other supporters went from class to class and led students to evacuate the building like a fire drill. Virtually every student and teacher stood outside the school for forty-five minutes before returning to class. Although some white teachers opposed the demands, many supported them because they saw them as improving the lot of all the teachers.[125] They won their demands for the appointment of a black assistant principal, a black disciplinarian, and a black guidance counselor after they threatened a school boycott. With no movement on the other demands, in December the fifty-five black teachers and fifteen white teachers held a two-day teach-in on black culture in the auditorium to an overflow crowd of black students. In response, the principal agreed to incorporate black studies into the curriculum.[126]

The revolt at Farragut quickly spread to other schools in the city. In January 1968, a group of students at Harrison High School formed an organization called the New Breed and demanded that a black history class start in the fall of 1968. They also insisted upon the removal of the white principal, the employment of more black faculty members, and the establishment of an Afro-American club. On October 7, the black students walked out of the school in protest over the principal's refusal to discuss their grievances.[127] The following day, five hundred black students at Austin High School joined with five hundred students from Harrison and marched to the Board of Education office. The Austin students demanded a black principal, a black assistant principal, more black teachers, a black homecoming queen, and regular meetings with black students.[128] Subsequently, students across the city made written demands to principals calling for a black studies curriculum and more black teachers and black principals. For the rest of the month, students held impromptu assemblies, picketed police stations to demand the release of arrested students, marched outside schools, and engaged in sporadic walkouts.[129] On October 13, the Concerned Black Students of Chicago, representing thirteen schools, called for a city-wide boycott of high schools by black students to take place each Monday until the board met their demands. They demanded black control of black schools (with a black school board running the black schools), black history classes, black administrators, better school buildings, holidays to honor black heroes, and black businesses to supply black schools. On Monday, October 14, 28,000 students, more than half the black high school students in the city, boycotted the schools, and many marched on the Board of Education and City Hall.[130]

The Woodlawn Organization, the Chicago Urban League, Operation Breadbasket, TCQE, and BTC supported the school boycotts and urged teachers to participate. On Monday, October 21, more than seven hundred teachers and 20,000 students boycotted the schools, and four hundred teachers attended a rally sponsored by Operation Breadbasket to hear student leaders, James McQuirter, Bobby Wright, and Timuel Black while other teachers set up "liberation schools" on the day of the boycotts to teach the students. On October 29, nine thousand students boycotted classes, and on the first Monday in November, immediately before the presidential elections, police broke up a city-wide "sit in" and "sleep in" of students. School officials closed all public schools early.[131] When the new school year began, sit-ins and boycotts spread to Philadelphia, Boston, and Seattle.[132] By the end of the year, sit-ins and boycotts occurred in schools in Cincinnati, Washington, D.C., New Jersey, and New York.[133]

The city-wide boycotts came to an end when General Superintendent Redmond punished boycotters but made concessions to student demands. Redmond threatened students and parents with court action unless they returned to school, and he expelled some of the student leaders. At the same time, the board met with student and community leaders and made concessions on introducing a black studies curriculum and employing more black teachers. The board quickly approved the deployment of black teachers, principals, and assistant principals and the appointment of African American Manford Byrd to the newly created position of deputy superintendent of Chicago schools, the highest educational position held by a black in the nation. Redmond further appointed African American principal and former teacher Frank Gardner to the Board of Examiners to replace the white retiree James Smith. The organized city-wide revolt ended, but individual schools still erupted over the next few months as parents, students, and teachers protested against racist textbooks and white principals and demanded more black faculty members and a black studies curriculum.[134]

1969 CTU Strike

In late 1968, as the negotiations for the 1969 contract drew near, John Desmond and the CTU leadership sought to appease the majority white teachers who wanted the union to prioritize pay in negotiations and oppose plans to curtail transfer rights. Teachers at Kelvyn Park High School and Lane Technical School, both schools with a largely white teaching force, petitioned Desmond to demand higher pay.[135] Student and community unrest created even deeper resentment among white teachers who complained about violence in the schools and that the board transferred some white teachers and principals on the demands of black students. There was animosity between black and white teachers after the student unrest and teachers appeared "ill at ease with each other."[136]

At the same time, the CTU came under great pressure from organized black teachers to concentrate on educational improvements in the negotiations with the board. With the achievement of collective bargaining, the CTU became a junior partner in the administration of the schools, and it could no longer distance itself from the policies of the Board of Education. In August 1968, the board announced it did not have enough money to fulfill all the provisions of the 1968 agreement negotiated with the CTU the previous January. With CTU leadership approval, the board cut back the few union-negotiated educational programs that could have improved conditions in the inner-city schools. The $60 per month pay raise negotiated by the union to start in September ($40 per month had already been paid) remained, but the board rescinded the promise to cut class sizes in the inner-city schools by hiring more teachers and teacher aides. The programs for socially maladjusted children, in-service training programs for the inner-city teachers, and free periods for elementary school teachers were reduced.[137] In response to the cutbacks and in the midst of a strike by mostly white New York City teachers against the Puerto Rican– and African American–controlled Ocean Hill–Brownsville school board, the BTC called for black teachers not to renew their CTU membership. "We have to admit that Whitey plans and fights very well, but our time is coming and we are going to be just as vicious and unmerciful," it declared. "Chicago is going to make New York's school problems look like a Sunday school picnic."[138] In light of these developments, John Kotsakis and the TAC insisted that the new contract negotiations should concentrate on educational improvements rather than teachers' pay. They called for the reinstatement of programs cut from the 1968 budget, a maximum class size of twenty-five, a daily preparation period, and abolition of the teacher certification policy.[139]

John Desmond responded to the pressure by announcing that educational improvements would gain priority over pay rises in the 1969 contract negotiations. The union called for the full implementation of the 1968 agreement that had been curtailed in August 1968, the elimination of the oral exam for certification of FTBs, reduction in class size, and additional employment of teacher aides.[140] In early January 1969, Desmond reached an agreement with the Board of Education that entailed no pay raise but included implementation of the 1968 contract, smaller class sizes, a pilot program for three inner-city schools, and the hiring of more substitute teachers. Even though the editor of the *Chicago Sun-Times* called for "overhauling an unfair and antiquated system" of teacher certification, the Board of Education announced it would only consider eliminating the oral exam for certification.[141]

The union contract appealed to neither the militants, who were disgusted that the union had not pushed hard enough for FTB certification or for improvements in the inner-city schools, nor to the white membership, who wanted a salary increase. Concerned FTBs, Operation Breadbasket, BTC, and TCQE all announced they would not strike with the "racist" union. The *Chicago Daily Defender,* the main black community paper in Chicago, backed the stance of the black teachers against the "injudicious unconscionable racial policy" of the CTU.[142] At the unions' contract ratification meeting, Desmond recommended approval of the board's offer while the TAC called for its rejection because there were insufficient educational improvements in the contract. Operation Breadbasket's Roy Stell and about seventy-five other black teachers walked out of the mass meeting.[143] Subsequently, the meeting voted 1,368 to 1,148 to reject the settlement and to strike. With fewer than three thousand out of a membership of 19,000 voting, Desmond decried, "We fought for educational improvements this year, and the teachers who should have cared didn't even bother to come and vote." This confirmed to Desmond that most teachers only cared about money. "We emphasized throughout negotiations that our members wanted some money in their pockets," but the board wouldn't listen.[144] After the membership refused to accept the agreement, the board offered the union a little more on educational improvements, but no further increase in pay. Desmond accepted an interim six-month contract. Against the advice of the TAC and the black teacher groups, who still argued that Desmond had not negotiated sufficient educational improvements, the membership accepted the contract by a vote of 9,622 to 5,206.[145]

In the spring of 1969, the threat of a teachers' strike resurfaced again as a financial crisis threatened school funding and put into jeopardy the union-negotiated 1969 contract. In a statement to the School Problems Commission (SPC) of the Illinois legislature on January 24 1969, James Redmond decried the board and legislature as "inheriting a state's accumulation of neglect of the financing of its school system."[146] Redmond and Desmond asked that state aid to Chicago schools be doubled from $400 per student to $800 per student just to pay for the contract they had negotiated. After a recommendation from the SPC, on April 2, 1969, Governor Richard Ogilvie announced that the state's school budget would only be increased from $400 to $500. As a result, the Board $28 was million short of covering the negotiated contract, and General Superintendent Redmond announced that the board would have to discharge an estimated seven thousand teachers, increase class size and teaching load, and make other educational cutbacks unless they received more money from the state legislature.[147]

The CTU sought more money from Springfield to pay for their demands and started a campaign based around the Save Our Schools slogan. On April 22, 1969, nearly ten thousand CTU members marched in the Loop calling for greater school funds, and in early May, two thousand union members descended on Springfield demanding more money from the state. Black teacher groups refused to join the campaign because they did not believe it was worth demanding more financing for a racist school system in which black schools did not get an equal share of the money. With the six-month interim agreement running out, the union asked the Chicago Board of Education to pay for full implementation of the 1968 agreement and the 1969 interim agreement, no layoffs, a $150 monthly wage increase starting in September 1969, and FTB certification after two years of service. A strike date of May 22 was set unless the board agreed to the demands. The membership voted in early May 10,944 to 5,438 to strike.[148]

The discussion of a strike occurred as the schools in the black inner-city areas exploded again. In April 1969, two hundred students walked out of Lindblom High School demanding more black faculty members and an extended African American history program.[149] In early May, the white principal of Englewood High School was transferred and replaced with a black principal after students sat down in the principal's office, smashed windows, and fought with police, demanding his removal.[150] Other parents picketed to demand new school buildings. In March 1969, the Organization for the

Southwest Community organized a student boycott of twelve schools to protest overcrowded and underfunded schools. While thousands of students stayed at home, more than a thousand parents attended a "probe-in" in their place in which they talked to teachers and janitors and surveyed the poor conditions in the schools.[151] Parents organized a week-long boycott of Vincennes Elementary School on the South Side protesting the conditions in the overcrowded school, which was built in 1892 and which the Building Department had characterized as "unsuitable for institutional use."[152] Fighting between white and black students erupted at Tilden High School and Gage Park High School and spread into the neighborhood as hundreds of students fought each other and the police on the southwest side.[153] On April 3, 1969, the day before the anniversary of Martin Luther King's assassination, unrest spread through the schools and into the black neighborhoods on the West Side and near North Side. Governor Ogilvie called out more than five thousand National Guard troops at the request of Mayor Daley, and during the day, 89 people suffered injuries and 263 were arrested.[154] After more student violence broke out on Malcolm X's birthday, the *Chicago Daily Defender* commented, "Practically every public high school in a predominantly white community with an increasingly large black enrollment has had incidents of racial violence since school started in September."[155]

With no movement from the Board of Education or the legislature in Springfield to pay for the salary increase or the improvements in the schools, on May 22 and May 23, 1969, the CTU undertook its first official strike. More than three-quarters of the teachers supported the union and many turned up at the schools to convince their wavering colleagues to strike. Many striking teachers held classes for their students in makeshift tents outside the schools, at the YMCA and the Chicago Boys Club. Some parents joined the picket lines and others opened their homes and served coffee and snacks to the pickets.[156] Just like their white colleagues, many black teachers, even if reluctantly, supported the union. At DuSable High School on the South Side, where black teachers made up 80 percent of the faculty and which had traditionally been a union stronghold, the teachers narrowly voted against the strike but only about a third crossed the picket line.[157] Many of these African American teachers had been active in the union for years and believed it was their duty to support it. One black female teacher recalled, "I just went along with the program, stuck with them."[158]

On balance, black teachers who supported the union did so more for educational improvements than did their white counterparts. With most black teachers working in the inner-city schools and white teachers located in the far north and south of the city, the *Chicago Sun-Times* reporter noted on his tour of the union picket lines that "salary increases were most important to striking teachers in the outlying areas of Chicago."[159] One black teacher claimed she supported the strike because "of the issues that were involved namely I felt that the black teachers were not being treated fairly . . . the FTB issue was one that had to be resolved." Striking was "the one way of accomplishing the issues that had to change."[160] Other black teachers walked out because they saw the need for both educational improvements and improved salaries for teachers. We "want better salaries, but we also want better conditions in the schools too, for us and the students," claimed one teacher at Bogan High School.[161] Mamie Till Mobley joined the strike because she "agreed with the issues that were on the table such as class size and salary. In unity there is strength," she concluded.[162]

It is clear, however, that many black teachers, and the communities they came from, refused to support the striking union. While overall only about 23.7 percent of schoolteachers crossed the picket lines, approximately 45 percent of the black teachers reported for work.[163] Particularly in the black neighborhoods on the south and west sides of the city, many schoolteachers refused to strike. Forty percent of elementary teachers in the thirteen "black" school districts worked during the strike, while just 13.3 percent in the fourteen "white" districts reported for work.[164] At Englewood High School, 95 percent of all teachers attended school, 60.9 percent at Kenwood High School, 50 percent at Forrestville and Calumet High Schools, and 48 percent at Hyde Park High School. On the West Side, Marshall High School saw 48 percent teacher attendance and 46.2 percent at Carver.[165] The specter of the Ocean Hill–Brownsville dispute of the previous fall haunted teachers from the black community and hung over the Chicago strike. In the minds of many in the black community, the teachers were privileged and powerful interests, striking at the expense of the weak and less fortunate, and in these black communities, teachers were under the most pressure to cross the picket lines.

Other black teachers proved more reluctant to follow the CTU because they either disapproved of labor unions or striking against black students. The discriminatory and exclusionary stance of building trades and apprenticeship programs in AFL unions and the inaction of many local labor organizations over civil rights convinced many African Americans that unions were part of the white establishment that denied them equal rights. A nationwide survey by *Newsweek* magazine taken in 1963 found that blacks in the North considered labor unions the second "most harmful" institution to the rights of blacks behind real estate companies.[166] Some black nationalist teachers, such as Harold Charles, staff coordinator for Operation Breadbasket and teacher at Farragut High School, never joined the CTU, which he saw as part of a racist establishment which supported white teachers but cared little about the black community. Charles declared, "We will defy the board of education and the union to educate our children."[167] Barbara Sizemore, a CTU member before she became a principal in the Chicago public schools, proclaimed she would never strike against the children.[168] Other black teachers, especially the low paid FTBs, claimed they did not have the funds for a sustained strike. Operation Breadbasket's David Harrison suggested that a poll of black teachers found that "most black teachers couldn't economically afford any strike."[169]

Other black teachers who had supported the union for years, like Roy Stell, felt they could not support the CTU at this time. The Teachers Committee for Quality Education, the Black Teachers Caucus, Operation Breadbasket, and the Concerned FTBs all opposed the strike and told black teachers to keep the predominantly black schools open in defiance of the union. They suggested that Desmond and the union had let the black community down by not supporting the FTB strike, the student boycotts of the fall of 1968, or the demands for black control of black schools. The Concerned FTBs struck in the winter of 1967–68 but refused to do so at this time. These teachers did not believe they supported the board over the union but sided with their own community. For Grady Jordan of the BTC, the "primary commitment was to the black community not the union. . . . I'm a member of the teachers union by choice. I'm a member of the black community by birth. I was born into it and I will die in it. So that was my first commitment."[170] Many black teachers boycotted the strike but hoped their stance would change the policies of the union. "We are not against unionism," said Operation Breadbasket's David Harrison, "but we cannot support the CTU in this strike since the union has been racist in dealing with problems of the black community."[171] A group of thirty-four working teachers at Dvorak Elementary School on the West Side asserted in a letter to the *Chicago Sun-Times* that they reported for work because they did not want to let their students down. They claimed that they would not strike at this time because they cared more about the black students' education than they did about gaining higher pay for teachers. "We need more programs, more aides and other educational improvements in the inner city schools—a raise in salary is not our priority."[172]

Even while the CTU was negotiating with the Board of Education to end the strike, many black teachers began to call for their own union. Leaders of Operation Breadbasket urged black workers to leave their unions and set up their own organizations. Roy Stell surveyed seven thousand black teachers about forming an all-black breakaway union of teachers, administrators, tradesmen, and clerical workers when the CTU dues period ended in August 1969. The coalition of groups wanted new procedures for hiring and promotion of black teachers and administrative personnel, hiring of more black tradesmen in black schools, and use of black products and services in black schools.[173]

After Governor Ogilvie agreed to give more funds to Chicago public schools in return for Mayor Daley's support for legislation in the state capital in Springfield, Daley mediated a settlement whereby all the demands of the CTU were met. The teachers' union gained a $100 monthly raise for teachers, the recruitment of 750 new teachers to be assigned to the overcrowded segregated schools, and the reduction of class size. In response to the threat of a permanent split, the CTU prodded the board and Mayor Daley to give in to the demands of the Concerned FTBs. Desmond and the board agreed that after three years of satisfactory service the FTBs would gain Chicago certification without an exam.[174] Over the weekend of May 24 and 25, the union membership voted 9,776 to 523 to accept the agreement and returned to work on Monday.[175]

Consequences of the May 1969 Strike

Faced with a divided union at best and a breakaway union at worst, the CTU leadership changed its orientation after the strike. The CTU purposely avoided inflammatory rhetoric and did not try to discipline strikebreakers. The agreement, which concluded the FTB issue and included school improvements, forestalled the breakaway union.[176] The BTC broke up in 1970 and the Concerned FTBs disbanded after its demands had been met. In the next union strike in January 1971, the union opposed teacher layoffs and called for more movement on educational improvements. The CTU won the four-day strike, and included in the contract were higher pay, more teacher aides, more movement on class size, and Martin Luther King, Jr.'s birthday as a designated school holiday. Approximately 90 percent of black teachers supported the strike in January 1971 and the differences in support between black and white teachers were less pronounced, with only 10.6 percent from the black districts working and 6.4 percent from the white districts.[177] The CTU leadership put more black teachers on election slates and in positions of power too. Jacqueline B. Vaughn, who served as vice president from 1972 following a term as recording secretary and negotiator for the CTU, replaced Robert Healey as CTU president in 1984, the first African American, woman, and elementary school teacher to hold the post. Vaughn served as CTU president until her death from cancer in 1994.

Subsequent to the strike, the Chicago Board of Education also responded to the militancy of black community activists and the demands of the union. The Chicago Board of Education introduced new special education programs for needy students, but the most dramatic change came in curriculum. In the late 1960s and early 1970s, the Chicago Board of Education and others across the country introduced new classes that focused on the African American experience and included black authors in the English curriculum. As author Jonathan Zimmerman suggested, "black students effected one of the most remarkable transformations of the public school curriculum in the twentieth century."[178] The Chicago Board of Education employed more black teachers and administrators. With a new performance-based principal's examination first undertaken in 1970, nearly half (73) of the 150 successful candidates were black, and more blacks passed this exam than all previous exams combined. In the previous exam of November 1967, 62 of those who passed were white and only 17 were non-white.[179] At the beginning of the school year in 1968, 33.9 percent of the 24,000 Chicago public school teachers, 25 percent of the assistant principals, 6 percent of the principals, two of the eight assistant superintendents, and 18 percent of the district superintendents were African American.[180] By September 1972, black employment had increased to 37.7 percent of the 26,000 teachers, 39 percent of the assistant principals, 17.5 percent of the principals, 33.3 percent of the assistant superintendents, and 29.3 percent of the district superintendents.[181] Mattie Hopkins, one of the leaders of the BTC, became a member of the Board of Education, while another BTC leader, Grady Jordan, became high school district superintendent in the Chicago public schools.[182] In 1980, Ruth Love became the first black superintendent of the Chicago public schools.

Conclusion

The significance of the events in late 1960s Chicago is that for the first time since the 1930s a large section of public school teachers, parents, and students entered into a campaign to improve the quality of public education. In contrast to the 1930s, however, teachers were now divided along racial lines. The majority of African American teachers working as FTBs wanted equal pay and status with full-time white teachers, but many also sought reform of the school system. Consequently, black teachers and their students within the inner-city schools tended to support educational improvements and community alliances, while most white teachers advocated spending the available money on higher wages. Because of the inability of the union to address issues connected with the black schools, many African American teachers refused to support the CTU when the union organized its first-ever strike in May 1969.

There were many problems with the rhetoric and practices of the Black Power movement as it related to the public schools. Many competent white teachers and principals were forced out of black schools, which induced resentment and further divisions along racial lines. Immediate certification of all FTBs probably meant some underperforming teachers gained full-time jobs in the schools. White teachers were accused of racism because they wanted to maintain the right to transfer even though many simply wanted to teach in schools with better working conditions. Yet as the case of Chicago illustrates, black teachers initiated some major changes in public education. While Black Power had dissipated by the mid-1970s, the fact that black teachers have gained a degree of equality with white teachers, more black principals and administrators work in the schools, students study courses in African American history and literature, and teachers' unions adopt the concerns of black teachers remains a legacy of this turbulent era.

Conclusion

Public school teachers in Chicago have a long tradition of labor organization dating back to 1902 when the Chicago Teachers Federation (CTF) allied with the Chicago Federation of Labor (CFL). When the CTF disaffiliated from organized labor, rival teacher unions remained attached to the CFL into the 1930s. With public school teachers facing payless paydays and the school system under attack by business elites and corrupt politicians, teachers pressured their weak and divided union leaders to form a united teachers' organization in 1937. Although the largest and most influential teachers' union in the country until the rise of the New York local in the 1960s, the CTU had to wait until 1966 to gain collective bargaining rights and until 1969 to engage in its first strike.

The actions of Chicago public school teachers call into question the role of professionalism in hindering teachers' militancy and unionization. In the early years of the century, school boards nationwide raised educational credentials for teachers and suggested that teachers should exhibit a commitment to serving the public and the school administration. Most public school teachers, however, believed that their expertise and training meant they should be given more control over their work in the classroom and be consulted about school policy, and that they deserved higher pay and greater public respect. As Martin Lawn found in his study of the British National Union of Teachers, "'Professionalism' was a particular term used by teachers to symbolize their attempts to define and control their work and was part and parcel of their opposition to employer control—over pay, tenure, cheap unskilled teachers and compulsory overtime."[1] Public school teachers wanted to improve their professional status through unionization, and as events in Chicago show, they were more open to unions than scholars of teacher unionism assume.

The formation of the CTU was a direct result of the deprivations of the Great Depression, but the strength of the city's labor movement through-out the early twentieth century helps to explain both the emergence of the CTU and its ability to persist while so many other teacher unions elsewhere collapsed. Teachers were often either born into families with traditions of unionism or had neighbors and friends who engaged in union activities, and they lived in a city where labor unions enjoyed legitimacy and political influence. The progressive quality of much of the early labor movement and its connections to the strong middle-class reform movements further nur-tured the activities of teachers like Margaret Haley. The accomplishments of Chicago's private sector unions convinced teachers that they too must resort to the strategy of traditional union practices. A strong labor movement in Chicago through the 1960s supported and fostered the successful campaign for collective bargaining.

Another major finding is that while bread-and-butter demands proved a constant commitment of all Chicago public school teachers, reform of the school system remained a continuous demand of many teachers. The first secretary of the CTU, Kermit Eby, and his supporters wanted to democratize the school system and urged teachers to play a major role in the political life of the city. Under the economic strains of the 1930s and the political impulses of progressive education and New Deal liberalism, many Chicago teachers also sought to introduce a more progressive liberal curriculum and end political and business control of the schools. In the 1950s, even under the relentless pressure of the red scare, some teachers fought the imposition of loyalty oaths and restrictions in the curriculum. No longer cowed by McCarthyism, radical teachers aligned with the civil rights movement and campaigned for collective bargaining in the early 1960s, and, under the influence of black nationalism, many teachers called for improvements in the black schools.

Race and gender influenced attitudes toward reform. The major distinction between the reform efforts of the early years of the century and the turbulent decade of the 1960s was that race rather than gender was a major impetus behind reform. In the years before the formation of the CTU, there was a dis-cernible difference in the policies and practices of male teachers, who focused more attention on pay and benefits, and female teachers, who concentrated greater energy on reform issues. In the 1930s teachers like Lillian Herstein and Mary Herrick carried this tradition into the new union. This difference between economic self-interest and reform took on racial overtones in the 1960s as the CTU leadership faced increasing opposition from black teachers, parents, and students. By the 1960s, black teachers were more concerned than white teachers with the problems of the African American community and prodded the union toward reform of the school system, while most, but not all, white teachers wanted the union to maintain its emphasis on gaining higher salaries for its members.

This study emphasizes the significance of race in the working lives of teachers and in teacher unionism. The second Great Migration of African Americans into racially segregated Chicago led to overcrowding and inequality in the public schools. It also ignited a civil rights movement that pressured Chicago teachers, the CTU, and local politicians to align with the struggle for racial equality. Both the white union leadership and white rank-and-file saw the civil rights movement and school integration as threats to teachers' classroom autonomy and working conditions. At the same time, deteriorating conditions in many schools contributed to the campaign for collective bargaining. With the civil rights movement pressuring Mayor Daley to improve conditions for African Americans in Chicago, the mayor ordered his supporters on the Board of Education to accede to the teachers' demands.

The influence of the civil rights movement on the campaign for collective bargaining in the 1960s has been ignored or misinterpreted by scholars. Most commentators have either seen little connection between these two campaigns or have, in some tenuous and undefined way, seen the civil rights movement as a direct inspiration for public school teachers to demand collective bargaining. The civil rights movement's willingness to break the law made civil disobedience acceptable and legitimized its use for public school teachers. The AFT undoubtedly had teachers who felt inspired by the civil rights struggle, but as this study suggests, the major connections between the schoolteachers and the civil rights movement concerned the threat the movement posed to teachers' working conditions and the influence it had on Mayor Daley's decision to accede to the teachers' demands.

Black public school teachers faced discrimination within the school system and the union. As African American teachers entered the Chicago school system, the Board of Education confined them to underfunded and overcrowded segregated schools and restricted their promotion prospects. As the number of black teachers increased dramatically in the postwar years, the board employed them as FTBs on less pay and fewer benefits than white teachers. Civil rights activists and black teachers demanded an end to racial discrimination and the right of black teachers to teach in any school they wanted. By the 1960s, the union leadership and the majority white membership were unconcerned with the black teachers' problems. Because of the unions' stance on racial issues, a gulf opened up between the union and the African American teachers, which was finally resolved with the union's adoption of many of the black teachers' demands.

The racial transformation of the schools is one of the major changes in public education. The school system today shows a greater commitment to multiculturalism and the number of non-white teachers and administrators in the Chicago public schools has increased dramatically. In 2002–03, only 31.7 percent of the 587 principals and 45.7 percent of the 26,548 teachers in the Chicago public schools were white.[2] At the same time, the student body has continued its racial transformation. As a 1980 federal desegregation case compelled integration of the Chicago schools, white families continued their flight to the suburbs and more Latinos moved into the city. In September 2004, only 8.8 percent of the 426,812 enrolled students in the Chicago public schools were white, 49.8 percent were black, and 38.0 percent were Latino.[3]

In addition to influencing attitudes toward reform, the study shows that gender crucially influenced other aspects of the occupation of teaching. At the beginning of the century, teachers were divided between men and women locals that reflected unequal pay between female elementary teachers and high school teachers. From 1937 to 1970, Chicago public school teachers were mostly female and the CTU's elected officials, if not the president, reflected this picture. Even though many men high school teachers were unwilling to accept equality, the union since its inception demanded equal pay for women elementary school teachers with high school teachers and defended the right of married teachers to teach. In the 1940s, female elementary school teachers prodded the CTU to successfully campaign for a single salary schedule for all Chicago public school teachers. Although some historians have characterized the union militancy of the 1960s as male-driven, women elementary school teachers played a major role in the campaign for collective bargaining rights.

Chicago paved the way for teacher unionism, but the trajectory of the CTU was not atypical of teacher unions in the twentieth century. Earlier in the century, teacher unions including the CTF had no legal right to bargain or strike, so they adopted different strategies to satisfy their demands, joining with local labor federations, building alliances with middle-class reform groups and community organizations, lobbying politicians, using the legal system, and petitioning the Board of Education. In the 1940s and 1950s, teacher unions moved away from a professional model of unions and sought traditional gains such as higher salaries and better benefits and working conditions through the adoption of a state collective bargaining law. Opposition to public sector bargaining receded as private sector unions gained legitimacy from politicians, employers, and the general public. In the 1960s and 1970s, teachers in Chicago and elsewhere prodded boards of education to grant collective bargaining rights, and their unions negotiated their first binding contracts. From the time the unions negotiated their first contracts, public school teachers eschewed the professional union model of teacher unionism and adopted traditional trade union militancy, which emphasized strikes and collective bargaining to pursue their demands.

The events in Chicago contribute to debates about the role of the law in encouraging public sector unions. Many labor and industrial relations experts have argued that changes in labor laws explain the rise in teacher militancy and growth in public sector collective bargaining contracts during the 1960s.[4] In Illinois, however, there were no changes in public sector laws that could have directly encouraged militancy or collective bargaining. Instead, as other scholars suggest, changes in the attitudes of public sector workers who voiced dissatisfaction with their careers was the chief cause of teacher militancy.[5]

The story of the CTU highlights the enormous opposition schoolteachers faced in their attempt to improve the pay, status, and working conditions of teachers and the quality of the public school system. Earlier in the century, politicians, school authorities, and the general public considered public sector bargaining and industrial action by government workers as undemocratic. At times, the union faced opposition from powerful politicians who used the schools as sources of patronage and from conservative and business groups who often sought to restrict the funding and content of public education. Taxpayers, many of whom were property owners and sent their children to parochial schools, were often unwilling to support higher taxes for public education. The CFL, with many of its affiliates protected by the political machine, gave less than full support to the teachers' cause. Finally the teachers, reluctant to strike or become involved in electoral politics, and CTU leaders, too often willing to compromise with those in power, further limited the success of the union.

Even though the Chicago public school teachers confronted many obstacles, they helped to change the city's education system. Through its close relationship with Chicago civic organizations, the CTU was able to curb some of the excesses of the Kelly-Nash political machine in the 1930s and partly influence the allocation of public education funding, the school curriculum, and teachers' salaries. During the Second World War, the union played its part in the home front, aiding in the defeat of fascism and helping to introduce a single salary schedule for all Chicago public school teachers by accommodating the Board of Education. In subsequent years, the CTU protected non-communist teachers and limited the attacks on academic freedom from McCarthyite witch hunters. Pressure from militant teachers in the 1960s prodded the union to campaign successfully for collective bargaining rights and go some way in meeting the demands of activists in the black community.

Examining public education and teacher unions in historical perspective helps put the problems faced by today's teachers into context. Some argue that U.S. public education had a golden era before teachers gained collective bargaining rights in the 1960s. In reality, before teacher unions bargained with school boards, schools were often controlled by self-serving politicians and business elites, and teachers' working lives were heavily circumscribed by administrators. Teachers enjoyed less control over what and how they taught and labored in overcrowded classrooms. They had no medical insurance or paid vacations, inadequate sick leave, and their pay was dependent on the whims of politicians. Public school teachers faced wage cuts and payless paydays during the Depression, and in the postwar era they endured smaller salaries and fewer benefits than unionized private sector workers. Women and black teachers had less pay and fewer promotion prospects than their white male counterparts.

Because of the adoption of collective bargaining, the working lives of public school teachers have been transformed. Paid vacations, health insurance, smaller class sizes, accumulated sick leave, and paid sabbaticals are now standard for teachers across the country. Collective bargaining has meant that teachers can no longer be arbitrarily made to conform to the dictates of board of educations or machine politicians. The board of education is now unable to simply inform the teachers of their pay and conditions of employment without input from the teachers, but instead has to enter into negotiations with their unions. A formal grievance procedure also allows teachers to deal more equally with principals and school administrators. Through an elaborate performance evaluation and appeal procedure, it is much more difficult to dismiss teachers and therefore their job security has increased.[6]

If the working lives of American schoolteachers have improved, they have been unable to overcome the persistent problem of public school funding. The Illinois legislature provides few resources for public education, which means the Chicago public school system is still overwhelmingly funded by a local property tax. Teacher unions have made few concerted attempts and had little success in persuading politicians to change the way public education is funded. As suburbs grew and whites fled Chicago in the post–World War II era, however, the tax revenue for the Chicago schools declined and poverty increased compared to wealthier communities. In 1999, New Trier Township, Illinois, for example, spent $13,528 per child on public education, while Chicago spent only $7,541.[7] *Education Week* in 2004 rated Illinois the worst state in the nation for equitable school funding.[8] As a result, the Board of Education and the union negotiate over meager resources, deciding whether funding should be spent on teachers' wages or school improvements.

The relationship between the union and the wider community has continually resurfaced as a problem for teacher unions. In the 1930s and 1940s, many parents signed petitions and demonstrated with the teachers as students left the classrooms to support the teachers' demand for regular pay. By the 1960s this relationship had broken down and neither students nor parents paid much attention to the union's demands for collective bargaining. The teachers increasingly blamed parental neglect for students' lack of discipline and educational failure, while the parents criticized uncaring teachers for student underachievement. During the campaign for collective bargaining, the CTU did not encourage school integration and received little support from the civil rights movement in return. With bargaining between teacher unions and the Board of Education often restricted to teachers' wages and working conditions, unions had little inclination to seek the support of the public or form coalitions with potentially powerful civic groups. Because teachers often undertook strikes to satisfy their demands, the union—not the school administrators, the state legislators, or the way the public education system was funded—was often blamed by the public for the deteriorating schools.[9]

The years that have followed the CTU's first strike in 1969 have confirmed the inadequacy of public school funding and the problematic relationship between the teachers and the wider community. Parents, blaming the school administrators and the union for the poor performance of the Chicago system of public education, campaigned for reform in the 1980s.[10] High dropout rates, low student achievement, bureaucracy, corruption, and financial crisis due to an overdependence on the property tax characterized the system. In 1987, U.S. secretary of education William Bennett proclaimed the Chicago public schools the worst in the country and the teachers embarked on a nineteen-day strike. Mayor Harold Washington, who was elected the city's first black mayor that same year, ushered in another phase of reform.[11] In 1988, the Chicago School Reform Act created elected Local School Councils

(LSC) consisting of six parents, two community members, two teachers, and the principals to take authority away from the central bureaucracy and hand power to local communities and parents. The councils had input into school programs and the power to hire and fire its own principal while the principal had the authority to assign teachers.[12] Although they were a success in some schools, too often there was little parental involvement and parents on the councils deferred to the principal or teachers. As a result, the councils had little overall impact in improving public education in Chicago.

With the Chicago public schools showing little signs of improvement in the 1990s, political leaders in the state capital of Springfield and in Chicago initiated another reform effort. In 1995, the state legislature gave Mayor Richard M. Daley, the son of Richard J. Daley, authority to name a new Board of Education and a chief executive officer to replace the school superintendent. The Illinois General Assembly also restricted the scope of collective bargaining in the Chicago public schools. The CTU could no longer bargain over charter schools, privatization of services, layoffs or reductions in force, class size, staffing and teaching assignments, class schedules, academic calendar, hours and places of instruction, pupil assessment policies, pilot programs, and educational technology.[13] School superintendent Argie Johnson was ousted and Paul Vallas, the mayor's budget director, was appointed chief executive officer. Subsequently, the new administration placed greater blame for school failure on underachieving principals and teachers and put more emphasis on magnet schools, test scores, summer schools for failing students, and an end to "social promotion." They also put schools on probation and reconstituted failing schools, and principals and teachers have been put under greater administrative control and some have been removed from the schools.[14]

The persistence of reform as a motivation for some public school teachers is confirmed by the significant role union teachers have played in the recent movement for reform of the public schools. In recognition of the demand for reform initiatives from teachers, CTU president Jacqueline Vaughn allowed veteran reformer John Kotsakis, a special assistant to Vaughn, to build the CTU Quest Center. Kotsakis, one of the young radicals who campaigned for collective bargaining in the 1960s and ran unsuccessfully for CTU president in 1972, sought to foster innovative school reforms. The Quest Center was opened in 1992 with a $1.1 million grant from the John D. and Catherine T. MacArthur Foundation to develop curriculum and school policies. Kotsakis and Deborah Walsh (Lynch), director of the Quest Center, were the driving force behind the center and subsequent educational initiatives until Kotsakis died in 1994 and Lynch left the center to work in a Chicago elementary school.[15]

The culmination of the recent reform initiative within the CTU came in May 2001 when Deborah Lynch, previously director of the Quest Center, won the CTU presidency, ousting Tom Reece and the caucus that had controlled the union for three decades. Lynch had defeated Reece because he had proved too pliant in his relationship with the Board of Education. Although she was no political radical, Lynch was associated with the Teacher Union Reform Network, a group of nationwide teacher union locals who wanted educational improvements in addition to salaries and benefits. She wanted the union to play a greater role in professional development and in decision making in the schools and at board level. As part of her reform initiative, Lynch increased the budget for the Quest Center, enlarged the center's role in training teachers, and won the restoration of many of the bargaining rights lost in 1995, including the right to bargain over class size, academic calendar, and staffing issues. In 2003, she forged a deal with the board that the union and the board would jointly run failing schools. If the schools did not show improvement within a year, the board would be allowed to close them.[16]

As Kermit Eby had found more than sixty years earlier, it proved difficult for Deborah Lynch to reconcile an emphasis on school reform and traditional union aims. In the 2004, CTU presidential election, challenger Marilyn Stewart capitalized on members' discontent with the 2003 contract negotiated by Lynch and particularly with an increase in health insurance payments. Just like many before her, Stewart argued that the union should focus on wages and benefits and not educational reform. The union "should go back to the traditional function of a union," she proclaimed. "We're a labor union, not a university." A majority of the membership seemed to agree as Stewart defeated Lynch in the election, ending another of the significant attempts at reform that has consistently marked the history of teacher unionism.[17]

Notes

Introduction

1. On teacher conservatism, see Willard Waller, *The Sociology of Teaching* (New York: Russell and Russell, 1932); Dan C. Lortie, *School Teacher: A Sociological Study* (Chicago: University of Chicago Press, 1975); and Larry Cuban, *How Teachers Taught: Constancy and Change in American Classrooms* (New York: Longman, 1984). For the implications of this conservatism for teachers' unions, see Wayne J. Urban, "Teacher Activism," in *American Teachers: Histories of a Profession at Work,* ed. Donald Warren, 190–209 (New York: Macmillan, 1989); Wayne J. Urban and Jennings Wagoner, Jr., *American Education: A History* (New York: McGraw-Hill, 1996), 261–65; The Commission on Educational Reconstruction, *Organizing the Teaching Profession: The Story of the American Federation of Teachers* (Glencoe, Ill.: The Free Press, 1955); and William Edward Eaton, *The American Federation of Teachers, 1916–1961: A History of the Movement* (Carbondale and Edwardsville: Southern Illinois University Press, 1975). Richard A. Quantz, "The Complex Vision of Female Teachers and the Failure of Unionization in the 1930s: An Oral History," *History of Education Quarterly* 25 (Winter 1985): 439–58; Stephen Cole, *The Unionization of Teachers: A Case Study of the AFT* (New York: Praeger, 1969); and Ronald G. Corwin, *Militant Professionalism: A Study of Organizational Conflict in High Schools* (New York: Appleton-Century-Crofts, 1970) address the issue of gender and teachers' unions.

2. Marjorie Murphy, *Blackboard Unions: The AFT and the NEA, 1900–1980* (Ithaca, N.Y., and London: Cornell University Press, 1990), 1.

3. Murphy, *Blackboard Unions,* 43.

4. Robert J. Braun, *Teachers and Power: The Story of the American Federation of Teachers* (New York: Simon and Schuster, 1972); William J. Grimshaw, *Union Rule in the Schools* (Lexington, Mass.: Lexington Books, 1979); and F. Howard Nelson and

Jewell C. Gould, "Teachers' Unions and Excellence in Education: Comment," *Journal of Labor Research* 9 (Fall 1988): 379–87.

5. Tom Loveless, ed., *Conflicting Missions: Teachers Unions and Educational Reform* (Washington, D.C.: Brookings Institute Press, 2000); Myron Lieberman, *Teacher Unions: How They Sabotage Educational Reform and Why* (San Francisco: Encounter Books, 2000); and Peter Brimelow, *The Worm in the Apple: How the Teacher Unions are Destroying American Education* (New York: HarperCollins, 2004).

6. Wayne J. Urban, *Why Teachers Organized* (Detroit, Mich.: Wayne State University Press, 1982), 10–11.

7. Wayne J. Urban, "The Effects of Ideology and Power on a Teacher Walkout: Florida 1968," *Journal of Collective Negotiations* 3 (Spring 1974): 133–46; Wayne J. Urban, "Merit Pay and Organized Teachers in the USA," in *The Politics of Teacher Unionism, International Perspectives,* ed. Martin Lawn, 193–212 (London: Croom Helm, 1985); Wayne J. Urban, "Essay Review: Old and New Problems in Teacher Unionism," *Educational Studies* 20 (Winter 1989): 355–64; and Urban, "Teacher Activism." Others support Urban's view. Russell C. Oakes, "Public and Professional Reactions to Teachers' Strikes, 1918–1954" (Ph.D. diss., New York University, 1958), in his study of teacher strikes between 1918 and 1954, found that "not a single teachers' group struck primarily for the improvement of overall school conditions or the improvement of the curriculum" (3). Albert Schiff, "A Study and Evaluation of Teachers' Strikes in the United States" (Ed.D. diss, Wayne [State] University, 1952); and William J. Moore and Ray Marshall. "Growth of Teachers' Organizations: A Conceptual Framework," *Journal of Collective Negotiations* 2 (Summer 1973): 271–97, found economic causes as the main reason for strikes and the growth in teachers' unions.

8. David Hogan, *Class and Reform: School and Society in Chicago, 1880–1930* (Philadelphia: University of Pennsylvania Press, 1985), 222–27; Julia Wrigley, *Class Politics and Public Schools, Chicago 1900–1950* (New Brunswick, N.J.: Rutgers University Press, 1982); Ira Katznelson and Margaret Weir, *Schooling For All: Class, Race, and the Decline of the Democratic Ideal* (New York: Basic Books, 1985); Marvin Lazerson, "Teachers Organize: What Margaret Haley Lost," *History of Education Quarterly* 24 (Summer 1984); 264; Marvin Lazerson, "If All the World Were Chicago," *History of Education Quarterly* 24 (Summer 1984): 174; and Murphy, *Blackboard Unions,* 6.

9. Paula O'Connor, "Grade-School Teachers Become Labor Leaders: Margaret Haley, Florence Rood, and Mary Barker of the AFT," *Labor's Heritage* 7 (Fall 1995): 4–17.

10. Celia Lewis Zitron, *The New York City Teachers Union 1916–1964: A Story of Educational and Social Commitment* (New York: Humanities Press, 1968).

11. David Selden, *The Teacher Rebellion* (Washington, D.C.: Howard University Press, 1985).

12. Steve Golin, *The Newark Teacher Strikes: Hopes on the Line* (New Brunswick, N.J., and London: Rutgers University Press, 2002), quote on page 3.

13. A. Urbanski, "Turning Unions Around," *Contemporary Education* 69 (Summer 1998): 186–90; and Bob Peterson and Michael Charney, *Transforming Teacher Unions: Fighting for Better Schools and Social Justice* (Milwaukee, Wisc.: Rethinking Schools, 1999).

14. See Charles Taylor Kerchner, Julia E. Koppich, and Joseph G. Weeres, *United Mind Workers: Unions and Teaching in the Knowledge Society* (San Francisco: Jossey-Bass Publishers, 1997); Joseph E. Slater, "The Court Does Not Know 'What a Labor Union Is': How State Structures and Judicial (Mis)constructions Deformed Public Sector Labor Law," *Oregon Law Review* 79 (Winter 2000): 981–1032; and Joseph E. Slater, *Public Workers: Government Employees Unions, the Law, and the State, 1900–1962* (Ithaca, N.Y.: Cornell University Press, 2004).

15. For an overview of the relevant literature on gender and working-class history, see Ava Baron, "Gender and Labor History: Learning From the Past, Looking to the Future," in *Work Engendered: Toward a New History of American Labor,* ed. Ava Baron, 1–46 (Ithaca, N.Y.: Cornell University Press. 1991); Mari Jo Buhle, "Gender and Labor History," in *Perspectives on American Labor History: The Problems of Synthesis,* ed. J. Carroll Moody and Alice Kessler-Harris, 55–79 (DeKalb: Northern Illinois University Press, 1990); Leon Fink, "Culture's Last Stand: Gender and the Search for Synthesis," *Labor History* 34 (Spring–Summer 1993): 178–89; Lois Rita Helmbold and Ann Schofield. "Women's Labor History, 1790–1945," *Reviews in American History* 17 (December 1989): 501–18; Ruth Milkman, "Gender and Trade Unionism in Historical Perspective," in *Women, Politics and Change,* ed. Patricia Gurin and Louise Tilly, 87–107 (New York: Russell Sage Foundation. 1990); and Ruth Milkman, "New Research In Women's Labor History," *Signs* 18 (Winter 1993): 376–88.

16. For more on women and teaching, see Kate Rousmaniere, *City Teachers: Teaching and School Reform in Historical Perspective* (New York: Teachers College Press, 1997); Jackie M. Blount, *Destined to Rule: Women and the Superintendency, 1873–1995* (New York: State University of New York Press, 1998); Ruth Markowitz, *My Daughter, the Teacher: Jewish Teachers in the New York City Schools* (New Brunswick, N.J.: Rutgers University Press, 1993); and John Rury, *Education and Women's Work: Female Schooling and the Division of Labor in Urban America, 1870–1930* (New York: State University of New York Press, 1991).

17. A number of historians have recently examined the role of black teachers in school reform in the 1960s. Jerald E. Podair, *The Strike That Changed New York: Blacks, Whites, and the Ocean Hill-Brownsville Crisis* (New Haven, Conn., and London: Yale University Press, 2002); Jane Anna Gordon, *Why They Couldn't Wait: A Critique of the Black-Jewish Conflict Over Community Control in Ocean Hill-Brownsville (1967–1971)* (New York and London: RoutledgeFalmer, 2001); Golin, *The Newark Teacher Strikes*; and Dionne A. Danns, *Something Better for Our Children: Black Organization in Chicago Public Schools, 1963–1971* (New York: Routledge, 2003).

Chapter 1: The Formation of the Chicago Teachers Union

1. Figures for union membership from U.S. Department of Commerce, Bureau of the Census, *Historical Statistics of the U.S.* (Washington, D.C.: Government Printing Office, 1975), 178; AFT figures from Moore and Marshall, "Growth of Teachers' Organizations."

2. Mary J. Herrick, *The Chicago Schools: A Social and Political History* (Beverly Hills, Calif.: Sage, 1971), 403.

3. U.S. Department of Commerce, *Historical Statistics of the United States,* 368–69; Chicago Board of Education, *Annual Reports;* George S. Counts, *School and Society in Chicago* (New York: Harcourt Brace, 1928), 28; and George D. Strayer et al., *Report of the Survey of the Schools of Chicago, Illinois,* vol. 2 (New York: Teachers College, Columbia University, 1932), 148. The reasons for this spectacular growth in school attendance are covered in Hogan, *Class and Reform;* and David J. Hogan, "Education and the Making of the Working Class in Chicago, 1880–1930," *History of Education Quarterly* 18 (Fall 1978): 227–70.

4. Counts, *School and Society in Chicago,* 39. For a detailed analysis of the centralization and bureaucratization of public education in Chicago during the Progressive Era, see Marjorie Murphy, "From Artisan to Semi-Professional: White Collar Unionism Among Chicago Public School Teachers, 1870–1930" (Ph.D. diss., University of California, Davis, 1981).

5. Charles Merriam, *Chicago, A More Intimate View of Urban Politics* (New York: Macmillan, 1920), 22.

6. Herrick, *The Chicago Schools,* 163–75; and Marjorie Murphy, "Taxation and Social Conflict," *Journal of the Illinois State Historical Society* 74 (Winter 1981): 254–55. For more on Mayor Thompson, see Lloyd Wendt and Herman Kogan, *Big Bill of Chicago* (New York: Bobbs Merrill Co., 1953); Paul M. Green and Melvin G. Holli, eds., *The Mayors: The Chicago Political Tradition* (Carbondale: Southern Illinois University Press, 1987); and Douglas Bukowski, *Big Bill Thompson, Chicago, and the Politics of Image* (Urbana and Chicago: University of Illinois Press, 1998).

7. Strayer et al., *Report of the Survey of the Schools of Chicago, Illinois,* vol. 1, 170 and 174. Comparisons are made with New York, Philadelphia, Detroit, and Cleveland, which are five of the largest six cities in the country. Los Angeles was excluded because climate and other factors made the costs comparisons useless.

8. Figures from Strayer et al., *Report of the Survey of the Schools of Chicago,* vol. 1, 139; and Wrigley, *Class Politics and Public Schools,* 209–10.

9. Strayer et al., *Report of the Survey of the Schools of Chicago,* vol. 4, 19–24.

10. Strayer et al., *Report of the Survey of the Schools of Chicago,* vol. 4, 14–15; and New York figures from Rousmaniere, *City Teachers,* 77.

11. John L. Rury, "Who Became Teachers? The Social Characteristics of Teachers in American History," in *American Teachers: Histories of a Profession at Work,* ed. Donald Warren, 9–48 (New York: Macmillan, 1989).

12. Strayer et al., *Report of the Survey of the Schools of Chicago*, vol. 1, 252–54.

13. Myra Strober and David Tyack, "Why Do Women Teach and Men Manage? A Report on Research on Schools," *Signs: Journal of Women in Culture and Society* 5, no. 3 (Spring 1980); 494–503; Myra H. Strober and Audri Gordon Langford, "The Feminization of Public School Teaching: A Cross-Sectional Analysis, 1850–1880" *Signs: Journal of Women in Culture and Society* 11 (Winter 1986); 212–35; Joel Perlmann and Robert A. Margo, *Women's Work? American Schoolteachers, 1650–1920* (Chicago and London: University of Chicago Press, 2001); Redding S. Sugg, Jr., *Motherteacher: The Feminization of American Education* (Charlottesville: University of Virginia Press, 1978); and Frances R. Donovan, *The Schoolma'am* (New York: Frederick A. Stokes, 1938).

14. John K. Folger and Charles B. Nam, *Education of the American Population* (Washington, D.C.: U.S. Department of Commerce, Bureau of the Census, 1967), 81; Strayer, *Report of the Survey of the Schools of Chicago*, vol. 1, 256.

15. Adam Fairclough, *Teaching Equality: Black Schools in the Age of Jim Crow* (Athens and London: University of Georgia Press, 2001), 5; and Mary J. Herrick, "Negro Employees of the Chicago Board of Education" (M.A. thesis, University of Chicago, 1931), 32.

16. Harold F. Gosnell, *Negro Politicians: The Rise of Negro Politics in Chicago* (Chicago and London: University of Chicago Press, originally published 1935, 1967), 283–86; and Michael Homel, *Down from Equality: Black Chicagoans and the Public Schools, 1920–1941* (Urbana: University of Illinois Press, 1984).

17. Gosnell, *Negro Politicians*, 292, 294, and 300; and James R. Grossman, *Land of Hope: Chicago, Black Southerners, and the Great Migration* (Chicago: University of Chicago Press, 1989), 350.

18. Murphy, *Blackboard Unions*, 40.

19. Strayer, *Report of the Survey of the Schools of Chicago*, vol. 2, 272.

20. In the mid-1920s, George Counts surveyed seven Chicago elementary schools with 181 teachers and found that 41 percent of the teachers were Catholic. Counts, *School and Society in Chicago*, 240.

21. James W. Sanders, *The Education of an Urban Minority, Catholics in Chicago, 1833–1965* (New York: Oxford University Press, 1977), 27; Janet Nolan, *Servants of the Poor: Teachers and Mobility in Ireland and Irish America* (Notre Dame, Ind.: University of Notre Dame Press, 2004); Janet Nolan, "A Patrick Henry in the Classroom: Margaret Haley and the Chicago Teachers' Federation," *Eire-Ireland* 30 (Summer 1995): 104–17; Counts, *School and Society in Chicago*, 105; and William W. Wattenberg, *On the Educational Front, The Reactions of Teacher Associations in New York and Chicago* (New York: Columbia University Press, 1936), 126–29.

22. Lotus Delta Coffman, *The Social Composition of the Teaching Population* (New York: Teachers College, Columbia University, 1911, AMS edition published in 1972), 57 and 73.

23. Strayer, *Report of the Survey of the Schools of Chicago*, vol. 2, 272.

24. Murphy, *"From Artisan to Semi-Professional,"* 106; and Murphy, *Blackboard Unions*, 38–39.

25. Strayer, *Report of the Survey of the Schools of Chicago*, vol. 2, 272–73.

26. Murphy, *Blackboard Unions*, 87–90; Edward Krug, *The Shaping of the American High School*, vol. 1 (New York: Harper and Row, 1964); Rury, "Who Became Teachers?" 28; and Arthur Walz, "Why the Union Single Salary Schedule for Chicago Teachers?" WCFL talk, February 12, 1944, in Chicago Historical Society, CTU Collection, Box 34, Folder 5.

27. Chicago Board of Education, *Proceedings*, June 8, 1931, 1882.

28. Herrick, *The Chicago Schools*, 95.

29. *Historical Statistics of the US: Colonial Times to 1970: Part 1* (Washington, D.C.: U.S. Bureau of the Census, 1975), 164; and *NEA Research Bulletin* 7 (May 1929): 113–15. The figures for the elementary school teachers include teachers of special subjects who were paid more than all other elementary school teachers.

30. Pamela Bolotin Joseph, "'The Ideal Teacher' Images of Paragons in Teacher Education Textbooks Before 1940," in *Images of Schoolteachers in Twentieth-Century America*, ed. Pamela Bolotin Joseph and Gail E. Burnaford, 265–74 (New York: St. Martin's Press, 1994).

31. *NEA Journal* 21 (May 1932): 160.

32. *Chicago School's Journal*, September 1930, 3–4.

33. Bessie Slutsky, "The Chicago Teachers' Union and Its Background" (M.A. thesis, Northwestern University, 1945), 14 and 21.

34. John A. Vieg, *The Government of Education in Metropolitan Chicago* (Chicago: University of Chicago Press, 1939), 222–23.

35. Robert L. Reid, ed., *Battleground: The Autobiography of Margaret Haley* (Urbana: University of Illinois Press, 1982), 91.

36. F. C. Smith, "Education as a Profession," *Peabody Journal of Education* 16 (September 1938): 85; and Aaron Kline, "Suggestions for Financial Relief for the Chicago Public Schools," *Chicago Principals' Club Reporter*, September 1931, 5.

37. Jeff Hearn, "Notes on Patriarchy: Professionalization and the Semi-Professions," *Sociology* 16 (May 1982): 195; and Rury, "Who Became Teachers?" 10.

38. Upton Sinclair, *The Goslings: A Study of the American Schools* (Pasadena, Calif.: Upton Sinclair, 1924), 405.

39. Waller, *The Sociology of Teaching*, 58.

40. Raymond E. Callaghan, *Education and the Cult of Efficiency* (Chicago: University of Chicago Press, 1962); and Michael Apple, *Education and Power* (New York and London: Routledge and Kegan Paul, 1986).

41. Strayer, *Report of the Survey of the Schools of Chicago*, vol. 1, 258.

42. Chicago Board of Education, *Proceedings*, June 8, 1931, 1882.

43. *American Teacher*, April 1927, 11.

44. Strayer, *Report of the Survey of the Schools of Chicago*, vol. 1, 167.

45. Strayer, *Report of the Survey of the Schools of Chicago*, vol. 1, 50.

46. Strayer, *Report of the Survey of the Schools of Chicago*, vol. 1, 267.

47. Richard Hofstadter, *Anti-Intellectualism in American Life* (New York: Vintage Books, 1963), 320.

48. Waller, *The Sociology of Teaching*, 50.

49. Chicago Board of Education 46th Annual Report, 1899–1900, 168; and Strayer, *Report of the Survey of the Schools of Chicago*, vol. 1, 253–54.

50. Blount, *Destined to Rule the Schools*, 96. See also Sari Biklen, *School Work: Gender and the Cultural Construction of Teaching* (New York: Teachers College Press, 1995).

51. *American Teacher*, April 1927, 6–7.

52. Chicago Board of Education, *Proceedings* (October 14, 1925), 266.

53. *American Teacher*, May 1928, 19.

54. Teachers in San Antonio, Texas, became the first teachers to join labor when they directly affiliated with the AFL in 1902, while the CFT affiliated with the CFL. Figures from Murphy, "From Artisan to Semi-Professional," 225.

55. For more on Margaret Haley, see Kate Rousmaniere, *Citizen Teacher: The Life and Leadership of Margaret Haley* (Albany: State University of New York Press, 2005); Janet Nolan, "Margaret Haley," in *Women Building Chicago, 1790–1990: A Biographical Dictionary*, ed. Adele Hast and Rima Schultz, 338–41 (Bloomington: Indiana University Press, 2001); and Nolan, "A Patrick Henry in the Classroom," 104–17.

56. *The Men Teachers Union of Chicago: Twenty First Anniversary* (Chicago, 1934); Blanche Rinehart, "Mr. Gompers and the Teachers," *Changing Education*, Summer 1966, 14–15; "Monthly Report to the Secretary Treasurer," August 1935, AFT collection, Archives of Labor and Urban Affairs, Walter P. Reuther Library, Wayne State University, Detroit, Michigan (hereafter cited as AFT Collection), Series V1, Box 2, "Chicago Women's Teachers Union, 1933–1937" folder; and "Monthly Report to the Secretary Treasurer," September 1934 to September 1937, AFT Collection, Series V1, Box 1, "Chicago Men Teachers Union 1935–1937" folder.

57. Elizabeth McKillen, *Chicago Labor and the Quest for a Democratic Diplomacy, 1914–1924* (Ithaca, N.Y.: Cornell University Press, 1995).

58. James Weinstein, *The Decline of Socialism in America, 1919–1925* (New York, Monthly Review Press, 1967); and Stanley Shapiro, "'Hand and Brain': The Farmer-Labor Party of 1920," *Labor History* 26 (1985): 405–22.

59. James R. Barrett, "Ethnic and Racial Fragmentation: Toward a Reinterpretation of a Local Labor Movement," in *The African-American Urban Experience: Perspectives From the Colonial Period to the Present*, ed. Joe Trotter, Earl Lewis, and Tera Hunter, 291 (New York: Pelgrave Macmillan, 2004).

60. David Montgomery, *Workers Control in America* (New York and London: Cambridge University Press, 1979), 57–58.

61. James R. Barrett, *Work and Community in the Jungle: Chicago's Packinghouse Workers, 1894–1922* (Urbana and Chicago: University of Illinois Press, 1987), 143.

62. Brigid O'Farrell and Joyce L. Kornbluh, eds. *Rocking the Boat: Union Women's*

Voices, 1915–1975 (New Brunswick, N.J.: Rutgers University Press, 1996), 17. For example, John Fitzpatrick's wife, Catherine, was a prominent member of the CTF.

63. Richard Schneirov, *Labor and Urban Politics: Class Conflict and the Origins of Modern Liberalism in Chicago, 1864–97* (Urbana: University of Illinois Press, 1998).

64. Maureen A. Flanagan, "Gender and Urban Political Reform: The City Club and the Woman's City Club of Chicago in the Progressive Era," *American Historical Review* 95 (October 1990): 1032–1050; and Counts, *School and Society in Chicago,* 216–19.

65. Philip Foner, *Women and the American Labor Movement from World War I to the Present* (New York: Free Press, 1980); Elizabeth Anne Payne, *Reform, Labor, and Feminism: Margaret Dreier Robins and the Women's Trade Union League* (Urbana and Chicago: University of Illinois Press, 1988); and "Report on Workers Education" Chicago Historical Society, Lillian Herstein papers, Box 1, "Workers education movement items" folder.

66. Sterling D. Spero, *Government as Employer* (New York: Remsen Press, 1948), 1–15; Morton R. Godine, *The Labor Problem in the Public Service* (Cambridge, Mass.: Harvard University Press, 1951); Slater, "The Court Does Not Know," 981–1032; and Slater, *Public Workers.*

67. *Chicago Daily News,* August 27, 1915. For similar views of school superintendents, see *The Nation's Schools,* March 1929, 45–46.

68. Reid, *Battleground,* 179.

69. Quoted in Murphy, "From Artisan to Semi-Professional," 72.

70. Robert L. Reid, "The Professionalization of Public School Teachers: The Chicago Experience, 1895–1920" (Ph.D. diss., Northwestern University, 1963), 168–84.

71. Oakes, "Public and Professional Reactions to Teachers' Strikes," 86–87; and Spero, *Government as Employer,* 4 and 29

72. Murphy, *Blackboard Unions,* 90–95.

73. MTU *Monthly Bulletin,* December 1933, 5, AFT Collection, Series V1, Box 1, "Chicago Men Teachers' Union 1916–1934" folder.

74. James Earl Clarke, "The American Federation of Teachers; Origins and History from 1870 to 1952" (Ph.D. diss., Cornell University, 1966), 123; and *American Teacher,* October 1933, 6.

75. James A. Meade, Lucie Schacht, and Agnes Clohesy to Building Representatives, October 25, 1928, AFT Collection, Series V1, Box 1, "MTU 1916–1934" folder; and "Stenograph report of meeting of the Playground Teachers Union" December 2, 1929, 7, CTU Collection, Box 31, Folder 3.

76. "Twenty Questions Answered," 1930, CTU Collection, Box 4, Folder 6.

77. "Monthly Report to the Secretary Treasurer," August 1935, AFT Collection, Series V1, Box 2, "Chicago Women's Teachers Union, 1933–1937" folder; and "Monthly Report to the Secretary Treasurer," September 1934 to September 1937, AFT Collection, Series V1, Box 1, "Chicago Men Teachers Union 1935–1937" folder.

78. Wattenberg, *On the Educational Front,* 125.

79. Maureen A. Flanagan, *Seeing With Their Hearts: Chicago Women and the Vision of the Good City, 1871–1933* (Princeton, N.J., and Oxford: Princeton University Press, 2002).

80. In 1934–35 there were 43,959 PTA members in Chicago. Of this number only 10 percent were fathers. "The Parent Teacher Associations and the Chicago Public Schools" Havighurst-McCaul Project on Society and Education in Chicago, no author, CSC papers, Box 29, Folder 3. Throughout the Depression, letters to newspapers concerning education continued to be overwhelmingly sent by women.

81. E. B. Collette, "100% and Democracy," *The Bulletin of the Chicago Federation of Men Teachers and of the Federation of Women High School Teachers,* November 1919, 12–14; *The Federation Bulletin* May 4, 1914, 6 (AFT series 1, Box 68); *The Federation Bulletin* September 11, 1914, 4 (AFT series 1, Box 68); E. B. Collette "Federation Needs," *The Bulletin of the Chicago Federation of Men Teachers and of the Federation of Women High School Teachers,* April 1920, 25–26 (AFT series 1, Box 68). Quote in letter from W. T. McCoy to Charles Stillman, n.d. but 1918–1921, AFT Collection, series V1, Box 1, MTU 1916–1934 folder.

82. "Radio Programs: F of WHST June 1933–June 1934" CSC Box 2, Folder 2; and *Bulletin of the Men Teachers Union of Chicago,* May 1932, Chicago Teachers' Federation collection, Chicago Historical Society, Chicago, Ill. (hereafter cited as CTF Collection), Box 63, Folder 1.

83. "Notes From a Telephone Conversation Between Miss Haley and Catherine Hannan," September 25, 1931, CTF Collection, Box 60; and CFT meeting minutes, January 24, 1933, 56, Box 16; Joan K. Smith, "Autobiography as Source: Some Methodological Cautions," *Vitae Scholasticae* 2 (Spring 1983): 182; Herrick, *The Chicago Schools,* 238.

84. "Margaret Haley Autobiography," 223–224, CTF Collection, Box 34, Folder 2

85. Nicholas R. Cannella, *171 Years of Teaching in Chicago, 1816–1987* (Chicago: CTU, 1987), 26.

86. "Illinois Support of Education Compared to Other States," Chicago Schools Committee (CSC) collection, Chicago Historical Society, Chicago, Ill. (hereafter cited as CSC Collection), Box 2, Folder 2. See Lyman B. Burbank, "Chicago Public Schools and the Depression Years of 1928–1937," *Journal of the Illinois State Historical Society* 64 (Winter 1971): 365–81, for an overview of the teachers in the Depression.

87. The Illinois state assembly decided the limits of taxation, which the Board of Education could impose on the city by a "pegged levy." The portion directly from the state was in the form of the state distributive fund. Herrick, *The Chicago Schools,* 180; and "Illinois Support of Education Compared to Other States," CSC Collection, Box 2, Folder 2.

88. Figures from Strayer, *Report of the Survey of the Schools of Chicago,* vol. 1, 139; Herrick, *The Chicago Schools,* 179–81; and Wrigley, *Class Politics and Public Schools,* 209–10.

89. Murphy, "Taxation and Social Conflict," 255–59; Penny Lipkin, "Payless Pay-

days: Financial Crisis of the Chicago Board of Education, 1930–1934" (M.A. thesis, Columbia University, 1967), 3–6; Burbank, "Chicago Public Schools and the Depression Years of 1928–1937," 371; and Herrick, *The Chicago Schools,* 195. For more on the Association of Real Estate Taxpayers, see *Cook County's Revenue Problem* (Chicago: Association of Real Estate Taxpayers, 1931); and David T. Beito, *Taxpayers in Revolt: Tax Resistance During the Great Depression* (Chapel Hill and London: University of North Carolina Press, 1989).

90. U.S. Bureau of the Census, *Historical Statistics of the United States: Colonial Times to 1970* (Washington, D.C.: GPO, 1975), 1 and 224.

91. Wrigley, *Class Politics and Public Schools,* 208; Roger Biles, *Big City Boss in Depression and War: Mayor Edward J. Kelly of Chicago* (DeKalb: Northern Illinois University Press, 1984), 22; and Beito, *Taxpayers in Revolt,* 70.

92. In June 1930, only 80 percent of the 1928 taxes had been collected, only 60 percent of the 1929 taxes, and only 50 percent of the 1930 taxes. Figures from Alex Gottfried, *Boss Cermak of Chicago: A Study of Political Leadership* (Seattle: University of Washington Press, 1962), 247; and Wrigley, *Class Politics and Public Schools,* 209.

93. The National Economic League, formed in the spring of 1932, organized in thirty-five states and had former presidents Herbert Hoover and Calvin Coolidge on its advisory council. The United States Chamber of Commerce coordinated with local chambers of commerce to cut expenditures. Eaton, *The American Federation of Teachers,* 44–46; S. Alexander Rippa, "Retrenchment in a Period of Defensive Opposition to the New Deal: The Business Community and the Public Schools, 1932–1934," *History of Education Quarterly* 2 (June 1962): 76–82; *American Teacher,* April 1933, 12–16; David B. Tyack et al., *Public Schools in Hard Times* (Cambridge, Mass.: Harvard University Press, 1984), 85–91; and Wattenberg, *On the Educational Front,* 21–29.

94. Fred W. Sargent, "The Taxpayer Takes Charge," *Saturday Evening Post,* January 14, 1933; and *American Teacher,* February 1933, 21 and 78. CCPE members included the directors of the four leading tax anticipation holding banks: the First National, the Harris Trust and Savings, the Continental Illinois, and the Northern Trust.

95. *Illinois Teacher,* March 1933, 195.

96. Herrick, *The Chicago Schools,* 189; and *Chicago Tribune,* July 28, 1932, 1, and January 18, 1933, 11. The role of Cermak in the development of the political machine in Chicago is covered in Harold Gosnell, *Machine Politics: Chicago Model* (Chicago: University of Chicago Press, 1937); and Gottfried, *Boss Cermak of Chicago.*

97. The council chose seventeenth ward alderman Francis J. Corr as temporary mayor until it selected Kelly in April. Once Kelly gained power, he was in a position to appoint five new members of the eleven-member Board of Education. Lewis E. Myers, president of the Board of Education, had announced his retirement in January 1933, Carter Blatchford retired due to ill health, and the terms of three other members of the board expired.

98. "The Kelly-Nash Political Machine," *Fortune* 14 (August 1936): 126; Wattenberg, *On the Educational Front*, 32–37; "The Assault on the Schoolhouse," *The Nation*, August 16, 1933, 173; and "Defrilled Chicago," *Time*, July 24, 1933, 31. The Board of Education had used a teacher tenure loophole that ensured that teachers were guaranteed continuous employment as long as satisfactory service was maintained. However, when the junior high schools were closed and some subjects abolished, teachers were not guaranteed employment and could be dismissed. Those holding certificates that allowed them to teach in the elementary or high schools were gradually absorbed into these schools, while the other teachers went to Normal School to obtain an elementary certificate or took the high school qualifying exam. Wrigley, *Class Politics and Public Schools*, 221, claims that at the same time 1,400 teachers were fired, approximately 700 new political appointees were added to the city payroll. See also Stephen D. London, "Business and the Chicago Public School System, 1890–1966" (Ph.D. diss., University of Chicago, 1968), 118.

99. *Teacher News and Views*, February 15, 1936, 1 and 3.

100. *Chicago Principals Club Reporter*, April 1932, 9–10.

101. *Nation*, May 10, 1933, 516.

102. *The Saturday Evening Post*, July 1, 1933, 68.

103. In the fall of 1933 and through 1934 a series of teacher strikes swept through the coal mining regions of Pennsylvania and Alabama, but these were isolated cases involving only a few hundred teachers. Oakes, "Public and Professional Reactions to Teachers' Strikes," 94–113.

104. *Chicago Tribune*, September 6, 1931, 4; Studs Terkel, *Hard Times: An Oral History of the Great Depression* (New York: Pantheon, 1970), 442; *American Teacher*, February 1931, 5; *New York Times*, June 19, 1931, 14; *Chicago Schools Journal*, March 1931, 348, and April 1931, 399; and Special Report issued by the Joint Board of Teachers Unions, June 22, 1931, CTU Collection, Box 1.

105. *Chicago Tribune*, October 20, 1931.

106. Minutes of All-City Publicity Committee mass meeting September 29, 1932, 73, CTF Collection, Box 63, "July–September 1932," Folder.

107. CTF leaflet, October 17, 1932, CTF Collection, Box 63; and *American Teacher*, February 1930, 6.

108. CTF leaflet, September 17, 1931, CTF Collection, Box 60; and *Chicago Daily News*, January 5, 1932, 1, and 6, and January 7, 1932, 3.

109. Paul E. Peterson, *The Politics of School Reform, 1870–1940* (Chicago: University of Chicago Press, 1985), 194.

110. Hogan, "Education and the Making of the Working Class in Chicago," 242–43.

111. Jeffrey Mirel, *The Rise and Fall of an Urban School System, Detroit, 1907–1981* (Ann Arbor: University of Michigan Press, 1993).

112. *NEA Research Bulletin* 10 (January 1932): 20.

113. *Commerce* 30 (August 1933): 24.

114. *Chicago Principals Club Reporter,* April 1933, 30.

115. Wrigley, *Class Politics and Public Schools,* 233–36. The historical collusion between Chicago politicians and construction unions is covered in Robert F. Pearse, "Studies in White Collar Unionism" (Ph.D. diss., University of Chicago, 1950), 57–60. For more on the janitors and their unions, see Herrick, "Negro Employees of the Chicago Board of Education," 61–69.

116. Elementary Teachers Union leaflet, March 28, 1932, CTU Collection, Box 35, Folder 9.

117. Men Teachers Union, *Special Bulletin,* 1932, CTU Collection, Box 3; Federation of Women High School Teachers, "Summary of Meetings," February 1932, CTU Collection, Box 4; Chicago High School Teachers Association leaflet, October 1932, CTU Collection, Box 18; and *American Teacher,* June 1933, 4.

118. Robert Russell to CTF, November 10, 1931, CTF Collection, Box 60; and South Side Teachers leaflet, March 9, 1932, and South Side Teachers Delegate meeting minutes, March 15, 1932, both in CTF Collection, Box 62.

119. CTF leaflet, undated, CTF Collection, Box 62; Emma Levitt, "The Activities of Local Teacher Organizations in Chicago Since 1929" (M.A. thesis, University of Chicago, 1936), 29–30; and All-City Delegates Group meeting minutes, October 21, 1932, CTF Collection, Box 63.

120. *Chicago Daily News,* July 13, 1932, 6; All-City Delegates Group meeting minutes, December 9, 1932, 52, CTF Collection, Box 64; and Wattenberg, *On the Educational Front,* 190.

121. *Chicago Schools Journal,* January 1933, 130.

122. *Bulletin of the MTU,* September 1932, 4

123. *Illinois Teacher,* December 1931, 124

124. *Chicago Herald and Examiner,* June 18, 1932, 7.

125. "Spasmodic Diary of a Chicago School-Teacher," *Atlantic Monthly* 152 (1933): 515.

126. CTF meeting, August 4, 1931, 56, CTF Collection, Box 12.

127. *Chicago Tribune,* May 8, 1932, 14.

128. Letter from C. L. Vestal, president of the Men Teachers Union, to Charles S. Dewey, chairman of the Committee for Sale of Tax Warrants, CTU Collection, Box 3.

129. *NEA Journal* 22 (April 1933): 125.

130. *Chicago Herald and Examiner,* March 17, 1933, 13, March 21, 1933, 13, and March 22, 1933, 26; VEC leaflet, May 8, 1933, CSC Collection, Box 1, Folder 6; and VEC membership card, CTF Collection, Box 65, "May 1933" folder. For the history of the VEC, see "VEC Disbands," June 1934, CSC Collection, Box 27, "Undated Items 1" folder; "The VEC Answers Some Questions," May 27, 1933, CTF Collection, Box 65; and Levitt, "The Activities of Local Teacher Organizations in Chicago Since 1929," 126–29.

131. VEC leaflet, May 8, 1933, CSC Collection, Box 1, Folder 6; and VEC membership card, CTF Collection, Box 65, "May 1933" folder. For the history of the VEC, see

"VEC Disbands," June 1934, CSC Collection, Box 27, "Undated Items 1" folder; "The VEC Answers Some Questions," May 27, 1933, CTF Collection, Box 65; and Levitt, "The Activities of Local Teacher Organizations in Chicago Since 1929," 126–29.

132. *Chicago Herald and Examiner,* March 17, 1933, 13, March 21, 1933, 13, and March 22, 1933, 26.

133. Wattenberg, *On the Educational Front.* 95; Clarke, "The American Federation of Teachers," 269; *Time,* May 8, 1933, 34, and November 8, 1937, 34; Progressive Party "Call for Change of Administration in the Men Teachers Union of Chicago," 1932, Chicago Historical Society library; Braun, *Teachers and Power,* 42–43; John Fewkes, interview by Renee Epstein, Transcript, July 30 and 31, 1986, 4, AFT Oral History Project, Archives of Labor and Urban Affairs, Walter Reuther Library, Wayne State University, Detroit, Mich. MTU membership list of August 1931 shows Fewkes as member 845, which indicates, according to the attached notation, that he joined in 1928. CTU Collection, Box 3, Folder 1. For Fewkes's attendance at meetings, see MTU minutes 1928–1937, CTU Collection, Box 2. The other three members of the central committee of the VEC were Milton Raymer, Roland Kehoe, and Earl Solem.

134. "Margaret Haley Autobiography," p. 493–95, CTF Collection, Box 34, Folder 3.

135. *City Club Bulletin,* May 8, 1933, CSC Collection, Scrapbook 1; VEC meeting, May 26, 1934, CTF Collection, Box 68; John Fewkes to Mary Abbe, May 15, 1933, CTU Collection, Box 67; Eaton, *The American Federation of Teachers,* 97–98; Robert Iversen, *The Communists and the Schools* (New York: Harcourt, Brace and Company, 1959), 113; "The VEC Answers Some Questions" leaflet, CTF Collection, Box 65, "May 1933" folder; and John Fewkes, interview by Renee Epstein, 6–7.

136. *Chicago Daily News,* April 5, 1933, 1 and 3, and April 6, 1933, 1; and *Time,* April 17, 1933, 24.

137. *Chicago Daily News,* April 11, 1933, 6; "Crane Junior College Bulletin," May 11, 1933 and "Crane College Javelin," May 16 and 23, 1933, CSC Collection, Scrapbook 1.

138. "Spasmodic Diary of a Chicago School Teacher," 517; Herrick, *The Chicago Schools,* 240; *Chicago Daily News,* April 15, 1933, 1 and 4.

139. Tyack et al., *Public Schools in Hard Times,* 43; and Braun, *Teachers and Power,* 45–46.

140. "Spasmodic Diary of a Chicago School Teacher," 521; *American Teacher,* June 1933, 18–19; and Braun, *Teachers and Power,* 46–48.

141. *Chicago Daily News,* May 4, 1933, 3; VEC leaflet, May 1933, CSC Collection, Scrapbook 1; *Chicago Tribune,* May 10, 1933, 9; and Spero, *Government as Employer,* 324.

142. *Chicago Tribune,* June 10, 1933, 1, and July 6, 1933, 3; and Burbank, "Chicago Public Schools and the Depression Years of 1928–1937," 374–75.

143. High School Teachers Association leaflet, April 15, 1933, CTF Collection, Box 63; MTU, *Monthly Bulletin,* May 1933, CTU Collection, Box 3; Elementary Teachers Union leaflet, January 21, 1934, CTF Collection, Box 63; *Chicago Herald and Exam-*

iner, July 7, 1933, 4; and MTU *Monthly Bulletin,* April 1933, 2, AFT Collection, Series V1, Box 1, "Chicago Men Teachers Union 1916–34" folder.

144. Herrick, *The Chicago Schools,* 209–57.

145. "The Activities of the 'Save Our Schools' Campaign," 1933, CTU Collection, Box 19.

146. MTU *Monthly Bulletin,* November 1933, CTU Collection, Box 3, Folder 3; and James S. Hazlett, "Crisis in School Government, Chicago 1933–1947" (Ph.D. diss., University of Chicago, 1968), 82.

147. Herrick, *The Chicago Schools,* 209–31.

148. Herrick, *The Chicago Schools,* 217–21.

149. Lipkin, "Payless Paydays," 53–54.

150. Vieg, *The Government of Education in Metropolitan Chicago,* 39.

151. "Spasmodic Diary of a Chicago School Teacher," 525.

152. Slutsky, "The Chicago Teachers Union and Its Background," 20; and Herrick, *The Chicago Schools,* 241–44. Figures for national AFT membership from William J. Moore and Ray Marshall, "Growth of Teachers' Organizations: A Conceptual Framework," *Journal of Collective Negotiations* 2 (Summer 1973): 274.

153. Slutsky, "The Chicago Teachers Union and Its Background," 21.

154. John Fewkes "An open letter to the Teachers of Chicago," n.d., but Jan–Feb 1934, CTF Collection, Box 65.

155. CTU circular, July 14, 1937, CTU Collection, Box 7, Folder 19.

156. Vieg, *The Government of Education in Metropolitan Chicago,* 218.

157. "The Chicago Teachers Union, 1938–39," n.d., no author, 3, CTU Collection, Box 34, Folder 3; and "Understanding the Chicago Teachers Union," CTU pamphlet, September 8, 1938, 1, CTU Collection, Box 34 Folder 3.

158. Johannsen to Fitzpatrick, May 20, 1937, CTF Collection, Box 69, folder 4.

159. "Why Teachers Do Not Want Their Calling Unionized," Association of Chicago Teachers leaflet, September 27, 1937; John Myers to J. Edward Huber, May 16, 1939, CTU Collection, Box 18; and *Chicago Tribune,* May 22, 1939.

160. Minutes of CTF meeting, May 15, 1937, 38–96, CTF Collection, Box 20; CTF meeting minutes, March 19, 1936, 9, CTF Collection, Box 19, and Minutes of CTU mass meeting, October 28 1938, 3, CTF Collection, Box 21.

161. Robert H. Zieger, *The CIO, 1935–1955* (Chapel Hill: University of North Carolina Press, 1995); and union membership figures from *Historical Statistics of the U.S.,* 177.

162. Minutes of Joint Board of Teachers Unions, April 21, 1937, 13, CTF Collection, Box 69, "January–April 1937" folder.

163. Slutsky, "The Chicago Teachers Union and Its Background," 20; Herrick, *The Chicago Schools,* 241–44; Terkel, *Hard Times,* 442. Figures for national AFT membership are from Moore and Marshall, "Growth of Teachers' Organizations," 274.

164. George H. Gallup, ed., *The Gallup Poll: Public Opinion, 1935–1971,* vol. 1, 1935–1948 (New York: Random House, 1972), 66–67.

165. Charles S. Rhyne, *Labor Unions and Municipal Employe Law* (Washington, D.C.: National Institute of Municipal Law Officers, 1946), 436. The legal status of teachers is covered in *NEA Research Bulletin*, April 1947, 25–72.

166. Richard N. Billings and John Greenya, *Power to the Public Worker* (Washington and New York: Robert B. Luce, 1974), 32.

167. Barbara Warne Newell, *Chicago and the Labor Movement: Metropolitan Unionism in the 1930s* (Urbana: University of Illinois Press, 1961), 198 and 205; and Cohen, *Making A New Deal.*

168. John Fewkes to John Fitzpatrick, December 6, 1938, and John Fewkes to William Johnson, March 25, 1939, CTU Collection, Box 19, Folder 2.

169. John Fewkes to James McCahey, October 17, 1938, and August 5, 1938, CTU Collection, Box 19, Folder 1. Without the protection of tenure or sympathetic politicians, education boards in Seattle, St. Louis, and Detroit dismissed or would not hire teachers who were union members. In 1938 only seventeen states had teacher tenure laws and the number of teachers covered by tenure was only 37.4 percent of the national workforce. Willard S. Elsbree, *The American Teacher: Evolution of a Profession in a Democracy* (New York: American Book Company, 1939), 478; Joseph Slater, "Down By Law: Public Sector Unions and the State in America, World War I to World War II" (Ph.D. diss., Georgetown University, 1998), 133–201, and 172; and Eaton, *The American Federation of Teachers,* 35.

170. *NEA Journal* 22 (April 1933): 125.

171. Levitt, "The Activities of Local Teacher Organizations in Chicago Since 1929," 1.

Chapter 2: Struggling for an Identity

1. *CTU Weekly News Bulletin,* November 10, 1937, 6; Minutes of Mass Meeting called by teachers welfare organizations, 14, May 19, 1937, CTF Collection, Box 69, Folder 4; J. C. Harger to John Fewkes, October 11, 1939, CTU Collection, Box 12, Folder 12; Minutes of CTU Union Council Meeting, October 25, 1937, 3, CTU Collection, Box 38, Folder 5.

2. Biles, *Big City Boss in Depression and War,* 3, 39, and 43. See also Gottfried, *Boss Cermak of Chicago*; Gosnell, *Machine Politics: Chicago Model*; and Wrigley, *Class Politics and Public Schools.*

3. *New York Times,* March 4, 1935, 16; and Biles, *Big City Boss in Depression and War,* 39.

4. *Chicago Daily Times,* May 23, 1937, 10.

5. Under the Otis Law of 1917, teachers seeking positions in the Chicago schools were required to pass an exam and join an eligible list until a vacancy appeared. However, when a teacher was sick or away on leave, it was permissible under the law to make a temporary, non-tenure, appointment of someone not on the eligible list. Report of the Education Committee City Club of Chicago, *The Record of William H.*

Johnson as Superintendent of Chicago Schools, April 9, 1940, 5, CTU Collection, Box 14, Folder 8.

6. See *Certain Personnel Practices in the Chicago Public Schools* (Washington, D.C.: National Commission for the Defense of Democracy through Education of the NEA, May 1945), 10–14; *Collier's Magazine,* July 6, 1940, 61; and *Chicago Tribune,* June 11, 1939, sec. 3, p. 5.

7. In the principals' exam that the newly appointed Johnson supervised in the fall of 1936 and spring of 1937, 122 out of the 155 who passed the oral exam were former pupils in Johnson's education classes he taught at Loyola University. Those who passed the exam included the sister of the board president, the secretary to Superintendent Johnson at Loyola University in Chicago, and a host of relatives of Chicago politicians and officials. Of the first fifteen appointed to positions as principals, fourteen were relatives or friends of board members or influential politicians. Report of the Education Committee City Club of Chicago, *The Record of William H. Johnson as Superintendent of Chicago Schools,* 3; Hazlett, "Crisis in School Government, 152–163; William C. Reavis, *Relations of School Principals to the Central Administration Office in Large Cities Department of School Principals of the NEA* (Chicago: NEA, 1937), 48 and 83.

8. *Certain Personnel Practices in the Chicago Public Schools,* 46 and 61; and *Chicago's Schools,* December 1941, 4.

9. Biles, *Big City Boss in Depression and War,* 26; *Chicago Herald and Examiner,* June 20, 1939, 16; L. R. Grimm, *State School Fund Payments in Illinois and Other States* (Springfield: Department of Research and Statistics, Illinois State Teachers Association, March 1936), 3. For more on Governor Henry Horner, see Thomas B. Littlewood, *Horner of Illinois* (Evanston, Ill.: Northwestern University Press, 1969).

10. *Chicago's Schools,* March 1937, 1–2; Herrick, *The Chicago Schools,* 228; and *CTU Weekly News Bulletin,* November 26, 1937, 1.

11. *Chicago Herald and Examiner,* October 20, 1937, 1 and 6, October 29, 1937, 1, and November 7, 1937, sec. 4, p. 3.

12. Report of the Education Committee City Club of Chicago, *The Record of William H. Johnson as Superintendent of Chicago Schools,* 6–7; and *Chicago Daily Times,* May 23, 1937, 10.

13. Report of the Education Committee City Club of Chicago, *The Record of William H. Johnson as Superintendent of Chicago Schools,* 7; *Chicago Herald and Examiner,* November 9, 1939, 7; and *Chicago Daily News,* December 15, 1939, 28, and May 21, 1940, 6.

14. *Propaganda Analysis,* February 25, 1941, 4, CTU Collection, Box 14, Folder 3; William Edward Eaton, "The Social and Educational Position of the American Federation of Teachers, 1929–1951" (Ph.D. diss., Washington University, 1971), 128–38; and Iversen, *The Communists and the Schools.*

15. *Christian Science Monitor,* October 4, 1937, 8.

16. Jonathan Zimmerman, *Whose America?: Culture Wars in the Public Schools*

(Cambridge Mass.: Harvard University Press, 2002), chapter 3; and Henry R. Linville, *Oaths of Loyalty for Teachers* (Chicago: AFT, 1935).

17. *Chicago Herald and Examiner,* May 9, 1934, 3 and 12, May 10, 1934, 1, June 30, 1935, 1, December 28, 1937, 3; and Chicago Board of Education, *Proceedings,* May 9, 1934, 1303.

18. Randi Jill Storch, "Shades of Red: The Communist Party and Chicago's Workers, 1928–1939" (Ph.D. diss., University of Illinois at Urbana-Champaign, 1998), 40–41.

19. John Fewkes to Irvin Kuenzli, February 15, 1941, CTU Collection, Box 12, Folder 2; "Education and Democracy in Crisis" Committee to Save the AFT leaflet, CTU Collection, Box 12, Folder 12.

20. Elizabeth Dilling, *Red Network: A Who's Who and Handbook of Radicalism for Patriots* (Chicago: Ayer Company Publishing, 1934).

21. John Fewkes, AFT Oral History Project, Tape 2, p. 2.

22. Iversen, *The Communists and the Schools,* 113.

23. Storch, "Shades of Red," 43–46. Tellingly, Randi Storch's study of the Communist Party in Chicago does not mention public school teachers at all.

24. Nathan Glazer, *The Social Basis of American Communism* (New York: Harcourt, Brace and World, 1961), 226. See Bella Dodd, *School of Darkness* (New York: P. J. Kennedy and Sons, 1954), 93 and 130. For Bella Dodd's testimony to the Senate Internal Security Subcommittee, see *Subversive Influence in the Educational Process. Hearings Before the Subcommittee to Investigate the Administration of the Internal Security Act and Other Internal Security Laws of the Committee on the Judiciary United States Senate,* 82nd Congress, September and October 1952 (Washington, D.C.: U.S. GPO, 1952), 2–40; and *Subversive Influence in the Educational Process. Hearings Before the Subcommittee to Investigate the Administration of the Internal Security Act and Other Internal Security Laws of the Committee on the Judiciary United States Senate,* 83rd Congress, March 1953 (Washington, D.C.: U.S. GPO, 1953), 511–46. For studies that show the foreign and Jewish nature of communism in the United States, see Harvey Klehr, *Communist Cadre: The Social Background of the American Communist Party Elite* (Stanford, Calif.: Hoover Institute Press, 1978), 41, 105–106 and 160; Dodd, *School of Darkness,* 110–111.

25. Kermit Eby, *Protests of an Ex-Organization Man* (Boston: Beacon Press, 1961), ix–x.

26. Kermit Eby, "The Practicability of the Ideal," WCFL radio talk, February 17, 1938, 1–3, CTF Collection, Box 71, 1938 folder; Kermit Eby, "Teachers' Unions," *Progressive Education* 20 (October 1943): 301; and Kermit Eby, "Teachers' Unions and School Administration," *American School Board Journal* 104 (June 1942): 20.

27. Kermit Eby, "Do Teachers Want Democracy?" *American School Board Journal,* February 1944, 26.

28. Kermit Eby, "Understanding the CTU," May 19, 1938, 3, CSC Collection, Box 3, Folder 7; and Kermit Eby, "Democracy, How Many Crimes . . .?" in *Miscellany Volume 1* (Bethany Theological Seminary), 12.

29. Minutes of VEC meeting, February 14, 1934, 10, CTF Collection, Box 67, "February 10–28 1934" folder.

30. Urban, *Why Teachers Organized.*

31. *Chicago Herald and Examiner,* October 29, 1937, 1, and December 12, 1937, 10; Kermit Eby, "A Picture of Union Activity," and Proceedings of CTU meeting, May 28, 1940, 21, CTU Collection, Box 29, Folder 2; "Study Class Report," August 31, 1938, CTU Collection, Box 39, Folder 1; and "Official Report by locals on referendum vote," AFT Secretary-Treasurer's Office Collection, Box 8, Folder 1.

32. Arthur W. Kornhauser, "Analysis of 'Class Structure' of Contemporary American Society-Psychological Bases of Class Divisions," in *Industrial Conflict: Psychological Interpretation,* ed. George W. Hartmann, 199–264 (New York: Cordon Company, 1939).

33. The concerns of workers in general is addressed by Melvyn Dubofsky, "Not So 'Turbulent Years': Another Look at the American 1930s," *Amerikastudien/American Studies* 24 (January 1979): 5–20; Sidney Verba and Kay Lehman Schlozman, "Unemployment, Class Consciousness, and Radical Politics: What Didn't Happen in the Thirties," *Journal of Politics* 39 (May 1977): 291–323; Zieger, *The CIO, 1935–1955;* Bernard Sternsher, "Victims of the Great Depression: Self-Blame/Non-Self-Blame, Radicalism, and Pre-1929 Experiences," *Social Science History* 1 (Winter 1977): 137–77; John Bodnar, "Immigration, Kinship and the Rise of Working-Class Realism in Industrial America," *Journal of Social History* 14 (Fall 1980): 45–66; Gary Gerstle, *Working Class Americanism: The Politics of Labor in a Textile City, 1914–1960* (Cambridge: Cambridge University Press, 1989), 96–150; and Cohen, *Making a New Deal,* 267–93.

34. George S. Counts, *Dare The Schools Build a New Social Order?* (New York: John Day 1932; republished with a preface by Wayne J. Urban (Carbondale and Edwardsville: Southern Illinois University Press, 1982), 25–26. For more on the Progressive educators and social reconstructionists in the 1930s, see C. A. Bowers, *The Progressive Educator and the Depression: The Radical Years* (New York: Random House, 1969); and Robert B. Westbrook, *John Dewey and American Democracy* (Ithaca, N.Y., and London: Cornell University Press, 1991), especially pp. 429–95.

35. *CTU Weekly News Bulletin,* October 14, 1939, 1.

36. Teachers often referred to the CCPE as "fascist." See Robert C. Moore, "Big Business Fascism in Illinois," *Journal of Educational Sociology* 8 (March 1935): 420; Llewellyn Jones, "The Chicago Interlude," *The New Republic,* July 5, 1933, described the CCPE as "unofficial fascism"; Charles Stillman, "Financial Fascism," *American Teacher,* April 1933, 10–11. See also Lipkin, "Payless Paydays," 33–34.

37. Lillian Herstein, "The Chicago Teachers Union Receives Its New Charter," October 28, 1937, p. 21, CTU Collection, Box 29, folder 1.

38. Mary Herrick to John M. Lee, May 6, 1935, CTU Collection, Box 45, Folder 4.

39. "Understanding the Chicago Teachers Union," September 8, 1938, CTU Collection, Box 34, Folder 3

40. *American Teacher,* March–April 1938, 28–29.

41. Hazlett, "Crisis in School Government," documents the struggle between the CTU and the school administration from 1937 to 1947.

42. Proceedings All Union Meeting, March 18, 1938, 41, CTU Collection, Box 29, Folder 1.

43. *Chicago Union Teacher,* April 1939, 8.

44. Hazlett, "Crisis in School Government," and Francis M. Landwermeyer, "Teacher Unionism—Chicago Style: A History of the Chicago Teachers' Union, 1937–1972" (Ph.D. diss., University of Chicago, 1978), make this point.

45. Some school boards made agreements with their local unions. The Macoupin County Federation of Teachers in Benald, Illinois, and the Proviso, Illinois, Council of the West Suburban Teachers Union negotiated agreements in 1934 and 1938 respectively. See *American Teacher,* November 1944, 6–7; and *Illinois Union Teacher,* November 1944, 2, and April 1987, 20.

46. Spero, *Government as Employer,* 346.

47. Lillian Herstein, "What Attitudes Should We Inculcate In Our Children," January 6, 1936, 7, Lillian Herstein Papers, Chicago Historical Society, Chicago, Box 1, Folder 2.

48. *American Teacher,* November 1938, 16–18.

49. *Chicago Union Teacher,* December 1938, 15.

50. *Chicago Union Teacher,* February 1939, 23.

51. Thos. M. Thompson, "Educate or Perish," transcript of talk on WCFL, October 21, 1933, 3–4, CSC Collection, Box 2, Folder 1.

52. Lillian Herstein, "What Attitudes Should We Inculcate In Our Children," 7.

53. *American Teacher,* November 1938, 19.

54. *The Nation,* September 19, 1934, 323; *Chicago Union Teacher,* February 1938, 4; *Chicago Daily News,* May 11, 1939, 12; and Robert C. Keohane, "The Social Studies in a Changing World," transcript of WCFL radio broadcast, March 31, 1938, CTU Collection, Box 31, Folder 6.

55. *Chicago Union Teacher,* February 1938, 3.

56. "Minutes of the Study Class Committee Meeting," October 16, 1939, CTU Collection, Box 39, Folder 1.

57. "The Educational Philosophy and Program of the Chicago Teachers Union," n.d. but late 1930s, CTU Collection, Box 34, Folder 3.

58. *Chicago Union Teacher,* February 1939, 9.

59. Wilson Boetticher and Raymond Lussenhop, "Social Attitudes in the Social Studies" transcript of talk on WCFL, May 8, 1940, CTU Collection, Box 31, Folder 6; and *CTU Weekly News Bulletin,* May 18, 1940, 3.

60. CTU Sub-Committee on the Single Salary Schedule and Publicity Committee, "A Report to the Whole Membership on 'the Single Salary Schedule,'" September 26, 1939, CTU Collection, Box 23, Folder 5; Slutsky, "The Chicago Teachers Union and Its Background," 46–50; The Commission on Educational Reconstruction, *Organizing the Teaching Profession,* 57; and *CTU Weekly News Bulletin,* April 1, 1939, 2.

61. *CTU Weekly News Bulletin,* November 26, 1937, 2, and May 11, 1940, 2–3; Membership lists from school delegates, CTU Collection, Box 29, Folder 5; CTU list of delegates to AFT conference 1938–1949, CTU Collection, Box 7, Folder 20, and Box 8, Folder 1.

62. May Lord, "Mary Herrick," in *Women Building Chicago 1790–1990: A Biographical Dictionary,* ed. Rima Schultz and Adele Hast, 382–85 (Bloomington: University of Indiana, 2001); Herrick, *The Chicago Schools,* 17–18.

63. Leon Despres, interview with the author, May 24, 2001; Betty Balanoff, telephone interview with the author, June 14, 2001; *Who's Who in Labor* (New York: Dryden Press, 1946), 161; O' Farrell and Kornbluh, *Rocking the Boat,* 10; Elizabeth Balanoff, "Lillian Herstein" in *Women Building Chicago 1790–1990: A Biographical Dictionary,* ed. Rima Schultz and Adele Hast, 387–91 (Bloomington: University of Indiana Press, 2001); Lester E. Engelbrecht, "Lillian Herstein: Teacher and Activist," *Labor's Heritage* 1 (April 1989): 66–75; and Carol Kleiman, "Labor Is Lillian's Love," *Chicago Tribune,* September 5, 1971, sec. 5, p. 11.

64. *American Teacher,* March 1939, 8.

65. Zieger, *The CIO 1935–1955,* 147–61; and Rick Halpern, *Down on the Killing Floor: Black and White Workers in Chicago's Packinghouses, 1904–54* (Urbana: University of Illinois Press, 1997).

66. Margaret Burroughs, interview with the author, September 27, 2001; Herrick, "Negro Employees of the Chicago Board of Education"; Lord "Mary Herrick," in *Women Building Chicago 1790–1990: A Biographical Dictionary,* ed. Rima Schultz and Adele Hast (Bloomington: University of Indiana Press, 2001).

67. Clarence Lee 1896–1961, Obituary in *Chicago Union Teacher,* May 1961, 1. See also *Chicago Union Teacher,* September 1938, 8–9, April 1939, 9, May 1949, 2 and 4, and September 1939, 24–25. Sterling Spero and Abraham Harris suggest that in the late 1920s there were only eleven black teachers in the desegregated AFT locals in the northern states. See Sterling D. Spero and Abraham L. Harris, *The Black Worker* (New York: Columbia University Press, 1931), 69. The figures for Chicago contradict this; see Herrick, "Negro Employees of the Chicago Board of Education," 77–79.

68. Charles Paul Skibbens, "The Chicago Teachers Union: A Study of its Program, Problems, and Possibilities" (M.A. thesis, Loyola University, 1956).

69. Martin Levitt, "The Chicago Citizens School Committee, A Study of a Pressure Group" (M.A. thesis, University of Chicago, 1947), 18 and 56.

70. *CTU Weekly News Bulletin,* May 11, 1940, 4.

71. Agnes Nestor to Ira Turley, November 1, 1943, CTU Collection, Box 64, Folder 3.

72. Counts, *School and Society in Chicago,* 216–19.

73. Morton Strassman, "The Activities of Parent-Teacher Associations in Elementary Schools in Chicago" (M.A. thesis, University of Chicago, 1936), 11.

74. Nathan Godfried, *WCFL Chicago's Voice of Labor* (Urbana and Chicago: University of Illinois Press, 1997), 114–15; *American Teacher,* March 1939, 8, and December

1939, 4; Kermit Eby, "A Picture of Union Activity" and "Proceedings of CTU meeting" May 28, 1940, 21, CTU Collection, Box 29, Folder 2.

75. Newell, *Chicago and the Labor Movement,* 198 and 205; Godfried, *WCFL Chicago's Voice of Labor,* 114–15; and *American Teacher,* December 1939, 4. The CTU radio program was the only weekly program by an AFT local, and they continued their Thursday night fifteen-minute program until 1949.

76. Wrigley, *Class Politics and Public Schools,* 240–48.

77. Robert A. Slayton, "Labor and Urban Politics: District 31, Steel Workers Organizing Committee, and the Chicago Machine," *Journal of Urban History* 23 (November 1996): 29–65.

78. Biles, *Big City Boss in Depression and War,* 63–64.

79. On August 2, 1939, Congress enacted the Hatch Act, which banned federal employees from taking part in national elections. A second Hatch Act, passed on July 19, 1940, extended the previous act to include any public employees at local or state level running for office at federal elections. Both could have been interpreted to include teachers. Subsequently, the Hatch Act was amended by the Brown amendment in 1942, which excluded teachers from certain parts of the law. Leo Hassenauer to John Fewkes, August 21, 1940, CTU Collection, Box 25, Folder 3; *NEA Research Bulletin* (April 1947): 58–59; Myron Tripp "Some Judicial Decisions Affecting Dismissal of Teachers for Political and Religious Reasons," n.d. 4, AFT Collection, Series V1, Box 1, "AFT History and Miscellaneous Bulletins" folder; and Hammond Indiana Board of Education to employees, March 1940, CTU Collection, Box 12, Folder 12.

80. Paul H. Douglas, *In the Fullness of Time: The Memoirs of Paul H. Douglas* (New York: Harcourt Brace Jovanovich, 1971), 415; Leaflet of "Independent Committee for Paul Douglas for Alderman," January 25, 1939, CSC Collection, Box 3, Folder 7; and *Chicago Daily News,* July 25, 1939, 5.

81. Harold L. Ickes, *The Secret Diary of Harold L. Ickes, Vol. 2, The Inside Struggle 1936–1939* (New York: Simon and Schuster, 1954), 512–15; Biles, *Big City Boss in Depression and War,* 68; and Douglas, *In the Fullness of Time,* 86.

82. *Chicago Union Teacher,* October 1948; John Fewkes to union member, March 25, 1940, CTU Collection, Box 42, Folder 1; "Questionnaire for all candidates for ward committeemen," n.d. but 1939, CTU Collection, Box 31, Folder 5; and *CTU Weekly News Bulletin,* April 6, 1940, 2–3, October 26, 1940, 3–4, and November 2, 1940, 3–4.

83. Raymond J. Peacock campaign leaflet, n.d., CTU Collection, Box 35, Folder 4.

84. "Proceedings of General Membership Meeting," April 2, 1940, CTU Collection, Box 29, Folder 2.

85. *Chicago Daily News,* June 22, 1937, 11; and John Fewkes to James B. McCahey, June 24, 1937, CTU Collection, Box 36, Folder 16.

86. Margaret Haley, "Report to the Group in the Conference of June 29th at the Bismarck Hotel," June 24, 1937, 4; and Margaret Haley, "Record of Events Leading Up to the McCahey Conferences," 22, both in CTF Collection, Box 71.

87. Elsie K. McElliott to Margaret Haley, June 24, 1937, Elsie K. McElliott to Margaret Haley, June 28, 1937, and CTF memo, July 1, 1937, all in CTF Collection, Box 70, "June to September 1937" folder; Margaret Haley, "Report to the Group in the Conference of June 29th at the Bismarck Hotel," June 29, 1937, 13, CTF Collection, Box 71; and Herrick, *The Chicago Schools*, 229.

88. John Fewkes to Mayor Kelly, July 13, 1937, Fewkes to Henry Horner, August 19, 1937, CTU Collection, Box 35, Folder 4; Fewkes to public official, November 23, 1937, and letters from various churches to Fewkes and to Mayor Kelly, November and December 1937, CTU Collection, Box 35, Folder 10; John Fewkes to citizens of Chicago, November 29, 1937, CTU Collection, Box 14, Folder 6; and Herrick, *The Chicago Schools*, 230.

89. John Fewkes "Uphill Struggle All the Way, The First Ten Years of the Chicago Teachers Union," *American Federationist* 55 (February 1948): 18–19.

90. *CTU Weekly News Bulletin*, September 13, 1941, 1.

91. *Chicago Herald and Examiner*, November 11, 1937, 1 and 4; and *Chicago American*, November 11, 1937, 2.

92. *Chicago Herald and Examiner*, December 8, 1937, 1.

93. *American Teacher*, March 1939, 8.

94. "Elementary Functional Group," March 3, 1939, CTU Collection, Box 115, "CTU minutes of functional meetings" folder; John Fewkes to Mayor Kelly, March 3, 1939, and Mayor Kelly to John Fewkes, March 6, 1939, CTU Collection, Box 20, Folder 6; and *Chicago Daily News*, May 12, 1939, 1 and 8.

95. All of this information is in handwritten notes in CTF Collection, Box 74, "June–Dec 1941" folder. See also *Chicago Tribune*, May 22, 1939, 2.

96. *Chicago Daily News*, May 16, 1939, 3.

97. *Chicago Daily News*, February 3, 1939, 1, May 12, 1939, 1 and 8. Lyle H. Wolf had been restored to the faculty of Chicago Teachers College in July 1938. Among new CTU members, the newspaper reported, was Marie McCahey, principal of Warren School and sister of the board president.

98. John Fewkes to William Johnson, September 12, 1939, CTU Collection, Box 19, Folder 2.

99. *Chicago Daily Times*, December 4, 1940, 34.

100. Herrick, *The Chicago Schools*, 253.

101. See numerous letters from John Fewkes and Ira Turley to William Johnson in CTU Collection, Box 14, Folders 8 and 9; John Fewkes to locals of the CFL, April 9, 1941, CTU Collection, Box 18, Folder 1; Kermit Eby, "Portrait of an Educator or Politics and Teacher Morale," July 8, 1940, 11, CTU Collection, Box 28, Folder 4; "Administrative Spying on Union Talks," CTU memo, n.d., CTU Collection, Box 14, Folder 8; John Fewkes to Henry Schweinhaut, April 11, 1940, CTU Collection, Box 14, Folder 8; and *Chicago Daily News*, December 11, 1940, 10.

102. Kristi Andersen, *The Creation of a Democratic Majority, 1928–1936* (Chicago and London: University of Chicago Press, 1979); and John M. Allswang, *A House for All Peoples* (Lexington: University Press of Kentucky, 1971).

103. In 1936, Chicago contained 927,000 Catholics, 363,000 Jews, and 505,000 Protestants (see U.S. Department of Commerce, Bureau of the Census, *Religious Bodies, 1936* (Washington, D.C.: Government Printing Office, 1936), 1: 480–82.

104. *NEA Research Bulletin,* November 1940.

105. *Chicago Tribune,* October 29, 1937.

106. Levitt, "The Chicago Citizens School Committee," 44.

107. John Fitzpatrick to John Fewkes, July 19, 1939, and John Fewkes to John Fitz-patrick, July 27, 1939, CFL/Fitzpatrick Papers, Chicago Historical Society, Box 27, Folder 10.

108. Lillian Herstein, interview, Roosevelt University.

109. Eby, *Protests of an Ex-Organization Man,* 49.

110. Esther F. Gibney, "The Public School Teacher in a Metropolis" (Ph.D. diss., Northwestern University, 1947), 221, 233, and 242.

111. Edna Siebert to CTU delegates, December 8, 1938, CTU Collection, Box 21, Folder 3.

112. "Membership in the CTU from 1937 to 1963," CTU Collection, Box 29, Folder 6; and *CTU Weekly News Bulletin,* November 15, 1941, 2.

113. Eby, "Democracy, How Many Crimes . . .?" 11.

114. "Memorandum to Fill the Gaps in the Discussion of the Meeting of the Execu-tive Board of the CTU January 3, 1940," and Lillian Herstein to John Fewkes, January 17, 1940, both in Mary J. Herrick Collection, Box 1, Folder 4, Archives of Labor and Urban Affairs, Walter Reuther Library, Wayne State University, Detroit, Mich.; and Lillian Herstein interview with Elizabeth Balanoff, October 30, 1970, 93–94, Roosevelt University, Chicago.

115. Letter from John Fewkes to Irvin Kuenzli, February 15, 1941, CTU Collection, Box 12, Folder 2; and "Education and Democracy in Crisis" Committee to Save the AFT leaflet, CTU Collection, Box 12, Folder 12.

116. Robert Speer to John Fewkes, March 24, 1941, and John Fewkes to Robert Speer, March 26, 1941, both in CTU Collection, Box 12, Folder 12; "Lawson School Petition," December 21, 1940, Sara Rubin to John Fewkes, March 4, 1941, Anna Recu to John Fewkes, March 3, 1941, Cecilie Beni to John Fewkes (n.d.) and Daisy Driss to John Fewkes, March 5, 1941, CTU Collection, Box 11, Folder 7; *Save the American Federation of Teachers News Bulletin,* March 12, 1941, CTU Collection, Box 12, Folder 2; and *CTU Weekly News Bulletin,* April 19, 1941, 1. For more on the communist issue in the AFT, see *American Teacher,* April 1941, 4–17; Iversen, *The Communists and the Schools.*

Chapter 3: World War II, Accommodation, and the Struggle for Equal Pay

1. Joan L. Rog, "Chicago Public Schools March Off to War: Participation of the City Public Schools in the Second World War: 1941–1945" (Ph.D. diss., Loyola University of Chicago, 1996), 170; *Annual Report of the Business Manager, 1943* (Chicago: Board

of Education, 1943); John Howatt, "Schools and the War," *Chicago Schools Journal,* September–December 1943, 12–15; William H. Johnson, "Chicago Public Schools Contribute to the War Effort," *Chicago Schools Journal,* January–June 1943, 49–56; Slutsky, "The Chicago Teachers Union and Its Background," 41; Paul G. Armstrong to Ira S. Turley, January 5, 1942, Ira S. Turley telegram to unknown, June 11, 1942, CTU Collection, Box 14, Folder 9; Ira Turley to Butler Laughlin, December 20, 1941, CTU Collection, Box 41, Folder 9; and *CTU Weekly News Bulletin,* June 6, 1942, 1.

2. *Saturday Evening Post,* September 2, 1939, 5, 6, 9, 32, 34, and 36; and *CTU Weekly News Bulletin,* September 9, 1939, 3. For more on the communist issue in the AFT, see *American Teacher,* April 1941, 4–17.

3. *CTU Weekly News Bulletin,* September 16, 1944, 1.

4. *CTU Weekly News Bulletin,* February 28, 1942, 2, September 19, 1942, 1–2, December 12, 1942, 2, September 23, 1944, 3, December 11, 1943, 1; CTU leaflet, May 1942, CTF Collection, Box 74, "January–May 1943" folder; Ira S. Turley to William Johnson, October 22, 1942, CTU Collection, Box 14; and Mayor Edward Kelly to Ira S. Turley, January 11, 1943, CTU Collection, Box 20, Folder 8. The money helped Kelly fund the Chicago Service Men's Center, which supplied food and lodging to off-duty servicemen.

5. *American Teacher,* November 1943, 30; Rog, "Chicago Public Schools March Off to War," 170; The Board of Education's contribution to the war effort is covered in *Annual Report of the Business Manager, 1943; CTU Weekly News Bulletin,* August 31, 1940, 1, November 23, 1940, 2, June 2, 1943, 2, September 2, 1944, 3; CTU leaflet, May 1942, CTF Collection, Box 74, "January–May 1943" folder; Ira Turley, "Report to the Membership on Civilian Defense," April 14, 1942, CTU Collection, Box 19, Folder 6; CTU leaflet January 29, 1942, CTU Collection, Box 41, Folder 9; Herrick, *The Chicago Schools,* 254; Harry C. McKinsie, "The Schools in the War Effort," June 9, 1945, WCFL talk, CTU Collection, Box 34, Folder 4; Irvin R. Kuenzli to Lucy Mellen, March 23, 1945, AFT Collection, Series III: Executive Council, Box 5, John M. Fewkes folder; and "The Chicago Teachers Contribution to the War Effort," n.d., CTU Collection, Box 49, Folder 9.

6. Biles, *Big City Boss in Depression and War,* 116–19; Harry C. McKinsie, "The Schools in the War Effort," June 9, 1945, WCFL talk, CTU Collection, Box 34, Folder 4; *Chicago Principals Club Reporter,* December 1945, 3–5; and Ira S. Turley telegram to unknown, June 11, 1942, CTU Collection, Box 14, Folder 9. For more on Chicago during the war, see Perry R. Duis and Scott La France, *We've Got a Job To Do: Chicagoans and World War II* (Chicago: Chicago Historical Society, 1992); Perry Duis's chapter in *The War in American Culture: Society and Consciousness During World War II,* ed. Lewis A. Erenberg and Susan E. Hirsch (Chicago and London: University of Chicago Press, 1996); and Paul M. Green and Melvin G. Holli, *World War II Chicago* (Chicago: Arcadia, 2003).

7. *Chicago Principals Club Reporter,* December 1945, 3–5; and Certificate in CTU Collection, Box 41, Folder 9.

8. *Certain Personnel Practices in the Chicago Public Schools,* 31 and 45.

9. *Certain Personnel Practices in the Chicago Public Schools,* 24. Butler Laughlin was president of the Chicago Teachers College from 1928 until his removal by Superintendent Johnson in 1936.

10. When the departments were closed and some subjects abolished, teachers were not guaranteed employment and could be dismissed. *Chicago Sun,* September 12, 1943, 28.

11. *Chicago Daily News,* January 28, 1943, 8.

12. *Certain Personnel Practices in the Chicago Public Schools,* 40.

13. Leon Despres, interview with the author, May 24, 2001.

14. *Certain Personnel Practices in the Chicago Public Schools,* 25.

15. *Chicago Herald American,* December 11, 1942, 1 and 2; and *Chicago Sun,* January 1, 1943, 6, September 12, 1943, 28.

16. Ira Turley to William Johnson, October 22, 1942, CTU Collection, Box 14, Folder 9; Mayor Kelly to Ira Turley, January 11, 1943, CTU Collection, Box 20, Folder 8; *Chicago Sun,* February 3, 1944, 12, accused the board of "playing ball" with the CTU.

17. Robert H. Zieger, *American Workers, American Unions* 2nd ed. (Baltimore and London: Johns Hopkins University Press, 1994), 86.

18. "Can Teachers' Unions Be Called Out On Strike," AFT pamphlet, Chicago, n.d., CTU Collection, Box 31–4; and unidentified news paper clippings in AFT series 111, Box 5, "Arthur Elder" folder; and Bernard Yabroff and Lily Mary David, "Collective Bargaining and Work Stoppages Involving Teachers," *Monthly Labor Review* 76 (May 1953): 478.

19. Kermit Eby to Ira Turley, August 19, 1942, and Ira Turley to Kermit Eby, August 21, 1942, CTU Executive Board memo, n.d., all in CTU Collection, Box 26, Folder 5; "The Facts and Controlling Considerations in the Case of Kermit Eby and the Chicago Teachers Union," CTU Collection, Box 64, Folder 3.

20. Leaflet, CTU Collection, Box 78, Folder 7; and *Chicago Sun,* January 27, 1943, 21, January 30, 1943, 5.

21. Ira Turley to Mayor Kelly, February 10, 1943, and Ira Turley to Mayor Kelly, February 23, 1943, CTU Collection, Box 20, Folder 8; and Ira Turley to William Johnson, September 16, 1943, William Johnson to commissioner of police James Allman, September 22, 1943, and William Johnson to Ira Turley, September 22, 1943, CTU Collection, Box 14, Folder 9; Committee for Continued Unity and Action to the membership, n.d., AFT collection, Series 1, Box 62, "Forward With Turley" folder.

22. *CTU Weekly News Bulletin,* February 15, 1943, 2; *Chicago Daily News,* February 2, 1943, 9, and *Chicago Sun,* January 29, 1943, 6.

23. *Chicago Daily News,* February 6, 1943, 6, February 12, 1943, 14, and February 16, 1943, 8.

24. Lydia Tilken to Ira Turley, March 3, 1942, CTU Collection, Box 42, Folder 5.

25. Kermit Eby, "Do Teachers Want Democracy?" *American School Board Journal,*

February 1944, 26; Eby, "Democracy, How Many Crimes . . . ?" 5 and 9. Immediately after his sacking, Eby became assistant director of research and education for the CIO in Washington, D.C., and director in 1945. In 1948 he became associate professor of social sciences at the University of Chicago and wrote on labor and religion. Eby died in Chicago on August 10, 1962, at age fifty-eight. See Philip G. Altbach, "Kermit Eby: Pragmatic Idealist," *Liberal Education* 50 (1964): 71–77; and John R. Steelman, *Who's Who In Labor* (New York: Dryden Press, 1946), 101.

26. *Chicago's Schools,* May–June 1944, 2.

27. Herrick, *The Chicago Schools,* 254; *CTU Weekly News Bulletin,* May 16, 1942, 2, October 23, 1943, 1; and Levitt, "The Chicago Citizens School Committee," 18, 47 and 55.

28. Murphy, *Blackboard Unions,* 87–90; Krug, *The Shaping of the American High School;* Rury, "Who Became Teachers?" 28; Arthur Walz, "Why the Union Single Salary Schedule for Chicago Teachers?" WCFL talk, February 12, 1944, CTU Collection, Box 34, Folder 5; and CTU Sub-Committee on the Single Salary Schedule and Publicity Committee, "A Report to the Whole Membership on 'the Single Salary Schedule,'" September 26, 1939, CTU Collection, Box 23, Folder 5.

29. U.S. Department of Commerce and Bureau of the Census, *Historical Statistics of the United States,* 368–69; NEA Committee on Equal Opportunity, *Progress and Problems in Equal Pay for Equal Work;* Murphy, *Blackboard Unions,* 88; and CTU Sub-Committee on the Single Salary Schedule and Publicity Committee, "A Report to the Whole Membership on 'the Single Salary Schedule,'" September 26, 1939, CTU Collection, Box 23, Folder 5.

30. Hazel Davis, "Single Salary Schedules Today," *NEA Journal,* December 1947, 638–39; C. C. Ball, "In Defense of a Single Salary Plan," *Nation's Schools* 15 (March 1935); E. E. Lewis, "Desirable Principles of Teachers' Salary Schedules," *American School Board Journal* 80 (May 1930): 45–46; W. C. McGinnis, "The Salary Schedule," *Schools and Society* 31 (January 11, 1930): 61–62; R. D. Shouse, "The Salary Question; Is It Fair that High School Instructors Are Paid More than Elementary Teachers," *Nation's Schools* 15 (January 1935): 25–26; W. W. Carpenter and A. G. Capps, "Unfair to Whom?" *Nation's Schools* 15 (April 1935): 33–34; Elbridge C. Grover, "Brief Resume of Studies on the Single Salary Schedule," *American School Board Journal* 91 (July 1935): 26 and 75; Ed Hurley, *The Single Salary Schedule* (NEA report, 1985), 7; Lyle L. Morris, *The Single Salary Schedule: An Analysis and Evaluation* (New York: Teachers College, Columbia University, 1930), 2–3; and The Civic Federation, *A Report on Teachers' Salaries in Chicago* (Chicago: Civic Federation, 1946), 37. For more on the NEA and its attitude toward the single salary schedule, see Wayne J. Urban, *More Than the Facts: The Research Division of the NEA 1922–1997* (Lanham, Md.: University Press of America, 1998), 56–57.

31. CTF meeting, December 6, 1930, 78, CTF Collection, Box 11; *Illinois Teacher,* December 1930, 142, and January 1938, 149; Russell L. Wise, "Organization and Administration in Chicago," *Chicago Schools Journal,* January 1933, 73; *NEA Research*

Bulletin 14 (March 1936): 59; *CTF Bulletin*, September 1940, 3; CTU Collection, Box 18, Folder 5; and CTF to Board of Education, CTF Collection, Box 71, Folder 1.

32. As a number of historians note, women wanted to end sex-based disadvantages and used labor unions as their vehicle. See Nancy Gabin, *Feminism in the Labor Movement: Women and the United Auto Workers, 1935–1975* (Ithaca, N.Y.: Cornell University Press, 1990); Annelise Orleck, *Common Sense and a Little Fire: Women and Working-Class Politics in the United States, 1900–1965* (Chapel Hill and London: University of North Carolina Press, 1995); and Dorothy Cobble, *The Other Women's Movement: Workplace Justice and Social Rights in Modern America* (Princeton, N.J., and Oxford: Princeton University Press, 2004).

33. Folger and Nam, *Education of the American Population*, 81–84; and Gibney, "The Public School Teacher in a Metropolis," 68 and 49.

34. Robert G. Spinney, *City of Big Shoulders, A History of Chicago* (DeKalb: Northern Illinois University Press, 2000), 200–201; and Duis and France, *We've Got a Job To Do*, 67–95.

35. Gibney, "The Public School Teacher in a Metropolis," 39.

36. Dennis A. Deslippe, *"Rights Not Roses" Unions and the Rise of Working-Class Feminism, 1945–80* (Urbana and Chicago: University of Illinois Press, 2000), 44–45; Karen Anderson, *Wartime Women: Sex Roles, Family Relations, and the Status of Women During World War II* (Westport, Conn.: Greenwood Press, 1981), 6 and 56; and Susan M. Hartmann, *The Home Front and Beyond: American Women in the 1940s* (Boston: Twayne Publishers, 1982), 61 and 65.

37. The Civic Federation, *A Report on Teachers' Salaries in Chicago*, 33; NEA report, "Salaries of City School Employees, 1942–43"; "More Money for Elementary Teachers," October 5, 1943, CTU Collection, Box 115; Sharon Hartman Strom, "'We're No Kitty Foyles': Organizing Office Workers for the Congress of Industrial Organizations, 1927–50," in *Women, Work and Protest: A Century of US Women's Labor History*, ed. Ruth Milkman, 225 (London: Routledge and Kegan Paul, 1985).

38. Stenographic report of "Regular Meeting of the CTF," December 11, 1943, 21, CTF Collection, Box 26; and CTF meeting minutes, December 12, 1942, 73, CTF Collection, Box 25.

39. CTF meeting minutes, June 14, 1941, 41, CTF Collection, Box 24.

40. Minutes of CTU Union Council Meeting, October 25, 1937, 4–5, and Minutes of CTU Union Council Meeting, November 1, 1937, 2–3, both in CTU Collection, Box 38, Folder 5; and stenographic report of "Regular Meeting of the CTF," December 11, 1943, 101, CTF Collection, Box 26.

41. CTU Sub-Committee on the Single Salary Schedule and Publicity Committee, "A Report to the Whole Membership on 'the Single Salary Schedule,'" September 26, 1939, CTU Collection, Box 23, Folder 5; Slutsky "The Chicago Teachers Union and Its Background," 46–50; *Chicago Union Teacher*, February 1943, 6; Ira Turley "The CTU Acts for Salary Restoration," November 5, 1941 CTU leaflet, AFT Collection, Series 1, Box 62, "Forward With Turley" folder.

42. Committee for Continued Unity and Action to the membership, n.d.; "Susan Scully Needs No Defense," *Election News,* May 17, 1943, 4; *Election News,* May 11, 1944, 2, all in AFT Collection, Series 1, Box 62, "Forward With Turley" folder. The three winners on the opposition slate were Arthur N. Turnbull, Samuel Barth, and Helen C. Campbell.

43. Slutsky, "The Chicago Teachers Union and Its Background," 48–49; and *Chicago Union Teacher,* November 1944, 7.

44. *Illinois Union Teacher,* May 1944, 3; *American Teacher,* January 1944, 7; and CTF meeting minutes, December 12, 1942, 85, CTF Collection, Box 25.

45. Attendance in Chicago elementary schools fell 12 percent, from 318,445 in 1940 to 279,030 in 1945, and, because of greater job opportunities for older students, high school attendance fell 20 percent from 144,671 to 115,715 (see Table 5). In 1945, 437 high school teachers and 2,913 elementary teachers still waited for employment on an assigned list. The Civic Federation, *A Report on Teachers' Salaries in Chicago,* 1.

46. Benjamin C. Willis, *Report on the Chicago Teachers College to the Chicago Board of Education* (Chicago: Board of Education, 1956), 11–12.

47. Irvin R. Kuenzli to members of the AFT Executive Council, March 7, 1946, CTU Collection, Box 28, Folder 6.

48. The Civic Federation, *A Report on Teachers' Salaries in Chicago,* 57–58.

49. *CTU Weekly News Bulletin,* January 15, 1944, 1; Slutsky, "The Chicago Teachers Union and its Background," 49; and *Election News,* May 11, 1944, 1, AFT Collection, Series 1, Box 62, "Forward With Turley" folder.

50. Arthur Walz to Arlie Swender, February 26, 1945, CTU Collection, Box 28, Folder 6.

51. Hartmann, *The Home Front and Beyond,* 212–13.

52. *CTU Weekly News Bulletin,* December 3 1945, 2; and Chicago Board of Education, *Proceedings,* January 14, 1946, 511–12.

53. Chicago Board of Education, *Facts and Figures 1956,* 33.

54. *CTU Weekly News Bulletin,* February 11, 1946, 2–3.

55. Gibney, "The Public School Teacher in a Metropolis," 31, 252, 262, and 268.

56. Gibney, "The Public School Teacher in a Metropolis," 37–42.

57. Henry G. Borchardt, "A Teacher Looks at His Job," *Life,* January 6, 1947, 84.

58. Robert E. Rogers, "Feminization of Our Schools," *Pictorial Review,* September 1930, 67.

59. Borchardt, "A Teacher Looks at His Job," 77–78 and 82.

60. CTF meeting minutes, December 8, 1945, 30, CTF Collection, Box 28.

61. *CTU Weekly News Bulletin,* October 14, 1946, 4.

62. Arthur Walz to CTU delegates, January 7, 1947, CTU Collection, Box 3, Folder 4; Men Teachers Club, "Attention-All Men Teachers" leaflet, 1945, CTF Collection, Box 76, "June–December 1945" folder; *Chicago Sun,* February 4, 1947, 1 and 2; Men Teachers Club, "A Message of Great Importance to All High School Teachers," leaflet,

1947, and "A Report to our members," 1947, both in CTF Collection, Box 78, "July–December 17 1948" folder.

63. Miss Doyle, Phillips High School petition, October 31, 1946, and November 1, 1946, CTU Collection, Box 26, Folder 6.

64. *Chicago Daily News,* January 7, 1947, 4; *CTU Weekly News Bulletin,* January 20, 1947, 6; CTU Policies Committee meeting minutes, May 5, 1947, CTU Collection, Box 64, Folder 3; and newspaper cutting in Carl Megel Papers, Box 21, Folder 13.

65. Deslippe, *"Rights Not Roses" Unions and the Rise of Working-Class Feminism,* 44–45; and Cannella, *171 Years of Teaching in Chicago,* 14.

66. Zieger, *The CIO, 1935–1955,* 213; and Myron Lieberman and Michael H. Moskow, *Collective Negotiations for Teachers: An Approach to School Administration* (Chicago: Rand McNally, 1966), 80–81.

67. Milton Derber, *Labor In Illinois: The Affluent Years, 1945–80* (Urbana and Chicago, University of Illinois Press, 1989), 242–44.

68. Marshall O. Donley, Jr., *Power to the Teacher: How America's Educators Became Militant* (Bloomington and London: Indiana University Press. 1976), 38–39; and *Life,* March 10, 1947, 36–37.

69. Donley, *Power to the Teacher,* 38–39; and *Life,* March 10, 1947, 36–37.

70. Spero, *Government as Employer,* 332–37; Lieberman and Moskow, *Collective Negotiations for Teachers,* 290; Oakes, "Public and Professional Reactions to Teachers' Strikes," 256; Donley, *Power to the Teacher,* 36; and Philip Kochman, "The Developing Role of Teachers Unions" (Ph.D. diss., Columbia University, Teachers College, 1947), 25.

71. *Illinois Union Teacher,* November 1946, 1.

72. *Readers Digest,* October 1945, 89; *Life,* September 16, 1946, 36; and *Saturday Evening Post,* November 9, 1946, 16, 17, 110, 111, and 113.

73. Gibney, "The Public School Teacher in a Metropolis," 278.

74. "Salary Schedule Survey, 1956–57," n.d., no author, Illinois State Federation of Labor Collection, Box 93, AFT Folder; Benjamin Fine, *Our Children Are Cheated: The Crisis In American Education* (New York: Henry Holt and Company, 1947), 43–44. See also I. L. Kandel, *The Impact of the War Upon American Education* (Chapel Hill: University of North Carolina Press, 1948).

75. Gibney, "The Public School Teacher in a Metropolis," 194 and 170–71.

76. Gibney, "The Public School Teacher in a Metropolis," 41.

77. Fine, *Our Children Are Cheated,* 3–4 and 10; and Willard B. Spalding, "Teachers' Organizations Are Poor Stuff," AFT collection, Series 1X: Miscellaneous, Box 1, "Misc. copies of older bulletins" folder.

78. CTF minutes, September 13, 1947, 29, CTF Collection, Box 29.

79. See petitions in CTU Collection, Box 14, Folder 9, Box 26, Folder 6, Box 39, Folder 5; Mildred M. Lynch to CTU, February 8, 1946, Gertrude Berger, Stockton School to CTU Executive Board, February 4, 1946, and transcript of WCFL radio

talk by Charlotte Russell, "The Progress of the CTU," 4, May 18, 1946, all in CTU Collection, Box 26, Folder 6; and *CTU Weekly News Bulletin,* January 19, 1946, 3, and March 25, 1946, 2.

80. *American Teacher,* November 1944, 6–7; and *Illinois Union Teacher,* November 1944, 2, and April 1987, 20.

81. Donley, *Power to the Teacher,* 38–39; and Robert J. Thornton, "U.S. Teachers' Organizations and the Salary Issue: 1900–1960," *Research in Economic History* (Supplement 2, 1982): 139–40.

82. Spero, *Government as Employer,* 28, 71, 76, 198, and 214; Marvin J. Levine and Eugene C. Hagburg, *Public Sector Labor Relations* (St. Paul, Minn.: West Publishing Company, 1979), 15; and Richard C. Kearney, *Labor Relations in the Public Sector* (New York: Marcel Dekker, 1984), 43.

83. Englewood High School, Bateman Elementary School, Kelly High School petitions, February 1946, CTU Collection, Box 39, Folder 5; *CTU Weekly News Bulletin,* June 3, 1946, 1; *Illinois Union Teacher,* September 1948, 1; *American Teacher,* April 1959, 7; and *Chicago Union Teacher,* October 1948, 7.

84. Richard C. McFadden, *Labor Management Relations in the Illinois State Service* (Urbana: Institute of Labor and Industrial Relations, University of Illinois, 1952), 25–26.

85. American Federation of Teachers, "Monthly Report," October 1937–April 1965, AFT, Series X11: AFT Locals Collection, Box 6, CTU folders; *Chicago Herald American,* January 5, 1947, 6; and *Chicago Daily News,* January 6, 1947, 1, January 7, 1947, 1 and 4, January 8, 1947, 1, and January 9, 1947, 4.

86. American Schoolmen's Association leaflet, November 1948, CTF Collection, Box 78, "July–December 17 1948" folder; Herschel N. Scott, "Boys Must Be Taught By Men," n.d., CTF Collection, Box 93, "Undated Items" folder; *Chicago Herald American,* September 9, 1952; Ed Hurley, *The Single Salary Schedule* (NEA report 1985), 7. With the introduction of the single salary schedule in January 1954, the high school teachers worked longer hours than elementary school teachers for the same pay.

87. For more on labor feminism, see Dorothy Sue Cobble, "Recapturing Working-Class Feminism: Union Women in the Postwar Era," in *Not June Cleaver: Women and Gender in Postwar America, 1945–1960,* ed. Joanne Meyerowitz, 57–83 (Philadelphia, Temple University Press, 1994); Dorothy Sue Cobble, "'A Spontaneous Loss of Enthusiasm'": Workplace Feminism and the Transformation of Women's Service Jobs in the 1970s," *International Labor and Working-Class History* 56 (Fall 1999): 23–44: Cobble, *The Other Women's Movement*; Orleck, *Common Sense and a Little Fire*; and Gabin, *Feminism in the Labor Movement.*

88. The exception here is Urban, *More Than the Facts.*

Chapter 4: The Cold War in the Chicago Public Schools

1. Murphy, *Blackboard Unions,* chapter 9.

2. *Certain Personnel Practices in the Chicago Public Schools,* 35, 40, and 62.

3. Herrick, *The Chicago Schools,* 271–74.

4. *Chicago Sun,* May 19, 1946, 1, and May 29, 1946, 1.

5. *Chicago Tribune,* July 11, 1946, 6.

6. Wrigley, *Class Politics and Public Schools,* 252–56.

7. *Chicago Sun,* November 10, 1944, 21.

8. "The Facts of the Chicago Investigation," CTU leaflet, August 23, 1946, CTU Collection, Box 7, folder 25.

9. *Chicago Sun,* May 29, 1946, 1.

10. Wrigley, *Class Politics and Public Schools,* 254.

11. Grimshaw, *Union Rule in the Schools,* 38.

12. Grimshaw, *Union Rule in the Schools,* 38.

13. Kay H. Kamin, "A History of the Hunt Administration of the Chicago Public Schools, 1947–1953" (Ph.D. diss., University of Chicago, 1970), 6–7; and *Chicago's Schools,* September 1947, 2.

14. Herrick, *The Chicago Schools,* 279 and 290.

15. Transcript of Herold C. Hunt radio talk on WCFL, September 14, 1948, CTU Collection, Box 24, Folder 4; and Mary Herrick talk on WCFL, January 27, 1948, CTU Collection, Box 31, Folder 9.

16. *Chicago Union Teacher,* November 1950, 3.

17. *Chicago Board of Education Proceedings,* January 20, 1948, 976–79.

18. *Chicago Union Teacher,* January 1948, 5, and February 1948, 1.

19. *Chicago Union Teacher,* February 1948, 1.

20. *Chicago Daily News,* January 23, 1948, 1.

21. Transcript of WDGY radio speech, March 20, 1948, Lillian Herstein Collection, Box 1, Folder 5.

22. *Chicago Sun,* January 24, 1948, 1 and 48; and CTU leaflet, January 24, 1948, CTU Collection, Box 24, Folder 1.

23. John Fewkes to CTU delegates, January 30, 1948, CTU Collection, Box 21, Folder 4.

24. Minutes of high school functional meeting, February 16, 1949, p. 3, CTU Collection, Box 23, Folder 7.

25. *Chicago Union Teacher,* October 1948, 7, and November 1948, 3.

26. Herrick, *The Chicago Schools,* 191–93.

27. *Chicago Union Teacher,* February 1948, 9.

28. "Membership in the CTU from 1937 to 1963," CTU Collection, Box 29, Folder 6; and Herrick, *The Chicago Schools,* 291.

29. "Membership in the CTU from 1937 to 1963," CTU Collection, Box 29, Folder 6; and Herrick, *The Chicago Schools,* 291.

30. Introduction to CTF Papers, CHS. Figures from Herrick, *The Chicago Schools,* 291.

31. Figures from Bureau of Labor Statistics quoted in *Chicago Union Teacher,* December 1953.

32. *Facts and Figures* (Chicago Board of Education, 1951), 17.

33. Cannella, *171 Years of Teaching in Chicago,* 9, 10, and 15–17; Braun, *Teachers and Power.*

34. Paul E. Peterson, *School Politics Chicago Style* (Chicago and London: University of Chicago Press, 1976), 187, for the salaries of Chicago teachers.

35. *Chicago's Schools* (December–January 1950), 3.

36. *Facts and Figures* (Chicago Board of Education, 1956), 20.

37. Zieger, *The CIO, 1935–1955,* chapter 8.

38. Richard M. Fried, *Nightmare in Red: The McCarthy Era in Perspective* (New York: Oxford University Press, 1990), chapter 4; and Ellen Schrecker, *Many Are the Crimes: McCarthyism in America* (Boston: Little, Brown and Company, 1998).

39. Fried, *Nightmare in Red,* chapter 6.

40. Gilbert E. Smith, *The Limits of Reform: Political and Federal Aid to Education, 1937–1950* (New York and London: Garland, 1982), 186–88; and Murphy, *Blackboard Unions,* 179–82.

41. Murphy, *Blackboard Unions,* 181. After the *Brown v. Board of Education* Supreme Court decision of 1954, blacks and liberals opposed federal aid for segregated schools and southerners refused to support any bill that tried to alter the structure of school segregation. Only after the Soviet Union had launched Sputnik in October 1957 and several books and journals noted that the Soviets were leading the United States in academic achievement did Congress pass the National Defense Education Act in 1958. The act provided financial assistance to college students in the form of loans and fellowships and federal aid for states to improve instruction in the schools in the sciences and technology. See Urban and Wagoner, *American Education,* 281–83.

42. Levine and Hagburg, *Public Sector Labor Relations,* 15; and Spero, *Government as Employer,* 28.

43. Urban and Wagoner, *American Education,* 291–92; John Ligtenberg to Irvin Kuenzli, October 31, 1947, AFT Secretary-Treasurer's Office Collection, Box 7, Folder 3; and Kearney, *Labor Relations in the Public Sector,* 218.

44. Yabroff and David, "Collective Bargaining and Work Stoppages Involving Teachers," 478.

45. Iversen, *The Communists and the Schools,* 360.

46. George H. Gallup, ed., *The Gallup Poll: Public Opinion, 1935–1971,* vol. 2, 1949–1958 (New York: Random House, 1972), 853 and 1135–1136.

47. Stuart J. Foster, *Red Alert! Educators Confront the Red Scare in American Public Schools, 1947–1954* (New York: Peter Lang, 2000), 87. See *Subversive Influence in the Educational Process. Hearings Before the Subcommittee to Investigate the Administration of the Internal Security Act and Other Internal Security Laws of the Committee on the Judiciary United States Senate* (Washington, D.C.: U.S. GPO, 1952–1955).

48. Iversen, *The Communists and the Schools,* 264–69 and 336–40; and Mary Herrick, "Oaths Required of Teachers," July 1957, 1, AFT Collection, Series 1: President's Department, Box 72, "Research Reports 1957" folder.

49. *Los Angeles Evening Herald and Express,* January 24, 1950, sec. C, p. 1.

50. Zimmerman, *Whose America?,* chapter 4; Urban and Wagoner, *American Education,* 277–78; and Iversen, *The Communists and the Schools,* 255.

51. Arnold R. Hirsch, *Making the Second Ghetto: Race and Housing in Chicago, 1940–1960* (Cambridge: Cambridge University Press, 1983), 202.

52. Iversen, *The Communists and the Schools,* 276–81.

53. Walter Gellhorn, ed., *The States and Subversion* (Ithaca, N.Y.: Cornell University Press, 1952), 54–139.

54. *Chicago Union Teacher,* February 1951, 6.

55. *Chicago Tribune,* October 7, 1947, 1 and 12, October 8, 1947, 1–2, October 9, 1947, 1 and 19. See also James T. Selcraig, *The Red Scare in the Midwest, 1945–55: A State and Local Study* (Ann Arbor, Mich.: UMI Research Press, 1982), 77.

56. Mary J. Herrick, "The Civics Course in the Chicago Public Schools," January 13, 1953, 2, CSC Collection, Box 12, Folder 2.

57. Herrick, "The Civics Course in the Chicago Public Schools," 3; *Chicago Tribune,* August 26, 1950, 3, and October 10, 1950, 1.

58. *Chicago Union Teacher,* October 13, 1950, 3; and Selcraig, *The Red Scare in the Midwest,* 79.

59. Selcraig, *The Red Scare in the Midwest,* 79.

60. *Chicago Tribune,* October 12, 1950, 7.

61. *Chicago Tribune,* September 8, 1948, 10.

62. *Chicago Schools Journal,* March–April 1954, 163–64.

63. Robert Havighurst, *The Public Schools of Chicago: A Survey for the Board of Education of the City of Chicago* (Chicago: Chicago Board of Education, 1964), 129.

64. *Chicago Daily News,* September 8, 1948.

65. *Chicago Tribune,* October 7, 1949.

66. *Chicago Tribune,* June 13, 1950.

67. *Chicago Tribune,* December 14, 1949, and August 27, 1949.

68. Entry No. 10, February 22, 1951, Box 114, File #600, 1949–54; Entry No. 10, February 14, 1953, and April 29, 1953, Box 114 File #600, 1949–54, both in Chicago Police Department, Red Squad selected records, Chicago Historical Society (hereafter Red Squad selected records); newspaper cutting in Illinois State Federation of Labor and Congress of Industrial Organizations papers, Box 50, AFT Folder; and *Chicago Tribune,* October 12, 1950, 7.

69. *Chicago Herald American,* May 24, 1948, 1 and 2, and May 25, 1948, 1 and 2.

70. *Chicago Sunday Tribune,* December 9, 1951, sec. 3, p. 1.

71. Red Squad selected records.

72. Entry No. 10, February 22, 1951, Box 114, File #600, 1949–54; Series of Letters dated May 19, 1951, Box 114, File #600, 1949–54; Entry No. 10, December 17, 1952, Box 114, File #600, 1949–54; Entry No. 10, January 19, 1953, Box 114, File #600, 1949–54; Detective to commanding officer, June 27, 1953, Box 114, File #600, 1949–54; Letter, May 5, 1955, Box 114, File #600, 1955–56, all in Red Squad selected records.

73. Entry No. 9, February 20, 1951, Box 114, File #600, 1949–54; Letter, October 18, 1956, Box 114, File #600, 1956–58; Letter, May 15, 1953, and May 22, 1953, Box 114, File #600, 1949–54; and Letter, April 19, 1951, Box 114, File #600, 1949–54, all in Red Squad selected records.

74. Margaret Burroughs, interview with the author, September 27, 2001.

75. Barbara Sizemore, telephone interview with the author, October 29, 2002.

76. Detective to commanding officer, June 12, 1953, Box 114, File #600, 1949–54; and Letter, February 17, 1956, Box 114, File #600, 1955–56, Red Squad selected records.

77. Commanding officer, industrial detail, to commissioner of police, March 9, 1951, Box 114, File #600, 1949–54, Red Squad selected records.

78. Mary Sperling McAuliffe, *Crisis on the Left: Cold War Politics and American Liberals, 1947–1954* (Amherst: University of Massachusetts Press, 1978), 90–103.

79. File #744, Box 72, "Citizens Schools Committee" folder, Red Squad selected records; *Chicago Tribune,* March 16, 1951, 11.

80. John Fewkes to Carl Harris, February 11, 1941, CTU Collection, Box 14, Folder 1.

81. Harvey A. Swets to John Fewkes, March 10, 1941, CTU Collection, Box 11, Folder 7.

82. John Fewkes to E. L. Kimball, March 10, 1949, CTU Collection, Box 20, Folder 10.

83. Herrick, "The Civics Course in the Chicago Public Schools," 1 and 4.

84. *Chicago Union Teacher,* April 1951, 5.

85. *Chicago Union Teacher,* June 1953, 3.

86. AFT Proceedings 34th Annual Convention 1951, 429.

87. Herrick, *The Chicago Schools,* 293–300.

88. *Chicago Union Teacher,* June 1948, 2, and September 1948, 1.

89. *Chicago Sun-Times,* April 16, 1953, 55.

90. *Chicago Sun-Times,* June 26, 1955, 3.

91. *Illinois Union Teacher,* September 1952, 6.

92. *Chicago Sun-Times,* June 26, 1955, 3; John Fewkes interview, AFT Oral History Project, Tape 2, 11; and William James Hurley, "Professional Growth Through Activities of the CTU" (M.A. thesis, DePaul University, 1952), 47.

93. *Chicago Union Teacher,* March 1949, 3.

94. *Chicago Union Teacher,* February 1951, 6.

95. *Chicago Union Teacher,* April 1951, 5; and *Chicago Tribune,* August 10, 1950, 20, and March 16, 1951, 10.

96. *Chicago Union Teacher,* September 1953, 1.

97. *Chicago Tribune,* July 19, 1955, 16.

98. Mary Cannon, "Tobey Silbert Schein Prinz," in *Women Building Chicago, 1790–1990, A Biographical Dictionary,* ed. Rima Lunin Schultz and Adele Hast, 719–22 (Bloomington and Indianapolis: Indiana University Press, 2001).

99. Isabelle McErlean, interview with Matthew Salvador, December 4, 2002, in Joliet Area Historical Museum Archives.

100. Herrick, "The Civics Course in the Chicago Public Schools," 5.

101. *Chicago Union Teacher,* June 1948, 2, and September 1948, 1.

102. Tommie Martin, interview with the author, August 9, 2002.

103. Margaret Burroughs, interview with the author, September 27, 2001.

104. Timuel Black, interview with the author, May 16, 2000.

105. Mary Cannon's notes of interview with Gertrude Berger, February 11, 1995, in possession of author; and Cannon, "Tobey Silbert Schein Prinz," 720.

106. Ken Brown, interview with the author, April 7, 2000, and Timuel Black, interview with the author, May 16, 2000.

107. Letters, September 29, 1955, and November 10, 1955, Box 114, File #600, 1955–56, Red Squad selected records; and Meyer Weinberg, interview with the author, May 24, 2000.

108. "The Fight Against the Broyles Test Oath" leaflet, April 1956, CTU Collection, Box 28, Folder 10.

109. *Chicago Daily News,* September 8, 1955, 37; *Chicago American,* March 4, 1956, 1; *Chicago Tribune,* December 18, 1956, F sec. 2, p. 1, and December 19, 1956, F part 2 p. 5; Shirley Lens, "Statement," December 17, 1956, Sidney Lens Collection, Chicago Historical Society, Box 2, Folder 6; and Shirley Lens to CTU delegates, March 27, 1956, CTU Collection, Box 28, Folder 10.

110. Harvey Klehr, John Earl Haynes, and Fridrikh Igorevich Firsov, *The Secret World of American Communism,* Russian trans. Timothy D. Sergay (New Haven, Conn., and London: Yale University Press, 1995), 13.

Chapter 5: The Campaign for Collective Bargaining Rights and the Civil Rights Movement

1. Pete Seeger, "Teacher's Blues," various artists, *American History in Ballad and Song,* vol. 2 (Folkways Records, 1962).

2. *Time,* August 16, 1963, 45.

3. Murphy, *Blackboard Unions,* 277; and Robert C. O'Reilly, *Understanding Collective Bargaining in Education: Negotiations, Contracts and Disputes Between Teachers and Boards* (Metuchen, N.J., and London: Scarecrow Press, 1978), 123–24.

4. Murphy, *Blackboard Unions,* 209.

5. London, "Business and the Chicago Public School System," 127.

6. Spinney, *City of Big Shoulders,* 204–208; Hirsch, *Making the Second Ghetto*; Arnold R. Hirsch, "Massive Resistance in the Urban North: Trumbull Park, Chicago, 1953–1966," *Journal of American History* 82 (September 1995).

7. See Melvin G. Holli, *The American Mayor: The Best and Worst Big-City Leaders* (Philadelphia: Pennsylvania University Press, 1999), 107–16. For more on Mayor Daley, see also Roger Biles, *Richard J. Daley: Politics, Race and the Governing of Chicago* (DeKalb: Northern Illinois University Press, 1995); Mike Royko, *Boss: Richard J. Daley of Chicago* (New York: Dutton, 1971); and Adam Cohen and Elizabeth Taylor, *American Pharaoh. Mayor Richard J. Daley: His Battle for Chicago and the Nation* (Boston: Little Brown and Company, 2000).

8. Havighurst, *The Public Schools of Chicago,* 54.

9. Herrick, *The Chicago Schools,* 346.

10. Homel, *Down From Equality,* 27.

11. City of Chicago, Board of Education, Advisory Panel on Integration of the Public Schools, Report, "Integration of the Public Schools, Chicago," March 31, 1964, Philip M. Hauser, chairman, 15.

12. City of Chicago, Board of Education, Advisory Panel on Integration of the Public Schools, Report, "Integration of the Public Schools, Chicago," March 31, 1964, Philip M. Hauser, chairman, 16. After complaints from the Urban League, NAACP, CORE, TFIS, and others in January 1963, the board appointed the first black principal at a non-black school, Whittier Elementary School. *Integrated Education* 1 (June 1963): 53.

13. New York, Los Angeles, Philadelphia, and Detroit being the other four cities. Gary Orfield, *Must We Bus? Segregated Schools and National Policy* (Washington, D.C.: Brookings Institute, 1978), 158, 162.

14. "De Facto Segregation in the Chicago Public Schools," *Crisis* 65 (February 1958): 88–92.

15. Report on Office of Education Analysis of Certain Aspects of Chicago Public Schools Under Title VI of the Civil Rights Act of 1964 (U.S. Department of Health, Education and Welfare, January 1967), 13.

16. *Chicago Tribune,* May 12, 1962, sec. 3 p. 9.

17. Homel, *Down From Equality,* 35–40; and "De Facto Segregation in the Chicago Public Schools," 92. For examples of gerrymandering school boundaries to maintain racial segregation, see *Hearings Before a Special Subcommittee of the Committee on Education and Labor House of Representatives, 89th Congress, First Session on Investigation of De Facto Racial Segregation in Chicago's Public Schools,* July 27 and 28, 1965 (Washington, D.C.: GPO, 1965), 154–60 and 207–10; and *Integrated Education* 3 (December 1965–January 1966), 24–28. In 1979 the Office of Civil Rights of the Department of Health, Education and Welfare (HEW) confirmed these charges. For example, rather than transfer black students from overcrowded Jenner Elementary School in the 1950s to empty classrooms in nearby white Ogden, Lincoln, and La Salle Elementary Schools, the report stated, the board built two additions to Jenner. See *Chicago Tribune,* April 12, 1979, 1.

18. Report on Office of Education Analysis of Certain Aspects of Chicago Public Schools Under Title VI of the Civil Rights Act of 1964 (U.S. Department of Health, Education and Welfare, January 1967), 9.

19. *Integrated Education* 2 (April–May 1964): 23.

20. Robert Havighurst, *The Public Schools of Chicago: A Survey for the Board of Education of the City of Chicago* (Chicago: Chicago Board of Education, 1964), 2; Cannella, *171 Years of Teaching in Chicago,* 28–29; and Herrick, *The Chicago Schools,* 306–10.

21. Larry Cuban, *Urban School Chiefs Under Fire* (Chicago: University of Chicago Press, 1976), 2.

22. U.S. Commission on Civil Rights, *Civil Rights USA, Public School North and West, 1962* (Washington, D.C.: GPO 1962), 230.

23. Christopher Robert Reed, *The Chicago NAACP and the Rise of Black Professional Leadership, 1910–1966* (Bloomington and Indianapolis: Indiana University Press, 1997). 189–90; "De Facto Segregation in the Chicago Public Schools," 87–93; Charles and Bonnie Remsberg, "Chicago: Legacy of an Ice Age," *Saturday Review,* May 20, 1967, 75; James R. Ralph, *Northern Protest: Martin Luther King, Jr., Chicago, and the Civil Rights Movement* (Cambridge, Mass.: Harvard University Press, 1993), 15; and Cuban, *Urban School Chiefs Under Fire,* 8–11. The main studies of the civil rights movement in Chicago are Ralph, *Northern Protest;* and David J. Garrow, *Chicago 1966: Open Housing Marches, Summit Negotiations and Operation Breadbasket* (New York: Carlson, 1989), both of which concentrate on the King movement in Chicago often at the expense of local grassroots organizing; Alan B. Anderson and George W. Pickering, *Confronting the Color Line: The Broken Promise of the Civil Rights Movement in Chicago* (Athens: University of Georgia Press, 1986); and Danns, *Something Better for Our Children,* which both argue that the early civil rights movement in Chicago achieved little.

24. "De Facto Segregation in the Chicago Public Schools," 87–93; Remsberg "Chicago: Legacy of an Ice Age," 75; Ralph, *Northern Protest,* 15; Cuban, *Urban School Chiefs Under Fire,* 8–11; City of Chicago, Board of Education, Advisory Panel on Integration of the Public Schools, Report, "Integration of the Public Schools, Chicago," March 31, 1964, Philip M. Hauser, chairman.

25. *Chicago Tribune,* July 11, 1–2, July 12, 1–2, July 13, 5, July 16, 3, July 17, 7, July 18, 1–2, July 19, 1–2, and July 20, 3, 1963, August 3, 2, August 13, 1–2, August 14, 1–2, August 15, 1 and 10, August 16, 1–2, August 20, 6, and August 24, 7, 1963; *Chicago Sun-Times,* August 13, 1963, 1 and 4, and *Chicago Tribune,* September 7, 1–2, September 9, 4, and September 10, 2, 1963. For more on CORE, see August Meier and Elliot Rudwick, *CORE, A Study in the Civil Rights Movement, 1942–1968* (New York: Oxford University Press, 1973); and on the Chicago Urban League, see Arvarh E. Strickland, *History of the Chicago Urban League* (Columbia and London: University of Missouri Press, 2001).

26. Anderson and Pickering, *Confronting the Color Line,* 157; *Chicago Sun-Times,* October 23, 1963, 1; and *Integrated Education* 1 (December 1963–January 1964): 10–11, and *Integrated Education* 2 (April–May 1964), 23.

27. McFadden, *Labor Management Relations,* 27; Illinois State Federation of Teachers to Rueben Soderstrom, May 3, 1951, Illinois State Federation of Labor and Congress of Industrial Organizations papers, Box 111, Teacher Bills Folder, Springfield Ill.; and *Illinois Union Teacher,* September 1950, 4, and March 1953, 1.

28. Ron Patterson, interview with the author, April 7, 2000.

29. Anthony Grosch, interview with the author, August 15, 2002.

30. Remsberg, "Chicago: Legacy of an Ice Age," 73–75 and 91–92; Alan Rosenthal, *Pedagogues and Power: Teacher Groups in School Politics* (Syracuse, N.Y.: Syracuse University Press, 1969), 151; and Cuban, *Urban School Chiefs Under Fire,* 2.

31. *Chicago Union Teacher,* January 1961, 2.

32. Cannella, *171 Years of Teaching in Chicago,* 9, 10, and 15–17. See also Braun, *Teachers and Power.*

33. Peterson, *School Politics Chicago Style,* 186.

34. Peterson, *School Politics Chicago Style,* 212.

35. *Caucus Comments,* May 1960, 3, in CSC Collection, Box 18, Folder 1.

36. David Farber, *The Age of Great Dreams, America in the 1960s* (New York: Hill and Wang, 1994), 8.

37. Sanders, *The Education of an Urban Minority,* 204.

38. John Fewkes, interview broadcast on WAIT radio, February 17, 1961, CTU Collection. See Donley, *Power to the Teacher,* 195–97, for similar problems elsewhere.

39. *Chicago Union Teacher,* February 1960, 1.

40. Havighurst, *The Public Schools of Chicago.*

41. Anna Anthony, interview with the author, August 22, 2002.

42. *Chicago Sun-Times,* September 8, 1968, sec. 2, p. 3.

43. Havighurst, *The Public Schools of Chicago,* 352–53.

44. Ron Brown, interview with the author, April 7, 2000.

45. *Illinois Education,* May 1959, 366.

46. NEA, *What Teachers Think: A Summary of Teacher Opinion Poll Findings 1960–65* (Washington, D.C.: NEA, 1965), 19.

47. *Chicago's American,* March 24, 1964, 6.

48. *Chicago Union Teacher,* June 1961, 1–2.

49. *Chicago Daily News,* March 6, 1964, 1.

50. *Chicago's American,* March 5, 1964, 3.

51. *Chicago Daily News,* February 8, and 9, 1954. Katznelson and Weir, *Schooling for All*; and Mirel, *The Rise and Fall of an Urban School System.*

52. Robert E. Doherty and Walter E. Oberer, *Teachers, School Boards, and Collective Bargaining: A Changing of the Guard* (Ithaca: New York State School of Industrial and Labor Relations, a Statutory College of the State University, Cornell University, 1967), 21.

53. Herrick, *The Chicago Schools,* 379.

54. Lichtenstein, *State of the Union,* 136–37.

55. Havighurst, *The Public Schools of Chicago,* 418; and Marlowe Mogill, telephone interview with the author, June 19, 2001.

56. Ron Patterson, interview with the author, April 7, 2000.

57. "Proceedings of CTU Conference with Negro American Labor Council," March 19, 1964, 81, CTU Collection, Box 30, Folder 8; "Why the Parents of this Community (Englewood) are Demonstrating against the Beale School Principal," PACE and ECCA petition, CTU Collection, Box 14, Folder 14; *Chicago Tribune,* September 14, 1963, 1; *Chicago Sun-Times,* September 20, 1963, 3 and 5; and *Chicago Sun-Times,* March 24, 1964, 3.

58. Virginia Johnson, "Teachers' Conceptions of Pupil-Discipline" (M.A. thesis, University of Chicago, 1951), 83, 88, 107, 108, and 112.

59. *Chicago Daily News,* December 1, 1965, 8.

60. Havighurst, *The Public Schools of Chicago,* 418.

61. Jerald E. Podair, "'White' Values, 'Black' Values: The Ocean Hill–Brownsville Controversy and the New York City Culture, 1965–1975" *Radical History Review* 59 (Spring 1994), also makes this point about the different cultural values of white teachers and black students. In New York, however, the teachers were overwhelmingly Jewish teachers from eastern Europe inspired by socialist and radical ideals.

62. *Chicago Daily News,* December 1, 1965, 8.

63. *Chicago's American,* March 5, 1964.

64. *Chicago Schools Journal,* February 1961, 217–18.

65. Gerard Joseph Heing, "A Study of Certain Attitudes of Elementary School Teachers Who Have Remained in Two Chicago Public School Districts That Contrast in Pupil Transiency" (Ph.D. diss., Northwestern University, 1965), 2, 12–14, and 133.

66. John Winget, "Teacher Inter-School Mobility Aspirations: Elementary Teachers, Chicago Public School System, 1947–48" (Ph.D. diss., University of Chicago, 1952).

67. Howard Becker, "Role and Career Problems of the Chicago Public School Teacher" (Ph.D. diss., University of Chicago, 1951), 16, 19, and 310. See also Howard Becker, "Social Class Variation in Teacher-Pupil Relationships," *Journal of Educational Sociology* 25 (April 1952): 451–65; and Howard Becker, "The Teacher in the Authority System of the Public School," *Journal of Educational Sociology* 27 (November 1953): 129–41.

68. Earl C. Valentine, "The Occupational Expectations of Three Normal School Student Groups" (M.A. thesis: University of Chicago, 1950), 49.

69. Havighurst, *The Public Schools of Chicago,* 165 and 352–53.

70. *Chicago Daily News,* January 16, 1965, 4.

71. *Chicago Tribune,* October 7, 1963, 1 and 2.

72. Newspaper cuttings, CTU Collection, Box 88, Folder 3.

73. T. F. Connery, Open Letter, n.d., CTF Collection, Box 89, "Nov–Dec 1963" folder.

74. Rolland Dewing, "Teacher Organizations and Desegregation, 1954–1964" (Ph.D. diss., Ball State University, 1967).

75. Patrick J. Groff, "Teacher Organizations and School Segregation," *School and Society* 90 (December 15, 1962): 441–42.

76. *New York Times,* December 11, 1961, 26.

77. Cecile S. Oliver to Carl Megel, December 21, 1952, Megel Collection, Box 3, "Segregation 1952" folder.

78. AFT Proceedings, 40th Annual Convention 1956, 307.

79. Timuel Black, interview with the author, May 16, 2000. Between 1956 and 1958, Herrick took a leave from teaching to be full-time director of national research for the American Federation of Teachers. She served as vice president of the AFT between 1958 and 1962.

80. Meyer Weinberg, interview with the author, May 24, 2000.

81. In a roundtable discussion undertaken by the *Chicago American* in 1961 with Raymond Pasnick, member of the Board of Education, and Edwin Berry, executive director of the Chicago Urban League, Fewkes alone refused to highlight these issues. *Chicago American,* December 17, 1961, 1 and 6.

82. "CTU Position on Integration Within Chicago Public Schools," May 21, 1962, CTU Collection, Box 26, Folder 4.

83. Barry Shapiro, "The Chicago Teachers Union and the Ghetto" (M.A. thesis, University of Chicago, 1968), 73–74.

84. *Chicago Tribune,* August 12, 1963.

85. Hurley, "Professional Growth Through Activities of the CTU," 47.

86. Shapiro, "The Chicago Teachers Union and the Ghetto," 24.

87. *Integrated Education* 1 (December 1963–January 1964): 43.

88. *Chicago Union Teacher,* November 1963, 2.

89. "Proceedings of CTU Conference with Negro American Labor Council," March 19, 1964, 45, CTU Collection, Box 30, Folder 8.

90. *Chicago's American,* March 12, 1964, 1.

91. *Integrated Education* 1 (January 1963): 22; *Chicago Daily News,* May 21, 1965, 1; and *Chicago Union Teacher,* May 1965, 1.

92. *Chicago Union Teacher,* December–January 1966, 3.

93. CTU scrapbook collection, Box 92, Folder 5.

94. *American Teacher,* February 1955, 19; *Chicago Union Teacher,* June 1961, 1, and "Chicago Teachers Union's Position on Discipline in the Schools," March 28, 1960, CSC Collection, Box 18, Folder 2.

95. "Chicago Teachers Union's Position on Discipline in the Schools," March 28, 1960, CSC Collection, Box 18, Folder 2; *Chicago Union Teacher,* October 1954, 6, and November 1954–December 1960; "Tomorrow's Exploding Schools," CTU program, May 1961, CSC Collection, Box 18, Folder 1; and "Proceedings of CTU Conference with Negro American Labor Council," March 19, 1964, 46 and 82, CTU Collection, Box 30, Folder 8.

96. *Chicago Sun-Times,* January 22, 1965, 22.

97. *Chicago's American,* May 8, 1961, 3.

98. *Chicago Sun-Times,* February 4, 1966, 29; and *Chicago Union Teacher,* February 1966, 1.

99. *Chicago Sun-Times,* September 14, 1963, 5.

100. Wayne Urban, *Gender, Race, and the National Education Association* (New York and London: RoutledgeFalmer, 2000), 201.

101. Cole, *The Unionization of Teachers.* See also William T. Lowe, "Who Joins Which Teachers' Group?" *Teacher College Record* 66 (1965): 614–19; William S. Fox and Michael H. Wince, "The Structure and Determinants of Occupational Militancy Among Public School Teachers," *Industrial and Labor Relations Review* 30 (1976): 47–58.

102. *NEA Journal,* February 1963, 17–20.

103. Havighurst, *The Public Schools of Chicago,* 339; and Donley, *Power to the Teacher,* 195.

104. *Facts and Figures* (Chicago Board of Education, 1964), 47; and *Facts and Figures* (Chicago Board of Education, 1967), 65.

105. NEA Research Division, *The American Public-School Teacher, 1965–66* (Washington, D.C.: NEA, 1967), 51.

106. Havighurst, *The Public Schools of Chicago,* 339.

107. *Facts and Figures* (Chicago Board of Education, 1964), 47; and *Facts and Figures* (Chicago Board of Education, 1967), 65.

108. Havighurst, *The Public Schools of Chicago,* 170, 236, 339, 342–43, and quote on 340.

109. *The Nation,* September 25, 1967, 260.

110. Robert J. Hoder to Charles Cogen, May 21, 1966, AFT Office of the President Collection 1960–1974, Box 14, "Chicago, Volume 1" folder, Archives of Labor and Urban Affairs, Walter Reuther Library, Wayne State University, Detroit, Mich.

111. Arthur Marwick, *The Sixties: Cultural Revolution in Britain, France, Italy and the United States, c. 1958–c. 1974* (New York: Oxford University Press, 1998); Theodore Roszak, *The Making of a Counterculture: Reflections of the Technocratic Society and Its Youthful Opposition* (New York: Doubleday, 1969); Terry H. Anderson, *The Sixties* (New York: Longman, 1999); and Stewart Burns, *Social Movements of the 1960s: Searching for Democracy* (Boston: Twayne Publishers, 1990).

112. Anthony Grosch, interview with the author, August 15, 2002.

113. Melvin Urofsky ed., *Why Teachers Strike* (New York: Doubleday Anchor Book, 1970), 3.

114. James Chiakulas, interview with the author, May 16, 2001.

115. Havighurst, *The Public Schools of Chicago,* 159, 161, and 344.

116. *Chicago Daily News,* April 21, 1966, 3; and Anthony Grosch, interview with the author, August 15, 2002.

117. Ron Brown, interview with the author, April 7, 2000.

118. Timuel Black, interview with the author, May 16, 2000.

119. Timuel Black, interview with the author, May 16, 2000.

120. Timuel Black, interview with the author, May 16, 2000; Anna Anthony, interview with the author, August 22, 2002; and Letter, April 19, 1951, Box 114, File #600, 1949–54, Red Squad selected records.

121. Anna Anthony, interview with the author, August 22, 2002.

122. Ron Patterson, interview with the author, April 7, 2000.

123. Ken Brown, interview with the author, April 7, 2000.

124. Newspaper cuttings, CTU Collection, Box 88, Folder 5.

125. Reed, *The Chicago NAACP and the Rise of Black Professional Leadership,* 116.

126. Reed, *The Chicago NAACP and the Rise of Black Professional Leadership,* 122 and 176.

127. Anderson and Pickering, *Confronting the Color Line,* 454.

128. Meyer Weinberg, interview with the author, May 24, 2000; *Chicago Union Teacher*, May 1958, 2; Red Squad selected records, Box 231, "1139 Teachers Action Committee 1968–1970" folder, Box 72, "Chicago Teachers Union" folder, and Box 77, "Teachers for Integrated Schools" folder, Chicago Historical Society; *Caucus Comments*, February 1960, 3–4, and May 1960, 4, both in CSC Collection, Box 18, Folder 1; and Timuel Black, interview with the author, May 16, 2000.

129. *Chicago Union Teacher*, June 1958, 1.

130. *Caucus Comments*, June 1960, 1, CSC Collection, Box 19, Folder 1; and *Chicago Union Teacher*, January 1959, 1 and 2, and June 1960, 1.

131. Meyer Weinberg, interview with the author, May 24, 2000; *Integrated Education* 1 (January 1963); *Integrated Education* 2 (December 1963–January 1964): 10–11.

132. Gallup, *The Gallup Poll: Public Opinion, 1935–1971*, vol. 1, 1935–1948, 66–67; George H. Gallup, ed., *The Gallup Poll: Public Opinion, 1935–1971*, vol. 3, 1959–1971 (New York: Random House, 1972), 1970. At the same time, 36 percent believed that teachers should be able to strike while 53 percent opposed teachers' strikes. See Gallup *The Gallup Poll*, vol. 3, 1591–92.

133. *Illinois Union Teacher*, January 1955; and *American School Board Journal*, January 1955.

134. "Memorandum of Understanding," December 1959, AFT Secretary-Treasurer's Office, Collection, Box 8, Folder 24.

135. James L. Fletcher, "The Judicial and Legislative History of Public School Employees Collective Bargaining in Illinois, 1921–1971" (Ph.D. diss., Northwestern University, 1971), chapter 4.

136. Murphy, *Blackboard Unions*, 212–18; Philip Taft, *United They Teach: The Story of the United Federation of Teachers* (Los Angeles: Nash Publishing, 1974); and the website of the UFT at <www.uft.org>.

137. T. M. Stinnett, *Turmoil in Teaching: A History of the Organizational Struggle for America's Teachers* (New York; Macmillan, 1968), 72 and 145.

138. J. Joseph Loewenberg and Michael H. Moskow, *Collective Bargaining in Government: Readings and Cases* (Englewood Cliffs, N.J.: Prentice-Hall, 1972), 1.

139. Rosenthal, *Pedagogues and Power*; Doherty and Oberer, *Teachers, School Boards, and Collective Bargaining*, 21; and Charles Cogen, interview, AFT Oral History Collection, Tape 2, October 24, 1986, 4.

140. Newspaper cuttings, CTU Collection, Box 88, Folder 4.

141. Donley, *Power to the Teacher*, 197–202.

142. Zieger, *American Workers, American Unions*, 163–64. See also Mark McCulloch, *White Collar Workers in Transition: The Boom Years, 1940–1970* (Westport, Conn.: Greenwood Press, 1983).

143. Landwermeyer, "Teacher Unionism—Chicago Style," 212–15 and 222; and *Chicago Union Teacher*, January 1963, 1.

144. James Chiakulas, interview with the author, May 16, 2001.

145. James Chiakulas, interview with the author, May 16, 2001; CTU Collection,

Box 37, Folder 2; and "The Legacy of a Unique Union Leader," *Catalyst,* November 1999.

146. Doherty and Oberer, *Teachers, School Boards, and Collective Bargaining,* 32.

147. Peterson, *School Politics Chicago Style,* 190–91; Landwermeyer, "Teacher Unionism—Chicago Style," 210–21; and *Chicago Union Teacher,* February 1964, 1–10.

148. Fletcher, "The Judicial and Legislative History of Public School Employees Collective Bargaining in Illinois," 194 and chapter 5.

149. Peterson, *School Politics Chicago Style,* 190; and Grimshaw, *Union Rule in the Schools,* 44 and 100–1.

150. Landwermeyer, "Teacher Unionism—Chicago Style," 246–47.

151. Peterson, *School Politics Chicago Style,* 192.

152. Landwermeyer, "Teacher Unionism—Chicago Style," 268–74.

153. See various letters from teacher to Fewkes in CTU Collection, Box 27, Folder 3; and *Chicago Union Teacher,* May 1964, 4, and June 1964, 1.

154. On December 18, 1964, a dozen police were called to the house of representatives meeting from which fifty members of the United Teachers Committee were barred. *Chicago Sun-Times,* December 19, 1964, 1 and 10.

155. *Renewal,* July 4, 1965, 16; and quoted in Arvarh E. Strickland, "The Schools Controversy and the Beginning of the Civil Rights Movement in Chicago," *Historian* 58 (Summer 1996): 722.

156. *Chicago's American,* August 15, 1965, 4; Ralph, *Northern Protest,* 26 and 34–38.

157. Anderson and Pickering, *Confronting the Color Line,* 159–60, 179, and 180.

158. *Teachers Action News,* n.d., AFT Office of the President Collection, Box 14, "Chicago, Volume 1" folder.

159. Ironically, James Chiakulas, whose temporary teaching certificate the Chicago Board of Education had refused to renew in July 1965 because he had made "unprofessional statements" on a television program when he alleged discrimination against black teachers by the Board of Education, could no longer be a union representative, and he sat in a local bar alone while the historic vote took place, without a job or a position in the union. Chiakulas subsequently filed a grievance against the Board of Education but lost the case. Between 1965 and 1968, he worked full-time for the American Federation of State, County, and Municipal Employees Union (AFSCME) before he rejoined the Chicago public schools as an FTB in 1968. In 1974, he left to work as regional director for the Illinois Education Association. See James Chiakulas, interview with the author, May 16, 2001; and affidavit of James Chiakulas, n.d., AFT Office of the President Collection, Box 14, "Chicago, Volume 1" folder.

160. Anderson and Pickering, *Confronting the Color Line,* 188–94.

161. Sol Tax, ed., *The People vs. the System: A Dialogue in Urban Conflict* (Chicago: Acme Press, 1968), 167–68.

162. After the Board of Education recognized the CTU as the sole bargaining agent for the Chicago public school teachers, the Chicago Education Association filed suit,

and in 1966 a circuit court judge ruled that the board could grant exclusive bargaining rights to the CTU even without a state law. Indeed, it was only in 1983 that the Illinois General Assembly passed the Illinois Education Labor Relations Act and the Illinois Public Employee Labor Relations Act, which required public sector unions and management to bargain in good faith.

Chapter 6: Teacher Power and Black Power Reform the Public Education System

1. *Chicago Sun-Times,* May 23, 1969, sec. 1, p. 20.

2. Wendell Pritchett, *Brownsville, Brooklyn: Blacks, Jews, and the Changing Face of the Ghetto* (Chicago and London: University of Chicago Press, 2002); Podair, "'White' Values, 'Black' Values; Podair, *The Strike That Changed New York*; Gordon, *Why They Couldn't Wait*; Joshua B. Freeman, *Working-Class New York: Life and Labor Since World War II* (New York: New Press, 2000), chapter 12; Diane Ravitch, *The Great School Wars, New York City, 1805–1973: A History of the Public Schools as Battlefield of Social Change* (New York: Basic Books, 1974); and Murphy, *Blackboard Unions*, 236–37.

3. Gary Orfield and Susan E. Eaton, *Dismantling Desegregation: The Quiet Reversal of Brown v. Board of Education* (New York: New Press, 1996); Peter Irons, *Jim Crow's Children: The Broken Promise of the Brown Decision* (New York: Viking, 2002); Anderson and Pickering, *Confronting the Color Line*; and Ralph, *Northern Protest*. Danns, *Something Better for Our Children,* argues that while the early civil rights movement in Chicago achieved little in terms of school reform, the Black Power turn after 1966 led to major school reform. She overstates the support of parents and teachers for community control, overplays the amount of unity in the black community between teachers, parents, and students, and downplays the role of labor organizations in school reform.

4. Anderson and Pickering, *Confronting the Color Line,* 107 and 301–04.

5. U.S. Office of Education, Report on Office of Education Analysis of Certain Aspects of Chicago Public Schools Under Title VI of The Civil Rights Act of 1964, January 1967.

6. In 1966, the property owner in Illinois paid 71.8 percent of school costs, fourth highest among the fifty states; 6 percent of school revenue came from the federal government, and 22.2 percent from the state. A school bond issue of $25 million passed a referendum in November 1966, in March 1967 a referendum approved an increase in the city's educational tax, and in June 1968 a bond issue passed for school supplies. See *Chicago Union Teacher,* March 1967, 3.

7. *Chicago Sun-Times,* January 8, 1969, 37.

8. James Redmond, "Increasing De Segregation of Faculty, Students and Vocational Educational Program," Chicago Board of Education, August 1967; and Herrick, *The Chicago Schools,* 342, 345–46, and 430.

9. Peterson, *School Politics Chicago Style*, chapter 7.

10. Herrick, *The Chicago Schools*, 343–50.

11. *Chicago Daily News*, March 11, 1968, 1; and Katznelson and Weir, *Schooling For All*, 189.

12. *Saturday Review*, November 20, 1971, 90.

13. Chicago Urban League, "Racial Segregation in the Chicago Public Schools, 1965–1966," (Chicago, September 1966), 17.

14. Chicago Board of Education, Report, "Racial Survey, Administrative and Teaching Personnel," 1968–1972.

15. Herrick, *The Chicago Schools*, 342 and 430; and "The Elusive Black Educator," *School Management*, March 1969, 56.

16. In 1969, Alvin Boutte replaced Green, and the three black members and Latina Mrs. David Cerda made a voting block on the board. Peterson, *School Politics Chicago Style*, 32.

17. James Redmond, "Increasing De Segregation of Faculty, Students and Vocational Educational Program," Chicago Board of Education, August 1967; and Herrick, *The Chicago Schools*, 342, 345–46, and 430.

18. John Hall Fish, *Black Power/White Control: The Struggle of the Woodlawn Organization in Chicago* (Princeton, N.J.: Princeton University Press, 1973), chapter 4; and Barbara Sizemore, telephone interview with the author, October 29, 2002. African Americans in Los Angeles established their own unofficial school board, parents in Boston and Washington, D.C., set up alternative schools, and cities like San Francisco had other forms of local control experiments. Mario Fantini, Marilyn Gittell, and Richard Magat, *Community Control and the Urban School* (New York, Washington, and London: Praeger, 1970), 82–99; and *Newsweek*, October 28, 1968, 84–85.

19. *Chicago's American*, August 25, 1966, 8.

20. Desmond and the CTU were not alone in this. W. Clayton Hall and Norman E. Carroll found in their analysis of 118 elementary school districts in suburban Cook County, Illinois, in 1968–69 that unions had little impact on pupil-to-teacher ratios in the classrooms because they traded higher salaries for class size. W. Clayton Hall and Norman E. Carroll, "The Effects of Teachers' Organizations on Salaries and Class Size," *Industrial and Labor Relations Review* 26, (1973): 834–41.

21. Grimshaw, *Union Rule in the Schools*, 46–48.

22. Peterson, *School Politics Chicago Style*, 191–93.

23. Herrick, *The Chicago Schools*, 353.

24. *Chicago Union Teacher*, February 1968, 14–15.

25. Shapiro, "The Chicago Teachers Union and the Ghetto," 23.

26. *Chicago Tribune*, November 21, 1967, sec. 2, p. 8.

27. Cannella, *171 Years of Teaching in Chicago*, 17–18 and 29.

28. Peterson, *School Politics Chicago Style*, 195; and figures for 1963 from Havighurst, *The Public Schools of Chicago*, 176.

29. Mamie Till Mobley, telephone interview with the author, November 5, 2002.

30. James Chiakulas, interview with the author, May 16, 2001; Grady Jordan, interview with the author, June 7, 2001; and U.S. Commission on Civil Rights, *Civil Rights USA, Public School North and West, 1962* (Washington, D.C.: GPO, 1962), 105–07.

31. *Chicago Sun-Times,* January 9, 1968, 10.

32. "The Elusive Black Educator," *School Management,* March 1969, 74.

33. Harold Charles, telephone interview with the author, April 15, 2002.

34. *Roosevelt Torch,* April 14, 1969, in Red Squad selected records, "FTB, 1968–1969" folder.

35. Harold Charles, telephone interview with the author, April 15, 2002.

36. Tommie Martin, interview with the author, August 9, 2002.

37. Grady Jordan, interview with the author, June 7, 2001.

38. Peterson, *School Politics Chicago Style,* 195.

39. Peterson, *School Politics Chicago Style,* 195.

40. *Chicago Sun-Times,* March 20, 1965, 34; *Chicago Union Teacher,* February 1965, 1, and March 1965, 2.

41. Shapiro, "The Chicago Teachers Union and the Ghetto," 73–74. For more on the MES program, see "Total School Plan That Works," *American Teacher,* May 1970.

42. David Farber, *The Age of Great Dreams, America in the 1960s* (New York: Hill and Wang, 1994), 111.

43. Maurice Isserman and Michael Kazin, *America Divided, The Civil War of the 1960s* (New York: Oxford University Press, 2000), 199; William L. O'Neill, *Coming Apart: An Informal History of America in the 1960s* (Chicago: Quadrangle Books, 1971), 170–73, 176–77; and Paul A. Gilje, *Rioting in America* (Bloomington and Indianapolis: Indiana University Press, 1996), 158.

44. Anderson and Pickering, *Confronting the Color Line,* 163; and Cohen and Taylor, *American Pharaoh,* 349.

45. Anderson and Pickering, *Confronting the Color Line,* 214; and Cohen and Taylor, *American Pharaoh,* 387–91.

46. See Stokely Carmichael and Charles V. Hamilton, *Black Power: The Politics of Liberation in America* (New York: Random House, 1967); Robert Lee Scott and Wayne Brockriede, eds., *The Rhetoric of Black Power* (New York: Harper and Row, 1969); William L. Van Deburg, *New Day in Babylon: The Black Power Movement and American Culture, 1965–1975* (Chicago and London: University of Chicago Press, 1992), 40–51; Daniel Wynn, *The Black Protest Movement* (New York: Philosophical Library, 1974), chapter 6; and Allen J. Matusow, *The Unraveling of America: A History of Liberalism in the 1960s* (New York: Harper and Row, 1984), chapter 12. For a more critical view of Black Power, see David Burner, *Making Peace with the 60s* (Princeton, N.J.: Princeton University Press, 1996), chapter 2.

47. Clayborne Carson, *In Struggle, SNCC and the Black Awakening of the 1960s* (Cambridge, Mass: Harvard University Press, 1981); and Meier and Rudwick, *CORE: A Study in the Civil Rights Movement.*

48. Charles E. Jones, ed., *The Black Panther Party* (Baltimore: Black Classics Press, 1998).

49. In a survey of black opinion undertaken in fifteen major cities in 1968, the authors found that "[m]ost Negroes of all age groups today reject separatist thinking both in the political and in the personal sense." In the survey only 14 percent of blacks "approved" of Stokely Carmichael and 14 percent of H. Rap Brown, but 72 percent "approved" of Martin Luther King. Angus Campbell and Howard Schuman, *Racial Attitudes in Fifteen American Cities* (Ann Arbor: University of Michigan, Survey Research Center Institute for Social Research, 1970), 19–21.

50. Van DeBurg, *New Day in Babylon;* and Gary T. Marx, *Protest and Prejudice: A Study of Belief in the Black Community* (New York: Harper Torchbook, 1969), 227–28.

51. *Handbook of Chicago School Segregation* (Coordinating Council of Community Organizations, August 1963), 29, in CORE: Chicago Chapter Collection, Chicago Historical Society, Box 1, Folder 5.

52. Zimmerman, *Whose America?*, 42–54 and chapter 5; and Van Deburg, *New Day in Babylon,* 65–66.

53. *Chicago Daily Defender,* March 24, 1969, 4, and April 16, 1969, 2.

54. Jerome H. Skolnick, "Black Militancy," in *Majority and Minority: The Dynamics of Racial and Ethnic Relations,* ed. Norman R. Yetman and C. Hoy Steele, 566–68 (Boston: Allyn and Bacon, 1971).

55. *Chicago Tribune,* September 15, 1967, 1.

56. *Chicago Daily Defender,* November 30, 1967, 1 and 4.

57. *Chicago Daily Defender,* January 17, 1968, 3.

58. *Chicago Daily Defender,* April 3, 1968, 3–5, and April 4, 1968, 3.

59. James S. Coleman et al., *Equality of Educational Opportunity* (Washington, D.C.: GPO, 1966), 21.

60. Herrick, *The Chicago Schools,* 342.

61. *Chicago Today,* May 24, 1969, 5–6.

62. *Chicago Sun-Times,* September 8, 1968, sec. 2, p. 3.

63. *Chicago Daily News,* January 19, 1966, 13, and April 21, 1966, 3. Anthony Grosch, interview with the author, August 15, 2002.

64. Kenneth F. Misquitta, "A Study of the Unionization of School Principals in Chicago and Detroit From 1961–1981" (Ph.D. diss., Loyola University of Chicago, 1983), 85.

65. *Chicago Daily News,* March 6, 1968, 1 and 4; and *Chicago Tribune,* March 8, 1968, 1–2.

66. *Chicago Tribune,* March 8, 1968, 2.

67. E. Franklin Frazier, *Black Bourgeoisie* (New York: Free Press, 1997, originally published in 1957), 235–36.

68. Timuel Black, interview with the author, May 16, 2000.

69. *Chicago Daily Defender,* January 29, 1969, 24. Joshua B. Freeman makes the point that there was little support for community control experiments in New York either. Freeman, *Working-Class New York: Life and Labor Since World War II,* 226. For more on community control, see Alan A. Altschuler, *Community Control: The*

Black Demand for Participation in Large American Cities (New York: Pegasus, 1970); Henry M. Levin, ed., *Community Control of Schools* (Washington, D.C.: Brookings Institute, 1970); Fantini, Gittell, and Magat, *Community Control and the Urban School*; Joseph M. Cronin, *The Control of Urban Schools: Perspective on the Power of Educational Reformers* (New York: Free Press, 1973); and Thomas E. Glass and William A. Sanders, *Community Control in Education: A Study in Power Transition* (Midland, Mich.: Pendell, 1978).

70. Tommie Martin, interview with the author, August 9, 2002.

71. *Chicago Daily Defender,* November 29, 1967, 1 and 3.

72. See clippings in Red Squad selected records, Box 213, "Parker High School, 1968–1971."

73. Philip S. Foner, *Organized Labor and the Black Worker, 1619–1981* (New York: International Publishers, 1981), 408–24; and Herbert Hill, "Black Dissent in Organized Labor" in *Seasons of Rebellion: Protest and Radicalism in Recent America, ed.* Joseph Boskin and Robert A. Rosenstone, 75–80 (Washington, D.C.: University Press of America, 1980).

74. Philip S. Foner, *Organized Labor and the Black Worker, 1619–1981* (New York: International Publishers, 1981), 401.

75. Grady Jordan, interview with the author, June 7, 2001; Red Squads selected records, "Bobby Eugene Wright, 1968" folder; and quote in Bobby E. Wright, *The Psychopathic Racial Personality and Other Essays* (Chicago: Third World Press: 1984, revised edition 1994), xi.

76. Grady Jordan, interview with the author, June 7, 2001.

77. Robert L. Mason, "Mason's Manifesto," n.d., Red Squad selected records, Box 218, "FTB's folder"; and Shapiro, "The Chicago Teachers Union and the Ghetto," 47.

78. Robert L. Mason, "Mason's Manifesto," n.d., Red Squad selected records, Box 218, "FTB's folder."

79. *Chicago Union Teacher,* November 1968, 2.

80. Robert L. Mason, "Mason's Manifesto," n.d., Red Squad selected records, Box 218, "FTB's folder."

81. Grady Jordan, interview with the author, June 7, 2001.

82. Robert L. Mason, "Mason's Manifesto," n.d., Red Squad selected records, Box 218, "FTB's folder"

83. Shapiro, "The Chicago Teachers Union and the Ghetto," 82.

84. Robert L. Mason, "Mason's Manifesto," n.d., Red Squad selected records, Box 218, "FTB's folder."

85. Travis T. Johnson, "Race, Politics and Money: School Reform Chicago Style" (Ph.D. diss., Kent State University, 1993), 262; and *Chicago Daily Defender,* April 23, 1968, 3.

86. Shapiro, "The Chicago Teachers Union and the Ghetto," 48.

87. Out of fifteen leaders of the BTC, only two were women. See BTC leaflet, Red Squad selected records, Box 208, "Misc., ca 1968–1972" folder.

88. Robert L. Mason, "Mason's Manifesto," n.d., Red Squad selected records, Box 218, "FTB's folder."

89. See Steve Estes, "'I *AM* A MAN!': Race, Masculinity, and the 1968 Memphis Sanitation Strike," *Labor History* 41 (May 2000): 153–70; and Beth Tompkins Bates, *Pullman Porters and the Rise of Protest Politics in Black America, 1925–1945* (Chapel Hill and London: University of North Carolina Press, 2001), for wider discussions of gendered language in the civil rights struggle.

90. Chicago African-American Teachers Association *Newsletter,* Spring 1969, 1.

91. Robert E. Lewis Obituary in *Chicago Sun-Times* May 11, 2001, 80; and Chicago African-American Teachers Association *Newsletter,* Spring 1976, 4, for list of African American principals.

92. Grady Jordan, interview with the author, June 7, 2001.

93. Mattie Hopkins Obituary "CPS-Biography (Board Members)" Box, Chicago Board of Education archives, Chicago.

94. *Operation Breadbasket News* 1 (October 3, 1969): 2; and *Commerce,* April 1968, 24–25, 49, 50, 52, 54, 64, and 65.

95. Harold Charles, telephone interview with the author, April 15, 2002; and Ralph, *Northern Protest,* 68–69, 228–29; and Gary Massoni, "Perspectives on Operation Breadbasket," in *Chicago 1966: Martin Luther King, Jr. and the Civil Rights Movement,* ed. David J. Garrow, 179–346 (New York: Carlson, 1989).

96. "Statement to the press given on behalf of the TCQE," Timuel D. Black collection, CHS, Box 4, "Teachers Committee for Quality Education, 1964–1969"; Timuel Black, interview with the author, August 30, 2002; *Chicago Today,* May 24 1969, 5–6; and *Chicago Daily Defender,* March 12, 1969, 4.

97. *Chicago Union Teacher,* June 1968, 1; and Shapiro, "The Chicago Teachers Union and the Ghetto," 13 and 24–37.

98. Red Squad selected records, Box 230, "Teachers for Radical Change in Education" folder; and *Chicago Sun-Times* November 9, 1968, sec 1, p. 38.

99. Landwermeyer, "Teacher Unionism-Chicago Style," 350–54.

100. *Chicago Union Teacher,* June 1968, 1; and Shapiro, "The Chicago Teachers Union and the Ghetto," 24–37.

101. Golin, *The Newark Teacher Strikes,* 44.

102. William F. Gardner, "The History, Role and Operation of the Board of Examiners, Chicago Public Schools, 1917–1974" (Ph.D. diss., Northwestern University, 1975), 201.

103. *Chicago Tribune,* February 13, 1969, sec. B, p. 1.

104. *Chicago Sun-Times,* August 6, 1967, 38.

105. Donald M. Medley and Thomas J. Quirk, "The Application of a Factorial Design to the Study of Cultural Bias in General Culture Items on the National Teacher Examination," *Journal of Educational Measurement* 11 (Winter 1974): 235–45, quote on page 244. Subsequently, cultural bias in teacher exams became an issue of national concern. See Richard G. Allan, Paula M. Nassif, and Scott M. Elliot, eds., *Bias Issues in Teacher Certification Testing* (Hillsdale, N.J.: Lawrence Erlbaum, 1988). In 1971, a

Mississippi court found that a school district could not adopt passing scores on the National Teacher Examination as a requirement for employment and retention in employment because it meant hiring more whites than blacks (A. W. VanderMeer, "Legislators, the Courts, and Teacher Education," *School Review* 82 (February 1974): 285).

106. Marlowe Mogill, telephone interview with the author, June 19, 2001.

107. Timuel Black, interview with the author, August 30, 2002.

108. *Chicago Daily Defender,* January 29, 1969, 24.

109. *Chicago Union Teacher,* November 1967, 2; and *Chicago Sun-Times,* November 22, 1967, 4 and 17.

110. *Chicago Daily Defender,* January 17, 1968, 3. See also newspaper cuttings in Red Squad selected records, Box 218, "Full Time Basis Substitutes" file.

111. See newspaper cuttings in Red Squad selected records, Box 218, "Full Time Basis Substitutes" file.

112. Gardner, "The History, Role and Operation of the Board of Examiners, 107–09; and John B. Mack, III et al. v. James F. Redmond et al. (1968), United States District Court for the Northern District of Illinois Eastern Division, case number 68C751, National Archives and Records Administration, Great Lakes Region.

113. *Chicago Tribune,* August 9, 1968, 2. See also newspaper cuttings in Red Squad selected records, Box 218, "Full Time Basis Substitutes" file; and *Chicago Tribune,* February 13, 1969, sec. B, p. 1.

114. Timuel Black to John Desmond, February 3, 1969; Neva Howard to John Desmond, February 8, 1969. Quote in Timuel D. Black to John Desmond, February 3, 1969, Timuel Black collection, CHS, "Teachers for Quality Education" folder.

115. Gilje, *Rioting in America,* 158.

116. Cohen and Taylor, *American Pharaoh,* 452–57.

117. *Report of the Chicago Riot Study Committee to the Hon. Richard J. Daley,* August 1, 1968, 29.

118. *Report of the Chicago Riot Study Committee to the Hon. Richard J. Daley,* August 1, 1968, 32, and 115.

119. *Chicago Daily Defender,* May 25, 1968, 1.

120. *Chicago Sun-Times,* May 28, 1968, 22.

121. *Chicago Daily Defender,* May 25, 1968, 1.

122. Elizabeth Anders, "Everybody Run Farragut," Black Spears Press, Chicago, Occasional Paper 10, August 2000, reprinted from *Evergreen* magazine, 1971, quotes on page 68.

123. Harold Charles, telephone interview with the author, April 15, 2002.

124. Copy of Black Manifesto in Red Squad selected records, Box 210 "Farragut High School, 1968–1969."

125. Harold Charles, telephone interview with the author, April 15, 2002.

126. *Chicago Daily Defender,* December 21–27, 1968, 1.

127. *Chicago Daily Defender,* October 8, 1968, 1 and 3. See copy of Harrison High

School Black Manifesto in Red Squad selected records, Box 211 "Harrison High School, 1968–1970" folder.

128. *Chicago Daily Defender,* October 9, 1968, 1 and 3.

129. Joseph A. Taylor, "Should We Treat the Symptom or the Disease?" *Chicago Principals Reporter* 58 (Winter 1968): 5.

130. *Chicago Tribune,* October 15, 1–2, October 18, 1–2, October 22, 1–2, and October 25, 3, 1968.

131. *Chicago Daily Defender,* October 21, 1968, 1 and 3; *Chicago Daily Defender,* October 22, 1968, 1 and 3; and *Chicago Daily Defender,* November 5, 1968, 3 and 8.

132. *Chicago Daily Defender,* October 3, 8, October 9, 15, October 15, 5, October 16, 3, October 17, 6, and October 24, 12, 1968.

133. Jerome H. Skolnick, "Black Militancy," in *Majority and Minority: The Dynamics of Racial and Ethnic Relations,* ed. Norman R. Yetman and C. Hoy Steele, 566–68 (Boston: Allyn and Bacon, 1971).

134. *Chicago Tribune,* October 18, 1968, 1, and October 25, 1968, 3; *Chicago Daily News,* October 24, 1968, 14; Johnson, "Race, Politics and Money," 182–84 and 256; Earl Ogletree, "Plight of the Chicago Schools," *Phi Delta Kappan,* February 1969, 325; and *Chicago Daily Defender,* November 14, 1968, 3, November 20, 1968, 3.

135. Landwermeyer, "Teacher Unionism—Chicago Style," 389.

136. Marlowe Mogill, telephone interview with the author, June 19, 2001.

137. Landwermeyer, "Teacher Unionism—Chicago Style," 350–54.

138. *Chicago Union Teacher,* October 1968, 2.

139. *Chicago Sun-Times,* November 9, 1968, sec. 1, p. 38.

140. *Chicago Sun-Times,* May 23, 1969, 52.

141. *Chicago Sun-Times,* November 26, 1968, sec. 1, p. 29; and *Chicago Tribune,* January 7, 1969, sec. 1, p. 1.

142. *Chicago Daily Defender,* January 7, 1969, 2; and *Chicago Daily Defender,* January 13, 1969, 13.

143. *Chicago Sun-Times,* January 7, 1969, sec. 1, pp. 1 and 4.

144. *Chicago Tribune,* January 7, 1969, sec., 1, p. 1.

145. *Chicago Sun-Times,* January 21, 1969, 2.

146. "Statement to the School Problems Commission by James F. Redmond General Superintendent of Schools January 24 1969," Chicago Board of Education archives.

147. See Landwermeyer, "Teacher Unionism—Chicago Style," for a detailed description of the 1969 strike.

148. See Landwermeyer, "Teacher Unionism—Chicago Style," for a detailed description of the 1969 strike.

149. *Chicago Sun-Times,* April 11, 1969, 36.

150. *Chicago Sun-Times,* May 8, 1969, 6.

151. *Chicago Sun-Times,* March 14, 1969, 30.

152. *Chicago Daily Defender,* April 22, 1969, 4.

153. *Chicago Sun-Times,* April 26, 1969, 1, 5, 17 and 22.

154. *Chicago Tribune,* April 4, 1969, 1.

155. *Chicago Daily Defender,* May 20, 1969, 20.

156. *Chicago Sun-Times,* May 23, 1969 sec. 1, pp. 20 and 52.

157. Landwermeyer, "Teacher Unionism—Chicago Style," 443–47; *Chicago Today,* May 23, 1969, 8 and 12; and *Chicago Sun-Times,* May 23, 1969, sec. 1, p. 20.

158. Tommie Martin, interview with the author, August 9, 2002.

159. *Chicago Sun-Times,* May 23, 1969, sec. 1, p. 20.

160. Anna Anthony, interview with the author, August 22, 2002.

161. *Chicago Sun-Times,* May 22, 1969, 45.

162. Mamie Till Mobley, telephone interview with the author, November 5, 2002.

163. Landwermeyer, "Teacher Unionism—Chicago Style," 443–47; *Chicago Today,* May 23, 1969, 8 and 12; and *Chicago Sun-Times,* May 23, 1969, sec. 1, p. 20.

164. "Chronicle of Race and Schools in Chicago, 1962–1976," 1976 *Integrated Education Magazine,* CHS, 28.

165. Landwermeyer, "Teacher Unionism—Chicago Style," 443–47; *Chicago Today,* May 23, 1969, 8 and 12; and *Chicago Sun-Times,* May 23, 1969, sec. 1, p. 20.

166. William Brink and Louis Harris, *The Negro Revolution in America* (New York: Simon and Schuster, 1964), 234.

167. Quote in *Chicago Today,* May 22, 1969, 3; and Harold Charles, telephone interview with the author, April 15, 2002.

168. Barbara Sizemore, telephone interview with the author, October 29, 2002.

169. *Chicago Daily Defender,* May 17, 1969, 2.

170. Grady Jordan, interview with the author, June 7, 2001.

171. *Chicago Daily Defender,* May 22, 1969, 2.

172. *Chicago Sun-Times,* May 22, 1969, 45.

173. Landwermeyer, "Teacher Unionism—Chicago Style," 443–47; *Chicago Today,* May 23, 1969, 12; and *Chicago Today,* May 27, 1969, 6.

174. *Chicago Sun-Times,* May 24, 1969, 1, 3, and 12.

175. *Chicago Today,* May 26, 1969, 1

176. Thomas R. Brooks, "Black Upsurge in the Unions," *Dissent* 17 (March–April 1970): 131–32.

177. "Chronicle of Race and Schools in Chicago, 1962–1976," 1976 *Integrated Education Magazine,* CHS, 28.

178. Zimmerman, *Whose America?,* 123.

179. Gardner, "The History, Role and Operation of the Board of Examiners," 92 and 134.

180. Chicago Board of Education, Report, "Racial Survey, Administrative and Teaching Personnel," 1968–1972.

181. Chicago Board of Education, Report, "Racial Survey, Administrative and Teaching Personnel," 1968–1972.

182. Grady Jordan, interview with the author, June 7, 2001.

Conclusion

1. Martin Lawn, *Servants of the State: The Contested Control of Teaching, 1900–1930* (London: Falmer Press, 1987), 15–16. For more on this approach to the study of British teacher unionism, see Jenny Ozga and Martin Lawn, *Teachers, Professionalism and Class* (London: Falmer Press, 1981); and Jenny Ozga, ed., *Schoolwork: Approaches to the Labour Process of Teaching* (Milton Keynes: Open University Press, 1988).

2. Chicago Public Schools website, <http://www.cps.k12.il.us/AtAGlance.html>.

3. Chicago Public Schools website, <http://www.cps.k12.il.us/AtAGlance.html>.

4. Richard B. Freeman, "Unionism Comes to the Public Sector," *Journal of Economic Literature* 24 (1986): 41–86; and Gregory M. Saltzman, "Bargaining Laws as a Cause and Consequence of the Growth of Teacher Unionism," *Industrial and Labor Relations Review* 38 (April 1985): 335–51.

5. John F. Burton, Jr., "The Extent of Collective Bargaining in the Public Sector," in *Public Sector Bargaining*, ed. Benjamin Aaron, Joseph R. Grodin, and James L. Stern (Madison, Wisc.: Industrial Relations Research Association, 1979), 1–43; Michael Goldfield and Jonathan Plotkin, *Public Sector Unionism in the United States: The Reasons for its Take-off in the Early 1960s* (Ithaca, N.Y.: Cornell University Press, 1987); and Michael Goldfield, "Public Sector Union Growth and Public Polity," *Policy Studies Journal* 18 (Winter 1989–90): 404–20.

6. Grimshaw, *Union Rule in the Schools,* 62–65.

7. Edna Pardo, "When Do Children Get Golden Parachutes?" *Catalyst,* December 1999, <www.catalyst-chicago.org>.

8. Education Week website, <www.edweek.org>.

9. G. A. Hess, Jr., *School Restructuring, Chicago Style* (Newbury Park, Calif.: Corwin Press, 1991).

10. Lichtenstein, *State of the Union;* and Charles Taylor Kerchner and Douglas E. Mitchell, *The Changing Idea of a Teachers' Union* (New York, The Falmer Press, 1988).

11. Chicago Tribune, *Chicago Schools: Worst In America?* (Chicago: Chicago Tribune, 1988).

12. *Catalyst Chicago* (February 2000), 7; William Ayers, "Chicago: A Restless Sea of Social Forces," in Charles Taylor Kerchner and Julia E. Koppich, *A Union of Professionals: Labor Relations and Educational Reform* (New York and London: Columbia University, 1993), 177–93; Maribeth Vander Weele, *Reclaiming Our Schools: The Struggle for Chicago School Reform* (Chicago: Loyola University Press, 1994); and Anthony S. Bryk et al., *Charting Chicago School Reform: Democratic Localism as a Lever for Change* (Boulder, Colo.: Westview Press, 1998).

13. *Catalyst Chicago,* September 1995.

14. *Catalyst Chicago,* February 2000, 10–19.

15. *Catalyst Chicago,* February 2000, 22.

16. Deborah Lynch Walsh, *Labor of Love: One Chicago Teacher's Experience* (New York: Writers Club Press, 2000); *Catalyst Chicago,* November 1995; and *Catalyst Chicago,* September 2001.

17. *Chicago Sun-Times,* June 20, 2004.

Index

JOHN F. LYONS is an associate professor of history at Joliet Junior College.

The University of Illinois Press
is a founding member of the
Association of American University Presses.

_____

Composed in 10.5/13 Adobe Minion Pro
with FF Meta display
by Jim Proefrock
at the University of Illinois Press
Manufactured by Thomson-Shore, Inc.

University of Illinois Press
1325 South Oak Street
Champaign, IL 61820-6903
www.press.uillinois.edu